Black Light

Black Light

Revealing the Hidden History of Photography and Cinema

Christophe Wall-Romana

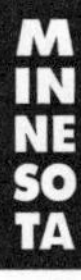

University of Minnesota Press
Minneapolis
London

This book is freely available in an open access edition thanks to TOME (Toward an Open Monograph Ecosystem)—a collaboration of the Association of American Universities, the Association of University Presses, and the Association of Research Libraries—and the generous support of the College of Liberal Arts at the University of Minnesota, Twin Cities. Learn more at the TOME website, available at openmonographs.org.

Every effort was made to obtain permission to reproduce material in this book. If any proper acknowledgment has not been included here, we encourage copyright holders to notify the publisher.

Portions of chapters 3 and 6 were previously published in a different form in "Kinemorphic Cursives: Self-Imaging and the Non-Mimetic Source of Photo-imaging," *Philosophy of Photography* 13 (2022): 35–59, https://doi.org/10.1386/pop_00038_1. Portions of chapter 7 were previously published in a different form in "Camille Flammarion's Flash-Forward: The Cinematicization of French Thought and Aesthetics (1867–1913)," in *1913: The Year of French Modernism,* ed. Effie Rentzou and André Benhaïm (Manchester, England: Manchester University Press, 2020); reproduced with permission of Manchester University Press.

Copyright 2026 by the Regents of the University of Minnesota

Black Light: Revealing the Hidden History of Photography and Cinema is licensed under a Creative Commons Attribution-NonCommercial-NoDerivatives 4.0 International License (CC BY-NC-ND 4.0): https://creativecommons.org/licenses/by-nc-nd/4.0/

Published by the University of Minnesota Press
111 Third Avenue South, Suite 290
Minneapolis, MN 55401-2520
http://www.upress.umn.edu

Available as a Manifold edition at manifold.umn.edu

ISBN 978-1-5179-1775-3 (hc)
ISBN 978-1-5179-1776-0 (pb)

A Cataloging-in-Publication record for this book is available from the Library of Congress.

Printed in the United States of America on acid-free paper

The University of Minnesota is an equal-opportunity educator and employer.

35 34 33 32 31 30 29 28 27 26 10 9 8 7 6 5 4 3 2 1

Contents

Acknowledgments

During the near decade it took this project to mature, many institutions and individuals and various voices (some of them not just in my head) have provided invaluable feedback, advice, and much-needed prodding. The first nudge was occasioned by an invitation from Ann Smock to her colloquium "Music, Letters, and Moving Shadows" at Berkeley in 2010. It was in 2015–2016 that I drafted the first iteration of this study, thanks to a fellowship from the American Council of Learned Societies. Final development of the book manuscript benefitted from a Samuel Russell Chair in the Humanities from the College of Liberal Arts at the University of Minnesota (2020–2023). Key members of the sounding board for this research were Juliette Cherbuliez, Michael Iarocci, Matthias Rothe, Debarati Sanyal, Ann Smock, Bill Smock, and Margaret Wall-Romana, who always either firmed up or redirected some of my flimsier ideas. For their generous invitations to talk about or publish preparatory work for this project, I want to thank Éric Méchoulan, André Benhaïm and Effie Rentzou, Nicholas Paige, Cécile Bishop and Zoe Roth, Jane Gaines, Noam Elcott, Thomas Elsaesser, Matthew Dodd, and the Bell Museum at the University of Minnesota. Archival research for this project was conducted at the Bibliothèque Nationale de France, the British Library, the Cambridge University Library, the Conservatoire National des Arts et Métiers, the Harry

Ransom Center of the University of Texas, the library of the Institut de France, the Paris Observatory Library, the Royal Astronomical Society, the Royal Society of London, and the St John's College Library at Cambridge University. I also want to thank Francis Oger and Anne Mayeur at the Société Astronomique de France for a visit of Flammarion's observatory and Ellen Embleton, Dena Goodman, James Lequeux, Omar W. Nasim, and Beverley F. Ronalds for kindly answering detailed queries. This book got immensely better thanks to anonymous readers of the manuscript working with the University of Minnesota Press, as well as Elizabeth Ault and anonymous readers working for Duke University Press. I owe a personal debt of gratitude to Brandy Monk-Payton for asking whether and how an earlier version of this project accounted for the violence of racism. I thank my editor, Leah Pennywark, for her support and patience. Finally, my deepest bow to my life partner and uncompromising "schmeditor," Margaret.

Introduction

The Matrix of Photography and Cinema

This study aims to revise our understanding of the origination of photography and cinema. Rather than the accepted thesis that each medium stemmed from a yearning to reproduce what we can see, it proposes the opposite: that they were developed to make visible what we cannot see. It suggests, furthermore, that the developmental paths of photography and cinema closely intersected, and it traces them back to two specific domains: inquiries about the structure and origins of the cosmos and conjectures regarding human diversity and racial difference. There is, of course, no question that photography and cinema became dominant media in the nineteenth and twentieth centuries through their unbounded ability to copy and mass-reproduce their own copies. But this vaunted double reproducibility proves to be a late affordance within the three-century-long matrix of ideas, practices, and devices whose overarching concern was to image the unseeable foundations of the universe—a universe in which race was a surprisingly cardinal feature.

This is a far-reaching and many-faceted thesis. This introduction takes readers through some of its key components and aspects, which the chapters will evidence more fully. We open with the importance of visualization and how it entwines the history of the universe, human history, and preoccupations with the cause of skin color and the exact nature of light. We then revisit current scholarship on media prehistory before delving deeper into the pivotal role of race and racism in the genesis of photography and cinema.

Visualization

Historians agree on the broad outlines of how technicians and industrialists implemented photography and cinema, in the 1820s–1830s for the former and the 1880s–1890s for the latter. What prompted these innovations, however, is far from established. Until recently, it was assumed that reproducing the visible world was a universal dream that technological advances at last made feasible. This conjecture is now no longer tenable, for several reasons. First, visual reality in its crude ordinariness wasn't regarded very highly prior to photography; it never warranted such a dream.[1] Second, media archaeology shows that optical apparatuses after the Renaissance developed out of a myriad of motives, including wonder and magic, entertainment and aesthetics, and occult and polymath quests—none of which felt the need to privilege visual verisimilitude.[2] Finally, photography and cinema emerged during the era of positivism that invoked supposedly universal history to justify Western hegemonic politics, tainting any common dream of visual reproduction. For all these reasons, an alternate scenario is needed.

Today, nearly everything from deep space to the atom and the brain has become picturable and seeable. But from the seventeenth to the nineteenth centuries, the unseeable held a powerful cultural appeal in Europe, in part through the Christian injunction of attending to "the evidence of things unseen." With the shocking early seventeenth-century revelation of heliocentrism, the introduction of the telescope, and faraway lands and peoples newly accessed, unseen reality grew exponentially, with spiritual realms still in play in the background.[3] Novel kinds of inquiry fastened on the new contours of the unseeable to make it imaginable: inquiries about how the universe came about and developed, how humans appeared on Earth and diversified, and whether human history conformed to or diverged from natural history as reconstructed then. Such questions induced new modes of visualization consonant with the "scientific revolution," and I claim that the long maturation of photography and cinema can be traced back to them. Recent scholarship justifiably appends scare quotes to "the scientific revolution" because it never had been disinterested or "pure" science.[4] Rather, it tended to mold natural and human history in order to legitimize white peoples' cultural and geopolitical domination, enabling the three-century-long transatlantic industrialization of slavery that figures centrally in this book.[5]

What is notable about seventeenth-century visualization practices is that they generally deprioritized present states of affair.[6] They were deployed instead to render the long past of the cosmos, Earth, and humankind tangible, the better to prepare for the organization of the future under the naturalized dominion of white Europe.[7] In other words, the new art of visualization was bookended by the divine and natural origin of the cosmos at one end and Europe's hegemony-to-come at the other. The chapters of this book rethink the long emergence of photography and cinema from the arrival of the telescope onward through this alternative purview: visualizing and imaging within the broad context of racial and global supremacy what lies beyond the currently observable.

Natural Philosophy

At stake, then, is the worldview of so-called natural philosophy, an umbrella term for antecedent scientific practices from the early 1600s to the early 1800s. While it begat our modern technoscientific approach, which rests in principle on actual, neutral, measurable, and replicable facts, natural philosophy's spirit of investigation was rife with competitive attachments. It cleaved often expressly to diverse preoccupations from theology, aesthetics, systematization, and analogism, to antiquarianism, mercantilism, jingoism, white supremacy, etc.[8] These were not considered extraneous because reality was never taken to be neutral, objective, or autonomous. Reality was not data (meaning "givens") but rather a divine gift meant to be deciphered by unraveling signs to better approach the invisible transcendent order. Rationality in the seventeenth century conformed to such preconceptions about harmonious relations (ratio) in a deistic universe. For René Descartes and his contemporaries, *reason* was synonymous with "natural light." Enlightenment methods favored extrapolating the invisible or unseeable from accepted models of the visible, of vision, and of light—whose problematic nature is at the core of this study. This is why astronomy, the discipline of both optics and space-time, was preeminent for visualization practices and germinal for the matrix of photocinema.

This method of extrapolation entangled astronomy with race. One supposedly rational conviction of most natural philosophers in the wake of heliocentrism was that all planets must surely be inhabited like Earth. This came to be known as the multiple worlds hypothesis. Its correlate was that extraterrestrial inhabitants could be envisioned by simply extrapolating earthly races, resulting in a natural universe conceptualized through racial lenses for nearly three centuries. The rational invention of racialized extraterrestrials was a crucial step for how visualization, astrophysics, light research, and racist constructs began coalescing in the 1600s into a substrate for long-maturing technologies of visual reproduction. By the 1700s, more recognizably pre-photographic and precinematic insights began emerging, further crystalizing the matrix of photography and cinema by the early 1800s. This last step took place within a transformational epistemic tension. On the wane was the legacy of natural philosophy's overreliance on approaching the nonobservable from unreliable extrapolation; on the rise was nineteenth-century technocratic science grounded in observation, mathematics, and precision instrumentation, culminating in the ideal of mechanical objectivity.[9] It is within that tension that the common episteme of photocinema yielded innovations after the first decades of the nineteenth century.

To make these ideas more tangible, let us consider Samuel Taylor Coleridge, an emblematic figure of this hinge. Belonging to the first generation of white thinkers for whom slavery finally lost its supposedly rational basis, he was a lifelong abolitionist from his days at Cambridge in the 1790s. At the inaugural meeting of the British Association for the Advancement of Science at the same university in 1833, he called upon scientific specialists to drop the title "philosopher" and leave it to actual practitioners of philosophy. The word *scientist* was adopted soon after.[10] His mature work as a poet-philosopher focused on the faculty of imagination and the cognitive dimension of poetic images. He debated those ideas in the late 1790s with his close friend Thomas Wedgwood, the vaunted inceptor of photography. Wedgwood's photochemical experiments, however, proceeded more from his father's ceramic plating business and the conceptual ambiguity of image-making probed by Coleridge and others in the Darwin–Wedgwood circle than from the project of copying the visible (see chapter 4). I argue that the views on race, supposed science, and imaging held by Coleridge and contemporaries are just as structurally interrelated to the development of photography and cinema as Wedgwood's marginal experiments.[11]

Fostering visualization over vision, this book relativizes the weak imperative of copying while offering a more comprehensive rationale for the emergence of photography and cinema.[12] The term *visualization* itself dates from 1816, just as Nicéphore Niépce in Burgundy, France, was experimenting on the earliest working photographic process. It was indeed Coleridge who coined the verb *to visualize* to denote the perceptual tangibility and philosophical import of envisioning.[13] The *Oxford English Dictionary* defines *visualization* as "the power or process of forming a mental picture or vision of something not actually present to the sight; a picture thus formed."[14] The clause "not actually present to the sight" is germane. It accentuates the multiple temporalities of visualization in contrast with the present of vision. It also brings attention to one central puzzle of natural philosophy: how light forms and carries images through the eyes into the brain and, even more fundamentally, what light really is. This remained a fundamental mystery until about the 1820s. Prior to that, the uncertain nature of light fostered wide skepticism regarding the reliability of optical images—another factor for the devaluation of the visually mundane.[15] We should note too that "not actually present to the sight" points equally to unseeable but real facts—the physical universe, the development of an embryo, or the physiological abnormality of Blackness (a given for Enlightenment racial thinking, as we will see)—and to mystical or fabulous realms, traces of the divine within a universe seen as a Creation, and false reports on animals and peoples, such as tiny homunculi thought to be observed swimming in sperm and human-animal hybrids.[16] Finally, visualizations form equally and synthetically from texts, ideas, biases, exchanges, visual aids, imagination, instrumentation, and projective geometry.[17] The coining of *visualizing* by Coleridge as a central mode of knowledge-making marks the end of natural philosophy, as visualizing began splitting into heuristic theorization, imagination as a cognitive and philosophical faculty, and emergent technologies of imaging.

Photoimaging

This study articulates the development of photocinema around two interrelated streams: photoimaging and kinemorphic visualization (explored in the next section). *Photoimaging* is my term for a protoformation from the seventeenth to the early nineteenth centuries that was part visualization and part image-making technic. It is defined as images made by light, whether actually or conjecturally, with two overarching characteristics: they are produced by spontaneous alterations within a material substrate that displays a pattern or image and they are caused by "light" (in scare quotes for reasons explained below). Photoimages straddled the divide between experimental and mystical branches of natural philosophy, especially in the German tradition of Naturphilosophie. For that metaphysical movement, light was the central cosmic riddle linking human and transcendental realms. It was thought to encompass all forces of nature: electricity, magnetism, chemical reactions, heat, sound, perhaps ideation and even the life principle itself. Yet because this transcendental unity of light was unseeable, metaphysical experimenters were in search of physical-chemical patterns materializing its hidden nature.

The most paradigmatic of such photoimages were produced by physicist and philosopher Georg Christoph Lichtenberg in the 1770s. He pressed sheets of sticky black paper on the body of an electrical machine to retain the fantastic electrostatic patterns formed by dust. His comments show that he thought they were windows into the unity of nature. They were unlike other images previously produced and, importantly, could not be considered direct copies. As chapter 3 explains, such images were often called natural "hieroglyphs."[18] Curiously, in 1769 Lichtenberg noted that an acquaintance named Jøns Matthias Ljungberg had mused about

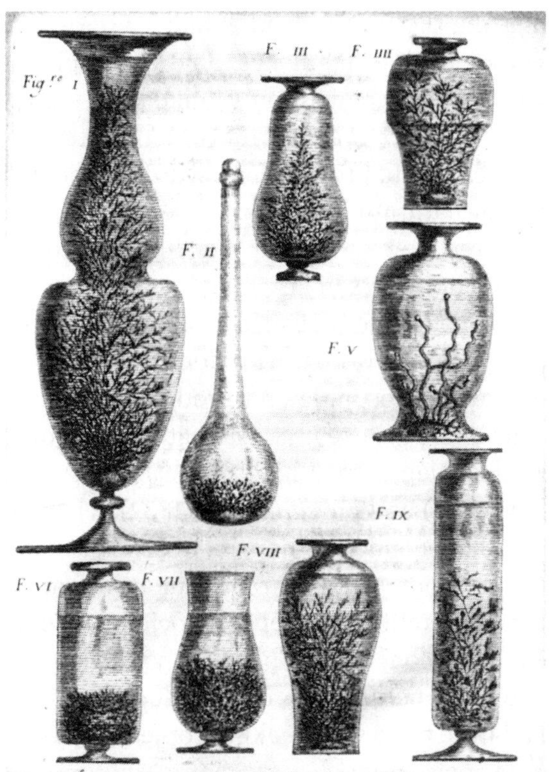

Figure I.1. **Arborescent crystallized metals. Diana's Tree (F. III) is made of silver nitrate. Wilhelm Homberg, "Réflexions sur différentes végétations métalliques,"** ***Mémoires de mathématique et de physique tirés des registres de l'Académie des sciences*** **(November 1692): 166. Courtesy of La Bibliothèque Nationale de France Gallica.**

"making the images of the camera obscura remain on paper," leading Lichtenberg himself "to imagine landscapes and other illuminated unmoving objects remaining still for a short time by means of a camera obscura."[19] Significantly, Lichtenberg did not pursue this prescient photoreprographic insight. For him, the electrostatic prints that he called "projections" were more akin to Diana's Tree (Arbor Dianae). In this spectacular chemical reaction treasured by seventeenth-century alchemists, silver nitrate—the prime reactive of photochemistry as it happens—precipitates into awe-inspiring arborescent crystals.[20] Like Lichtenberg's electrical prints, these concretions were sneak peeks into the metaphysical script of the Book of Nature. Such photoimages, I claim, are the true antecedents of proto-photographic prints.

One of the central actors in this book is doctor and physicist Thomas Young, who made decisive advances in understanding light.

Sharing the holistic and analogical creed of Naturphilosophie, he worked across linguistics, physiology, physics, and acoustics. Convinced that light and sound alike were wave phenomena, in 1804 he made photochemical prints of light interference patterns in a camera obscura to prove it. These unfixed photo prints, at the hinge between natural philosophy and science, are the first photographic pictures ever described. Yet like Lichtenberg's projections, they were not images of anything known but rather visual specimens or tests opening new realms of knowledge. As such, they served twin purposes: disclosing the hidden nature of "light" in the framework of Naturphilosophie and producing evidence that light is a wave. This dual purpose is attested at the core of pre-photography by the names Niépce gave his earliest photographic processes: *heliography* (1825) and *physautotype* (1832). The first means "sun writing" and the second "self-imprint of physical nature."[21] None of their five Greek roots indexes either human vision or copying. To make his novelty intelligible, Niépce associated it with the established class of chemical concretions, physical patterns, graphs, silhouettes, sparks, and other natural figures transducing the unseeable. Such attempts had little to do with making copies—although not nothing.

Apposite to such hieroglyphs, photoimaging stems from a second path: the long association of silver nitrate with Black skin. Known since at least the Islamic Golden Age (eleventh to twelfth centuries), photosensitive substrates were never used in the context of imaging until the late eighteenth century. Prior to this, they were exclusively connected to human skin and skin Blackness, because it was common knowledge that both silver nitrate (AgNO3, also called "lunar caustic" or "lapis infernalis," "hell stone") and silver chloride (AgCl, luna cornea, "horned silver" or "horned Moon")—the whitish compounds that became central for modern photochemistry—darken light skin. They were widely used to treat skin ailments and at times other conditions, always accompanied with a warning regarding their darkening properties.[22] In his 1664 book on color theory, Robert Boyle mentions a "merry" experiment with silver nitrate described as "a Snow-white body [substance]" that when laid upon "White Skin should presently produce a deep Blackness."[23] Right after mentioning this paradoxical equation—white + white =

black—Boyle segues into his next chapter: "The Cause of the Blackness of Negroes." Photography historians have never considered this racial discourse as integral to the genealogy of photography. This study recovers and elucidates the constitutive role of race for both proto-photography and protocinema.

Let us consider this decisive point in more detail. In late 1827, Niépce traveled to the Royal Observatory town of Kew to present his new photographic process (heliography) to British optical physicists and instrument-makers. They found his low-contrast artwork reproductions on tin plates underwhelming and did not encourage commercialization. After fruitless months, he returned to France and began collaborating with Louis Daguerre, who finalized photography in 1838. A single British scholar, the anatomist Everard Home, was intrigued enough by Niépce's plates to report on them. The then-secretary of the Royal Society (later disgraced for plagiarizing the manuscripts of his dead brother-in-law, the colonial surgeon and anatomist John Hunter), Home published the following passage in 1828, without mentioning heliography or Niépce by name: "A French gentleman has just discovered a substance by means of which he can so prepare any polished surface of silver or tin, that the sun's rays reflected from any object will be so fixed as to leave its image. The discovery he considers not brought to perfection, and therefore has not promulgated it: he has presented me with a specimen of this art, which will prove a very valuable discovery, since the outline of the representation must be perfectly accurate, however much it is diminished."[24] It has long been known that this measured endorsement is the earliest known reference to working photography in print. Yet no historian to my knowledge has mentioned the title of the section of Home's anatomy manual where it appears: "On the Rete Mucosum." This is the infamous Latin name of the epidermal layer in which white natural philosophers obsessively sought to locate the wellspring of Blackness. Home affirms that since in utero "the child of a black woman" is indistinguishable from that of a white woman, Blackness must "require light for its formation, or, at least, for its being rendered visible" (Home, "On the Rete Mucosum," 280). For Home, the main utility of photography is to confirm white thinkers' racial constructs: Blackness is latent before birth and is a complication of native whiteness. Photography entered the archive not as a means of visual reproduction but as a new cipher of Black subalternity.

Home had already conducted experiments in 1820 on himself and two unnamed Black men, seeking to quantify the effects of sunlight on their respective skin.[25] Availing himself of a partial annular solar eclipse, he employed on his own skin "two lenses" (a field telescope) to focus sunrays. The article detailing his results has a single illustration: the serial phases of that solar eclipse, drawn by Francis Bauer (coincidentally, Niépce's 1827 contact at Kew). Observing that only his own skin reacted intensely and painfully, Home consulted one of the most celebrated scientists of the day, Humphry Davy. He confirmed his hypothesis that Black skin absorbs the heat of sunlight better than white skin and most likely mentioned to Home the article he'd written in 1802 on the pre-photographic experiments of

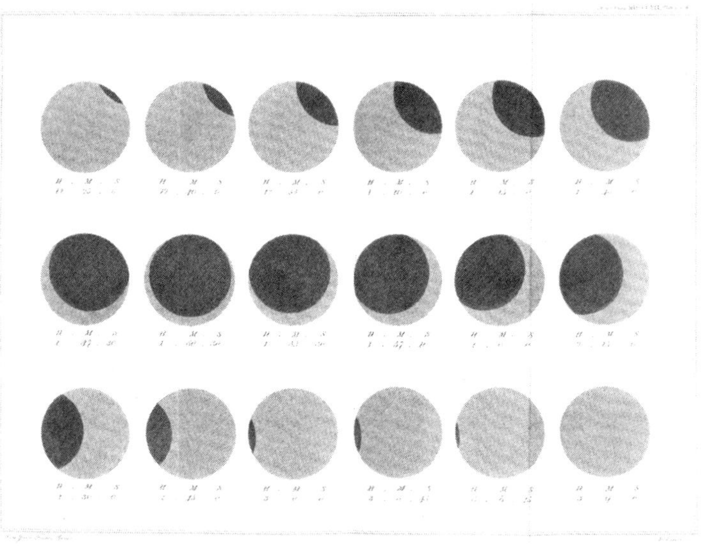

Figure I.2. **Francis Bauer, engraving of phases of the September 7, 1820, solar eclipse. Everard Home, "On the Black Rete Mucosum of the Negro, Being a Defence Against the Scorching Effects of the Sun's Rays,"** ***Philosophical Transactions of the Royal Society*** **111 (1821): 6, plate 1. Courtesy of the Royal Society.**

Wedgwood. Home and Davy thus represent a direct connection between Wedgwood's 1790s photonegative stencils and Niépce's 1827 heliographic plates. Their connection is not the desire to automatize visual copies but the enduring compulsion to explain Black pathology.

Photoimaging helps relativize notions that photography is an objective media. When film historian André Bazin defined the "objective character" of photography in 1945, he famously wrote: "For the first time an image of the world is formed automatically, without the creative intervention of man."[26] Bazin glosses over the history of automatic photoimages outlined above and mischaracterizes the objectivity of photography. As Charles Sanders Peirce astutely notes, photographs are "physically forced to correspond point by point to nature."[27] In other words, their copies are not spontaneous but calibrated to the range of the human eye. Indeed, recent scholars show how photography was always calibrated for white subjects and white viewers.[28] But photography does not register the objective world for a more fundamental reason: There is no objective world, visually speaking.[29] Flies, owls, humans, and x-ray satellites do not just see the world differently, they access separate windows of the electromagnetic radiation spectrum, which is unseeable as a whole. The realization early in the nineteenth century that "light" comprises not only invisible ranges but also black components and blackening properties was a major inducement for taking photoimaging toward photography and for beginning to depathologize Blackness (see chapter 4).

Kinemorphosis and Animated Visualization

The second mode of visualization we focus on concerns protocinema formations stemming from natural history. Natural history comprised investigations of the development and diversification of both the inanimate (cosmology and geology) and the animate (plants, animals, and humans). In the wake of the Copernican turn, natural history increasingly sidestepped biblical origin scenarios in search of other logics explaining the genesis of animate and inanimate beings. Jessica Riskin documents how a hybrid construct of biology and clocklike mechanics came to govern the explanation of animate beings well into the nineteenth century.[30] What I suggest in this study is that, for post-Copernican cosmology and astronomy, the new logic was not a construct but a new modality of visualization that I call "kinemorphosis." I define it as envisioning the sequential and uneven plastic transformation of matter and structures over time. Think of the growth of an embryo or the malleability of clouds. Emerging in astronomy around the beginning of the eighteenth century, I argue that kinemorphosis acted as a potent inducement toward visual animation heuristics and constituted a tangible source of protocinematic sensorium.

We are today so thoroughly shaped by moving images that it is a challenge to imagine an era when visual animation had zero conceptual and sensorial power and no human-made analog. Yet until roughly the second half of the seventeenth century, notions of animated images and visual plasticity were nearly unthinkable. Let's recall that none of the evolving processes we take for granted—the Big Bang, geomorphology, organic evolution, embryogenesis—were yet understood. Cinematic visualization arose in astronomy when interest in the path of comets confirming the heliocentric model produced a momentous new word and concept—*a trajectory*—highlighting visual motion. At the same time, precise illustrations of Moon phases, drifting sunspots, and solar eclipse phases leveraged sequential pictorial strategies. In medicine, William Harvey modeled blood circulation and especially epigenesis, the uneven growth and aggregation of embryos, eschewing the preformist theory of tiny homunculi inflating in the womb. However, these ways of visualizing dynamic metamorphosis remained marginal in the seventeenth century. For the early Enlightenment, René Descartes's attributes of reason as "clear and distinct" were projected on the world itself, implying that true states of fact could only be static or in captive motion.[31] As Klaas van Berkel, a scholar of seventeenth-century theories of motion, puts it: "Motion requires an explanation because it is not normal."[32] Visual motion as such remained nigh unpicturable, as philosopher George Berkeley neatly summarized in 1709: "Visible Motion is not of the same Sort with Tangible Motion."[33] While things are obviously moving, for Berkeley the eye can only register

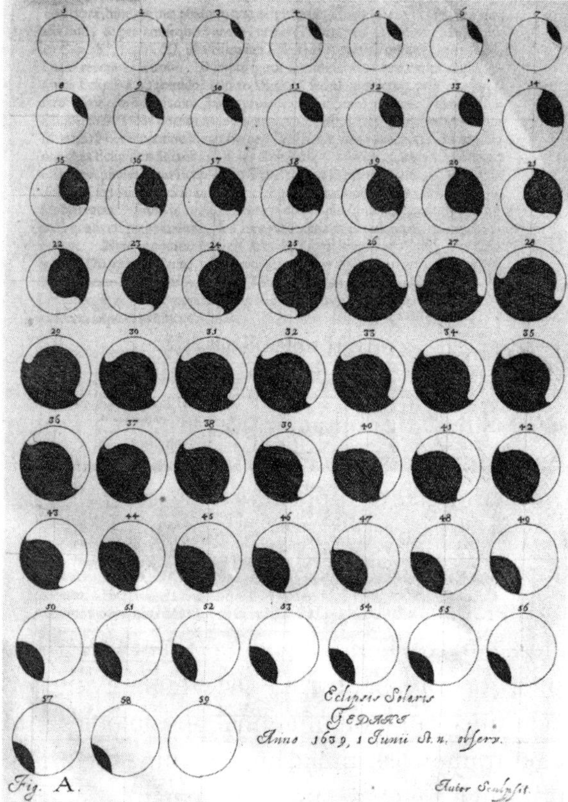

Figure I.3. **Phases of a solar eclipse observed in Gdańsk, Poland, in 1639. Johannes Hevelius, *Machinae Coelestis*, vol. 2 (Gdańsk, Poland: Simon Reiniger, 1679), fig. A, 2. Courtesy of La Bibliothèque Nationale de France Gallica.**

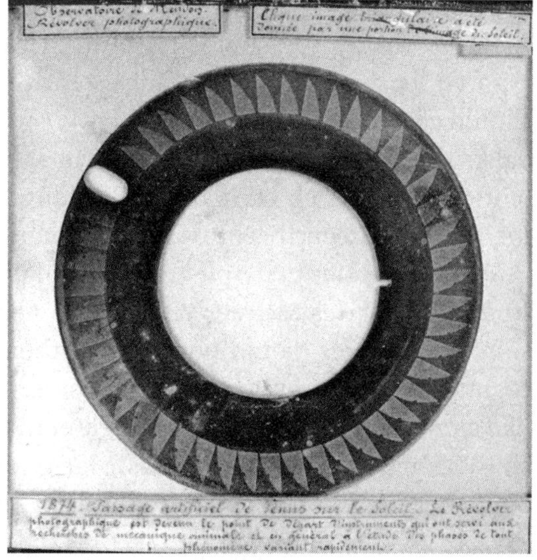

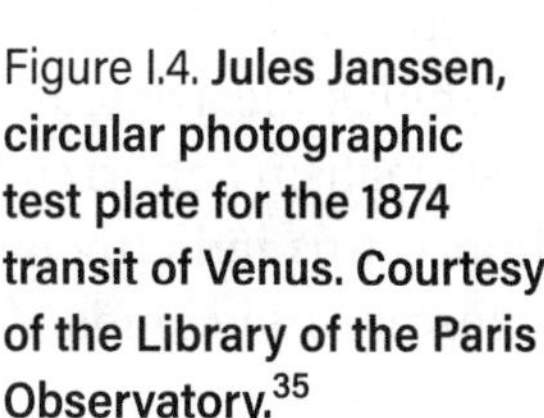

Figure I.4. **Jules Janssen, circular photographic test plate for the 1874 transit of Venus. Courtesy of the Library of the Paris Observatory.**[35]

clear and distinct sights, making visual motion a derivative formation, if not some kind of hallucination or illusion.[34]

Kinemorphosis gradually normalized after the 1730s, under the impetus of the new cosmology (see chapter 2).[36] It was recognized as such around 1802 when two natural philosophers independently published studies of paradigmatically kinemorphic objects—clouds.[37] London pharmacist Luke Howard stated that "the power of connecting [cloud types] . . . resides only in the mind before which their relations have passed, though perhaps imperceptibly, in review."[38] This comment symptomatically fuses the malleability of clouds with their comparative observation and visualization as though all share the same cinematic character. The other researcher was French botanist and anatomist Jean-Baptiste Lamarck, who studied cloud taxonomy through a setup used for observing astronomical trajectories: "A visual line having one end at the observer's eye and the other at the examined portion of the cloud" allows for "the movement of the observed cloud [to be] better sensed."[39] Lamarck's work on clouds partook of his general theory of transformism.[40] He is known for foreshadowing Darwinian evolution by positing the gradual transformation of animal physiologies into each other. But his larger framework aimed at explaining the origin of the Earth and life through long duration and dynamic interactions between gravitation, sunlight, and organic chemistry.[41]

Meteorology, the new science that Howard and Lamarck inaugurated, became a subset of nineteenth-century astronomy. So it should come as no surprise that a key inspiration for both meteorologists was the astronomer William Herschel and especially his revolutionary research on nebulae (literally, "cloud-like things").[42] In the late seventeenth century, astronomers began using *nebula* and *nebulosity* to refer to perplexing blobs of light in the firmament. Astronomer Charles Messier published a nebulae catalog in 1771 just so his colleagues would not mistake them for comets.[43] Formless cosmic chaff with neither rhyme nor reason, nebulae incarnated—like clouds at the time—what Enlightenment rationalism abhorred: shifty things and nebulous ideas. Herschel flipped this indictment on its head after observing thousands of star clusters and clouds of dust and stars, concluding that they all followed a similar process of kinemorphic development. In summing up that process, he outlined the cognitive and technical prerequisite for cinema: that thousands of discrete dissimilar static shapes can be understood through a single sequence of temporal metamorphosis (see chapter 3). This very formula underpins the animation of sequential chronophotographs in the late 1880s.

By the beginning of the nineteenth century, kinemorphic visualization and visual displays of motion—such as phantasmagoria shows, the Diorama of Daguerre, and moving panoramas—permeated visual culture. Media scholars have long acknowledged their protocinematic character. Visual motion was further mainstreamed by the 1830s, when physicist André-Marie Ampère coined the word *kinematics* (cinématique) for the study of all motions irrespective of force (thus distinct from mechanics). The term was then applied in the 1860s to the inner movements and design of all machines.[44] By the 1860s and 1870s, kinemorphic visualization pervaded scientific practices. It was theorized, for instance, by science popularizer G. F. Rodwell in "On the Perception of the Unseen" (1873):

> Let our eye revolve with infinite velocity in a circle, and let the circle rotate upon one of its diameters. A sphere whose surface consists of eyes will be the result, and let this be our instrument of vision; and let us call it for avoidance of repetition the Oculus, and with it travel space. Grant also to the Oculus power of contraction to the size of the atom, expansion to the size of the sun, infinite velocity in every direction, faculty of seeing in the dark, of distinguishing the most rapid motion, of seeing the imagined but unseen. . . . In the study of nature there are many unseen actions which it behoves us to visualise.[45]

Rodwell's mind experiment describes not vision or picturing or, strictly speaking, visual reality but a virtual, transscalar optics navigating through the space-time continuum to visualize it. My claim is that cinema emerged neither solely nor directly from chronophotography, as is premised by the canon of media history. Rather, its long maturation began somewhere around the 1650s with the visual animation insights of astronomers and physiologists; it was articulated in 1784 by astronomer Herschel's equation of static observations with a kinemorphic array in time; and it was technologically incepted by astronomer Camille Flammarion in 1867.

The Matrix of Photocinema

In 1807, three years after producing ephemeral photochemical prints, Thomas Young imagined a "chronometer." It was a weight-driven cylinder upon which a sensitive stylus attached to a vibrating body traced a sinuous graph of its vibration. Young's chronometer is recognized as a prototype that inspired early phonograph design in the 1870s. Yet, before that it served as the paradigmatic setup for a class of instruments that has been overlooked in the prehistory of cinema: chronoscopes and chronographs. Developed in the 1840s, these machines transduced moving phenomena into visual and measurable traces and directly influenced the invention of chronophotography (see chapter 6). Indeed, the cinematic apparatus Flammarion described in 1867 was an imaginary planet-size chronoscope (see chapter 7).

Young's preeminent role in both photoimaging and kinemorphic visualization signals the convolution of both paths. Though this study will characterize and reconstruct them separately for more clarity, they should be thought of as intertwined. The final technical emergences of photography and of cinema have traditionally been split into distinct disciplinary historiographies. Yet recent scholars of media in the long duration question this divide. Laurent Mannoni shows that protocinema insights are in fact much older and wider than comparable insights regarding proto-photography.[46] A key premise of this book is that photoimaging and kinemorphosis, though developed from separate insights, gradually combined into a common matrix—roughly from the arrival of the telescope as a paradigmatic visualization media onward (1608).[47] One further reason to soften the differentiation between photoimaging and kinemorphosis is that they refracted in very similar ways the entanglements of history and race within the macrocosm of natural history.

Synopsis of the Historiography of Photography and Cinema

Before moving to the fullest version of this book's argument and especially the place of racial discourses in it, a quick historical overview of scholarship on the origins of photography and cinema is in order.

Canonical History of Pre-Photography

1791–1797: Thomas Wedgwood makes unfixed silver nitrate contact prints of objects and of images painted on glass

1816: Nicéphore Niépce makes unfixed photographs of the view from his bedroom window

1816–1826: Niépce experiments with various substrates (metal, limestone, glass) and chemical compounds (gum arabic, guaiac, bitumen of Judea, etc.)

1826: A mysterious actor affirms he has fixed images in the camera obscura (according to Charles Chevalier)

1827: Niépce commits to "viewpoints from nature," renouncing reprography at the behest of Louis Daguerre

1827–1828: At Kew, Niépce presents low-contrast, fixed "heliography" plates to British optical scientists; Alphonse Eugène Hubert (later working with Daguerre) experiments with silver chloride imaging

1829: Collaborating with Niépce, Daguerre critiques the poor quality and lack of progress of heliography

1831: Daguerre, using iodine on a silver-coated metal plate, compares copies using a camera obscura and a solar microscope (a mirror reflecting solar rays into a lens)

1833: Niépce dies

1834: William Henry Fox Talbot makes "photogenic engravings" in Geneva, advised by astronomer John Herschel

1835: Daguerre makes a positive from a negative; Talbot reduces exposure time to ten minutes in miniature cameras but soon stops experimenting

1837: Daguerre takes exposure time down to seven to ten minutes; isolated experimenters explore photographic processes (John William Draper, Paul Gustave Froment, etc.)

1838: Daguerreotype perfected

1839: François Arago, head of the Paris Observatory and member of Parliament, makes Daguerre's process public and open source; John Herschel quickly retroengineers Daguerre's process and coins the word *photography*

Canonical History of Precinema

1860s: Plans and patents for setups of animated photography by several researchers (Louis Ducos du Hauron, Charles Cros)

1873: Astronomer Jules Janssen has Eugène Deschiens build a photographic revolver to record the passage of Venus across the Sun

1875: Astronomer Camille Flammarion publishes the authoritative description of Janssen's apparatus in the journal *La Nature*

1878: Eadweard Muybridge takes sequential photographs with a twelve-camera battery, projecting them in a magic lantern, later a zoopraxiscope; Étienne-Jules Marey publishes *The Graphic Method* based on drum electro-chronographs

1881: Muybridge meets Marey and shows him 1/500th-second exposures

1882: Marey constructs a single-camera chronophotographic setup to document animal and human locomotion

1885: Marey republishes *The Graphic Method* with a new section on the use of chronophotography; Kodak innovates celluloid film

1887: Muybridge publishes *Animal Locomotion,* a compendium of chronophotographic research

1888: Thomas Edison and William Kennedy Laurie Dickson patent the kinetograph/kinetoscope, a cylinder that can record and project as animation microphotographs arranged in a spiral

1888: Émile Reynaud projects canvas strips holding painted gelatin slides in a magic lantern

1889: Ottomar Anschütz exhibits his electrical tachyscope; Edison procures Kodak celluloid film for a new design of the kinetoscope

1891: Edison demonstrates the celluloid kinetoscope; several animated photographic projection patents and setups (e.g., Victor von Reitzner)

1893: Edison commercializes the celluloid kinetoscope

1894–1895: Several experimenters and showmen display cinematographic projection setups (Max Skladanowski, Grey and Otway Latham, etc.)

1895: Auguste and Louis Lumière commercialize a compact camera/projector with a cam and Maltese cross projecting celluloid films

For historians, until the mid-twentieth century, photography and cinema were inventions, the product of technical geniuses who realized the ageless dream of picturing reality. Proprietary and nationalistic biases were the norm. In the late nineteenth century, a pair of French advocates dethroned Daguerre, until then the official inventor of photography. They did so in favor of Niépce but without considering William Henry Fox Talbot.[48] Similarly, in the 1870s Eliza Meteyard proclaimed Thomas Wedgwood to be the inventor of photography, as did R. B. Litchfield in the 1900s (a Wedgwood descendant).[49] In the 1930s, Austrian chemist Josef Maria Eder attributed photography entirely to the German chemist Johann Heinrich Schulze's 1720s dabbling in photochemistry.[50]

Postwar historians like Beaumont Newhall, Helmut Gernsheim, André Bazin, and Georges Sadoul offer more nuanced genealogies focusing on better-documented technological developments.[51] They invoke a convergence model: for photography, the camera obscura combined with photochemistry; for cinema, still photography combined with serial projection via Muybridge and Marey. An important turn occurred in the early 1980s when the historiographic paradigm of early cinema shifted toward empirical research, the study of early spectatorial experience, and the polyvalence of "attraction" in the apparatus. Personal computing and the internet then enlarged notions of media beyond traditional audiovisual models. Deac Rossell's conclusions that "everything written before 1980 is suspect, and much that was written thereafter," reflects the mindset of current media scholarship.[52]

In the 1980s and 1990s, the influence of Michel Foucault and other critical theorists opened media studies to cultural studies in works by Paul Virilio, Friedrich Kittler, Jonathan Crary, and François Albéra and Maria Tortajada, among others.[53] They balanced archival documentation of technogenesis with social and cultural analysis. They bracketed grand narratives in favor of finer-grained studies on subsegments of media apparatuses, such as screen practices, spectacular culture, sound studies, magic lantern exhibitions, moving panoramas, etc. Simultaneously, well-researched monographs on individual precursors began dispelling the clichés and approximations of earlier biographers.[54]

The more recent trend of media archaeology reopens horizons far and wide. Gabriel Rockhill summarizes this approach as favoring "metastatic emergence" through "a variable-speed transformation unevenly distributed across social space" and a combination of heterogeneous factors.[55] Media archaeology currently rejects biological/genealogical models relying on birth, growth, death, inheritance, lineage, etc., finding such metaphorical language complicit with Western biopolitical hegemony. Instead of a vertical logic of preexisting ideas about separate media waiting for implementation, the field favors horizontal rhizomes of intersecting and transnational media practices and variants. Media archaeologists probe long durations down to the medieval era with growing attention to non-Western sources.[56] They also develop original research motifs such as vital temporality, insects, or geology while often dialoguing with contemporary art practices.[57] This strategy was summarized by Vivian Sobchack as "re-presencing" media history with the stated goal of advocating for diverse origins in the face of alarming industrial uniformization in audiovisual media.[58] One tenet of media archaeology is that no media variant is valued over another, since their final success reflects contingent cultural discourses and commercial pressures, not necessarily a superior technical potential. Introducing the English translation of Mannoni's 1995 cinema archaeology *The Great Art of Light and Shadow,* Tom Gunning explains this stance as ridding media history of back-shadowing and the fallacy of preformism.[59]

Today's studies of media prehistory, in sum, rest on an inverted funnel model in which implemented media at the tip are de-emphasized while the broad base of alternative antecedents, components, motivations, and practitioners are revalued. Media archaeology accordingly abstains from unifying scenarios. While this book is beholden to the new perspectives inaugurated by the field, it breaks with it in two significant ways: First, it proposes a comprehensive matrix accounting for the development of photocinematic ideas, practices, and technics over nearly three centuries; second, it delves into the racist underpinnings that have shaped much of media prehistory but have scarcely been investigated at all.

Race and Astronomy in the Matrix of Photocinema

This book is premised on the idea that the matrix of photocinema was coextensive with premodern and modern Europe's imperatives to visualize the world within a horizon of power. We should first qualify the concept of "world" as polysemic, multilayered, and fragmented. The Earth had long been visualized as a globe by the seventeenth century, but it included large terrae incognitae (unknown lands) and its distances and longitudes remained approximate. Lands previously unknown (the Americas, Australia) and more actively accessed (West Africa, East Asia) had not yet coalesced into a global sense of smooth geography that became a hallmark of the mid-nineteenth century—notably in Alexander von Humboldt's four-volume *Kosmos* (1844–1856). As Benjamin Schmidt suggests, in the seventeenth century such lands were envisioned through an exoticizing lens of travel accounts, fanciful illustrations, and merchandise flows, all of which contributed to a contrastive Eurocentric identity.[60] Hence, geographical, racial, and cultural otherness did not add more difference to a global commons. They were different worlds, truly otherworldly by European norms, reinforcing the racialized multiple worlds hypothesis.[61] Indeed, in most European languages, *world* denoted disparate objects, from Earth to the whole universe.[62] *A world* could also mean any planet or star, the secular realm of human life, a continent, its peoples, even an era of the past. *The world* was also synonymous with high society—earthlings that matter.

Such a composite world picture facilitated speculative cross-linkages by natural philosophers from one layer to another.[63] A single session at the newly formed Royal Society in the 1660s, for instance, intermixed discussions about the Moon and gravitation, the hypothesis of beings inhabiting other planets (other worlds), conjectures regarding "pre-Adamites"—thought to be a prehuman species—and the origin of skin color differences.[64] These were not pell-mell topics belonging to different disciplines but complementary inquiries about world constitution. For instance, as we will see in chapter 1, in the seventeenth century the term *species* denoted not only sets of humans or animals but also varieties of light and imaging.

This epistemic fluidity makes it less surprising that the first application of the word *race* for subdivisions of humankind came from an astronomical purview. It occurred in a short text of 1684 by François Bernier, a French doctor who long resided at the Mughal court, titled "A New Division of the Earth According to the Various Species or Races of Men Inhabiting It."[65] This foundational essay distributes peoples into four "races": sub-Saharan Africans, Far East Asians, Lapps, and a capacious fourth race composed of Europeans as well as Maghrebi, Levantines, subcontinental Indians, Southeast Asians, and northern Native Americans—in spite of their being "different from us in the shape of their face and their color."[66] Commentators interpret this odd racial distribution as crossing phenotypical boundaries (Robert Bernasconi), fragmenting Christianity's human unity (Justin E. H. Smith), or weakening monogenism.[67] Siep Stuurman emphasizes its prurient exoticizing of nonwhite women.[68] But no commentators provide a rationale for this confounding fourth race.

Its source was Bernier's teacher, the astronomer and natural philosopher Pierre Gassendi, whose Latin works Bernier edited and translated into French. An anti-Cartesian empiricist and atomist, Gassendi believed that other planets were inhabited, making explicit the link between racialization and conjectural extraterrestrials: "&

if . . . things born in Europe, Africa & America are wholly different from each other it is believable that those born on the Moon would be even more different. . . . If those born and raised in cold lands have such difficulty living in hot ones, and those from hot ones in cold ones, what would happen to a man whom we imagine was transported to the Moon whose torrid zone is so much more intemperate than ours?"[69] For Gassendi, latitude was a better index for classifying people than skin color or climate. He established a system of correspondence between peoples living at equal distances from the equator, whether in the same hemisphere but opposite meridians ("Periscians"), opposite hemispheres and the same meridian ("Antoecians"), or opposite hemispheres and opposite meridians ("Antipodes"). For Gassendi and Bernier, race was not primarily phenotypical but astronomical: It grouped humans together according to the length of the shadow their bodies project at noon.[70] It is only in this gnomonic perspective that European, Middle Eastern, Indian, and Native American peoples were deemed coracial. Modern racialization was ushered in by a procrustean photocinematic apparatus projecting human silhouettes on an earthly screen.

The larger stakes of racial classification lay of course in Europe's most consequent practice from the seventeenth to the nineteenth centuries: the mass-scale enslavement of Africans and Afrodescendants. The origin and global distribution of Black peoples and the optics, physiology, and feared mutability of Black skin were pivotal for envisaging the natural history of Earth within the solar system—and justifying slavery. For white natural philosophers, not a few of whom (like Boyle or Pierre-Louis Moreau de Maupertuis) were personally beholden to the transatlantic slave trade, Blackness was enmeshed in the maintenance of wealth and class, national, and civilizational standing. As the example of Home makes plain, Black peoples were ready subjects of investigation in both mind experiments and medical experimentation because the conjectural etiology of Blackness amounted to a central test for the validity of any system of natural philosophy. This resulted in a twin presumption shadowing the Enlightenment period: Humans were naturally white—in an aboriginal and exemplary sense—and Blackness was unnatural and in need of pathological explanation.[71]

While recent media scholars have increasingly examined racialized discourses and representations in early photographs and movies, almost no existing research addresses the role of racialization in the long emergence of media. This book outlines some of the racial constructs hardwired into the architectonics of photocinematic media. Part of its aim is to keep undoing "the investment in [the] exclusion" of race as an explanatory factor—an investment still extant in much early media and early science studies.[72] I adhere to the premise of race studies: All aspects of the Western episteme since at least the seventeenth century should be gauged for their reliance on racial and racist assemblages. Sylvia Wynter and Denise Ferreira da Silva, notably, rearticulated the "scientific revolution" through such racial analytics. They show how the sociohistorical death and ontological subalternity of peoples of color resulted from an epistemic program of reserving subjective transparency for white people. By objectifying racial others, the white Enlightenment legitimated its position of absolute legislator over the visible. Ferreira da Silva states that "the racial is an effect and a tool of the productive violent act that produces the global as a modern context of signification" (*Toward a Global Idea of Race,* 29). In this global racial context, what she calls the "play of universal reason" tames human inner motions (affects) in philosophy and outer motions (Newtonian laws) in astronomy to position white scientific subjectivity as an unaffectable and unmovable center for universal cognitive dominion. This accounts for why, as in Bernier's text published the same year as Isaac Newton's "De Motu" (1684), vision, visualization, astronomy, motion, projection, and race coalesced into a tight and powerful discursive formation, as Wynter points out.[73] It is from within that same formation, I argue, that the matrix of photocinematic media unfolded.

We are now equipped to formulate the central argument of this book: astronomical and cosmological visualization within the purview of natural history—together with the accounts of racial differentiation and Blackness that linked Earth to the cosmos, as well as photochemistry to skin color—were integral to the new modes of imaging that progressively shaped the matrix of photocinema from the seventeenth to the nineteenth centuries. There were three main racial discourses in this process, all focusing on Blackness as the polar opposite of aboriginal and normal whiteness.

The first is the thermo-metabolic thesis of Blackness, which concerned the purported cause of Black skin, associated with hot climate and nutrition since Aristotle. It breaks down into several components: one is the notion that Blackness proceeds from an unseen or latent biological structure not found among white people and that must be located in Black bodies (the crypto-latency thesis). A later hypothesis—inflected by the new photochemistry of the 1780s—is that Black skin results from photosensitivity alone: the photological thesis of Home. The latter was strongly reinforced by the arrival of photonegative images making white people look Black.

The second is the astro-racial thesis, tied to heliocentric astronomy. If other planets revolve around the Sun like the Earth does, they too must be inhabited, and their inhabitants should be envisioned through the same thermo-metabolic thesis of race, using a planet's distance from the Sun instead of latitude. Though purely speculative, it had a strong perverting effect: It confirmed racism as if it were dictated by the cosmos itself.

Finally, there is transracial and panracial morphism. This was an evolutionary and teleological discourse fomented in reaction to white fears of collective devolution and occasioned by mixed-race populations in Caribbean colonies. As neither the purported cause of Blackness nor the genetics of race-mixing were known, white fears included at times individual transracial morphism, with tanning as an early symptom. In panracial morphism, nature—assisted by nefarious means including conquest, so-called civilizing, eugenics, and extermination—directs the future mutation of all human races into whiteness as a universal telos. Present for instance in the work of Immanuel Kant (see chapter 3), panracial morphism was boosted in the nineteenth century by Georg Wilhelm Friedrich Hegel's philosophy of history and later by biased interpretations of Darwinism. It played an active and sustained role in cinematic visualization.

It should be added that these various racial constructs were invoked at various times by proslavery and polygenic views (considering humanity as formed of separate species) and by proponents

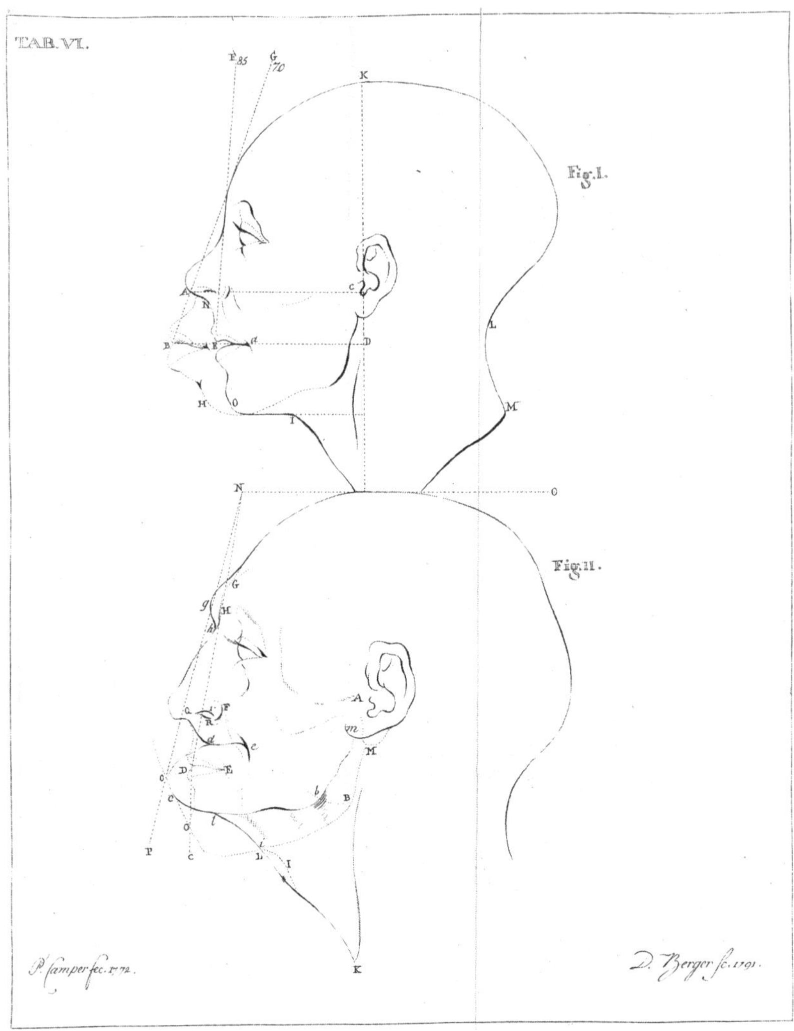

Figure I.5. **Petrus Camper, visualization of a human head morphing kinetically across races and ages, 1772. Courtesy of ETH-Bibliothek Zürich.**

of abolitionism and monogenism (humanity as a single species). In this regard, the matrix of photocinema was just as contested as the dominant culture it refracted.

Such racial discourses may seem at first far afield from tangible reconstructions of photography and cinema. However, while this book's insights into long duration intersections between race and visuality are novel in media studies, they are old news for race studies and diasporic Black thought. Thinkers of color have always known that optics and the visual sphere at large were forcibly policed in racial terms through modes ranging from total invisibility to hypervisible profiling.[74] In 1791, African American astronomer Benjamin Banneker argued to Thomas Jefferson that the "deepest dye" of his skin was irrelevant in gauging his intellectual capacities.[75] Frederick Douglass pointedly leveraged photographic portraiture as an active antidote to visual prejudice, while Frantz Fanon made plain how Black existence felt photographically "fixed" by white people's gaze, and Édouard Glissant famously claimed opacity as a right and a poetics of resistance (see chapter 5).[76]

That Blackness has long been culturally enmeshed in protomedia is the original proposal put forward by philosopher Fred Moten with "the black apparatus." "It's no accident," he writes, "that the story of the disciplinary animation of the image comes more fully into its own by way of the black apparatus."[77] This statement points in part to the biopolitical coercion of Black bodies coeval with Étienne-Jules Marey's chronophotographic work on human locomotion. More generally it directs us toward the mechanized surveillance of racialized laboring bodies. For Moten, a constant historical constraint on Black life was that "the Negro must be still, but still be moving"—that is, kept socially inert the better to extract forced labor (*Black and Blur,* 71). This suggests that the still/moving dialectic central to photocinema is also at the core of the black apparatus.[78] Moten defines the latter as "the sound/image of the black in the modern Euro-American audiovisual imagination," encompassing, for instance, "motion capture and composite imaging" in connection with "seriality and esthetic criminality," as well as plantocracy's "reproductive reproduction" (74, 76).[79] That expression refers to the sexual exploitation of Black women and the control of childbearing on the plantation, as a subtext for any articulation of media reproducibility. He suggests that the "montagic, dissonant, syncopated abstract; the criminal disruption of narrative; the grapho-reproductive improvisation of narrative," constitute a "portable dark continent" (120). In that virtual space, Black experience can signify and reappropriate the black apparatus while it keeps struggling against its strictures. For Moten, modernity at large needs to be retheorized, taking full account of enslavement, abolition, segregation, and discrimination in their reciprocal relations with media technicity.

He calls this recursive relationality "the anorigin of modernity" since it reaches to and keeps reviving earlier eras (Moten, *Black and Blur,* 120). This premise resonates with the media "anarchaeology" of theoretician Siegfried Zielinski in his critique of any media history that discounts Western autofoundation (arché meaning "foundation"). Significantly, Zielinski and Moten derive some of their inspiration expressly from Caribbean philosopher Édouard Glissant, whose poetics of relation refigures the Middle Passage and the Black Atlantic as the sunken subsurface of modernity.[80]

Early formations of photocinema proceeded from this subsurface as well. For instance, Thomas Wedgwood came from one of the most actively proabolitionist families of Georgian England. The British abolitionist movement famously adopted a cameo produced in the ceramics factory of his father, Josiah Wedgwood, that depicted a kneeling, enchained Black man encircled by the motto "Am I not a man and a brother?" Thomas Wedgwood most likely conducted his pre-photographic experiments there too. This opens the possibility of direct connections between abolition and photocinema. Several striking coincidences reinforce this possibility: Henry Peter Brougham and François Arago, the two state officials responsible for the passage of abolition legislation (England in 1833 and France in 1848), also conducted pre-photographic experiments (see chapter 4). A correlation between the context of abolition and the emergence of photography appears, therefore, to exist. But what is its exact tenor? Wedgwood toured the Caribbean in 1799 without making the slightest mention of slavery or enslaved peoples in his correspondence. As for Brougham and Arago, they made at times strikingly racist statements and, as state politicians, their abolitionist motivations were mixed with expediency and compromises. Such correlations must remain for now noncausal, though they do illustrate the continuous connective tissue between photocinema, Blackness, and slavery. Overall, while this connective tissue occasionally yielded arguments for emancipation and, in rarer instances,

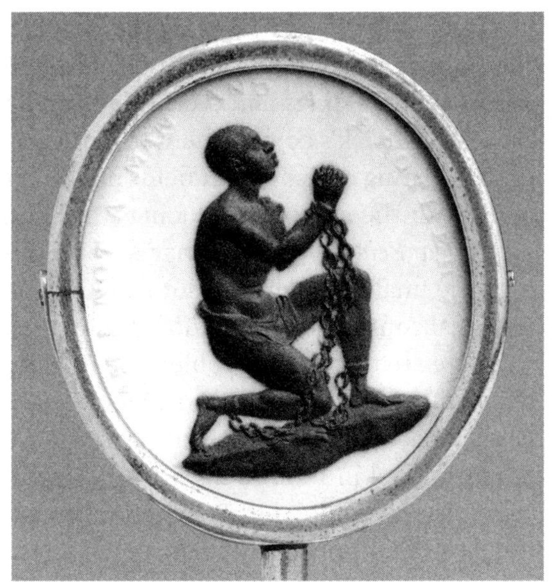

Figure I.6. **William Hackwood, *Am I Not a Man and a Brother?,* antislavery cameo, Wedgwood Works, ca. 1787. Courtesy of the Metropolitan Museum of Art.**

for equality, it was overwhelmingly rife with brutal anti-Blackness and so-called scientific—that is, unscientific—racism.

One of the most cynical aspects of Western modernity is its endless capacity to conceal the violence of its autoproduction. This concealment, Charles W. Mills notes, means that Black students studying philosophy in college who "have grown up in a universe" centered on the "African-American experience" of racial discrimination are suddenly "asked to pretend they are living in the other."[81] This split world informs the history of photocinema. Katherine McKittrick reminds us in *Dear Science,* with pressure on the word *dear,* that our academic work today remains beholden to the disinterested pursuit of Enlightenment science in continuing to elide at once nonwhite peoples and the history of their elision. This study takes such interpellations to heart by continuing to document "the unmet promise of modernity" from the depths of its own archive.[82]

Methodology

This book adopts a transhistorical scope and a panoramic method, relying on multiple case studies to reach a critical mass of material shoring up its central argument. Ranging across centuries and disciplines—foremost being media studies, science studies, and race studies—presents significant challenges in terms of the composite nature of the findings and their reception by disciplinary readers. I share McKittrick's commitment to explore "disobedient relationality" by locating crossovers in fields not usually dialoguing with each other, with the aim of "producing work at the edge of new meanings" (*Dear Science,* 45, 48). That is to say, this book's ambition is not to be the final word about photocinema's origination but to center historical connective tissue too long left unexamined.

There are two signal problems in media prehistory studies. The first is the problematic constructs of origins and origination that media archaeology has rejected—perhaps hastily. In taking the telescope's arrival in 1608 as a starting point, I am not subscribing to strict origins. Following Foucault's genealogical debunking, this study retraces lines of descent down to this overlooked paradigmatic setup for photocinema media only in order "to make visible all of those discontinuities that traverse us."[83] The notion of *matrix* points to this discontinuous rhizome of formation processes. These include, per the *Oxford English Dictionary,* "a place or medium in which something is originated," "the epidermal layer," "the elements which make up a particular system," "any mould in which something is cast or shaped," "a copy (positive or negative) of an original disc recording," "an array of symbols," "an array of circuit elements," "a rectangular array of potential image points," and finally the unseeable substrate of visual reality as in *The Matrix* trilogy.[84] The matrix of photocinema amounts to a complex set of media, epidermal layers, systems, molds, copies, arrays, circuits, and image points within sources that include texts, pictures, events, and instruments.

The second problem is historicization. While technical innovations and their components may be dated often quite precisely, it is more difficult to articulate the larger cultural and political processes conditioning their formation. This book attempts to do just that by locating specific cultural paths of emergence at specific hinge periods for specific features of the racialized photocinema matrix. The roughly chronological exposition begins with the arrival of the telescope in 1608 and ends in 1867 with Flammarion's fictive cinema apparatus, the telechronoscope, twenty years prior to Edison's kinetoscope with the same cylinder design. This chronological arc, meant to ease the task of readers confronted with a vast amount of new material, should not be mistaken for a vector of historical necessity. Indeed, for Flammarion, the cinema apparatus was inherently antitelic since it was predominantly a machine for traveling back in time to visualize at last the whole of human and natural history (see the conclusion).

Envisioning human history as a whole was a major imperative of the Western matrix of photocinema. Methodologically, this fractured wholeness remains present in this book's racial nomenclature. There is much productive disagreement among Black studies thinkers regarding the capitalization of *Black/black*. For instance, La Marr Jurelle Bruce writes: "I use a lowercase *b* because I want to emphasize an improper blackness: a blackness that is a 'critique of the proper'; . . . a blackness that is neither capitalized nor propertized via the protocols of Western grammar; a blackness that centers those who are typically regarded as lesser and *lower cases,* as it were."[85] Fred Moten makes the same choice along similar philosophical lines. Others, such as Lori L. Tharps and Kwame Anthony Appiah, adduce quite different reasons for capitalizing *Black*. A secondary but apposite debate is whether to capitalize *white/whiteness.* Nicholas Whittaker provides a useful encapsulation of the debate in "Case Sensitive: Why We Shouldn't Capitalize 'Black.'"[86]

The usage I opted for in this book should not be considered normative. I use *black* and *blackness* to refer to chromatic blackness outside of an overt racial context—at the same time as this study shows ostensibly nonracial blackness to have been racialized since at least the seventeenth century. Conversely, I use *Black* and *Blackness* whenever there is an overt racial context. Hence, I always use *Black skin,* even though, as we know, there is no such a thing because it is neither black nor different from any other human skin.

I do not capitalize *white* and *whiteness* in racial contexts for three antithetical reasons. First, whiteness was an unexamined historical norm until Black peoples rebelled against that norm. Thus, whiteness must be conceptually and historically regarded as subordinate to Blackness. Second, whiteness needs no elevation from social justice and, consequently, not in terms of stylistics either. Finally, most of the white thinkers treated in this book did not capitalize *white/whiteness,* but they often capitalized *Black/Blackness* to differentiate both races and reject Blackness as nonhuman and quasi-animal. My overall style choice is, then, in Fred Moten's apt phrase, to keep open "the case of blackness" rather than to renormalize it for the purposes of consistency or equity—cruelly latecomer directives in the Western historical record.[87]

In his 1785 indictment of slavery, British abolitionist Thomas Clarkson wrote: "Suppose we were to take a common globe; then begin at the equator to paint every country along the meridian line in succession from thence to the poles; and to paint them with the same colour which prevails in the respective inhabitants of each, we should see black, with which we had been obliged to begin, insensibly turn to an olive, and the olive, through as many intermediate colours, to a white. . . . The difference would consist wholly in shades of the same colour."[88] Visualizing our globe's continuum from white to black as if he were on the Moon, Clarkson affirms that it is—that we are—"the same colour." Instrumental for the development of photocinema since the seventeenth century, this racial overview effect remained deeply ambivalent in motivating both the maintenance of white supremacy and its unravelling.

Chapter Outline

Chapter 1, "Photosophia: Visualizing the Racialized Cosmos in the Seventeenth Century," addresses entanglements of astronomy, instrumentation, illustration, and anti-Blackness in seventeenth-century natural philosophy. I examine the racial subtext of the telescope's arrival and its early combinations with the camera obscura, before reviewing key sources of visualization: Athanasius Kircher's "photosophia," in *Ars Magna Lucis et Umbrae* (1644)—the first word with the prefix *photo-*—and sequential illustration strategies in Johannes Hevelius's *Selenographia* (1647), Christiaan Huygens's *Systema Saturnium* (1659), and Huygens's magic lantern slides (1659). With Robert Hooke's *Micrographia* (1665), we turn toward the intersection of racial discourses and astronomical visualization present in Johannes Kepler's *Somnium* (1634), Francis Godwin's *The Man in the Moone* (1638), Cyrano de Bergerac's *The Comical History of the States and Empires of the Moon* (1657), and Bernard Le Bovier, sieur de Fontenelle's racist treatise *Conversations on the Plurality of Worlds* (1686).

Chapter 2, "Kinemorphosis: Cosmological Animation and History's Whiteness," expands this protocinema path via the role of animated visualization in eighteenth-century cosmogenesis from Thomas Wright to Kant. It shows how Kant embedded anti-Blackness as a structural feature in the first truly kinemorphic cosmology. After examining William Herschel and Caroline Herschel's nebular cosmology, which provided the base equation of cinema, I turn to the first two-reel prototype of cinema: Jacques Barbeu-Dubourg's chronographic machine. It opens up interrelations between astronomy, race, abolitionism, and progressive models of history in David Rittenhouse, Adam Smith, Marie-Jean-Antoine-Nicolas de Caritat, marquis de Condorcet, and L.-M. Henriquez.

Chapter 3, "Photoimaging Hieroglyphs: Blackening, Anti-Blackness, and Proto-Photography," explores the paths of emergence of photography in the context of enslaved rebellions in the Caribbean. We connect the earliest fiction about photo-picturing, sited in Africa (1760), to Jean-Baptiste Demanet, a slave-trader in Senegal whose racist 1767 mineral theory of Blackness reshaped late eighteenth-century views on race. The chapter segues to photoimaging unseen forces of nature through nonmimetic traces, often called "hieroglyphs," from Lichtenberg's electrostatic figures to the anti-Black silhouette theory of Johann Kaspar Lavater, the photochemistry of Jean Senebier, and the photochemical silhouetting of Jacques Charles.

Chapter 4, "Photology: Black Light, the Wave Theory of Light, and Pre-Photography," documents the role of photochemistry in British physical optics (1800–1803) and French physical optics (1807–1839). After the discoveries of infrared and ultraviolet, new species of so-called black light emerged, including William Herschel's "black-making rays" (which have never been analyzed). We reexamine the photochemical picturing of Wedgwood, Davy, and

Young, together with the wave theory of light (WTL), against the background of abolitionism and the new photological paradigm of Black skin. The second part turns to French photochemical experiments in the 1810s. They were conducted while confirming the WTL and inflected pre-photography through Parisian instrument-makers who worked with Niépce, Daguerre, and the Paris Observatory. François Arago figures centrally as the leader of research on photochemistry, astronomy, and the WTL. He was also a precursor of photography who trained William Henry Fox Talbot in 1824, advised Daguerre in 1838, and was entrusted by John Herschel to reveal his father's "black-making rays."

Chapter 5, "Selenography: The Moon, Slavery, and the Dark Side of Photography," contrasts the scientific emergence of "heliography" or "sun writing" with an apposite path focused on moonlight. We examine photonegative discourses in early photography and in the work of Haitian thinker Pompée Valentin Vastey and abolitionist Jacques-Henri Bernardin de Saint-Pierre, who both debunked anti-Blackness. Racial selenography resurfaces in the infamous 1835 Great Moon Hoax written on the heel of race riots, which describes the racial hierarchy of Lunarians on the Moon. They are observed through a telescope supposedly built by John Herschel that displays a mobile vision and cinematic telepresence. The chapter ends with Brougham and Arago, who each conducted photoimaging research and ushered in abolition legislation in England (1833) and France (1848). To elucidate the problematic connection between photography and abolition, we turn to Frederick Douglass, who leveraged the daguerreotype and "tracings of time" to combat racist stereotypes.

Chapter 6, "The Graphic Method: Time-Tracing, Colonial Supremacy, and Astrophotography," amends the accepted view that Marey's chronophotography is the proximal source for cinema. Examining the history of self-tracing apparatuses since the seventeenth century, the chapter argues that Young's cylinder chronometer recorder, John Herschel's 1840 cylinder-camera, electro-chronograph drums, and moving-plate photography in the 1850s qualify Marey's "graphic method." The chapter segues into the role of time and ophthalmic hieroglyphs in optical perception and simulation instruments from the 1830s to the 1850s. Marey is also approached as a proponent of dynamic physiology, in parallel with John William Draper, a pre-photographic experimenter whose racist theories include transracial morphism, while leveraging photoimaging and kinemorphosis. The chapter closes with colonial astrophotography in the 1860s, when sequential photography was first deployed (for capturing solar eclipses), which inspired Jules Janssen's photographic revolver for the 1874 transit of Venus.

Chapter 7, "Flammarion's Telechronoscope: The End of Natural History and the Beginning of Cinema," argues that the astronomer Flammarion was instrumental for precinema, the inception of cinema, and early film. His mind experiment *Lumen* (1867) describes a photosensitive planet on which the animated history of Earth is optically imprinted—an astronomical conceit formulating a working cinema apparatus. Edison would use the same setup—spiraling microphotographs on a rotating cylinder—twenty years later. I document Flammarion's familiarity with all aspects of physical optics, his cylinder photometer, various fictional models of cinema (1867, 1891, 1894), and the astronomical animation shorts he created and exhibited (1897–1898). Flammarion interacted closely with four other precursors of precinema: Marey, photographer and balloonist Nadar, media inventor Cros, and Janssen. A key popularizer of science mixed with parascientific beliefs, he promulgated a macrohistorical model of history as an alternative to the supremacist ideology of positivist progress.

"Conclusion: The Matrix of Photocinema and the Moral Universe" steps back from this study's scholarship to reflect on its overarching thesis in connection with contemporary views on racial justice, especially Olúfẹ́mi O. Táíwò's proposals for global reparations. I also examine how important films like Georges Méliès's *A Trip to the Moon* (1902)—refracting the French conquest of Madagascar in 1896—dovetailed with the racist matrix of photocinema. Finally, I focus on a recurring feature in this study: intertwinements between protocinematic forms and modern history. I examine two stories of W. E. B. Du Bois and a short film by Jean Renoir showing how the film apparatus, racial injustice, and astronomy remained entangled in the postcinema era. One of Du Bois's stories includes a virtual movie of racism that was inspired by a cinema technology he discovered at the 1899 Paris Exhibition where his booth was not far from Marey's, the "chromo-megascope"—a film apparatus prototype bringing color to the big picture.

1

Photosophia

Visualizing the Racialized Cosmos in the Seventeenth Century

The Telescope in Racial Context

Innovative and striking means of visualizing the heliocentric solar system—its outer planets, the Moon, the Earth, and light itself—appeared during the seventeenth century. They contributed to a new universal framework linking physics, politics, visual culture, and race, within which the first lineaments of photocinema began to combine. The telescope's arrival in the early 1600s was a catalyst, obviously improving upon older astronomical instruments but also profoundly altering the texture and reach of visualization.[1] Since that apparatus is found at every stage in the development of photography and cinema down to Camille Flammarion's 1867 telechronoscope, we will regard it as a prototype for the entire matrix. However, a careful archaeology of the instrument complicates its paradigmatic role in the "scientific revolution."

First, there was never such a thing as *the* telescope. Optician Hans Lippershey built the first models in the fall of 1608 in The Hague, but various apparatuses were then quickly put together by others in France, Italy, and England. Bearing different names attesting to different uses and conceptual framing ("spyglass," "perspective cylinder," "lunettes," "occhiale," etc.), they came in both monocular and binocular configurations. While synonymous with astronomy, their initial application was in fact battlefield weaponry. We know this from an anonymous pamphlet in French that describes Lippershey offering his new device to Maurice of Nassau, the leader of Dutch states in rebellion against their Spanish occupiers. With these "field-glasses [lunettes]," the pamphlet states, "we can distinctly [distinctement] discover and see things distant from three or four leagues, as if we saw them a hundred yards from us."[2] Applications for reconnaissance and sharpshooting were instantly recognized by the warring parties, and both Maurice's brother Henry and the Spanish general Ambrogio di Filippo Spinola offered to pay Lippershey not to divulge his new technology.[3] The pamphleteer muses in passing that telescopes could magnify "even stars." About a year later, Galileo pointed his three-foot-long wooden tube with two lenses toward Jupiter, discerning four orbiting blobs that he concluded were moons. Only eight celestial bodies were then known in the solar system—Earth, the Sun and Moon, Mercury, Venus, Mars, Jupiter, and Saturn. The telescope increased that number by a whopping 50 percent. More importantly, because these four celestial bodies did not orbit Earth, their discovery challenged the Church's geocentric orthodoxy.

Historians of the telescope have paid little attention to this military context and disregarded the other two-thirds of the pamphlet that concerns lavish gifts Maurice received from two ambassadors from Siam. The latter are portrayed as "of a brown color, the nose pushed in, with thick hair black and coarse like a horse-mane," while "their language is very barbarous & very difficult to interpret, & letters are all the same: words are not distinct [distinguez]" (*Ambassades du Roy de Siam*, 11). This last word discloses the tacit logic of the pamphlet. Precisely what the racialized and animalized envoys lack—distinguishability—becomes the new power the telescope provides to white Europeans: enhanced optical distinction. Signaling Holland's ramped-up ambitions among colonial powers, the pamphlet is a geopolitical and racial declaration.[4] As is well established, European governments from the seventeenth century onward funded astronomical research to foster the global navigation technology requisite for intercontinental commerce, colonization, and the trading of enslaved peoples.[5] Astronomy was never

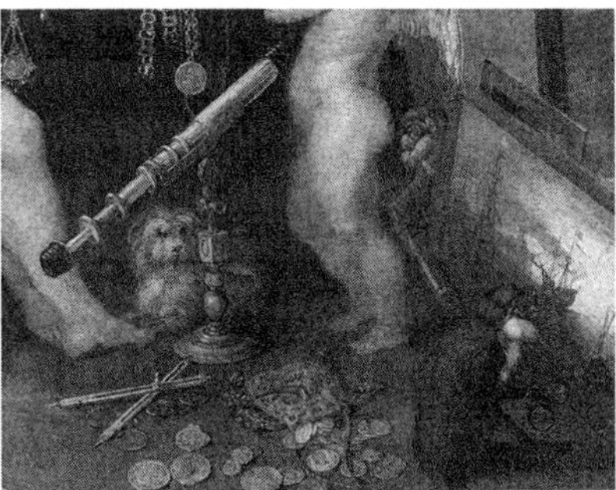
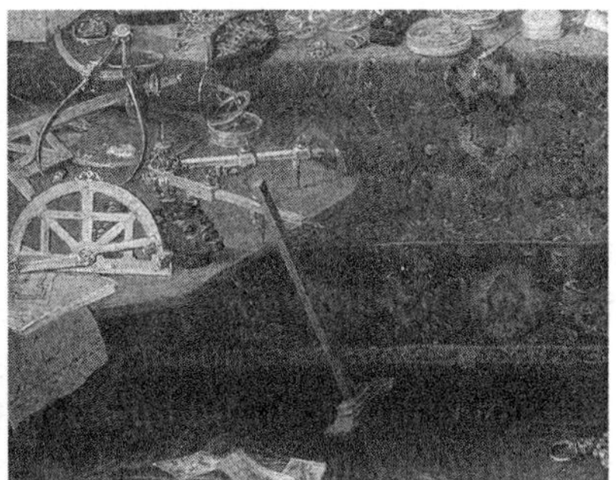

Figure 1.1. **Jan Bruegel and Peter Paul Rubens, *The Allegory of Sight,* 1617 (details). Courtesy of Museo del Prado.**

disinterested. The following vignette from an eighteenth-century play bears this point: "Are you not dispatched, said John the Black, to observe the Transit of Venus?—Pray God, answered the Captain, I carry out upon the coast of Africa both below and above the line, the trade of Negroes, which is much more interesting & lucrative than all your astronomical observations."[6] "Interesting [intéressant]" is to be read here as synonymous not with "knowledge-seeking" but with "interest-bearing." Massive slaving enterprises kept European states afloat and a number of Enlightenment thinkers solvent.[7]

This stark polyvalence of astronomy and telescopes did not go unnoticed. In 1617, Peter Paul Rubens worked with Jan Bruegel the Elder on *The Allegory of Sight,* featuring among the earliest depictions of telescopes.[8] Rubens was a close friend of Nicolas-Claude Fabri de Peiresc, who purchased a telescope in 1610 and corresponded with Galileo. In the painting, two such instruments lay amid Holland's colonial panoply: a compass, coins, a ship painting, and two capuchin monkeys with poor eyesight and tacit exotic and racial overtones. At the left edge of the canvas lies a confounding exhibit: the sculpted head of a Black "Moor," mouth frozen in a shout, surrounded by sharp-edged astronomical instruments looking like tools of torture. Among the few premodern European artists to depict a Black person with keen dignity (*Four Studies of a Head of a Moor,* 1614–1616), Rubens took for granted the telescope's entwinement with colonial and slaving enterprises.

The Camera Obscura and Telescope Setup: Motion, Visualization, Illustration

Telescopes were not the first astronomical instrument with a lens; the camera obscura was. Likely developed in China and mentioned in the thirteenth century by Ibn al-Haytham and Roger Bacon, the camera obscura rendered visible astronomical phenomena hitherto unwatchable with the naked eye—solar eclipses. The earliest known illustration dates from 1544 and shows a solar eclipse with the Moon in "blackface."[9] In 1567, Venetian astronomer and architect Daniele Barbaro designed a camera obscura equipped with a convex lens.[10] Johannes Kepler built a similar device in 1607 to observe a transit of Mercury across the Sun, and Lippershey may have gotten wind of it.[11]

By the 1630s, telescopes were routinely combined with camera obscuras to form a projection device that proves critical for media prehistory because it inaugurated an objective and automatic regime of mediated vision (I return to this key topic shortly). As a historian of premodern optics puts it: "The use of the camera obscura for solar observation is thus an important, and long-standing precedent

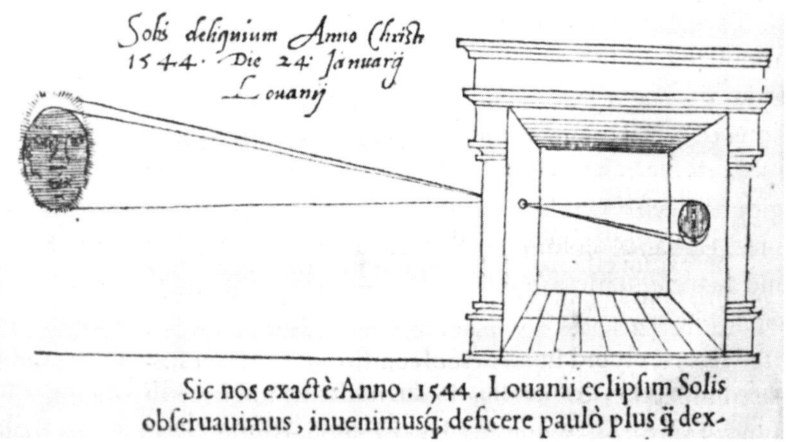

Figure 1.2. **Earliest known illustration of a camera obscura. Gemma Frisius, *De Radio Astronomico & Geometrico Liber* (Antwerp, 1545), 31. Courtesy of ETH-Bibliothek Zürich.**

to telescopic astronomy, and the publicly visible projected image, as a source of astronomical knowledge, precedes the privately discernible telescopic image. Small wonder, then, that both Scheiner and Galileo would use the telescope to project images of the sun onto a screen, to observe the movements of sunspots."[12] The magnified image of the Moon, the Sun, or its spots spontaneously moving on a screen in the dark represents an underappreciated precedent for projected cinema, especially since it brought attention to "continuous motion [mouvement continu]" in optics.[13] It also heightened the telescope's sense of projected telepresence, which instrument designer Johann Zahn, who devised the first portable camera obscura, called "telediopticus," lensed observation at a distance.[14] This dynamic aspect of celestial phenomena dovetailed with new objects and concepts such as that of *trajectory,* a word coined for comets in the 1660s. Comets' eccentric orbits in turn confirmed heliocentrism and were crucial to Isaac Newton's modeling of universal gravitation.[15] Late Renaissance astronomical handbooks trained students to "transform representations of specific heavenly phenomena into moving mental images of the structure of the cosmos," like Tycho Brahe's infamous epicycles.[16] But such images were merely of captive or cyclic motion, as in armillary spheres.[17] Continuous visual motion phenomena tracked by camera-obscura-telescope setups, such as drifting sunspots and arching trajectories, acculturated seventeenth-century vision to three-dimensional time-lapse and plastic deformation. They were the first kinemorphic objects attended to as such.

Camera-obscura-telescope observations also helped transform practices of visual record. Trigonometric coordinates with textual descriptions were increasingly complemented with sketches, diagrams, trajectories, multiphases, and finely rendered illustrations by the mid-seventeenth century. A signal issue was how to reconcile multiple and disparate observations of an object or phenomenon into a single image disclosing its contours and structure. Omar W. Nasim documents how, by the mid-eighteenth century, astronomers engaged in skillful composite picturing, crafting "working images" through a serial process of drafts, touch-ups, collation, and

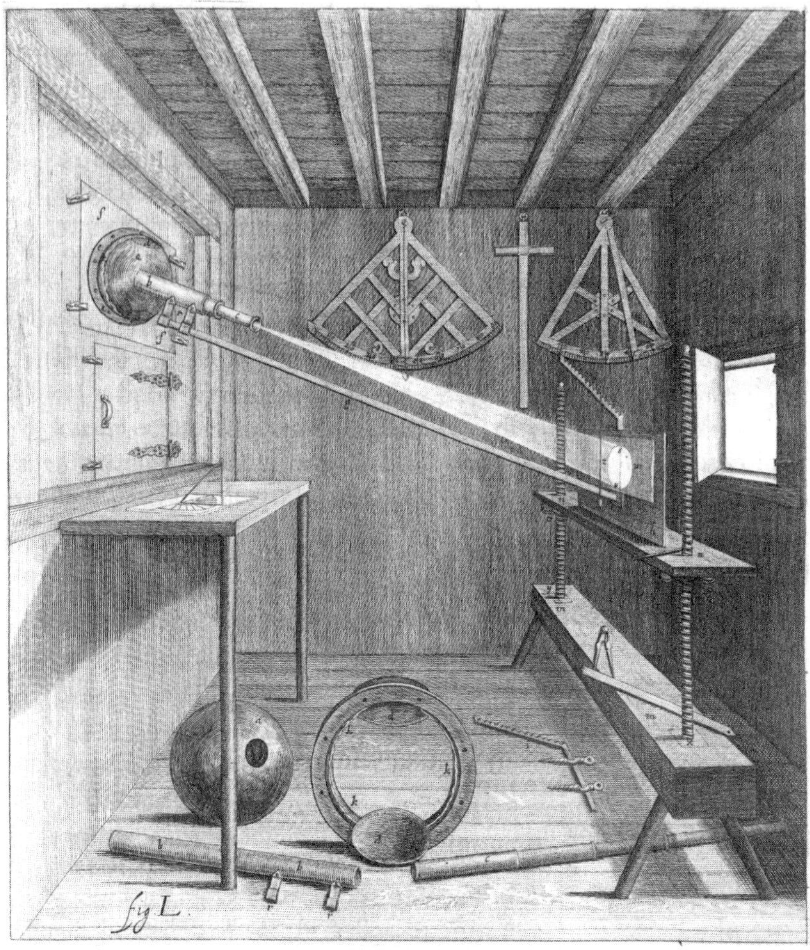

Figure 1.3. **Telescopic projection of sunspots in a room-size camera obscura. Johannes Hevelius, *Selenographia: Sive lunae descriptio* (Gdańsk, Poland: Hünefeld, 1647), 149. Courtesy of ETH-Bibliothek Zürich.**

synthesis. The resulting images were not mimetic copies but synthetic visualizations of what the object ought to look like.[18] Behind their apparent stasis, such images concealed visual continua and mitigated observational discontinuities. Astronomers like Christoph Scheiner and later Johann Heinrich Lambert symptomatically developed scalar devices called pantographs that replicated a line drawing at a larger scale. Telescopic observations, camera obscuras, composite illustrations, and early reprographics technics were thus coextensive.[19] Such assemblages, I claim, represent early and recognizable iterations of the matrix of photocinema.

A case in point is Athanasius Kircher's 1646 *Ars Magna Lucis et Umbrae,* which is especially pertinent since Laurent Mannoni borrowed its title for his own 1981 study *The Great Art of Light and Shadow: Archaeology of the Cinema.* Mannoni's book ambitions to track "the dream of being able to project moving illuminated images" across four centuries of sources, ranging from optics and philosophical toys to spectacles of magic. It emphasizes visual pleasure, wonder, philosophical toys, and illusion (Mannoni, *Great Art of Light and Shadow,* xvi). Mannoni describes Kircher's opus thus: "With its 935 folio pages, thirty-six engraved plates and over 500 drawings, Kircher's work is certainly one of the best optical compendia of the seventeenth century. All aspects of catoptrics and dioptrics are dealt with: light, shadow, illusions, colours, refraction, reflection, projection, distortion, mirrors, lenses, and so on. It also

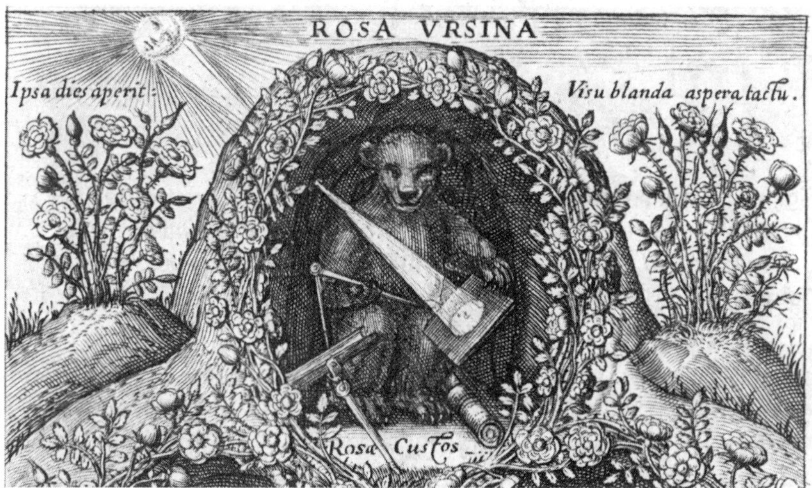

Figure 1.4. **The Sun's image projected into a camera obscura from a concealed refracting telescope. Christoph Scheiner, *Rosa Ursina: Observing Various Phenomena of the Sun's Flares and Spots,* vol. 3 (Bracciano, Italy: Andreas Phaeus, 1630), title page frontispiece. Courtesy of ETH-Bibliothek Zürich.**

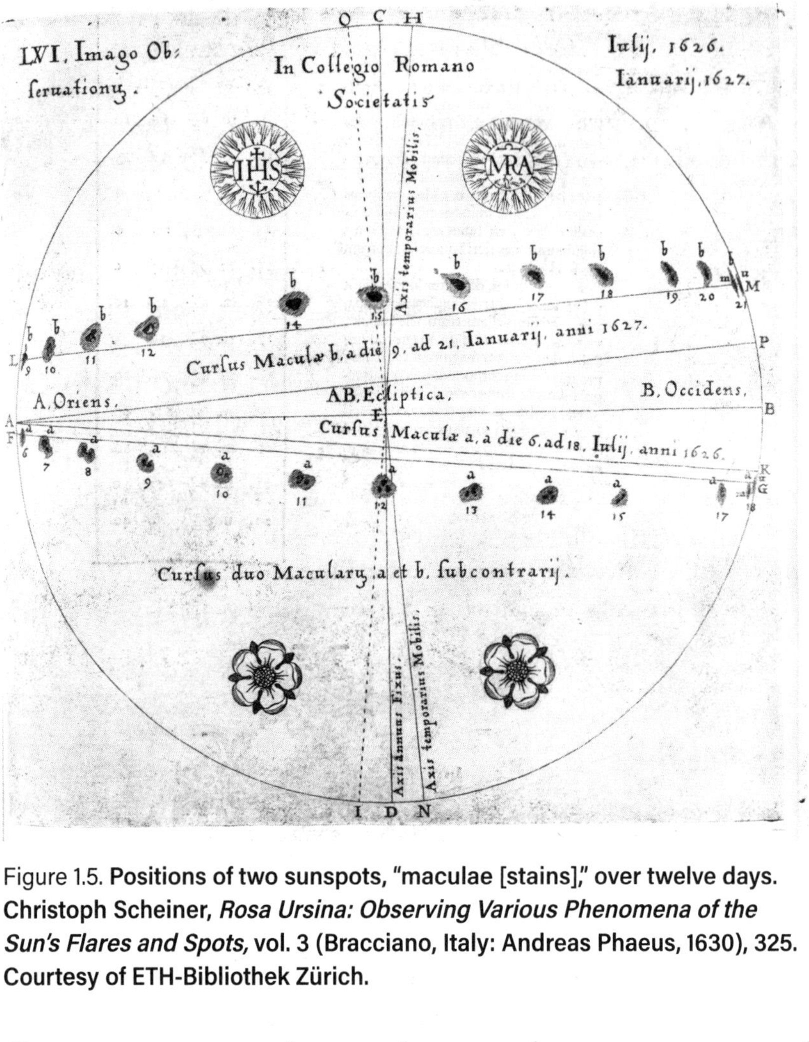

Figure 1.5. **Positions of two sunspots, "maculae [stains]," over twelve days. Christoph Scheiner, *Rosa Ursina: Observing Various Phenomena of the Sun's Flares and Spots,* vol. 3 (Bracciano, Italy: Andreas Phaeus, 1630), 325. Courtesy of ETH-Bibliothek Zürich.**

discusses astronomy: the sun, the stars, the moon, comets, and eclipses" (21). This account is rather misleading, since the ten parts of Kircher's book respectively address light, optical science, astronomy, astrology, horology, projective geometry, gnomons, cartography and comparative ephemeris, geodesy, and telescopes. His book thus represents a systematic program of investigation of how light and vision properly understood through projective geometry disclose the three-dimensional structure of the visible macrocosm.[20]

A Jesuit from Germany, Kircher is legendary for his automatons, firework displays, and polymath interests in Egyptian hieroglyphs, China, music, and volcanoes. Both Siegfried Zielinski and Mannoni consider him a subversive parascientific bricoleur who complicates linear models of media history.[21] However, astronomy and cosmology were Kircher's main concerns. He held the prestigious chair of mathematics at the Rome Collegium, counting René Descartes and Christiaan Huygens among interlocutors. In Avignon, France, he built a planetarium with mirrors projecting the light of the Sun and Moon and the exact time at various locations around the globe: an early cosmorama. He also collated accounts of comets and meteors, becoming the "acknowledged if unofficial clearinghouse for all eclipse sightings."[22] According to a recent biographer, his covert activity in spreading Copernican astronomy remains underacknowledged.[23] Even the last part of *Ars Magna Lucis et Umbrae,* titled "Magia [magic]," concerns telescopes, parabolic mirrors, and their combination with camera obscuras under the label of "helioscopes."[24] Mannoni mentions neologisms by Kircher but omits the determinant coinage: photosophia (Kircheri, *Ars Magna Lucis et Umbrae,* 17). This word denotes wisdom *from* light as a divine principle, *through* light via observation and visualization, and *about* light as a still enigmatic element. It is the first compound with the prefix *photo-*. Subsequently, Lambert coined the term *photometria* in 1760, while John Herschel crafted the words *photology* (1827) for research on light and *photography* in 1840. The lexical continuum in light inquiries from wise knowledge (*-sophy*), to quantification (*-metria*), discipline (*-logy*), and finally imaging (*-graphy*) outlines the broad arc of astronomy's shaping of the matrix of photocinema. Yet the prefix *photo-* also conceals a deeply racialized subtext in visualizing the universe and understanding light.

On the Origin of *Species*

In a later work of 1664 (*The Subterranean World*), Kircher examines the formation of all being. He invokes a hypothetical divine seed made of "salino-sulfuro-mercurial vapor" and endowing through "plastic power [virtus plastica]" its specific shape, color, and characteristics to each mineral, plant, and animal.[25] To explain how a single seed can contain so many forms, Kircher defers to the camera obscura through whose pinhole all parts of a landscape and all "species" of light pass through before recomposing a detailed colored image on screen (Hirai, "Kircher's Chymical Interpretation," 83). Kircher's conjecture shows that the problem of the generation of living species intersected with the epistemology of light. This conceptual intersection was also lexical, through the Latin word *species* from the verb specere ("to look"). Since at least Saint Augustine (fourth century CE), *species* denoted various aspects of the transmission of verisimilitude from light in the world to the eyes and the brain. Well into the eighteenth century, the term conflated images, reflections, refractions, distortions, colors, impressions, misperceptions, even ideations, whether in the world, the viewer's mind, or the viewing apparatus. Roger Bacon's late thirteenth-century treatise *De multiplicatione specierum* (On the multiplication of species) already debated this plurality of visual information channels.[26] Premodern discussions of optical matters still centered the term *species.*[27] The long subtitle of Christoph Scheiner's 1619 watermark opus *The Eye, That Is, the Foundation of Optics* includes: "the unseen spectacles of visible species both inverted and upright."[28] A French Copernican author explained in 1627 how the camera obscura produces images "because visible species [espèces visibles] are only perceived in darkness."[29] The developer of the microscope argued in 1675 that "there should be a cavity in the Optic Nerve, through which the Animal Spirits, representing the species of images in the Eye, might pass into the brain."[30] Even in his 1704 *Opticks,* Isaac Newton still described colors as "Species" while referring to "one entire Species or Picture."[31] Until the physics of light and the physiology of visual perception were better understood in the first half of the nineteenth century, *species* was the skeleton key unifying light, vision, imaging, and visualization.

For Kircher, species of light and animal species were directly connected because they could be classified only through their aspects (a word coming from "specere" too) and also because light was the divine principle of animation. The biological meaning gradually supplanted its optical precedent, starting with Carolus Linnaeus's 1753 *Species Plantarum* (*On Plant Species*) down to Charles Darwin's *On the Origin of Species* (1859).[32] For our purpose, optical and living species relied on the same cognitive model of making visible what cannot be seen, whether it be the hidden mechanisms of light and vision or the long-duration diversification of plants, animals, and humans around the globe. The threaded polysemy of *species* forms the epistemic substrate against which, for more contextual reasons, racial discourses and astronomy became intertwined along the seventeenth century.

Astronomical Illustration and Visual Motion

One of Kircher's correspondents and followers was Copernican astronomer Johannes Hevelius of Danzig. In 1647, he published *Selenographia*, a vanguard review of astronomical technologies aiming to optimize Moon (Selene) recording (*-graphia*) through both text and images.[33] The monograph probes the eye, vision, lenses, telescopes, drawing practices, etching and printing technics, even the composition of astronomy books.[34] *Selenographia* opens with a frontispiece showing Ibn al-Haytham next to Galileo, a rare acknowledgment of astronomy's non-European sources. It displays forty sequential illustrations of phases of the Moon drawn by Hevelius himself. They are shown waxing from a sliver to full, then back to a sliver. A second series shows another cycle of phases with a different lunar tilt. By focusing on only one section of lunar surface at a time and leaving the dark part blank, Hevelius underscored the ever-shifting appearance of the Moon—from its relative diameter, shadow angles, and the variable size of its overall visible area to its complex motions.[35] Our satellite was no longer a flat disk going through a sequence of illuminated sectors but a complexly moving sphere whose appearance was constantly morphing. This is partly why the Moon became a paradigmatic object in the genealogy of photocinema.

The sequential images of the Moon suggest a flipbook (also called a "mutoscope"), a nineteenth-century device in which a sheaf of pages with serial morphing images, when riffled quickly with the thumb, induce a visual motion effect. Although the images scattered

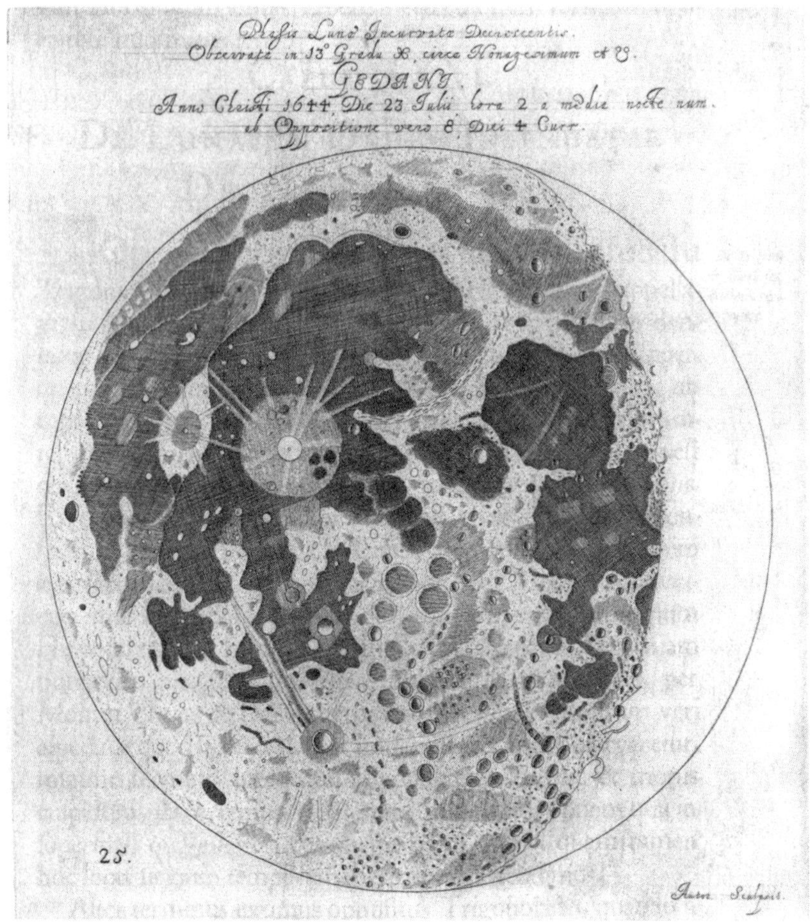

Figure 1.6. **Moon phase, Johannis Hevelii, *Selenographia: Sive lunae descriptio* (Gdańsk, Poland: Hünefeld, 1647), 500. Courtesy of ETH-Bibliothek Zürich.**

through Hevelius's book render such an application difficult, subsequent works of his—including *Cometographia* (1668) and *Machinae Coelestis* (1673)—show sequential illustrations together, inviting readers to visualize for themselves the dynamics of the phenomenon. Indeed, sequential illustrations of phases of a solar eclipse drawn by Hevelius can now be animated into a striking motion picture.[36]

Animated visualizations and sequential illustration soon produced scientific knowledge of their own. Astronomer Christiaan

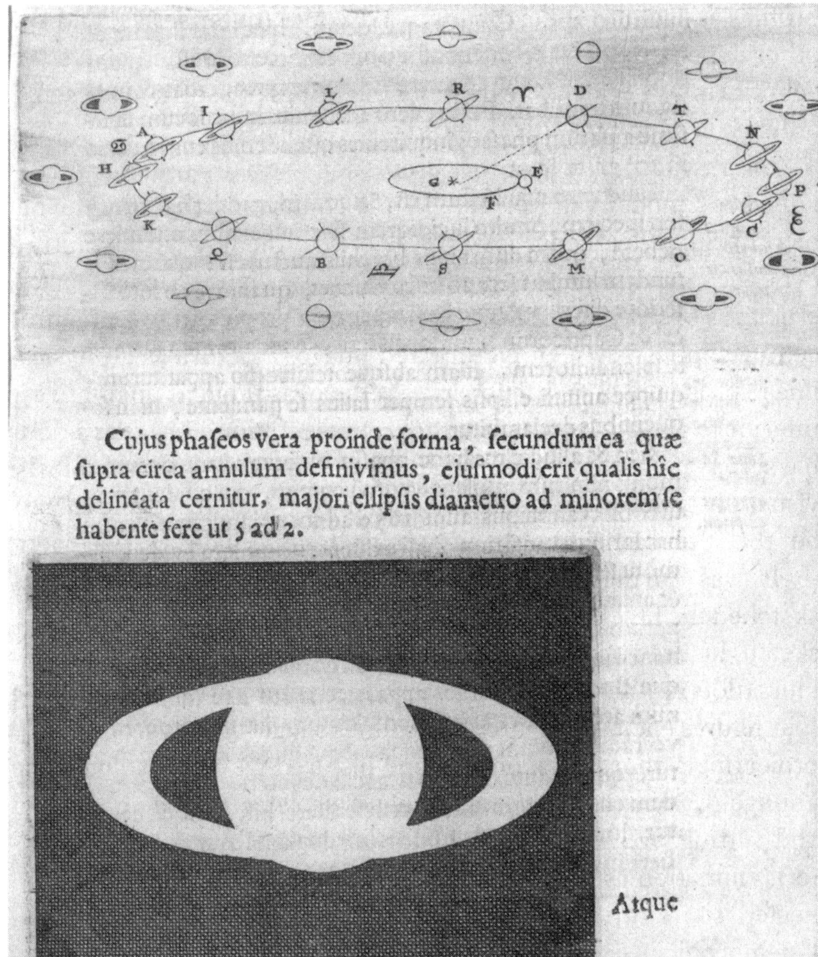

Cujus phaſeos vera proinde forma, ſecundum ea quæ ſupra circa annulum definivimus, ejuſmodi erit qualis hîc delineata cernitur, majori ellipſis diametro ad minorem ſe habente fere ut 5 ad 2.

Atque

Figure 1.7. **Two series of profiles of Saturn. Christiaan Huygens, *Systema Saturnium* (Den Haag, Netherlands: Adriani Vlacq, 1659), 55. Courtesy of ETH-Bibliothek Zürich.**

Huygens, another correspondent of Hevelius, is a case in point. In 1659, he solved the riddle of Saturn's puzzling changes of appearance. The story is well-known: telescopic observations showed Saturn at different times resembling a circle, an oval, a circle with two symmetrical outside dots, or a jug shape with two handles. Galileo was befuddled. To reconcile the data, Huygens visualized the orbit of Saturn from two parallactic purviews. One shows Saturnian profiles as seen from Earthbound telescopes (outer series) and the other depicts them as seen from a point of view located above the ecliptic (inner series). The irrational sightings of Saturn made sense only when simultaneously viewed and visualized.

After twenty-nine years of observations—a half orbit of Saturn—Huygens's model was verified. While confirming that Jupiter orbits the Sun, the deeper lesson was that in the new visual culture of heliocentric astronomy, precise pictorial visualization was just as crucial as observation. This troubled the difference in seventeenth-century optics between pictura and imago.[37] Pictura as a physical image projected on a screen or the retina was thought qualitatively inferior to imago, its truer mental representation. Huygens's double series of drawing demonstrated a new and complex symbiosis: visual observation productively enhanced by an unseeable imago, but the latter being in fact a pictura itself: a real, albeit virtual, view.

It was during work on his Saturn pamphlet that Huygens sketched the first known depiction of the magic lantern.[38] Below the sketch, he drew ten skeleton figures, four of which display motion blurs (dots) while three others show overlapping arm contours. The four figures enclosed in circular outlines suggest slides sequentially projecting a short tragicomic scene inspired by Hans Holbein the Younger's *Dance of Death* engravings: a skeleton taking off its head and putting it back on. Media historians hold Huygens's magic lantern animation as a protocinematic device, yet they have not connected it to Saturn's sequential profiles that derive from a common kinemorphic insight. It matters little which came first. The point is that precinematic pictorial animation and astronomical visualization were entangled from the start. Huygens certainly understood the yield of dynamic visualization. In the late 1660s, he went on developing a new theory of light. Rather than made of atomistic corpuscles or instant rays, Huygens envisioned light as a kinemorphic phenomenon: a propagating wave. As chapter 4 will show, reworking Huygens's model in the early nineteenth century proved instrumental for the emergence of both the wave theory of light and working photography.

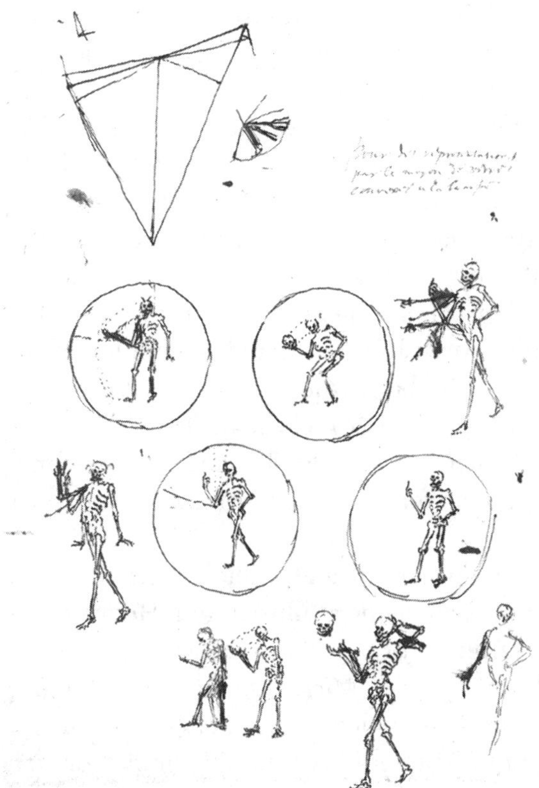

Figure 1.8. **Christiaan Huygens, magic lantern slides from 1659. Christiaan Huygens, *Œuvres complètes,* vol. 22 (La Haye, Netherlands: M. Nijhoff, 1950), 197. Courtesy of Leiden University Library.**

Micrographia: Magnification, Objectivity, and Blackness

Few books better instantiate how lensed medias reorganized seventeenth-century relationships between vision, imaging, and the macrocosm than the 1665 *Micrographia* of Robert Hooke. As it happens, it was one of the explicit sources for Huygens's wave theory of light.[39] We must not be misled by the monograph's title: It concerns not just the microscopic realm but magnification as such, Hooke's primary occupation being astronomy.[40] His work endeavors to reflect on and document the full scalar range of lensed optics through "Ocular experiments": "Hence there is a new visible World discovered to the understanding. By this means the Heavens are opened, and a vast number of new Stars, and new Motions, and new Productions appear in them, to which all the ancient Astronomers were

Strangers. By this the Earth it self, which lies so near us, under our feet, shows quite a new thing to us, and in every little particle of its matter, we now behold almost as great a variety of Creatures, as we were able to reckon up in the whole Universe it self."[41] Like Kircher, for Hooke the varieties of seeing become coextensive with varieties of the living. In such hermeneutics, empirical observation through "Hands and Eyes"—experiments, drawings, and observations—inform deductions of "Reason" through a "continual passage round from one Faculty to another." Hooke metaphorizes this hermeneutic circle as blood circulation within the "grand Oeconomy of the Universe" where we can find no "body whose particles are at rest, or lazy and unactive" (*Micrographia,* vii, 16). The main lesson of magnification is then all at once far-ranging scalability and relentless motion: the words *to move* and *motion* figure over three hundred times in *Micrographia.*

Exemplifying what Lorraine Daston and Peter L. Galison call the "truth-to-nature" creed of early modern illustration, Hooke seeks access to the "true appearance" of objects to transmit to readers their "plain representation" (Hooke, *Micrographia,* xxiv).[42] Hooke is proficient with optical projection devices, including the camera-obscura-telescope assembly, pantographs, and the perspectograph of his friend Christopher Wren. That last device allows an operator looking through an eyepiece to trace the contours of an object in her sight line with a stylus connected to an articulated pencil simultaneously drawing the object downscaled.[43] The remarkably three-dimensional rendition of *Micrographia*'s illustrations belie a combination of lensed observation with mechanically aided drawing. His practice thus also conforms to the imperative of "mechanical objectivity" that Daston and Galison locate mostly in the post-photographic era (*Objectivity,* 27). Yet, projective apparatuses such as the camera-obscura-telescope assembly and the perspectograph, as well as late seventeenth-century axonometric perspective that mitigates foreshortening to produce "orthographic" drawings, already integrated a form of mechanical objectivity.[44] They did so by foregrounding the actual geometrical "apparentia [appearance]" of objects over their seeable "proiectione [projection]" distorted by distance and stereoscopic vision.[45]

This overlooked early stage of mechanical objectivity produced what human vision cannot see: the parallel rays of the sun (and stars) shaping and shading an object. It is a strange kind of seeing as if from the viewpoint of a celestial object—as in the second series in Huygens's drawing—that sees objectively (i.e., without the distortions of human vision). The word *objectivity* stems from this view by the object. It was catalyzed by the French verre objectif (objective glass), which denotes the lens closest to the object, in contrast to the eyepiece, le verre oculaire (ocular glass or eyepiece), closest to the eye.[46] In *Micrographia*, Hooke was among the first to champion the expression "Object-Glass," and over the following decades parallel light rays were called "objective lines."[47] The tensions between this mode of nonhuman objective seeing and human vision undergirds our reconstruction of photocinema's origins.[48]

Hooke tackled this objective seeing through lunar shadows cast by the objective lines of sunlight in order to solve the problem of how to read the three-dimensional structures shadows both reveal and conceal.[49] Like Hevelius and Kircher, he was trained in drawing, etching, and printing techniques, in particular perspectival rendering.[50] He was particularly interested in shading techniques, leading him to digress about why certain bodies "look black." Starting from a statement he attributes to Aristotle, "black being nothing else but a privation of light," Hooke speculates on the microchemical process of light absorption. Invoking Aristotle's equation of whiteness with water and blackness with fire, he reasons that heat, by "agitating and rarifying the waterish, transparent and volatile water . . . which before filled the pores," leaves "burnt bodies" empty and "opacous" with "all [light rays] that enter into the pores of the body, never returning, but being lost in it." While his pragmatic concern is how to interpret shadows seen through his eyepiece, Hooke invokes an implicit racial discourse in which light becomes objectively "lost" in the "pores" of a black "body." Writer and scientist Margaret Cavendish, for one, saw through Hooke's racial implications. When he affirmed that in black bodies the "reflective quality is deficient," Cavendish countered that "black was as much a colour as any other colour," so that "saying that black is made by want of reflection" is optically nonsensical (Hooke, *Micrographia,* 101–2).[51] In another work, she adds that if Hooke were right, then "a black Moor would have larger Pores than a man of white complexion," suggesting that both were acutely aware of the slippage between chromatic blackness and racial Blackness.[52] Indeed, it was no slippage at all. As suggested by Robert Boyle's transition from silver nitrate medicine to Black skin, within late seventeenth-century debates at the Royal Society, racial Blackness, optics, and astronomy directly bore on each other from multiple directions, which I unfold in this chapter and the next.[53]

Hooke explicitly addresses racial Blackness only once in *Micrographia,* in a tangent that reveals the racial underlayment in much seventeenth- and eighteenth-century speculations about light and the macrocosm. A section titled "On the Wandring Mite" considers microorganisms and tiny insects, collectively called "mites," that adopt different forms depending on soil and food sources. Hooke postulates that they correspond to bioadaptations of a single nomadic stem species (akin to Kircher's "plastic seed"). He adds that mites "might leave their off-spring behind them, which by the change of the soil and Country they now inhabit might be quite altered from the hew of their *primogenitors,* and, like *Mores* translated into Northern *European* Climates, after a little time, change both their skin and shape" (*Micrographia,* 205). Such a flip comment demonstrates the shared currency of the thermometabolic etiology of skin color among his readers, together with the fiction that Black people transplanted to northern climates turn into white people—not just with respect to skin color but also phenotypically ("shape"). Hooke returns to the topic a few paragraphs later: "We find by relations how much the *Negro* Women do besmeer the of-spring of the *Spaniard,* bringing forth neither white-skinn'd nor black, but tawny hided *Mulattos*" (206–7). After alluding to environmentally triggered racial morphism, Hooke contradicts himself with an alternative cause of mutation through mixed parentage, with a doubly racist disparagement of staining ("besmeer") and animality ("tawny hided"). Earlier, Hooke wrote breezily of "Black, or some dark and dirty colour," making explicit his subjacent anti-Black prejudice (78). The absence of a reliable theory of reproduction and inheritance of traits makes either of Hooke's scenarios of racial mutability plausible for the time (Malcolmson, *Studies of Skin Color,* 43–58, 87–89). Of course, racial mutability was no disinterested matter. It correlated to a rising anxiety in Caribbean plantocracies concerning mixed-race offspring resulting from the sexual exploitation of enslaved women by white planters. Among other things, it troubled the ontological separateness of white people since it invalidated polygenesis—then widely held. My overall point is this: From the moment *Micrographia* turns to "intermixtures of *Black* and *White*" as a matter of pictorial reproduction of the objective world, the stakes of mixed-race reproduction in slaving colonies pop up, framed by anti-Blackness (Hooke, *Micrographia,* 68).[54]

Toward the end of his treatise, Hooke turns to the riddle of lunar features seen in telescopes. Are they convex mountains or concave craters? The optical and chromatic challenge "to distinguish between a *prominency* and a *depression,* between a *shadow* and a *black stain,* or a *reflection* and a *whiteness in the colour*" again evinces the

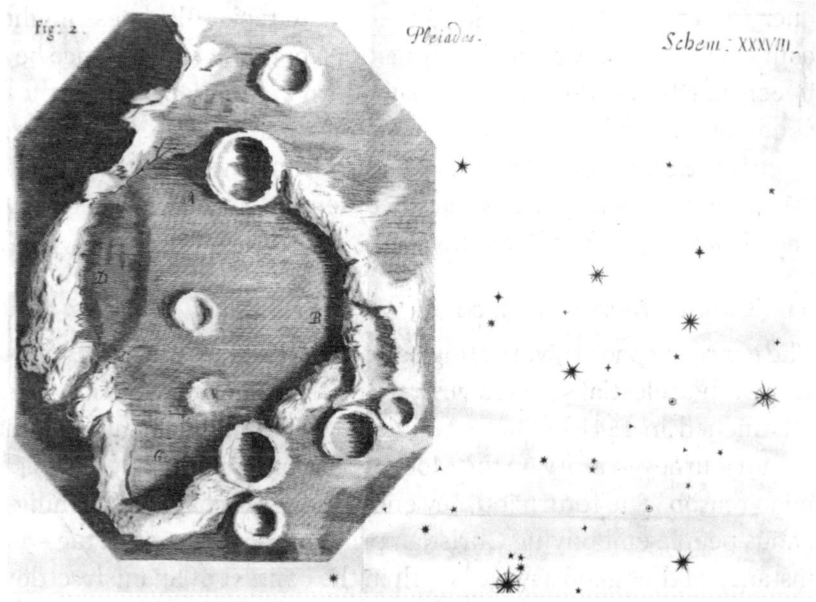

Figure 1.9. **Lunar craters and star magnitudes. Robert Hooke, *Micrographia, or Some Physiological Descriptions of Minute Bodies Made by Magnifying Glasses with Observations and Inquiries Thereupon* (London: John Martyn & James Allestry, 1665). Courtesy of ETH-Bibliothek Zürich.**

racist register of reflection and staining, as well as the rhetoric of distinction from the 1608 pamphlet on the telescope (Hooke, *Micrographia,* xxiv). To assay 3D lunar reliefs, Hooke experimented with boiling alabaster, concluding that lunar reliefs must be volcanic craters. This led him to muse that "could we look upon the Earth from the Moon, with a good Telescope, we might easily enough perceive its surface to be very much like that of the Moon" (246).

This statement is rather puzzling. Our planet was thought already to look bluish from space, quite unlike the silver-yellow Moon, even though astronomers of the time took for granted—some even observed—the presence of seas, mountains, and forests on our satellite. While Hooke emphasized the resemblance between Earth and Moon, recognizing, for instance, that the latter is held together by gravitation like the former, he also noted that the Moon is "only secondary, or attendant, on the bigger, and more considerable body of the Earth" (Hooke, *Micrographia,* 244). The question I will follow in the next sections is the extent to which Hooke's objective pictorial query about chromatic blackness veering to racial Blackness might connect to the widespread interrogation about the resemblance between Earth and the Moon, its subaltern ("attendant"), and thus about the resemblance between humans and Selenites. At stake, then, is the inherence of racial thought within seventeenth-century astronomical visualizations that, I contend, shaped the conceptual and visual culture of photocinema.

The Lunar Theater of Race

The genre of space travel dating back to the "Dream of Scipio," a vision of the celestial spheres written by Cicero in North Africa, was relaunched in 1541 by Juan Maldonado's *Somnium.* It narrates a dream journey to a city on the Moon whose inhabitants rule by Erasmian reason. The return journey ends among Mesoamerican Indigenous people embodying Christian principles by natural virtue—an instance of the "good savage" myth in the context of Spanish settler colonialism.[55] Indeed, from the 1620s onward, hypothetical travel to the Moon was expressly envisaged as a colonial project.[56] Johannes Kepler likely knew Maldonado's work when he sketched his own *Somnium* in the 1590s (it was published posthumously in 1634)—a similar dream travel journey to the Moon, but with the didactic aim of undoing geocentric orthodoxy. Kepler's frame story concerns an Icelandic boy kidnapped by demons from the dark side of the Moon.[57] Its visible side is peopled by naive creatures taking Earth as their satellite, which they call "Volva" since they see it rotating.[58] Denizens of the dark side are monstrous crawling creatures. On the visible side constantly flooded by sunlight, Kepler construes Lunarians as comparable to "Africans" who "expose themselves naked to the sun." In a 1605 letter he opined that "Africans are akin to reptiles in nature," as solarization makes their skin purportedly thicker than that of white people.[59] While the bulk of Kepler's text consists of an astronomical mind experiment, the pointed association of Lunarians with Africans is highly significant. It shows that to probe the living conditions of celestial bodies, European thinkers leveraged their own prejudiced views of racialized peoples. Hooke's *Micrographia* and Kepler's *Somnium* refract race in the same tangent yet structural way. Raz Chen-Morris notes that to encourage his readers to flip their geocentric perspective, Kepler construed "the treatise itself as a camera obscura," projecting "an inverted picture of the terrestrial world view."[60] The depiction of Africanized Lunarians plays, to my mind, a congruent didactic role in evincing among white readers an inverted picture of the Moon as a Black world.[61] The camera obscura, forming the core of Kepler's celebrated theory of vision and imagery, thus comes with its own racial lens.

The emergence of heliocentrism in the first half of the seventeenth century gave a boost to the old hypothesis of the plurality of worlds, according to which celestial bodies must be inhabited like Earth. Both Kircher and Huygens wrote treatises on the topic. Now that our globe was but a planet among others, human exceptionality as divinely elected was put in doubt. This occurred at a historical hinge when encounters with Indigenous Peoples of the New World and East Asia upset the Bible's human classifications, and thus white exceptionalism, just as the latter was boosted by colonial appropriation and the trade of enslaved Africans. The relativization of whiteness concurrent with and compensated by its global hegemony informed what we may call astro-racialization: race-inflected conjectures about the makeup of extraterrestrials.

The first wave of astro-racialization occurred in lunar fictions in the wake of Kepler's *Somnium*. What interests me here is how reimagining the heliocentric solar system through travels to a nonhuman community on the Moon entailed foregrounding skin color and enslavement together with prekinemorphic insights. Francis Godwin's fanciful 1638 bestseller *The Man in the Moone* is the paradigm. It follows the tribulations of the protagonist-narrator Domingo Gonsales, a Spaniard returning to Europe after reaping wealth from the East Indies. Having fallen ill, Gonsales is "set ashore with a *Negro*" named Diego on Saint Helena Island in the mid-Atlantic.[62] Uninhabited until the 1500s, the island became a port of call for slaving ships coming from the Gulf of Guinea. By Godwin's time, it was a notorious haven for maroons, fugitives from slavery, and enslaved persons summarily discarded because of illness or insubordination.[63] Godwin did not choose it randomly. Gonsales mentions an attack from "a Savage kind of people" whom he calls "slaves" (Godwin, *Man in the Moone,* 85). While the narrative suggests that Diego is Gonsales's enslaved manservant, Gonsales describes him only as a "Blackmoore" who, "though hee were a fellow of good parts, was ever content to be ruled by me" (76–77). Before even launching on space travel, the narrative alludes to the geography of the slave trade and invokes the most perverse figment of slavery: willing subservience and beneficent enslavers.[64]

Godwin splits the two protagonists on Saint Helena to expound on a pet idea: telegraphic systems.[65] Like the telescope, his telegraph reinforces racial distinction, and indeed Diego soon vanishes from the narrative. Gonsales's telegraph consists in a flock of domesticated wild geese bearing messages, and they are repurposed for aerial locomotion to the Moon. Gaining altitude, he ponders on the similarity of the two celestial bodies, seeing Earth "like another Moon" and it like "another Earth," observing: "a Spot like a Pear, with a Morsel bit out on one side. . . . This is no doubt the mainland of *Africke*. . . . After this succeeded a Spot almost Oval, just as we see *America* described in our Maps . . . so that it seemed to me no other than a huge mathematical Globe turned around leisurely before me, wherein successively all the Countries of our earthly World were within twenty-four hours represented to my View" (Godwin, *Man in the Moone* [1640], 95–96). With partly consumed Africa as starting point, the tale revels in the rotation of Earth unfolding a cinematic spectacle that instantiates the paradigmatic formula of all precinema insights: an automatic spectacle "successively . . . represented to . . . View." Reaching the Moon, Gonsales makes out its "very body" with "his natural colours," contrasting with Earth's "lurid and deadly colour of blue" (97). The anthropomorphizing of celestial bodies, doubled with an insistence on surface differences, makes way to overt racialization. The Lunarians Gonsales soon meets are described as having a "colour and countenance most pleasing," which is "neither blacke, nor white, yellow nor red, green nor blew, nor any colour composed of them. . . . Neither can I decipher this Moon-Colour . . . a colour never seen in our earthly world, and therefore neither to be described unto us by any nor to be conceived of one that has never seen it" (100). While Lunarians' "never seen" skin color seemingly transcends human races, note that black and white top the antiphrastic list. Godwin's sketch of a colorblind utopic Lunarian society conceals a dirty secret: They maintain an egalitarian system through eugenics. They get rid of "children . . . who are like to be of a wicked and debauched Humour" and "send them, I know not by what Means, into the Earth, and change them for other Children." These lunar changelings are kept in limbo "till that the ayre of the Earth may alter their colour to be like unto ours," Gonsales stipulates. The substitutions occur mostly "in the North of America, whose People . . . are wholly descended from [Lunarians], both in regard of their Colour, and their continued use of Tobacco." Occasionally, Lunarians "mistake their aime" and the children land in "Christendome, Asia, or Affricke," explaining perhaps the puzzle of mixed-race children (111–13).

Beneath its exoticization of Native Americans as extraterrestrials, the narrative proposes a sophisticated model of racial latency. While Earth's "ayre" precipitates racial traits according to the thermometabolic model, on the Moon Lunarians remain neuters (literally, "neither nor") incarnating the zero degree of race and inviting readers to rethink racial classification. Lunarian language too is primeval, comprising but a few words that "signifie divers and several things, and they are distinguished onely by their tunes that are as it were sung" (Godwin, *Man in the Moone,* 108). Like the Siamese ambassadors' language, Lunarian speech is nigh indistinguishable, forming the zero degree of linguistic articulation: music. What is determinant for our purpose is that Godwin rethinks racial etiology from a neutral skin substrate that precipitates into various skin colors. Through the rhetoric of latency, exposure, development, and fixation that belongs to photochemistry, skin figures as filmstock from the perspective of Kepler's camera obscura of the Moon. Indeed, it is most likely that Godwin, like Boyle, was aware that silver nitrate darkens light skin. Either way, his fiction converges with Kircher's plastic seed and Hooke's mites in similarly retheorizing the origin of species from a photosophic perspective with prephotographic features.

Translated into French in 1648, Godwin's tale was sent up by libertine writer Cyrano de Bergerac in *The Comical History of the States and Empires of the Moon* (1656). Cyrano's tale opens on a French protagonist and narrator strapped with bottles of dew as he ascends the atmosphere, discovering anew that "the Moon is a world like this one to which ours serves as Moon."[66] When the ascent fails, he tumbles down among unclothed people, meeting an "olive-colored old man" whose language sounds like "the hoarse chirping of a deaf man" (Cyrano, *Histoire comique,* 9). Convinced he is on the Moon, the protagonist has in reality landed in Canada—then called "New France"—again associating First Nations peoples with extraterrestrials. A second try with fireworks succeeds and he reaches the hinge point between Earth and Moon where gravitation reverses: "I suddenly saw myself flipping heels over head without having fallen over in any way—and scarcely would I have noticed had not my head felt the load of my body" (27–28). This flipping viewpoint embodies the inversion of Kepler's didactic camera obscura in *Somnium.*

Cyrano's tale is a satire staging upheavals of gender and race. Brought to the Lunar Queen, the Frenchman is deemed "the female" of a caged "monkey" who turns out to be a male Spaniard. The Queen wants them to breed "the race [la race] of these small animals" (Cyrano, *Histoire comique,* 75, 93). So, we have a female Lunarian attempting to breed two males from colonial empires to breed monkeys. Cyrano holds up a sarcastic mirror to Europe, parroting claims by state-sponsored slave-trading companies that their noble enterprise means to enhance the "dignity of our nation on behalf of whom the Universe produces men only to give us slaves" (74). When the protagonist learns Lunarian language, a law is passed to remind Lunarians (in the protagonist's voice) that "it is forbidden to believe that I possess reason," showing how racism begets concepts and law. Enticed female Lunarians are warned to resist impulses of "mixing with beasts & shamelessly committing with me sins against nature," a prohibition conflating miscegenation and same-sex desire, since the protagonist is identified as female by the Lunarians (97, 107).

The protagonist is guided on the Moon by a mysterious spirit who reincarnates Socrates's demon and the transmigrated souls of philosophers like Pierre Gassendi—Cyrano's real-life teacher (Cyrano, *Histoire comique,* 30). The guide is an incorporeal inhabitant of the Sun who adopts the guise of a human body by using compressed air (55). This part of the satire comprises long disquisitions by the Sun-spirit on Lucretian atomism, while couching Lunar culture as a photonegative of European mores. The tale closes when the Sun-spirit gifts two boxed books to the narrator. One looks like a diamond and contains maxims of paradoxical solar philosophy such as "that white is black & that black is white," parenthetically undoing the color line (164). The second book looks like a large pearl and comes with a twist: "Upon opening the box I found something made of metal, akin to our clocks, full of little springs: it is indeed a book, but a miraculous book without pages or characters; a book for whose learning eyes are useless, only ears are required. When someone wants to read, they power the machine by tightening numerous strings [nerfs] then turn the needle on the chapter they want to hear and instantly there resounds as if out of a human mouth or musical instrument all the distinct [distincts] and different sounds which great Lunarians use to express language" (166).[67] Well-versed in physics, astronomy, and the arts through his mentor Gassendi, Cyrano was acquainted with the gamut of new portable devices (thermometers, barometers, pantographs, compasses, squares, telescopes, air pumps, etc.) that were the hallmark of mid-seventeenth-century instrumentalization.[68] His audiobook is certainly among the first portable audiovisual media to be imagined and technologically visualized. Young Lunarians walk around with "thirty" of these attached to their belts in lieu of attending school (167). Granting Lunarians learning and their language distinction, Cyrano adds in the voice of the white protagonist regaining Earth, "Already I could distinguish [distinguois] Europe from Africa," as if restoring the ontological distinction enabling slavery (188). The distinction axis remains ever-present when it comes to assessing the languages—and minds—of racialized peoples teleported to the Moon. It unites the telescope, Godwin's telegraph and proto-photographic theory of skin color, and Cyrano's portable media.[69]

Anti-Blackness in Popular Cosmology

Bernard Le Bovier, sieur de Fontenelle's 1686 blockbuster *Entretiens sur la pluralité des mondes* (*Conversations on the Plurality of Worlds*) expanded astro-racialization to the entire solar system and made it unapologetically racist. Plagiarizing the work of Gassendi and François Bernier, *Entretiens* was a watershed in astronomical vulgarization and visualization.[70] Below I examine how Fontenelle translates astronomical didacticism into advanced animated visualization while embedding racist discourses into late seventeenth-century popular cosmology.

The book comprises five conversations between the Marquise de G., curious about celestial matters, and a male narrator expert in astronomy—transparently Fontenelle—tasking himself with "ordering without confusion vortices and worlds in her head" (Fontenelle, *Entretiens,* ix). This theoretical insemination takes, since the Marquise confesses on the penultimate page, "I have in my head the whole system of the universe!" (358).[71] To properly reproduce the cosmos in her head, the narrator trains her in "pure imagination," ridding her of misconceptions like "Indian" cosmogony's stack of giant elephants (45, 62). Proper visualization of the macrocosm shows its civilizational cards. The Marquise becomes proficient enough to envision herself free-floating in space but is then overtaken by vertigo. The astronomer instructs her on how to develop her cinematic capability: "Sometimes for instance I figure myself suspended in the air & staying there motionless while the Earth turns under me in twenty-four hours, & I see passing under my

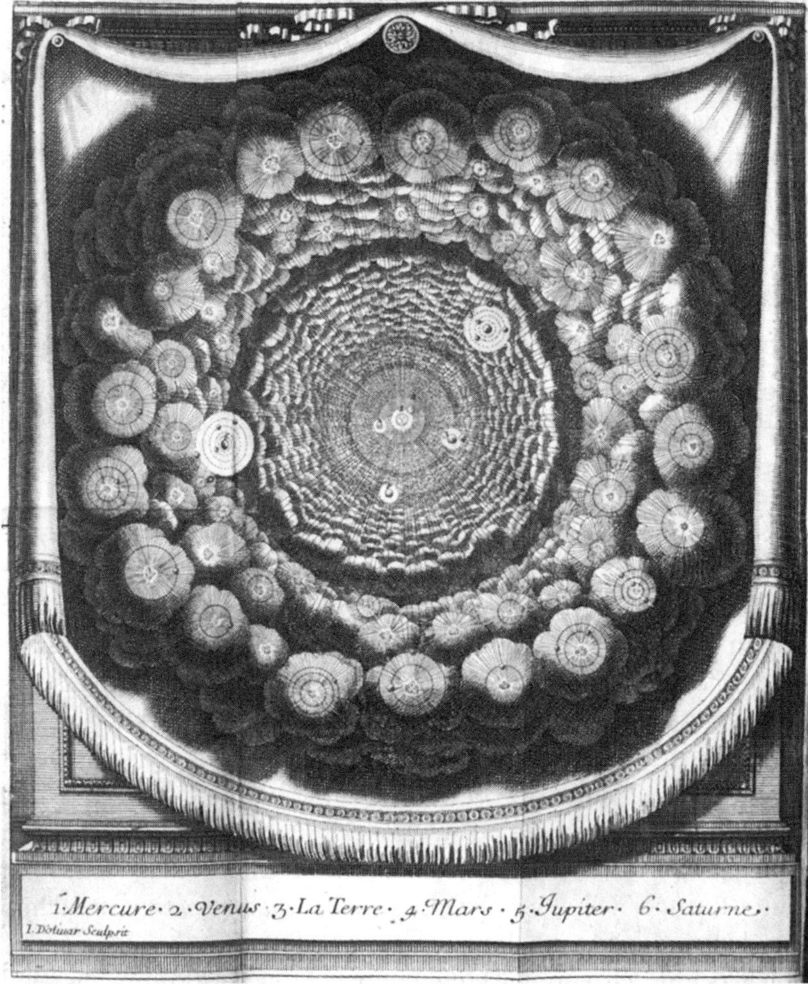

Figure 1.10. **Frontispieces to [Bernard Le Bovier, sieur de Fontenelle], *Entretiens sur la pluralité des mondes* (Paris: Veuve C. Blageart, 1686). Courtesy of La Bibliothèque Nationale de France Gallica.**

eyes all these different faces [visages différents], some white, others black, others dark, others olive-skinned, and I see first hats & then Turbans then hairy & shaven Heads, here Cities with belfries, there Cities with long needles and Crescents, here Cities with Porcelain Towers, there large Countries with only Huts; here vast seas, there awful deserts; in short, this infinite variety that is upon the Earth's surface" (69–70). The objective spectacle of rotating Earth visualized from orbit rehearses lunar journeys. But here, Fontenelle combines kinemorphic visualization with the rotational unfolding of earthly geographical, racial, and cultural diversity. The Marquise interprets his visualization as ethical and cosmopolitical interchangeability: "Hence in this very location where we are now, not in this park per se but in this location from an airborne purview [à le prendre dans l'air], other people have continuously gone through, taking our place, and after twenty-four hours we come back to it" (73). She also quips that it would be "quite pleasing" to have "the freedom to hasten or stop the motion of the Earth," a striking adumbration of cinema's accelerated motion and freeze-frame (76).

As the advertised topic of the *Entretiens* arises—inhabitants on other planets—Fontenelle leverages astro-racialization with unabashed prejudice: "I do not think that there are Men on the Moon. See how the face [face] of nature changes between here and China: other miens [visages], other figures, other mores, & almost other principles of reasoning. From here to the Moon the change must be much more considerable. When one goes to certain newly discovered lands, the inhabitants one finds are scarcely Men—they are animals with a human figure still rather imperfect but almost without human reason. Whoever could reach the Moon, surely they would no longer find Men there" (Fontenelle, *Entretiens,* 135). Fontenelle's radical racial distinction echoes Sylvia Wynter's diagnostic that white Europeans monopolized the term *Man,* rejecting nonwhite people to indistinct subaltern "humanity."[72] Fontenelle occasionally brackets his racism, remarking that the "faces" of "Europeans" and "Africans" follow "two particular models" but form nonetheless "a small family, in which all faces look alike" from the purview of cosmic speciation (210). This monogenic purview remains nonetheless racist and colonial, describing Mercurians as possessing "no more memory than most negroes, who never reflect on anything, act only by self-interest and with sudden movements" (223). The popularization of astronomical visualization with its protocinematic sensibility was of a piece with the epistemic promotion of anti-Blackness as a universal law not just on Earth but in the whole macrocosm.

The astronomer's biases were maybe not shared by the real-life friend of Fontenelle on which the Marquise is based.[73] After his racist exposé, she concludes: "There is not in men a fixed and determined character; some are like the inhabitants of Mercury, others like those of Saturn, & we are a mix of all the species [espèces] found on other planets" (Fontenelle, *Entretiens,* 289). That is certainly a subversive reading of the treatise: Humans devolve from universal miscegenation. Fontenelle quickly corrects this multiracial perspective by having her add that since "we" are "on the most temperate planet of the universe, & in one of the most temperate places of that planet," white peoples are supremely sited, thus supreme. The astronomer assents since from its middle position, Earth can panoptically "see all the other worlds in miniature" (290). The notion of Europe's central positioning on the globe, away from extremes, correlating with Earth's congruent central positioning in the solar system was a significant astronomical argument for white supremacy. Within this analogical framework, while Black and Inuit peoples are associated respectively with Mercury and Saturn, let us note that white people have no counterpart in the solar system. Hence, white people are the only true natives of planet Earth—all other races have cosmic affinities with another planet.

Fontenelle's racist conjectures acquired the status of scientific truth, especially after he became head of the French Academy of Sciences for forty-three years (1697–1740). The leap from fictional Moon travel to popular astronomy reflects a shift in cosmic visualization and its racial discourses toward universalization. At the same time his opus was published, France and England enacted new legislation regulating the enslaved people in Caribbean plantocracies, which were by then major economic engines for their superpower status. Before the Jamaica Slave Act of 1684 and the infamous Code Noir of 1685, enslaved people were regulated through a medley of local legislations. Fontenelle's 1686 astro-racialization partook of the same panoptic regulation of the universal macrocosm as Newton's publications from 1683 to 1685 on gravitation as a universal law.[74]

Cosmic Anti-Blackness

Before turning to the Ur-tale of photography, let us briefly see how universal astro-racialization migrated to the actual context of enslavement, on the one hand, and astronomy, on the other. In a vignette from 1684 by Thomas Tryon, an enslaver turned critic of slavery, an enslaved African man in Jamaica poses a rhetorical question to his enslaver:[75]

> Casting my Eyes to that *glorious Eye of Heaven,* which (they say) at one view beholds half the World . . . I had a thousand different Notions offered themselves to my Mind, and amongst the rest, I was thinking, what if the *Sun* should *forget to Rise* to morrow Morning, whether your Man, (our *Over-seer*) would make him get up, as he does us, by blowing his Horn? Or else how we should do to work in the Dark? Or if the Sea should swell a little higher, and wash the tops of your *Sugar-Canes,* I might not then lawfully swim Home to my own Country, without being beaten to a Jelly for a *Run-away*?[76]

This complex oration—which Tryon may have heard directly from an enslaved person—pits optics and the desperate dream of magical return to Africa against celestial mechanics. Acting like a magic lantern, the Sun projects into the narrator's mind a scenario of resistance whereby it refuses to shine on the plantation, sabotaging its forcible labor. In a complementary scenario, the Moon joins the revolt with a catastrophic tide enabling the narrator to rejoin Africa, eluding the vicious corporeal punishments listed ad nauseam in the new slave codes. The analogy hinges on the word *lawfully,* in that the Sun and Moon would be in the right to cause malfunctions in the laws of celestial mechanics on behalf of a higher justice. The stark moral of the tale, of course, is that no such ethical miracle ever takes place on the plantation—any more than in the heavens. Both are subject to unbreakable laws of force relations. No amount of solar projection or visualization can undo slave cosmology (even though emancipation ultimately resulted from envisioning such unthinkable scripts).

A contemporary book from 1690 shows, conversely, how arcane debates about universal cosmological laws evince race. A polemical fiction by anti-Cartesian Jesuit historian Gabriel Daniel, *A Voyage to the World of Descartes* sends the eponymous philosopher's soul on a cosmic journey to illustrate the shortcomings of the Cartesian theory of the cosmos and body-mind dualism. During the soul's absence, the body of Descartes is placed under the care of the soul of "a little negro [un petit nègre]," tersely stereotyped as "not a devil so much as black."[77] The fictional assistant of a real-life nemesis of Descartes (Henricus Regius from the University of Utrecht), the unnamed youth's scientific expertise is disparaged with another negative: "While a Negro, he is far from a fool [sot]" (Daniel, *Voyage du monde de Descartes,* 50–51). How the young man died attests to deep anti-Blackness: Two policemen (Dutch, it is assumed) found him asleep near the site of a rape and, extrajudicially, "instantly hung [him] to a tree" (47).

Daniel's intent in connecting Descartes to lynching is unclear. As Justin E. H. Smith points out, Cartesian dualism precludes the soul being racialized, so Daniel might be obliquely critiquing slavery.[78] More likely, however, Daniel ridicules such antiracist dualism through the obviously absurd exchangeability of Descartes's soul for that of a criminalized Black youth. After touring the dysfunctional Cartesian cosmos—in which Daniel demonstrates that vision and motion are equally preempted—Descartes's soul returns to its body. But the Black youth's soul refuses to leave it while claiming credit for having "rectified [Descartes's] ideas" (Daniel, *Voyage du monde de Descartes,* 246). Failing to resolve the cohabitation of these two souls in one white body, the narrative ends without another mention of the youth. Black subjectivity and agency—like Diego's in Godwin's fiction—become dispensable rhetorical ornaments.

We find a similarly callous juxtaposition of cosmology with expendable Black life in a work of Aphra Behn. The same year she published *Oroonoko, or the Royal Slave* (1688) celebrating the leader of a rebellion of enslaved people in Suriname, Behn translated Fontenelle's bestseller.[79] In her translator's introduction, she tries toning down Fontenelle's racism but dutifully renders the egregious passages cited. In 1687, Behn adapted a French farce, *Emperor of the Moon,* which culminates in a pageant not found in the original, with the following directions: "The Scene in the Front draws off, and shews the Hill of Parnassus; a noble large Walk of Trees leading to it, with eight or ten Negroes upon Pedestals, rang'd on each side of the Walks. Next Keplair and Gallileus descend on each side, opposite to each other, in Chariots, with Perspectives in their Hands, as viewing the Machine of the Zodiack. Soft Musick plays still."[80] While the play satirizes colonial enrichment schemes, this scene serves no purpose in the plot. Other, that is, than reifying Black persons as garden ornaments adorning Galileo and Newton, the new gods of the scientific revolution, brandishing their telescopes ("Perspectives") as scepters of white universalism.[81]

From Universal Anti-Blackness to Proto-Photography

It is against this same backdrop of anti-Black rhetorical ornamentation that we find what historians point to as the earliest reference to photography, from 1690. Its author is archbishop François de Salignac de La Mothe-Fénelon, a theologian and writer, and the tutor to the French dauphin (Louis XV). Titled "A Purported Journey," the tale depicts an island in the Red Sea reached after a trip from Marseille through Egypt. On the island, the air is always scented and the temperature ideal, sounds are melodious, and, made of chocolate, the ground is "black": "There was no painter in the land, but when one sought to make the portrait of a friend, a beautiful landscape, or a picture [tableau] representing some other object, one would pour water in large gold or silver basins, then place this water opposite the object to be painted. Soon, the water froze, turning into a mirror surface in which the image of that object was indelible."[82] Photography historians consider this the earliest origin of the dream of photography. But again, they disregard the rest of the tale, especially its intent. Fénelon adds that older men on the island go into a cave whence they emerged "blond" with their "wrinkles erased" and that to avoid intellectual labor, islanders "imported slaves from foreign countries and had them think for them" (Fénelon, *Oeuvres,* 4:572–73). The intent is clearly the same anti-Black pejoration as in Daniel or Behn. The story is not at all about utopia but rather about the toxicity of dreams. It is a cautionary tale against wish fulfillment eclipsing Christian virtue. The desires described—plenty, youth, thinking enslaved people, and fixed images—are poisonous to the faithful because they are against nature. The pointed location of the black-soil island between Asia and "Africa, where there are so many monsters," evinces all at once Islam, teratology, and Blackness (573). Archbishop Fénelon did not intuit photography at all: The basins' horizontal surface could capture only Narcissus's face—perhaps that is Fénelon's point.[83] This allegory makes the automatic reproduction of visual reality a theological and epistemic aberration comparable only to the possibility of Black agency and cogency. "A Purported Journey" is antiphotographic to the exact extent that it is anti-Black.

In prior heroic accounts of the scientific revolution and seventeenth-century media prehistory alike, disinterested thinkers using innovative scientific instruments effected a paradigm shift to uncover new truths (heliocentrism) and enact age-old dreams (copying human vision in fixed pictures). This chapter shows that military and colonial prospects, as well as the yield of human enslavement and concomitant anti-Blackness, inhered to and generalized within post-Copernican visualizations of the cosmos through the multiple world hypothesis. Old apparatuses like the camera obscura and new technologies of automatic visual objectivity were catalysts with telescopes in a slow shift in visual practices toward serial and synthetic visualizations of the visible world, with features of kinemorphosis present in Moon travel tales. Proto-photographic ideas were also present, notably by invoking chemical exposure followed by the slow development of a latent substrate into a fixed visual expression: skin color (Godwin). These precinematic and pre-photographic ideas had nothing yet to do with making pictural copies of visual reality. Instead, they dealt with organizing the global terrestrial polity by locating and controlling the mechanisms of skin color and racial difference to shore up colonization and slavery.

2

Kinemorphosis

Cosmological Animation and History's Whiteness

This chapter segues from flashes of animated visualization in seventeenth-century astronomical narratives and illustrations to the major innovation of eighteenth-century cosmology: kinemorphosis. That coinage denotes a specialized type of animated visualization in which the sequential but uneven developmental morphing of living beings, objects, or structures is envisioned as such. While heliocentric astronomy was limited to the solar system, eighteenth-century astronomy connected the latter to deep space, stars, and stellar structures, enabling a general theory of cosmology. I argue that it was in William Herschel's nebular cosmology of the 1780s that the root idea of the passage from chronophotography to cinema was formulated: static phases of a material continuum visualized as an animated sequence. This is one key reason why cosmology occupies a central role in the matrix of photocinema.

Kinemorphosis subsequently emerged in other domains of natural history from embryology to the modeling of the flow of human history, always inflecting and inflected by ideas of race at various scales.[1] By the 1760s, the legitimacy of slavery was finally overtly challenged. This redoubled debates by natural philosophers on the cause of Blackness and the biological processes of race mixing, while heightening conjectures regarding hypothetical race-shifting—white people becoming black, and Black people becoming white.

Chapter 3 delves into the pre-photographic context of the new photochemistry of the late eighteenth century. Chapter 6 examines the interactions of kinemorphic visuality with time-recording instruments in the context of precinema.

Eighteenth-Century Astronomy

While seventeenth-century astronomy focused on planets and comets orbiting the Sun, in the wake of Newtonian laws eighteenth-century astronomy began tackling deep space beyond the solar system. Very little was known circa 1700 about the distance, nature, and distribution of stars, apart from the conspicuous band of the Milky Way most astronomers considered the dominant structure of the universe. As to how the latter began, it remained largely a matter of divine creation shrouded in mystery. Isaac Newton envisioned a universe in perfect equilibrium between gravitation and centrifugal force, a well-regulated clockwork from past to future without a scenario for its origin.

Over the first decades of the eighteenth century, the clockwork began glitching. Astronomers detected countless irregularities in the Earth's axis, which wobbled three different ways, while the Moon's motions showed various perturbations in the plane of its orbit, its rotation, axis, etc. Newtonian mechanics proved unable to explain such secular inequalities soon understood to devolve from the way that more than two celestial bodies interact gravitationally (the three-body problem). All such perturbations suggested that cosmic states and cycles changed widely over time, but these changes were not yet articulated to the entire history of the cosmos.

There was a crisis in the firmament as well. Stars had been thought to be fixed lamps embedded in the celestial vault. But when Edmond Halley compared the positions of stars over time, he concluded not only that they seemed to move but that they did so in different directions, sometimes altering their brightness as well. In 1727, astronomer James Bradley decided to map out a year of daily positions of the star Gamma Draconis, always visible from London. He expected a specific set of measurements if it was fixed, another if it was moving. What he found was something in between. As a commentator puts it: "Something was awry either with the telescope or with the universe."[2] The issue was decided when Bradley realized that the discrepancy was caused by the "successive propagation of light"—the fact it was moving at a finite speed.[3] Demoting light from its prior abstract instantaneity to a fully physical phenomenon was instrumental in both shaping photocinema and directing it toward photography. It also occasioned fierce debates between supporters of Christiaan Huygens's wave theory—slowly gaining currency by the 1750s through mathematician Leonhard Euler's research on the dynamics of matter—and a traditionalist camp opining that light was a stream of corpuscles.

The more burning issue was observational: chromatic aberration. When light refracts through a lens it is partially decomposed, lengthening the blue end of the spectrum, fuzzing up telescopic images, and severely limiting magnification for stellar astronomy. In the 1750s, London optician John Dollond innovated combination lenses with two kinds of glass, lessening the blue shift. This boosted preparations for the main astronomical event of the century: the twin transits of Venus in 1761 and 1769. It was hoped that the proper timing of the black dot of Venus gliding across the Sun would yield by simple trigonometry the distance from Earth to the Sun, enabling the exact measurement of the solar system. It was during the following transits of Venus in 1874 and 1881 that Jules Janssen deployed a photographic revolver representing the proximate precursor device for cinema. In fact, photography was meant to palliate the unforeseen issue that arose in 1761 and 1769, when the black circle of Venus elongated into a drop as it crossed the edge of the Sun (see chapter 4).

What is light? How does it interact with optical glass or planets? Can it reliably relay the true appearance of faraway stars? And how did the universe form and evolve? Each of these astronomical queries contributed to the long maturation of photocinema.

Maupertuis's Plastic Visualization of Celestial and Raced Bodies

The word *cosmology* was scarcely used in its modern sense until the 1740s. The 1731 *Cosmologia generalis* of Christian, baron von Wolff rehearsed the "great chain of beings" of his teacher Gottfried

Wilhelm Leibniz with a new twist, as an exegete of Wolff explains: "The world, or the universe, is the series of finite beings, either simultaneous and coexisting, or successive, that are chained together."[4] While "simultaneous and coexisting" taxonomies were theorized by Carolus Linnaeus and Georges-Louis Leclerc, count de Buffon, the "successive" evolution of celestial and living bodies at long durations remained completely enigmatic. Pierre-Louis Moreau de Maupertuis took an important step toward visualizing their plastic formation over time by focusing on motion, asserting that "the greatest phenomenon of nature, the most marvelous, is motion: without it all would be plunged in eternal death."[5]

Maupertuis trained in astronomy in the 1720s, when Newtonian mechanics prevailed over Cartesianism and monadism in France.[6] He studied analytical mathematics in Basel, Switzerland, with Johann Bernoulli to better understand force, key to explaining unaccounted motions. Was force extrinsic like a billiard ball hitting another or intrinsic to matter, like the life force of animate beings known as vis viva? Newton's attraction between masses was vexingly halfway: an intrinsic force manifesting only extrinsically, through vision (trajectory) and time (clocks).[7] Ever since Galileo's studies of falling bodies, regular visual displacement—in ballistics, trajectories, rolling balls, comets, transits, eclipses, etc.—had acquired a commanding status. As Jessica Riskin demonstrates, quandaries of vis viva, mechanical motion, and biological growth became central to mid-eighteenth-century natural philosophy.[8]

Maupertuis contributed to that debate through a tangential but urgent question: the shape of Earth.[9] For René Descartes, ether vortices making celestial bodies spin squished them at the equator, while Newton asserted that centrifugal force should make them bulge. In *Discourse on the Different Figures of Celestial Bodies* published in 1732, Maupertuis posed the problem anew, asking what "the figure that a homogeneous and fluid mass rotating around an axis must take."[10] This heuristic premise broke with the Aristotelian logic of solids, still present in Emanuel Swedenborg's magnetic origin theory of the solar system. By visualizing the Earth's plastic kinemorphic transformation over long durations, Maupertuis concluded that Newton must be right. In 1736 he took part in an expedition to

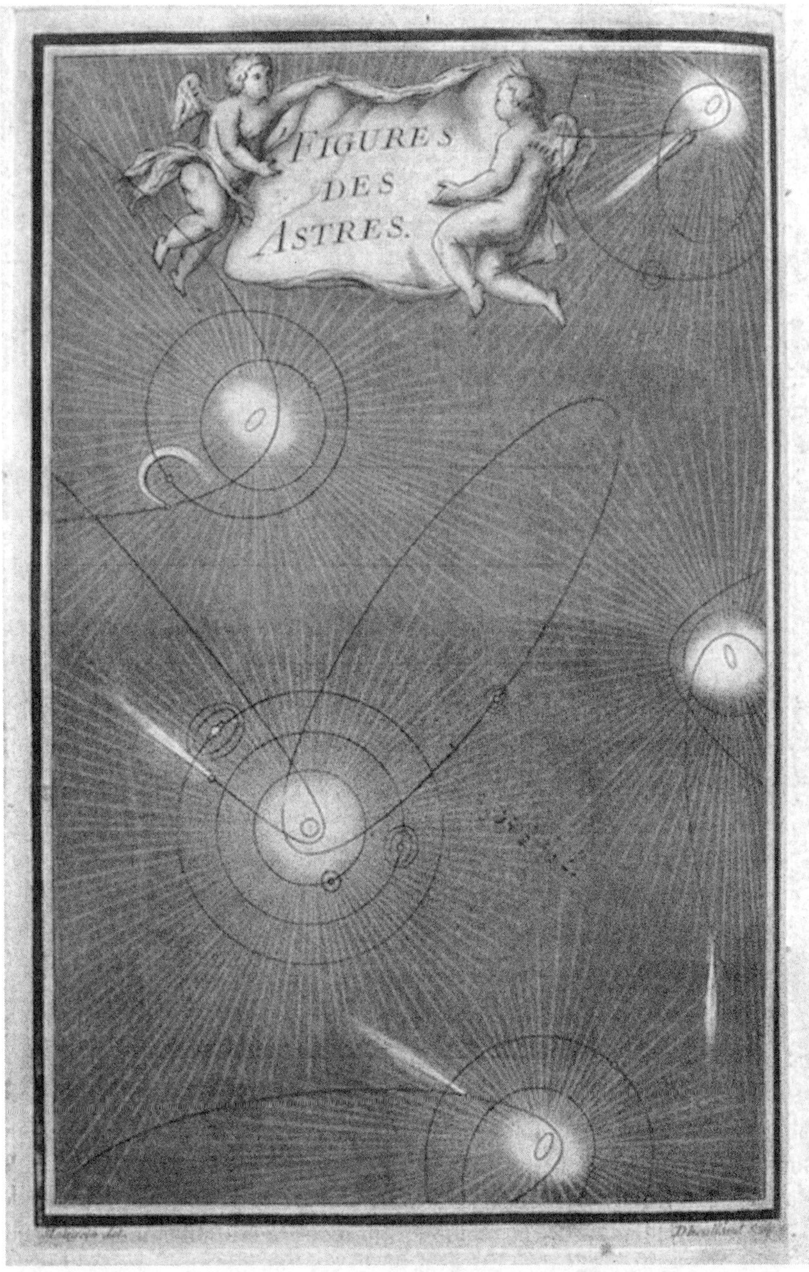

Figure 2.1. **Star systems with orbiting planets and comets. Maupertuis, *Discours sur les différentes figures des Astres* (Paris: Imprimerie royale, 1732), frontispiece. Courtesy of Bibliothèque Nationale de France Gallica.**

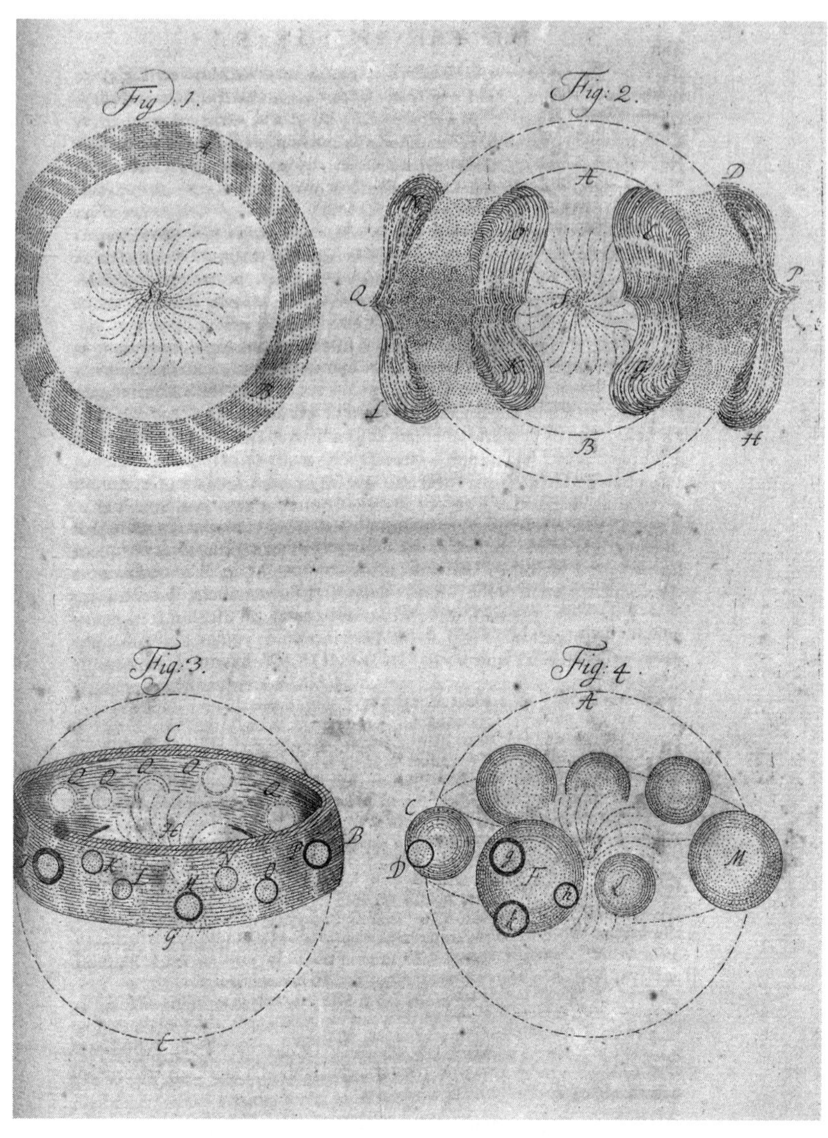

Figure 2.2. **Solid origin to the solar system from (1) a hard bulla around the Sun; (2) broken by magnetism; (3) forming a ring of matter; (4) forming planets. Emanuel Swedenborg, *Principia Rerum Naturalium* (Dresden, Germany: Friderici Hekelii, 1734), plate 26. Courtesy of ETH-Bibliothek Zürich.**

Lapland to measure the curvature of Earth, which confirmed Newton's hypothesis and his own visualization methodology.

Maupertuis's visualization experiment relied on time compression. It was concurrent with the gradual expansion of the conjectural age of the cosmos from six millennia in the mid-seventeenth century (based on the Bible) to several million years by the 1750s. Maupertuis extrapolated the long duration deformation of Earth to stars: "Fixed stars are suns like ours; it is very likely they have, like ours, a rotational motion around their axis. Hence, they are exposed to flattening given the rapidity of their motion; and why would there be no flat stars in the skies? Especially if we realize that we know from no observation the figure of the fixed stars" (*Discours,* 77). The default shape of all celestial bodies for Maupertuis was an ellipsoid, not an abstract geometrical sphere. While proven wrong about disk stars, he was right about larger structures: most clusters and galaxies are ellipsoids. Maupertuis was quite aware that visualizing the temporal plasticity of unseeable celestial bodies constituted a new method: "this art which extends our sight to the last places of space, taking it to the smallest parts of matter; & which makes us discover objects whose sight had appeared forbidden to humans" (*Oeuvres,* 4:5). The mechanical economy of such visual transformations suggested to him a more general law of physics, namely "a metaphysical principle upon which all the laws of motion are founded. And this is that, whenever there is a change in nature, the quantity of action employed for this change is always the smallest possible."[11] This "principle of least action" accounted for the optimal motion and shape of celestial bodies but also the optimal route of light refracting through various media.[12] Trusting the "spirit of system," Maupertuis sought to transduce this universal principle to other fields like psychology, linguistics, and biology.[13]

Notoriously, he applied least action visualization to sexual reproduction in a euphemistically titled book of 1745, *Physical Venus.* Again, visualization and reproduction proved coextensive. Rejecting preformism—the simple upscaling of an invariant pattern—as flippant, he argued for epigenesis, the complex development of tissue through uneven accretion and growth proponed by William Harvey.[14] One far-ranging implication of epigenesis was that it circumvented dualism since a coordinating "intelligent" force within organic matter was needed to structure and assemble the embryo. Maupertuis hoped that this vis viva shaping living bodies was akin to gravitation and centrifugal force shaping celestial bodies.[15]

Physical Venus has two parts: the first propones the epigenetic theory of reproduction, and the second expands on a best-selling pamphlet Maupertuis published (anonymously) the year before: "Physical Dissertation Occasioned by the White Negro." That text concerns a South American child with albinism who was paraded in Parisian salons, catalyzing anxieties in plantocracies about natural mutations breaching the color line.[16] Maupertuis approached processes of racial diversification according to the same dynamic purview as the developmental visualization of celestial bodies. He embraced the traditional thermometabolic model of racial mutation within the widespread premise of aboriginal whiteness. However, he was aware that the hypothesis that Blackness sprang from the "Malpighi layer" of skin had been debunked by capable anatomists.[17] The "white negro" occasioned in Maupertuis a reconsideration of his ideas on racial phylogeny. He asserts that "we cannot doubt" that all races come "from the same mother" and that "the difference between white and black, so conspicuous to our eyes, means very little to Nature" (Maupertuis, *Vénus physique,* 106, 118–19).[18] Yet this monogenic affirmation quickly devolves into a discourse of whiteness as cosmetic norm and Blackness as degenerative. Recycling racist tropes, he opines that "the black color lightens up but ugliness remains," venturing that non-Black races "relegated these deformed races to the least inhabitable climates of the Earth" (98, 123, 130). This unlikely historical conjecture blatantly contradicts his earlier mention of racial difference resulting from climate (130). When considering mixed-race children, Maupertuis comes up with another surprise: "If a black man marries a white woman, it seems that both colors are mixed; the child has an olive-colored hue, and features half from the mother and half from the father" (69). Three radical arguments are wrapped into this one statement. First, since the child of a Black parent and a white parent is viable, mixed children plainly confirm monogenism—in fact, they invalidate polygenism once and for all. Second, mother and father contribute equally their genetic material, making reproduction equiparental and epigenetic.[19] Finally, with his example of a Black man "marrying" a white woman, Maupertuis is willfully transgressive since the 1724 Code Noir stipulated (in the king's voice): "We forbid our white subjects of one or the other sex to contract marriage with blacks."[20] It is fair to say that Maupertuis's simple (and correct) statement was the most advanced affirmation of natural gender and racial equality.

What likely explains Maupertuis holding simultaneous antiracist and anti-Black sentiments is the fact that the wealth of his family came from the slave trade. His father, René Moreau, was a ship captain ennobled as Sieur de Maupertuis by Louis XIV for his privateering during the War of the Grand Alliance. Saint-Malo, France, where the Maupertuis family lived, endeavored at the time to rival Nantes and Bordeaux for the triangular trade. Moreau made multiple trips to the Caribbean in the 1680s and 1690s prior to being named director of Saint-Malo's chapter of the Compagnie des Indes Occidentales (West Indies Company). This leaves no doubt that he traded enslaved peoples.[21]

Maupertuis expressed opposition to slavery and recognized Black intelligence. In his *Essay on Moral Philosophy,* he sides with the "slave" abused by a "cruel master" and envisions how "a ship returning from Guinea is filled with Catos who prefer to die rather than survive their own freedom" (*Oeuvres,* 1:223, 225). He states that "the Negro & the Philosopher have but one and the same aim: to better their condition" (226). In another text, he celebrates Africa, "formerly inhabited by the most numerous and powerful nations, filled with the most superb cities" where "sciences and arts" were duly cultivated (2:364–65). Elsewhere, he frames white recognition of Black subjectivity by foregrounding ethical visual animation: "My body is animated [animé] by a mind [esprit] that perceives itself; thence I judge that other bodies similar to mine do the same. I would be ridiculous if a taller or smaller size or slightly different features made me refuse a soul to other men of my species [espèce]: even features more different still, black skin, would not authorize me to deprive of soul [âme] the inhabitants of Africa."[22] Visual perception of the racial other implies that their and my mindful self-animation are equal. That is Maupertuis's least action principle at its ethical best.

Having isolated animated visualization as a new method of inquiry into the origin of both racialized human and celestial bodies, Maupertuis failed his antiracist insights, falling back on the biased discourses of his familial, class, and intellectual milieu.

Three-Dimensional Cosmological Visualization in Wright and Lambert

What makes eighteenth-century cosmological thinking protocinematic was not local kinemorphic insights like Maupertuis's disk star but complete three-dimensional dynamic modeling at a macrocosmic scale. Two early contributors of this 3D pathway were Thomas Wright and Johann Heinrich Lambert. Wright was trained in projective geometry as a draftsman, landscape designer, and architect, and he transduced his skills to theoretical astronomy.[23] In 1734, he sketched a map "representing in a section of the Creation, eighteen

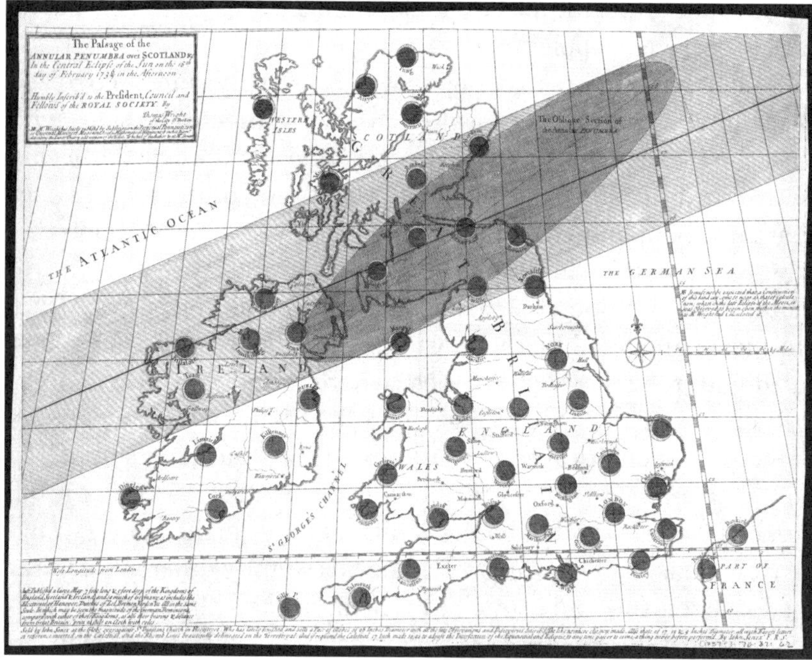

Figure 2.3. **Predictive map of eclipse path. Thomas Wright, broadside, 1737. Courtesy of Osher Map Library and Smith Center for Cartographic Education, University of Southern Maine.**

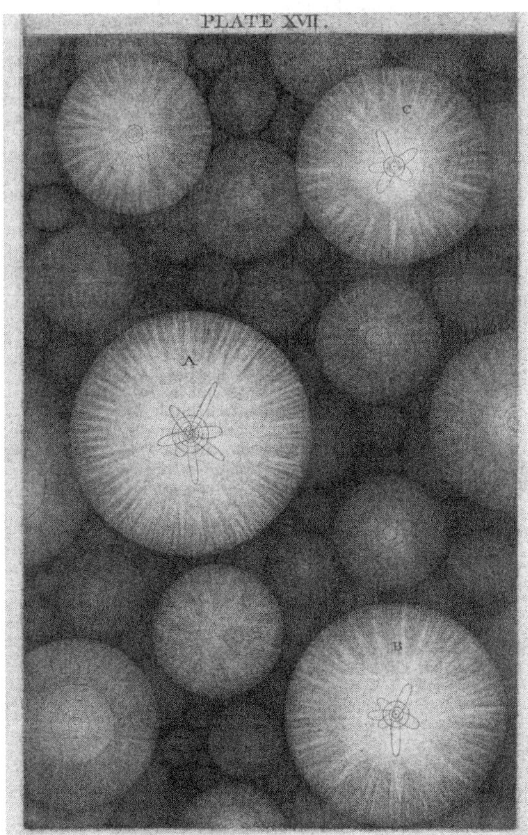

Figure 2.4. **Star systems in three dimensions. Thomas Wright of Durham, *An Original Theory or New Hypothesis of the Universe Founded upon the Laws of Nature and Solving by Mathematical Principles the General Phaenomena of the Visible Creation and Particularly the Via Lactea* (London: H. Chapelle, 1750), plate XVII (detail). Courtesy of ETH-Bibliothek Zürich.**

feet long and one broad, several thousand worlds and systems, and a great number of emblematic figures."[24] That map is lost, but a 1737 engraving illustrating the path of a solar eclipse shows his advanced skill at visually transducing orbital mathematics.[25] In 1750, he published *An Original Theory or New Hypothesis of the Universe,* printed and illustrated by himself.[26]

Like most astronomers of the time, Wright equates the Milky Way with the entire universe, envisioning it as a spherical structure with myriad solar systems orbiting around its center. As Simon Schaffer indicates, Wright presents "a picture of an evolving system" based on the circulation of fire and comets, altering Newton's "static world-view" and ushering in dynamic cosmology ("Phoenix of Nature," 189). Yet Wright's model is less about the physics of

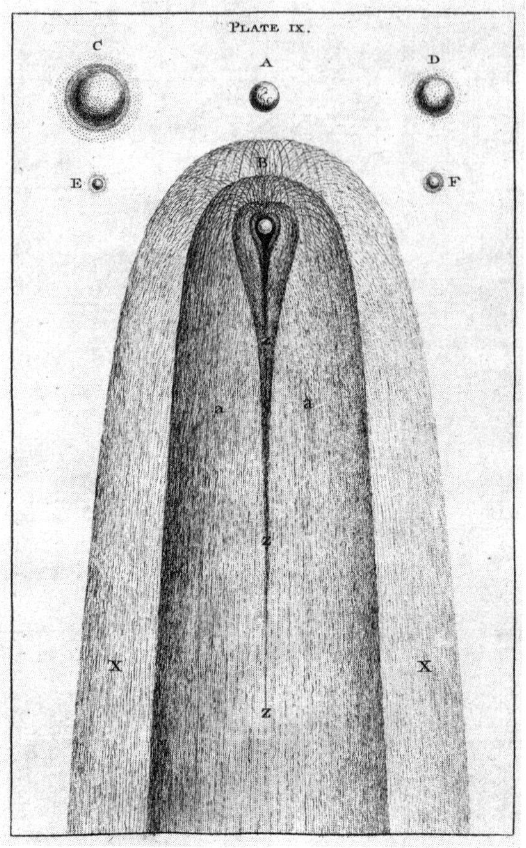

Figure 2.5. **Comet head. Thomas Wright of Durham, *An Original Theory or New Hypothesis of the Universe Founded upon the Laws of Nature and Solving by Mathematical Principles the General Phaenomena of the Visible Creation and Particularly the Via Lactea* (London: H. Chapelle, 1750), plate VIII. Courtesy of ETH-Bibliothek Zürich.**

celestial structures than their 3D visualization, as Figure 2.5 shows in his keenly extrapolated drawing of a comet's structure.[27] Wright was fully aware of the novelty of his virtual purview. He defines the latter as a "new-created mind, or thinking being . . . suspended in the Aether, exactly in the midway, betwixt Syrius and the Sun," who can observe the true shape of the Milky Way. This heuristic "being," at once theoretical figment and extraterrestrial, he adds, "can scarce be called less than an *ocular revelation*" (Wright, *Original Theory,* 34, 76). Wright was a follower of mystic Jakob Böhme and believed that after death the soul becomes a disembodied observer, a virtual Oculus roaming the universe. He confesses that "it isn't easy to know where to stop in such a scene of wonders" (61, 79). The book's best-known plate showing countless eyes at the center of planetary

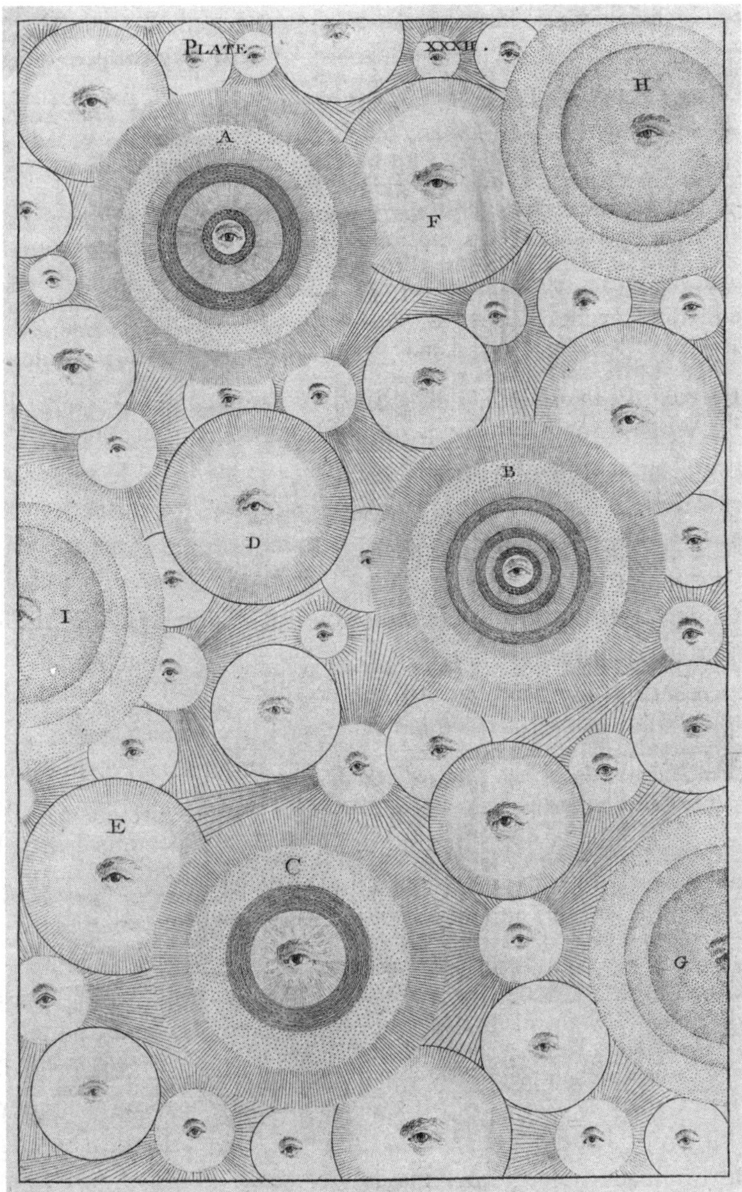

Figure 2.6. **The Oculus universe of Wright. Thomas Wright of Durham, *An Original Theory or New Hypothesis of the Universe Founded upon the Laws of Nature and Solving by Mathematical Principles the General Phaenomena of the Visible Creation and Particularly the Via Lactea* (London: H. Chapelle, 1750), plate XXXII. Courtesy of ETH-Bibliothek Zürich.**

systems should be read in its full polyvalence: all at once extraterrestrial observers, souls in their afterlife, deistic Eyes of Providence, and three-dimensional visualization making visible the unseeable cosmos.

Alsatian polymath Johann Heinrich Lambert also systematically investigated three-dimensional visualizations. A gifted mathematician, he researched perspective, optics, light, color theory, geometry, astronomy, and cosmology. His overarching concern harks back to Athanasius Kircher's: how to visualize the structure of the cosmos through projective geometry and the behavior of light in disclosing it. In the 1750s he theorized various kinds of perspectives, including aerial, while improving the design of the perspectograph—a modified pantograph producing elevation drawings from floor plans.[28] To improve the rendering of light and shadow in perspectival engraving, he built a quantified setup with candles and partial caches and screens to mathematize laws of surface reflectance and illuminance.[29] He also computed the amount of sunlight the Moon's surface reflects back to Earth. He called his new science of light quantification "photometria"—the second coinage of the prefix *photo-* after Kircher's *photosophia.*

After reading Wright's *Original Theory* and his friend Immanuel Kant's cosmology (see below), Lambert limned out his own cosmology in 1761. Like Wright, he highlighted visualization as a method and a drive: "In every situation that affords a point of view we will place an observatory and an observer."[30] Eschewing Wright's mysticism, Lambert latches on a real vehicle for his virtual visual exploration, comets, which "being attached to no particular system, are in common to all, and which, roaming from one world to another, make the tour of the universe" (Lambert, *System of the World,* 57). Born in the Swiss exclave of Mulhouse, Lambert became a wanderer working in Italy before landing at the Prussian Academy of Sciences in Berlin headed by Maupertuis. He writes: "I love to figure to myself those traveling globes, peopled with astronomers, who are stationed there for the express purpose of contemplating nature on a large as we contemplate it on a small scale. The moveable observatory cruising from Sun to Sun, carries them in succession through every different point of view, places them in a situation to survey all, to determine the position and motion of each star, to measure the orbits of the planets and comets which revolve round them" (57). It is as if the enticement of visualization produces a fictional excess—something like the James Webb Space Telescope meeting *Star Trek*'s USS *Enterprise*. This fictional excess was, as we'll see in chapter 7, instrumental for the inception of the cinema apparatus by Camille Flammarion, who drew direct inspiration from both Wright and Lambert.

Immanuel Kant's Protocinematic Cosmos (1755)

With Kant, both kinemorphic astronomical visualization (in this section) and astroracial discourses (next section) reached an apex in natural philosophy. Practicing neither observation nor mathematics, Kant acquired an advanced knowledge of astronomy early in his career as a teacher. In 1749, he joined the Maupertuisian debate about vis viva in his first published piece, concluding brashly: "We have as yet no dynamics."[31] He subsequently published essays on wind theory, earthquakes, and geological changes, showing his predilection for large dynamic phenomena at long durations. In *Universal Natural History and Theory of the Heavens* (1755), Kant expanded his entry for a prize question set by Maupertuis at the Academy of Sciences in Berlin regarding the future of Earth's spin.[32]

The nucleus of Kant's cosmology is Newtonian mechanics approached through modes of visualization developed by Maupertuis, Wright, and Lambert. The resulting model was qualitatively new in offering an exhaustive theory of the formation and evolution of the cosmos over time. It has three key features: all celestial bodies—stars, planets, moons, and comets—form through a gravitational process of accretion and centrifugal expulsion; the cosmos is in constant metamorphosis, not in a Newtonian static equilibrium; the cosmos is formed of embedded gravitational structures (planets and moons, planetary systems, galaxies, and galactic clusters). When Kant describes his visual simulation method, he tacitly couches it as a visual media setup: "I assume the matter of the whole world to be universally dispersed and I make complete chaos out of it. I see matter form in accordance with the established laws of attraction and modify its motion through repulsion. Without the assistance of any arbitrary inventions, I enjoy the pleasure of seeing the creation of a well-ordered whole by reason of established laws of motion which looks so much like the system of the world we have before our eyes that I cannot help but regard it as the same" ("Universal Natural History," 225–26). Virtual sequential imaging and time compression are the main operations. A panorama of disordered floating matter makes way for sharper pictorial patterns, then closely interlinked pictures, the last of which matches extant stellar maps. Visualization here resembles a magic lantern show with slides depicting the progressive steps of cosmic accretion and distension, from past states that are unseeable to present observations.[33] Like Wright and Lambert, he posits virtual viewpoints enabling him to envision cosmic features: "An eye situated in this plane of reference will perceive, in its view into the field of stars at the concave spherical surface of the firmament, this densest concentration of stars in the direction of such a drawn plane in the form of a zone illuminated by much more light" (249). Such visualizations rely expressly on motion parallax: "If such a world of fixed stars is viewed at such an immeasurable distance from the eye of the observer which is outside it, then it will appear under a small angle as a minute space illuminated by a weak light, the shape of which will be round as a circle when its plane presents itself straight to the eye and elliptical when it is seen from the side" (254–55). This lenticular shape of the Milky Way, echoing the lenticular shape of Maupertuis's disk stars, incites Kant to imagine the origin of the Sun as a spinning cloud of particles condensing into a sphere.[34] Planets replicate this process at a smaller scale while beginning to orbit the Sun's ecliptic plane, and comets form as well in eccentric orbits crossing the ecliptic. He conjectures that Saturn's rings resulted from particles emitted from that planet, which explains why they did not condense into moons. He then posits that the Milky Way itself formed through a similar process with smaller galaxies in various orbits in deep space. This cogent origin scenario combines gravitational and centrifugal forces through protracted kinemorphic modeling. It amounts to a virtual animation film. Recurring terms such as *perspective, angle of view, field of vision, unfolding/evolving* (Auswickelung), *gradual/ly, successive expansion, sequence,* and *series* emphasize this cinematic character.

Nebular formation hinges on the dynamic concretion and expansion of matter, which Kant simulates to its logical end: All orbiting bodies ultimately lose their centrifugal force and collapse into the central body whose hyperdensity causes it to conflagrate and redisperse into floating matter. A new cycle of nebular formation ensues, with subsequent collapses and regeneration ad infinitum (Kant, "Universal Natural History," 320–21).[35] This endless two-stroke engine of the universe leads Kant to entertain three major consequences (the third of which is discussed in the following section).

The first is sheer astonishment that this macrocosmic kinemorphic ballet really exists and, coextensively, that a human mind can visualize it. The two are often expressed together: "I represent the infinite nature of all creation, the formation of new worlds and the decline of the old ones and the unlimited realm of the chaos of the imagination"; "I find nothing that can raise the human spirit to nobler astonishment, by giving us a perspective on the unending field of the almighty, than this part of the theory that concerns the successive completion of creation" (Kant, "Universal Natural History," 235, 312). The miracle is that visualization and the cosmos in a way commune through the same process: a "self-forming nature in thought through the entire space of chaos" (264). This produces a vivid sense of kinesthetic pleasure verging on euphoria: "It is a not inconsiderable pleasure to allow one's imagination to roam freely beyond the limits of perfected creation into the realm of chaos and to see half raw nature in the proximity of the sphere of the formed world lose itself bit by bit through all stages and shadings of incompletion in the whole of unformed space" (315). Kant even wonders whether pleasure might not be the godhead's motivation for creating the universe: "Meanwhile, so that nature will beautify eternity with changeable scenes [veränderlichen Auftritten], God remains busy in ceaseless creation to make the material for the formation of even greater worlds" (318). These "changeable scenes," we should add, share a family resemblance with what Georges Méliès called "transformation views [vues à transformation]" (trick edits) in the 1890s.[36] Kant indeed digresses on scenes of optical wonder: "Let us have our imagination represent a wonderfully strange object such as a burning sun as it were from close-up. In one glance, we see broad lakes of fire lifting their flames up to the sky" (327). These include counterfactuals such as imagining a ring around Earth (303). As in Wright and Lambert, cosmology entwines the universe with imagination's jubilant powers of cinematic visualization.

The second consequence is that flights of visual fancy conceal the flipside of the cosmic scenario: the dysphoria of human finitude. If the universe is in an endless oscillating cycle, it has no specific aim, no end. Consequently, neither do human life and humanity, making the power to visualize the cosmos and see through God's works a useless if not perverse faculty: "We see the first members of a progressive relationship of worlds and systems, and the first part of this infinite progression already gives us to understand what we can suppose about the whole. There is no end here but rather an abyss of a true immeasurability into which all capacity of human concepts sinks even if it is raised with the help of mathematics" (Kant, "Universal Natural History," 256). This palpable ontological anxiety increases as the treatise goes on. Combining dizzying visualization and scientific simulation, it resembles Kant's later twin category of the sublime (dynamic and mathematic). We might call it Kant's dark kinemorphic sublime.

Because its publisher quickly went out of business, and because Kant turned away from natural philosophy to craft the modern foundation of epistemic critique, his cosmological book has remained on the historical sidelines. Its instrumental role in the eighteenth-century crystallization of ideas of photocinema is all the more crucial to reestablish.

Kant's Telos of Whiteness

Kant's third riposte to endless cosmic visualization is racial whiteness. Scholars have long probed the reasons for Kant's critical turn at the completion of his cosmology. According to Michael Friedman, Kant was left with ontological anxiety about balancing freedom and faith, together with the puzzle of anthropology: the meaning of humanity (Friedman, *Kant's Construction of Nature,* 590–91, 607). Kantian critique, in this view, recentered human life, reason, and historicity against the dark kinemorphic sublime. Yet between

Kant's precinematic cosmology and his critical anthropology there lies a submerged continuity: the structural role of race in orienting human ends.

Kant's cosmology, indeed, has an overlooked racial component. Kant took the plurality of worlds for granted: "Most of the planets are certainly inhabited . . . and those that are not will be at some stage," he affirms (Kant, "Universal Natural History," 354). Like Bernard Le Bovier, sieur de Fontenelle, he takes white supremacy as a universal that, in turns, discloses the architectonic of the universe:

> If a law is to be in place according to which the domiciles of intelligent creatures are distributed in the order of their relation to the common centre point, we shall have to place the lowest and least complete type that constitutes, as it were, the beginning of the type of the spiritual world, at that region that can be called the beginning of the entire universe in order to fill simultaneously with this and in equal progression all infinity of time and spaces with increasing degrees of perfection of the capacity to think and as it were gradually to approach the goal of the highest excellence, namely the divinity without, however, ever being able to attain it. (331)

In this somewhat opaque passage, Kant equates "lowest" intelligence with mass and pure embodiment, while higher intelligence is immaterial and close to the divinity. This directly translates the racist instrumentalization of Black peoples as reducible to their bodies and white peoples to their minds. Kant ascribed the center of the universe near the star Sirius, positioning Earth mid-universe: "Human nature, which occupies as it were the middle rung on the ladder of beings, sees itself as being between the two extreme limits of perfection" (329). As in Fontenelle, humans occupy the middle position in the cosmos and in the solar system insofar as white people occupy the temperate climatic lands on Earth. Kant blends all three cosmic scales together, exulting: "What an amazing sight! On the one hand, we saw thinking creatures among whom a Greenlander or Hottentot would be Newton, on the other hand, those who would admire him as an ape" (360–61). Rehearsing verses from Alexander Pope (which he quotes), Kant appears to relativize human intelligence from a cosmic perspective.[37] By the same token, however, he naturalizes at the scale of the universe the racial hierarchy established by white supremacy. For Kant, planets of any star system—and the life-forms and inhabitants they produce—reflect different biophysics due to their distance to the star. Beings on higher planets (Saturn and Jupiter) display a "fineness of the material, in the elasticity of the vessels and in the lightness and efficacy of the fluids . . . which delays far longer the frailty that is the consequence of the sluggishness of coarse matter," the latter characterizing beings on lower planets (Mercury and Venus). The difference extends to aesthetics as well. Kant contrasts Jupiter's multiple moons and Saturn's beautiful rings to "the lower planets [Mercury and Venus] on which this supply [of beauty] would be wasted uselessly, whose class borders more closely on the lack of reason" (363). Kant is not producing biophysical conjectures, he is rehearsing Fontenelle's astroracialization—he is racing the cosmos. Kant's chapter on multiple worlds indeed closes on a stark rhetorical question—namely, whether "those inhabiting the lower planets are attached too firmly to matter and equipped with far too few spiritual abilities to be permitted to bear the responsibility of their actions before the judgment seat of justice" (366). Again, decrypting this in racial terms plainly means that, from a cosmological vantage point, Black people and other people of color cannot self-govern and have no agency—are childishly irresponsible, justifying both white colonization and Black enslavement.

Insisting that inhabitants of the solar system "become more and more excellent and perfect in proportion to the distance of their domiciles from the Sun," Kant muses that "satellites orbiting around Jupiter will light our way in the future," perhaps after death ("Universal Natural History," 359, 367). This migration from less-perfect dense Earth to more-perfect cold Jupiter has a clear racial parallel too: instances of kidnapped African individuals transplanted to and educated in Europe who attained a so-called white intelligence. Kant was certainly aware of his colleague Anton Wilhelm Amo. Taken from Ghana as a child and brought to Germany, where he completed a doctorate in philosophy, Amo taught at the University of Jena in the 1740s—a few hundred miles from Kant in Königsberg, Germany.

Because the cosmology of Kant is the first full-fledged scientific work that is through and through kinemorphic (and because he is, after all, Kant), its astroracist discourse, echoing Fontenelle's, must be considered central for the racial foundations of the matrix of photocinema. Kant relied on two other racial constructs to anchor his idea of white supremacy, and both have a bearing on photocinema. He stated the first bluntly in unpublished notes from the 1780s: "All races will be wiped out . . . , except the white one." As Jon M. Mikkelsen indicates, in between the two parts of this quote, Kant wrote: "[Native] Americans and Negroes cannot govern themselves. Thus are only good as slaves," a comment interchangeable with lower extraterrestrials' inability "to bear the responsibility of their actions."[38] Besides the philosophical rationale that Sylvia Wynter and Denise Ferreira da Silva adduce—that thinking subjects were construed by the Enlightenment as necessarily white (see the introduction)—Kant's argument for the disappearance of nonwhite races comes from natural philosophy. Assenting to prevalent monogenism, Kant posited that all humans start from the same genetic germ or seed (Keime) and that, depending on thermometabolic conditions, this germ takes on different racial expressions manifested primarily by skin color: "white, black, red, and yellow."[39] We are returned to Francis Godwin's Lunarian children downing race by bioadaptation to the Earth's atmosphere.

Kant's lectures on physical geography, which he gave yearly for four decades, show that he embraced the idea that Black peoples are born white, the thermometabolic theory of skin color, and Johannes Kepler's notion that Black skin is thicker than white skin, together with Robert Hooke's version of chromatic/racial blackness as the disappearance of light into skin pores.[40] In the chapter on extraterrestrial inhabitants of his 1755 cosmology, Kant connects "the effect of light and heat" to "the ability of matter to accept them and more or less resist its drive" (Kant, "Universal Natural History," 303). In the 1802 version of his course on physical geography, Kant indicates that "recent chemical investigations" show that light "is something material," an acknowledgment of Jean Senebier's photochemical work (see chapter 3) (Kant, "Physical Geography," 498). Kant's theory of race thus became more fully photological in the 1780s: Skin color is caused by exposure to light and passed on via heredity.[41]

The question is why the bioexpression of Kant's common germ should favor the becoming-white of all races as a teleology of human history.[42] My conjecture is that Kant's photological racial telos is ultimately beholden to Newton's *Opticks,* which remained a lifelong reference.[43] James Delbourgo shows, for instance, that Newton's color theory of the spectrum inspired an influential model of Black skin by John Mitchell in the 1750s, which Olaudah Equiano and Thomas Clarkson still embraced in the 1780s.[44] What informs Kant's telic whiteness, I propose, is Newton's determinant experiment on the decomposition of white light into its color constituents and its subsequent synthesis back into white light.[45] Newton used a solar microscope in a camera obscura, letting the light beam decompose through a prism before bisecting it with a fast-moving comb and then a convex lens. The beam was then projected onto a screen as white light: "And these ranges of Colours, if the Comb was moved continually up and down with a reciprocal motion, ascended and descended in the Paper, and when the motion of the Comb was so quick, that the Colours could not be distinguished from one another, the whole Paper by their confusion and mixture in the Sensorium appeared white."[46] Let us note first that Newton's advanced apparatus—solar microscope, camera obscura, convex lens, shutter, and projection onto a screen—represents the core apparatus of pre-photography, while the shutter and screen projection belong to film technology. Newton adds that "every Body reflects the rays of its own Colour more copiously than the rest" (*Opticks,* 1:135). This lends itself to a racial interpretation in the sense that colored bodies belong only to their native emplacement in the spectrum while, by contrast, whiteness is synthetizing, unrestricted, and universal. Kant opined that Black people are born white (ontogeny) but also that "the first human lineal stem stock" closely resembled the phylogenetic makeup of "whites."[47] Kant's natural racial teleology thus follows Newton's decomposition of light to the letter: Racial whiteness is decomposed into people of color and then recomposed into telic whiteness.

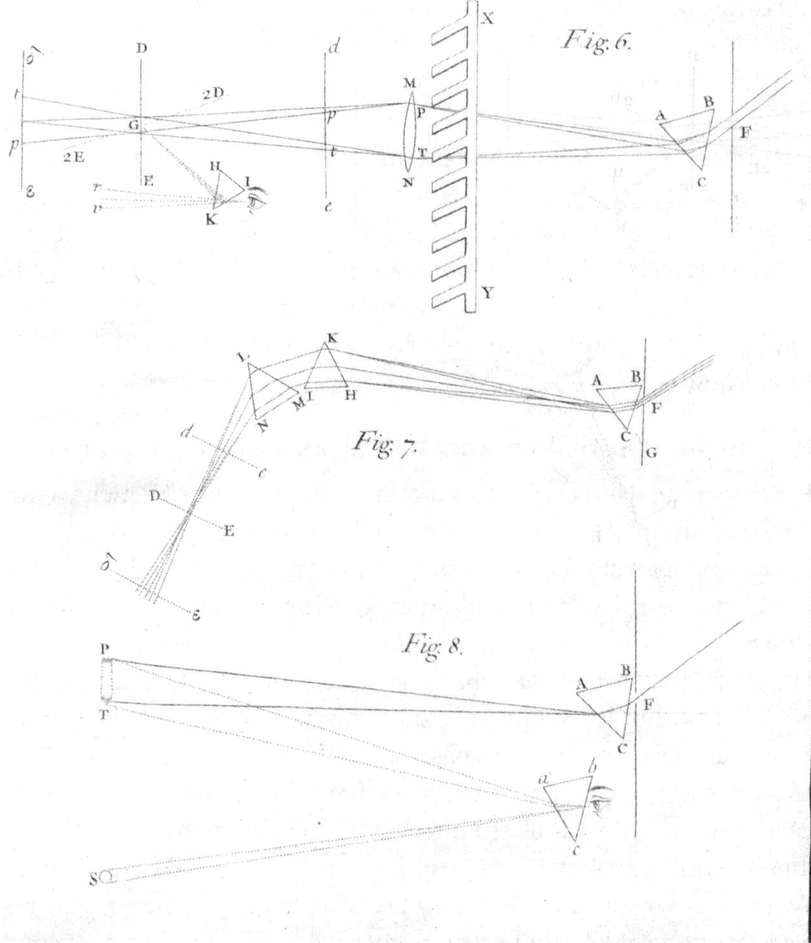

Figure 2.7. **Moving comb experiment. Isaac Newton, *Opticks*, vol. 1 (London: Smith & Walford, 1704), book 1, part 2, plate 2, figure 6. Courtesy of ETH-Bibliothek Zürich.**

Newton's *Opticks* ends with famous queries, one of which harks back to Hooke's redefinition of optical blackness (see chapter 1): "Do not black Bodies conceive heat more easily from Light than those of other Colours do, by reason that the Light falling on them is not reflected outwards but enters the Bodies, and is often reflected and refracted within them, until it be stifled and lost?" (*Opticks,* 3:133). Newton's photological language here is as racialized as Hooke's, making "black Bodies" supremely unfit to conceptualize light because they absorb heat. In his 1785 debate with Kant on race, Johann Gottfried von Herder rehearsed Thomas Clarkson's continuum theory of skin color: "Complexions run into each other. . . . All are at last but shades of the same great picture."[48] Kant insisted instead that Blackness rested outside of this continuum, invoking a recent chemical rationale for Black skin: excessive intake of phlogiston.[49] In the 1770s and 1780s, the explanation for photochemical blackening centered precisely on phlogiston (old model) or oxygenation (Antoine Lavoisier's new model), particularly via the work of Senebier, which Kant knew (see chapter 3).[50]

Herschelian Cosmology and the Chrono-Imaging Equation

It was William Herschel assisted by his sister Caroline Herschel who finalized kinemorphic cosmology while formulating the conceptual bridge between static and cinematic imaging. While John Herschel is recognized as key to pre-photography history—assisting William Henry Fox Talbot's research and giving photography its name—his father and aunt made contributions just as critical. Their saga needs no retelling, but let me provide salient points.[51] William was a German musician who became passionate for astronomy in the 1770s after moving to England during the Seven Years' War. An autodidact, he used reflector telescopes (parabolic mirror and lens) rather than the refractors (two lenses) almost exclusively used at that time. The mirrors he ground by hand were of such quality that in 1783 he became the first known person to discover a planet (Uranus), confounding the astronomical establishment. In the following years, always with Caroline's expert assistance—she forced him to secure for her a Crown salary, the first woman researcher ever paid by a state—they resolved hundreds of double stars (including Polaris), which no other telescope could do, revolutionizing stellar astronomy. William built the largest telescope to date in 1789, discovering two moons around Saturn—the first new moons of the solar system since 1670. He and Caroline recorded thousands of nebulae and star clusters, coming up with a novel typology of star systems enabling a reliable outline of the natural formation of the universe based on solid data.

For the educated public, the Herschels incarnated the freethinking Enlightenment remaking the world.[52]

William Herschel proceeded from a musical insight: fine-tuned rehearsed movement.[53] He contrived a new mirror-grinding machine, experimenting with various strokes, pressures, and directions painstakingly documented in hundreds of pages and drawings in Caroline's hand.[54] Observation was optimized with Caroline taking down coordinates so William would not lose night vision, while implementing new visual techniques (based on Nicolas Louis de Lacaille's): moving the telescope either horizontally counter to Earth's rotation to accelerate observation of a celestial band (a "sweep") or up and down across two adjacent bands (a "double swath"). To assess stellar distribution in the Milky Way, William conducted "star-gages"—that is, statistical approximations of 3D star density within a cone of observation. All such protocols combining vision, motion, and 3D visualization were unprecedented (Hoskin, *Discoverers of the Universe,* 82). During the day, William probed all aspects of observation, from the properties of glass and metal to the behavior of light, vision, and even ways of looking into the eyepiece—"practicing to see," as he put it (Hirshfeld, *Parallax,* 179).[55] This led him to experimenting in a camera obscura with lenses and prisms, wondering whether colors moved at different speeds by comparing the spectra of various stars—the beginning of spectroscopy. Noticing that red colors felt warmer to his eye, in 1799–1800 he measured the temperature of the spectrum and discovered a heat peak in the invisible margin beyond red: "calorific rays." They were later called "infrared" (see chapter 3).

With the finest and largest catalog of nebulae and stars compiled by Caroline, William began "analyzing the heavens" in 1789, classifying star clusters by sketching their contours.[56] With this vast panorama of shapes (over 2,500), the brother-sister team realized they held the key to the formation of star groupings. William uses an analogy with botany to explain it: "Is it not almost the same thing, whether we live successively to witness the germination, blooming, foliage, fecundity, fading, withering and corruption of a plant, or whether a vast number of specimens, selected from every stage

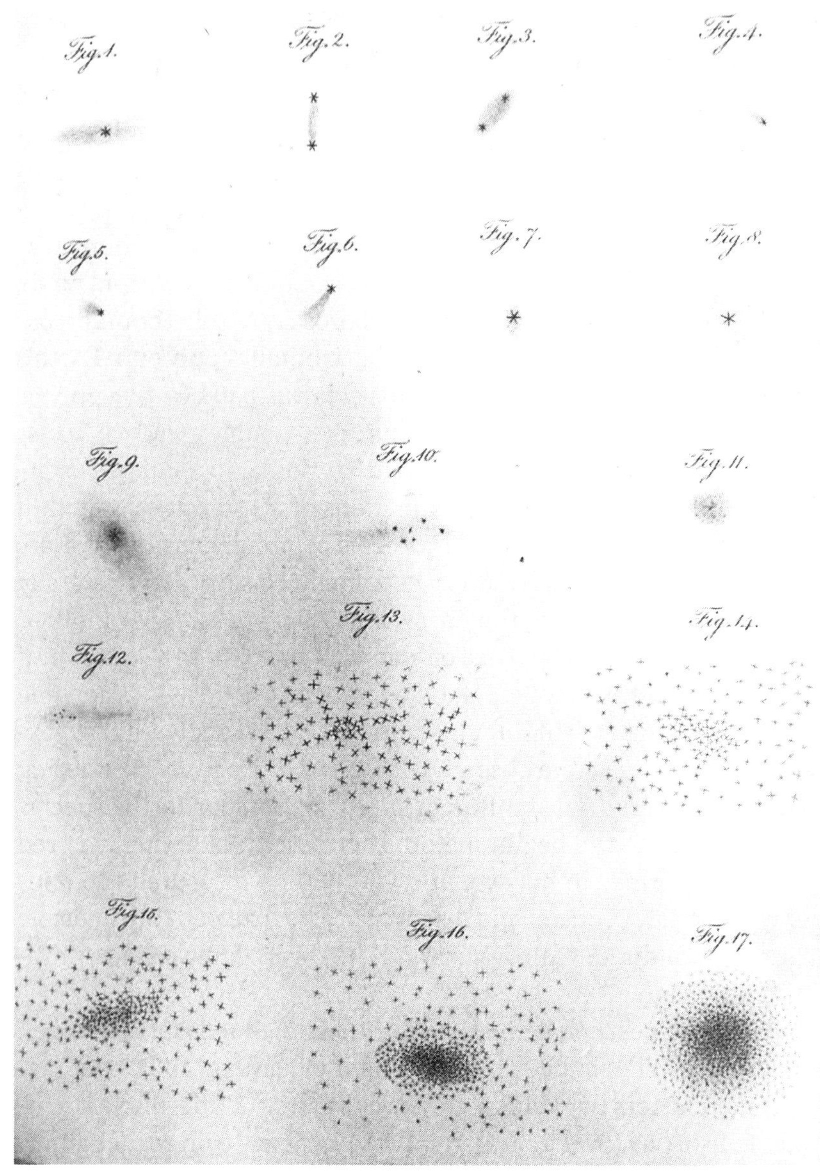

Figure 2.8. **Star clusters and nebulae correlating age and density. William Herschel, "Astronomical Observations Relating to the Sidereal Part of the Heavens,"** ***Philosophical Transactions of the Royal Society*** **104 (December 31, 1814): 248–84, plate 9. Courtesy of the Royal Society.**

through which the plant passes in the course of its existence, be brought at once to our view?" ("Catalogue," 226). If the maturation of galaxies and star clusters could not be directly observed, their kinemorphic evolution could be visualized through discrete cluster contours organized in morphic sequences. In other words, a survey of different objects of different ages distributed in space disclosed their common evolution in time. William was aware of this, writing: "After having shown the extent of the power of my 40ft telescope to penetrate into space, I should have added page 84, that this instrument may be said to have also the power of penetrating into time: at least with respect to what is past."[57] With this new "method of viewing the heavens," he adds, "we can, as it were, extend the range of our experience to immense duration" (226). Michael Hoskin points out that this purview "ushered in our modern astronomy in which everything—individual stars, clusters, even the universe itself—has a life history" (*Discoverers of the Universe,* 86).

William's equation is pivotal for media history: An array of static images was shown to be equivalent to an unseeable but visualizable kinemorphic sequence in time. This is the epistemic condition of possibility for transforming sequential photographs—via chronophotography—into motion pictures. In sum, the Herschels transformed the cosmos from a realm of discontinuous objects and shapes to a coherent virtual film of its natural history. We cannot overstate the importance of this Herschelian equation: Charles Darwin, Ernst Haeckel, Étienne-Jules Marey, and Flammarion each expanded its kinemorphic visualization, expressly attributing it to the Herschels.[58] Astronomy historians assert that William was not aware of the earlier dynamic cosmic models of Wright and Kant, but this is highly unlikely; more research will likely show that Berlin astronomer Johann Elert Bode was the bridge.[59]

Among other techniques of visualization, William used various pictorial strategies, from star cluster schematization to perspectival drawing and composite sketching. He writes: "The foregoing theoretical view, with all its consequential appearances, as seen by an eye inclosed in one of the nebulae, is no other than a drawing from nature, wherein the features of the original have been closely copied; and I hope the resemblance will not be called a bad one, when it shall be considered how very limited must be the pencil of the inhabitant of so small and retired a portion of an indefinite system in attempting the picture of so unbounded an extent" ("Catalogue," 220). As Omar W. Nasim shows in his examination of William's pictorial practices, *copy* is a summary term for a process of comparisons, collating and schematizing that synthesizes "composite pictorial representations, formed over time." These crafted images amount to "a whole series of controlled glimpses turned into an extended and steady gaze," another equation of discrete images with a dynamic process (Nasim, *Observing by Hand,* 17–18). William's extended metaphor—"drawing from nature," "copied," "pencil," "picture"—evokes rather remarkably the conceit of *The Pencil of Nature,* the title of the famous 1844 essay on photography by Talbot, who closely studied the work of William Herschel when training as an astronomer (see chapter 4). Yet the latter was never committed to static pictorial copies of the cosmos, and indeed "On the Construction of the Heavens" aimed foremost to provide "a section of our sidereal system" to sample cosmogenesis.[60] While the copy he

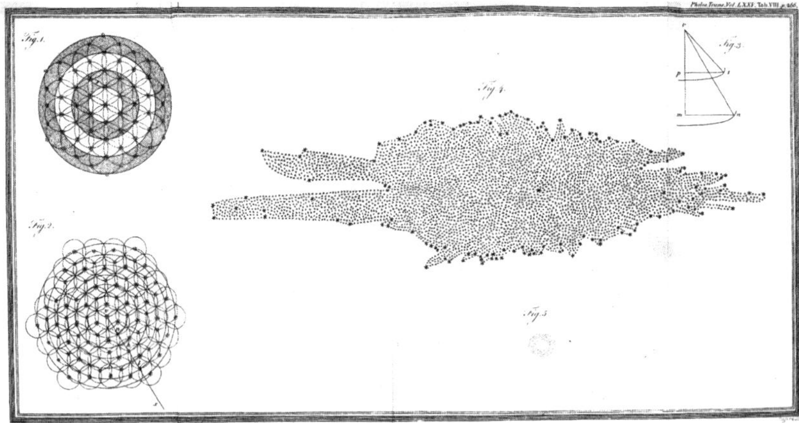

Figure 2.9. **3D structure of nebulae. William Herschel, "Accounts of Some Observations Tending to Investigate the Construction of the Heavens,"** ***Philosophical Transactions of the Royal Society*** **74 (January 1, 1784): 437–51, table 18. Courtesy of the Royal Society.**

refers to is from a nebulae's purview—that is, "objective" in the nonhuman model of vision I outlined in chapter 1—proto-photographic and protocinematic insights are closely entwined in his cosmology.

In the 1783 paper "On the Proper Motion of the Sun and Solar System," Herschel asserts that "there is not, in strictness of speaking, one *fixed* star in the heavens" and "there can hardly remain a doubt of the general motion of all the starry systems, and consequently of the solar one among them."[61] Expanding on Bradley's conjecture that the solar system orbits the center of the Milky Way, he muses: "A star, a sun, such as ours, may have a proper motion within its own system of stars, while at the same time the whole starry system to which it belongs may have another proper motion, totally different in quantity and direction" ("On the Proper Motion," 276). Calling such compound cosmic motions "intersystematical," William visualizes the cosmos as layers upon kinemorphic layers so that the motion of an object can only be relative to the scale of its structure. In other words, there is no proper motion in the cosmos since motion is ultimately dependent on a visual framework.[62] This means that the cosmos may be simulated, visualized in samples, and illustrated in small areas but not mimetically pictured as a whole.[63]

Animating History: Astronomical Culture and the Specter of Slavery

Astronomy in the eighteenth century was equally pivotal for colonial power, instrument innovation, and panoptic Enlightenment ideology.[64] The dynamic model of the universe that emerged from it altered public perception of the sensorium of space-time for both natural history and human history. Besides Kant, several philosophers intervened directly in astronomical culture. Voltaire studied Newtonian mechanics with Gabrielle-Émilie Le Tonnelier de Breteuil, marquise du Châtelet and penned *Micromégas* (1752) to satirize the multiple worlds hypothesis, while Georg Wilhelm Friedrich Hegel wrote his inaugural dissertation "On the Orbits of Planets" in 1801. Even a social philosopher like Adam Smith explored in the late 1750s, in "The Principles Which Lead and Direct Philosophical Enquiries; Illustrated by the History of Astronomy," to try to understand, in the words of a recent scholar, "the constituents and dynamics of human nature."[65] Smith puzzles in particular on the workings of the imagination: "The supposition of a chain of intermediate, though invisible, events, which succeed each other in a train similar to that in which the imagination has been accustomed to move, and which link together those two disjointed appearances, is the only means by which the imagination can fill up this interval, is the only bridge which, if one may say so, can smooth its passage from the one object to the other."[66] I want to insist on the expression "intermediate, though invisible, events" because it encapsulates the inspiration for animated visualization and recurs in my reconstruction of the development of photocinema (see chapter 6). Smith adds that "a system is an imaginary machine invented to connect together in the fancy those different movements and effects which are already in reality performed" ("Principles," 44). Contemporaneous with Kant's dynamic cosmology, this comment foregrounds mechanical simulation over visual reproduction—a key feature of precinema.

Smith's primary concern, however, was human history: understanding what dictates the conceptual progress of astronomy. Like Voltaire, Kant, and Hegel, he sought to derive from the achievements of natural philosophy new ways of modeling the dynamics of human conceptual evolution as a whole. This collective effort at modeling yielded an intriguing prototype of the cinema apparatus. In 1753, a medical doctor, linguist, experimental scientist, and gazetteer named Jacques Barbeu-Dubourg decided to construct an "imaginary machine" modeling history. A friend of Benjamin Franklin, he served as a conduit for French financial and logistic support to the American Revolution while translating and publishing the writings of Franklin and Benjamin Rush.[67] In 1753 he published *Chronography, or Description of Times,* a pamphlet listing political, cultural, and artistic figures of world history since "Creation," in parallel rows with columnar increments of ten years per inch.[68] To render the flow of events more vivid, he also designed "a chronographic machine [une machine chronographique]": an articulated casing with a fifty-four-foot scroll on two reels, which Denis Diderot describes in the *Encyclopédie* as comprising "two parallel cylinders, around one of which [the scroll] rolls itself at the same time that it unreels from the other, both exposing a quite large interval of time, & successively all the sequence of times & events, either descending from the creation of the world to us, or ascending from our time to that of creation."[69] In the pamphlet's preface, Barbeu-Dubourg asks: "Indeed, what is History? It is the Collection of all that the eyes have seen, all that the ears have heard" (*Chronographie,* 1). It is an archive of collective audiovisual perceptions, not just the list of great men and events he sketched. This machine was willfully cinematic, displaying "an entertaining & as it were mechanical science speaking to the eyes & the imagination, a moving & animated tableau [tableau

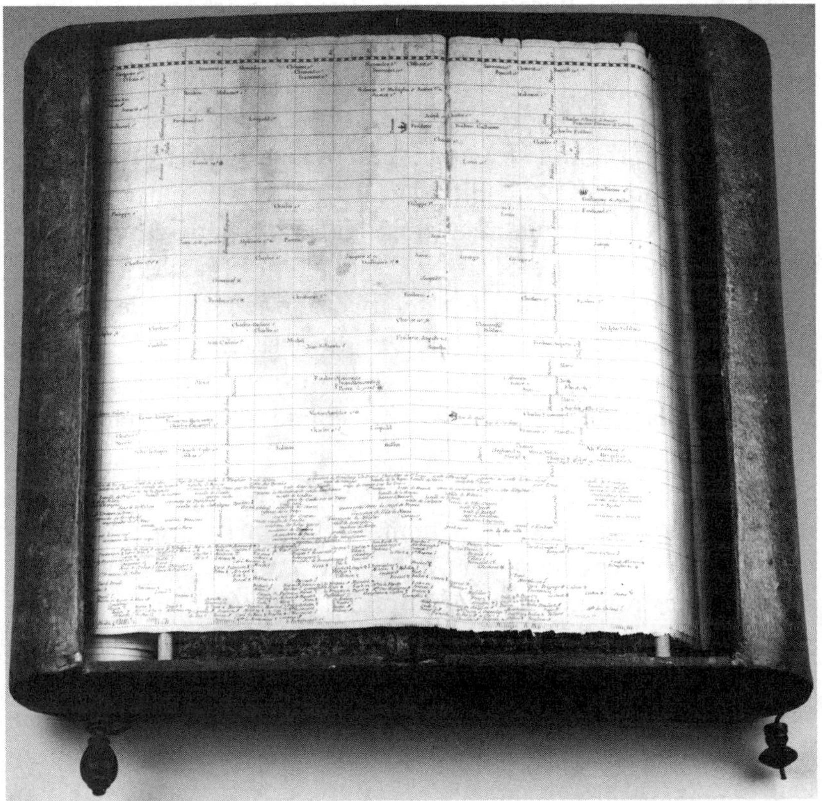

Figure 2.10. **Historical animation machine. Jacques Barbeu-Dubourg, *Machine chronographique* (Paris: Chez l'auteur, 1753). Courtesy of Princeton University Library, Rare Books Collection.**

mouvant & animé]" (8). Unnoticed by media historians, it is the prototype for all subsequent two-reel visual apparatuses from rolling panoramas to film projectors and photo cartridges. Diderot's astute comment about forward and reverse motion constitutes perhaps the earliest instance of this unique feature thought to be specific to the film apparatus. This chronographic machine is not a copying device, it is a history-visualizing media. As we see in subsequent chapters, visualizing the flow of history's past and future represents an overlooked enticement for the matrix of photocinema. When he learned in 1769 from Franklin that Quakers had renounced slavery, Barbeu-Dubourg marveled at this "good example for the universe." He believed that "all men are but one people made of Franco-Anglo-Negro-Sino-Turco-Russians," a rare long view of national-ethnic mélange, in lieu of the Enlightenment's segregated racial phylogeny.[70]

Around the mid-eighteenth century, astronomy's considerable lengthening of the time frame of human history precipitated various reevaluations of racial difference, first from the purview of astronomy—as we saw in Maupertuis and Kant—then within debates about the maintenance of slavery. Astronomer David Rittenhouse illustrates the linkage between the two purviews. The leading astronomer of the American colonies, he was responsible for the success of the 1769 Venus transit observation campaign in America, which convinced Europe that the colonies now formed an enlightened polity whose autonomy was worth supporting. As Eran Shalev shows, Newtonian mechanics and astronomy were instrumental for John Adams's and Thomas Jefferson's spirit of independence, explaining why revolutionary discourse disproportionately tapped the astronomical lexicon of *stars, Constellation, galaxy,* and *new planet* down to the constellated banner of the new republic.[71] In the words of Thomas Paine: "In no instance hath nature made the satellite larger than its primary planet; and as England and America . . . reverse the common order of nature, it is evident that they belong to different systems: England to Europe, America to itself."[72] In 1775, during the crucial Second Congress, Rittenhouse was recompensed with the keynote for the American Philosophical Association conference.[73] Through a Smith-like recitation of the conceptual progress of astronomy, he took his audience on an imaginary trip through the cosmos, commenting, for instance, on star systems "sufficiently removed from each other's attraction" as to cancel interaction—an echo of Paine's independentist rhetoric. He leveraged the multiple worlds hypothesis to figure America as an extraterrestrial world whose inhabitants "are wise enough to govern themselves according to the dictates of that reason their creator has given them." But then Rittenhouse addresses "real" aliens to critique America's anti-Blackness: "Happy people, and perhaps more happy still that all communication with us is denied. We have neither corrupted you with our vices nor injured you with violence. None of your sons and daughters, degraded from their native dignity, have been doomed to endless slavery by us in America merely because *their* bodies may be disposed to reflect or absorb the rays of light, in a way different from *ours*" (Rittenhouse, *Oration,* 19–20). As British authorities threatened rebellious colonies with emancipation as a form of retribution, Rittenhouse's antislavery dig came across as doubly anti-American to enslavers like Jefferson.[74] Rittenhouse's redefinition of *racial difference* as having merely to do with the physics of light reflection is nodal for this study. It explains why contemporaneous astronomers were often found at the forefront of abolitionism, why the new photochemistry became more racialized as antislavery movements arose, and why African American Benjamin Banneker embraced astronomy as a worthy pursuit in revolutionary times.[75]

In France, the leading antiabolitionist in the 1780s was Marie-Jean-Antoine-Nicolas de Caritat, marquis de Condorcet, who trained in mathematics and celestial mechanics under astronomers Alexis-Claude Clairaut and Jean Le Rond d'Alembert. He tackled the three-body problem of gravitational interactions between Earth, the Moon, and the Sun, requiring complex calculus and high visualization skills. In 1777, he became secretary of the Académie des Sciences, among the most powerful positions in the Republic of Letters.[76] In 1781, under the pseudonym "M. Schwartz" ("black" in German), Condorcet published *Reflections on the Enslavement of Negroes,* refuting key tenets of slavery: polygenesis, mental deficiency, and juridical rationales.[77] Calling slavery a "crime" and an "injustice," Condorcet nonetheless favored incremental emancipation with compensations for enslavers (Schwartz, *Réflexions,* 1, v).[78] In 1789, Condorcet radicalized his views on equality, writing: "Either no individual in humankind has true rights, or all have the same rights, and whoever votes against the right of another, whatever their religion, color or gender, thereby forfeits his."[79] This expression of inclusivity in our contemporary sense made him a strategic target of the plantocratic lobby. After the 1791 revolution by enslaved people in Saint-Domingue—the first successful overcoming of slavery by Black actors—the revolutionary assembly voted in 1794 to abolish slavery in the French colonies, where it had little control, and thus to little effect. Meanwhile, the Committee on Public Safety unleashed the Reign of Terror against its opponents, causing Condorcet to take his own life in 1794 while hiding in despair.

During that loaded hiatus, Condorcet jotted *Outlines of an Historical View of the Progress of the Human Mind,* proponing progress as a historical vector—that is, transforming astronomy-inflected natural history into social physics (he was the first to use the expression *social sciences*).[80] The *esquisse* (*outline*) and *tableau* (*view*) of the title accentuate the visualizability of history's flow:

> This picture [tableau], therefore, is historical since, as it must be subjected to perpetual variations, it is formed by the successive observation of human societies at the different eras through which they have passed. It will accordingly exhibit the order in which the changes have taken place, explain the influence of every past epoch upon that which follows it, and thus show, by the modifications which the human species has experienced, in its incessant renovation through the immensity of the ages, the course which it has pursued, and the steps which it has advanced towards truth and happiness. From these observations on what man has heretofore been, and what he is at present, we shall be led to the means of securing and accelerating the still further progresses, for which, from his nature, we may indulge the hope.[81]

Condorcet models history as the "successive observation" of a sequence of events morphing into one another in a way that parallels the Herschels' kinemorphic model of cosmic evolution. For Condorcet, human history is plainly coextensive with cosmology:

> The progress of this perfectibility, henceforth above the control of every power that would impede it, has no other limit than the duration of the globe upon which nature has placed us. The course of this progress may doubtless be more or less rapid, but it can never be retrograde; at least while the Earth retains its situation in the system of the universe, and the laws of this system shall neither effect upon the globe a general overthrow, nor introduce such changes as would no longer permit the human race to preserve and exercise therein the same faculties, and find the same resources. (*Outlines,* 4–5; *Esquisse,* 7–8)

This macrocosmic history model, of which this text is but a sketch, was to be printed in decimal columns, like Barbeu-Dubourg's chronography—its avowed model. Condorcet emphasizes the cognitive function of schematic visualization, meant "to gather a great number of objects systematically disposed so as to allow their relationships to be viewed at a glance" (*Esquisse,* 282). For him, the vector of history points unmistakably to a future devoid of slavery, colonialism, and religions, organized around a global and inclusive planetary republic (248–59). He developed this project further in a short summary titled "Fragment on Atlantis, or Combined Efforts by Humankind Towards the Progress of the Sciences," which limns out this "universal republic of science" (*Esquisse,* 383–431). Supported by networks of astronomical and meteorological observatories, the planetary republic would rely on demographic, eugenic, and epidemiological research meant to increase the life expectancy of world populations. For philosophers of history like Hegel and Auguste Comte, as well as for the entire nineteenth-century European agenda of world colonization, Condorcet's kinemorphic model was paradigmatic, albeit within an explicitly white suprematist view of world history that remains more tacit in Condorcet.

Western supremacy was not a given in cosmologically inflected models of history, as a frenetic 1799 novel attests, written by L.-M. Henriquez, a populist who satirized Jean-Paul Marat and Maximilien Robespierre and miraculously survived the Reign of Terror. Titled *Voyage and Adventures of Frondeabus, Son of Herschel, in the Fifth Part of the World, Translated from the Herschelic Language,* it is a picaresque satire of the lost utopia of the French Revolution.[82]

The hero Frondeabus (named after fronde et abus, or "rebellion and abuse," formerly a political crime against the Crown) comes from Uranus to visit Earth, where he is met by "an aerial flotilla, headed by the best aeronauts of the four parts of the world" (Henriquez, *Voyage et adventures de Frondeabus,* 199). He brings a hedonic message of freedom partly based on sexual liberation: "A celestial fire descends, from one pole to the other, electrifying the universe; everything loves in nature" (115). He champions women's rights and "the working industrious class, working like a machine" dreaming of liberating all people and ending slavery (194, 123). "In Africa," the protagonist claims, "I am sold with two thousand negroes; I cover them with a cloud and lift them into the air," also freeing Black enslaved people in America from hanging and Jews condemned by auto-da-fé in Portugal (207). The humans he brings back from Earth to Herchellipolis "are male and female, white, black, brown, olive-colored, of all hues and instincts," representatives of the full spectrum of humanity. The narrative ends on a pious note for the revolution: "May one day this infant republic become a model for all people" (215). The novel was favorably reviewed by the anti-Jacobin *Mercure de France* and by another main periodical for its second edition.[83] Substituting Herchellipolis, a new capital in Uranus named after the pioneer of modern cosmology, for the missed promise of the Revolution in Paris, Henriquez underlined the frailty of the revolutionary spirit allied with progress when antiracism vanishes from its core. But it also makes plain how kinemorphic visualization at the very end of the eighteenth century, as an antecedent to technologized moving images of the nineteenth century, intertwined the history of the universe and human history around the salient overcoming of anti-Blackness.

3

Photoimaging Hieroglyphs

Blackening, Anti-Blackness, and Proto-Photography

It is hard to shake the notion that the idea of photography was ambient in the eighteenth century, just waiting for the right alignment of technical possibilities. Historian François Brunet decisively debunks this "universal idea of photography," although he leaves the European ideology of universalism unchallenged.[1] This chapter reanalyzes late eighteenth-century discourses and practices of photochemical imaging research, which peaked in the 1810s and represent an overlooked context for Nicéphore Niépce's photographic experiments starting in 1816 (see chapter 4). Yet photochemistry was not the sole conduit for proto-photography. Arguably more determinant was natural philosophy's fascination for photoimaging, which I define as spontaneous visual imprints made by light or a physical force considered coextensive with it.[2] Such imprints, often referred to as natural "hieroglyphs," were investigated as metaphysical signs within the metaphorical conception of the Book of Nature in the seventeenth and eighteenth centuries. Chapter 5 shows how they intersected with a new stream of time-recording instruments from the late eighteenth century onward, bringing about the full emergence of photocinema during the nineteenth century. The photoimaging hieroglyphs I examine in this chapter range from magnetic, electrical, vibrational, and chemical patterns to the earliest technology of mass portraiture—the silhouette—with its spectacular application for the astronomical event of the century: the twin transits of Venus in 1761 and 1769.[3] Within both the new photochemical paradigm and the older photoimaging tradition, the nature of Blackness and the contestation of slavery were explicit concerns, especially with the onset of the Seven Years' War.

The Seven Years' War and Its Aftermath

The backdrop against which natural hieroglyphs took on new meaning was the Seven Years' War (1756–1763), a global conflict pitting France against England—the two superpowers of the day—and their respective allies. The war marked a decisive turn for enslaved populations and free peoples of color in Caribbean plantocracies, heightening debates about ending slavery. Resistance from enslaved peoples themselves amplified considerably during the war.[4] In Saint-Domingue, hundreds of peoples of all races died of poisoning in 1757–1758, as did cattle.[5] Enslavers held maroon leader François Mackandal responsible for a purported plot, and he and other rebels were captured, publicly tortured, and viciously executed. The spread of voodoo and obeah religious practices unifying enslaved communities—Mackandal was considered an oungan—as well as the forced enrollment of free and enslaved Black men during the war, which gave them field experience and insight into colonists' military practices, factored heavily in planned revolts by enslaved people.[6] In 1760–1761, a well-organized group of enslaved fighters launched Tacky's Revolt in Jamaica, an asymmetrical warfare that was one of the "major battles" of the war, according to historian Vincent Brown.[7] It was followed in 1763 by the Berbice Uprising in Dutch Guiana, led by the enslaved person Coffij and involving several thousands of enslaved and maroon rebels.[8] Leaders of all these armed revolts were caught, tortured, and publicly executed with such appalling atrocity that it jump-started early abolition movements.[9]

The war caused major shifts in the triangular trade. On the Senegambian coast, new-sprung trading networks rivaled national enslaving companies, increasing the sourcing of captives from inland Ceddo states but also occasioning more insurrections in staging camps and widespread marooning.[10] In the Caribbean, growing mixed-race and free Black communities vied for political representation, while the fear of uprisings led enslavers to harden the color line and rescind the social acceptance of passing. "The result was two societies [Jamaica and Saint-Domingue] that by the eve of the American Revolution were remarkably caste conscious, racially obsessed, and racially exclusive" (Burnard and Garrigus, *Plantation Machine,* 163). For Gene E. Ogle, across Caribbean colonies, "a visual economy relating subordination to skin color" overtook prior and more racially porous social markers like status, wealth, and education.[11] As Black diasporic intellectuals concomitantly began claiming their place in European and American public spheres, transatlantic culture in the decades following the 1760s saw growing tensions between abolitionists and enslavers. In turn, such debates heightened attention to skin Blackness and human reproduction, as well as chromatic blackness, portraiture, and visual reproduction.

About that time, the word *reproduction* mutated in both English and French. Until then, it narrowly denoted the replenishing of resources or the regrowth of a limb in animals and plants.[12] From the 1760s and into the 1800s, the word shifted to mean animal and human procreation from insemination to birth, a process exclusively denoted by *generation* prior to that. Then, new reprographic technics like mezzotint and lithography added the meaning "a copy" to *reproduction* around the turn of the nineteenth century.[13] What this double lexical shift suggests is that the enigmatic process, whereby new beings form from progenitors, resonated closely with innovations in visual reproduction.[14] In 1755, Louis de la Caze, a medical doctor from Montpellier, France, proposed a curious optical theory of embryogenesis. Since sexual pleasure feels intensely electrical, he reasoned that the male and female bodily contours of the procreators "were impressed into the seminal liquor, akin to how light rays reflected by objects, whose image they somehow carry, go and paint themselves upon various foci, & notably the retina."[15] He thus envisioned human reproduction as a photo composite within the camera obscura of the womb. That theory was far from marginal: In the article of *L'Encyclopédie* on "Génération," it bookends the authoritative model of Georges-Louis Leclerc, count de Buffon together with Pierre-Louis Moreau de Maupertuis's epigenetic model (see chapter 2).[16] The article's editor (Arnulphe d'Aumont) doubts that light "whose effects bear only on the surface of matters" (Diderot, "Génération," 7:573) could govern embryogenesis. But Buffon's own theory of reproduction hinges on a similar conflation of surface and depth, arguing that an "inner mold [moule intérieur]" shapes the embryo—a keen oxymoron.[17] The puzzles of genetic resemblance and embryogenesis may seem far afield from photocinema. What they have in common is a need to visualize unseen processes regarding the imprinting of matter by physical forces, with light as a model, on the one hand, and the uneven morphing of animate and inanimate matter over time, on the other. Photoimaging and animated visualization, I argue, became central and complementary modalities through which eighteenth-century natural philosophy envisioned the world, its racialized species, and their genetic and visual reproduction.

The Idea of Photography Comes from (the Idea of) Africa

Media historians have long ascribed the earliest fictional account of a recognizably photographic process to the 1760 picaresque fiction *Giphantie,* published anonymously by Charles François Tiphaigne de la Roche, a medical doctor from Normandy. His prior novel *Amilec* (1753) was quickly translated into English and German and favorably reviewed in leading European literary journals.[18] Narrated by an extraterrestrial with an Orientalist name (Zamar), *Amilec* reprises the seventeenth-century cosmic travel genre, but now combined with the new dynamic cosmology of Thomas Wright: "[The universe] was once contained in a seed no larger than a pea. . . . There are many worlds we can compare to young shoots as it were only beginning to grow. These star clusters, these whitish blobs you inhabitants of the Earth perceive in the heavenly vault and call milky ways are nothing else but sets of small worlds" (Tiphaigne, *Amilec,* 23–24). *Giphantie* transplants this astronomical frame story to Africa as similarly otherworldly. Written at the height of the Seven Years' War, the novel begins with an unnamed French narrator arriving on the "coasts of Guinea" (Tiphaigne, *Giphantie,* 1:6). A sandstorm teleports him to the center of Africa, where he awakens in a deserted city. A "benevolent shadow" in "human form" explains that his pre-Adamic "elemental spirit" people built sophisticated edifices and technologies (1:17–18). The latter include a giant glass replica of Earth that, by placing a glass rod at any spot, allows the operator to hear what is said at that location on the globe (1:46–47). Another device is equally panoptic: "By shifting the mirror in various directions, one can see different parts of the Earth's surface. One can see them all in succession if one places successively the mirror in all its possible positions" (1:79). The idea of Africa serves here as a phantasmatic origin site for audiovisual media, in a way congruent with the Moon for the seventeenth century (see chapter 1).

In a vast underground hall, large windows appear to open onto different landscapes, but the guide explains that they are not windows but a new kind of image:

> You know that light-rays reflected on various bodies form a picture [tableau] and paint these bodies upon any polished surface, the eye's retina, for instance, or water and mirrors. Elemental spirits sought to fix these fugitive images [fixer ces images passagères]; they fabricated a very subtle and viscous substance, which dries and hardens quickly, with which a picture is made in the wink of an eye. They coat a piece of canvas with this substance and present it to the objects they want to paint. The first effect on the canvas is that of a mirror: we can see all objects close and faraway whose images may be carried by light. But—what a mirror cannot do—the canvas, with its viscous coating, preserves the simulacra. A mirror faithfully renders objects but keeps none; our canvases render them no less faithfully and keep them all. This imprinting of images [cette impression des images] takes place in the first instant the canvas receives them. We quickly remove it to a dark place. One hour later, the coating is dry and a picture is obtained, all the more precious that no art can imitate its truth, and time can in no way damage it. . . . Nature . . . with its undeniably inflexible course, traces images on our canvases. (Tiphaigne, *Giphantie,* 1:132–33)

Media historians consider this a prescient account of photography—and they are quite right but also quite wrong. Certainly, fixing images of visual reality by chemical impression resembles a photographic process. However, the absence of a camera obscura with a pinhole precludes the formation of anything like a photographic image. Moreover, Tiphaigne's equation of such images with mirror images is plainly mistaken, since the latter display horizontal inversion. This lack of the basic knowledge of optics for the time disqualifies Tiphaigne's account as truly pre-photographic.

Indeed, the context of the novel makes clear that Tiphaigne's chemical impressions do not mean to copy visual reality at all. The hundreds of canvas prints, the guide explains, revive and illustrate the history of the world as it really happened: "Let your eyes run over . . . the most remarkable events that have shaken the Earth and made human destiny," he enjoins, confessing that this archive exhibits mostly "actions of violence" (Tiphaigne, *Giphantie,* 1:139–40). Hence, like the contemporaneous chronographic machine of Jacques Barbeu-Dubourg (see chapter 2), *Giphantie* envisions a totalizing perspective on humanity's history. It also trains the reader to adopt a cosmological purview by "seeing the Earth as a dot in the immensity of space, the spectacle of the centuries as an instant in eternal duration" (2:161). The guide denounces the slaughter of Native Americans (1:50) while calling on European monarchies to attend to the "public good" of the masses (2:129, 2:143). A tree that sheds lenses in lieu of leaves (the French feuilles means both "leaves" and "pages") brings attention to the biases of historiography: "Hence, according to the point of view [point de vue] through which these leaves will present themselves to the brain of the historian, he will see things as good or evil and write accordingly. Such books should not be titled, *History of What Happened in Such a Time,* but *Manner in Which Such Writer Saw What Happened*" (2:91). The chemical canvases, by comparison, purport to be objective renditions of historical facts—making unseeable past history visible at last. Tiphaigne himself is not devoid of the biases he denounces. He writes: "[Mahomet] soiled humankind with a stain that will likely never be erased," a formulation echoing Robert Hooke's racist tropes of staining while combining anti-Islam sentiment with a rhetoric of dye fixation (1:172).

The oddity of *Giphantie* is that it makes no reference whatsoever to Africans. The latter have simply vanished from the continent, engulfed by history's violent machinery that the novel both decries and emulates. This absence is symptomatic because slavery figures in palimpsest in the novel's narrative conceit. Readers of the time would have been fully aware that there is but one reason for a European to travel to Guinea circa 1760: to engage in the slave trade that was concentrated there. Slavery, in other words, is the very real flip side of a fictional and failed envisioning of photography. François de Salignac de La Mothe-Fénelon's anti-Blackness and Tiphaigne's ghosting of Africans both tether the notion of spontaneous fixation of images to what Christopher L. Miller aptly calls the "blank darkness" of Africanism—that is, European discourses imprinting fantasies upon Africa and its inhabitants.[19] *Giphantie* is an Africanist tale imagining the continent as a moonlike desert on Earth, emptied of the millions of actual peoples who disappeared into the Middle Passage.[20] As the origin text of photography, what it ultimately makes visible is the double violence of history: that which the West failed to acknowledge and represent and that which historians keep disavowing.

Nonetheless, Tiphaigne's photo-impressions, befitting more the metaphysical tradition of photoimaging than the prototechnics of photography, may well have had a direct influence on the latter. Literary journals of Paris, London, and Amsterdam favorably reviewed *Giphantie,* often citing from its magical photoimaging process.[21] There is no doubt that voracious readers belonging to the Lunar Society in the Midlands or the Masonic Lodge of the Nine Sisters in Paris would have taken notice of these periodicals.[22]

Blackness Mineralized and Metalized

Tiphaigne's evocation of Africa as an empty stage for future technics is directly connected to France's global geopolitical setbacks during the Seven Years' War and the hope that Africa might mitigate them. In 1763, a Catholic priest named Jean-Baptiste Demanet went to Senegal as chaplain for French troops reoccupying Gorée Island—the portal of the West African slave trade. Tasked with restoring Catholicism after years of British occupation, he freelanced in the trade of enslaved peoples. Back home, he published *A New History of French Africa* in 1767, calling on France—after its losses of Canada, India, and several Caribbean colonies—to relocate its plantation industry to Africa. The wishful formula "French Africa" is all the more eerie that it became the official name of West Africa under French domination from the mid-nineteenth century until the era of independences. Demanet returned to Africa in 1772 as a full-fledged enslaving entrepreneur with the "Société d'Affrique [*sic*]" and the Compagnie de la Guyane founded by French tax collectors—including chemist Antoine Lavoisier.[23] Demanet petitioned the pope to be named Bishop of Gorée, promising to gain new souls for the Church in exchange for a monopoly on the slave trade.[24]

A New History of French Africa quickly dispenses with geopolitics to prosecute its real aim: encouraging the commerce of human beings. It is a shameless brochure for would-be investors. The first volume provides a detailed how-to guide on the best business areas and local practices, including a blood-curdling table of bartering rates for purchasing "captives," given in the regional currency: an iron bar nine feet long by two inches wide and a half an inch thick.[25] The second volume closes on a topic that "I was advised to add to my *New History of Africa,*" the author states: namely, "Physical and Historical Dissertation on the Origin of Negroes and the Cause of Their Color" (Demanet, *Nouvelle histoire de l'Afrique françoise,* 2:329). Again, the justification for slavery rested on the unceasing pathologization of Black skin.

That long appendix revolves on an utterly paradoxical claim: "Blackness is so extrinsic & accidental to the Negroes that it vanishes in several ways" (Demanet, *Nouvelle histoire de l'Afrique françoise,* 2:243). Demanet mentions birth, migration, natural discoloration, excessive emotion, scarring, and old age as evidence. Africans are thus "really" white, albeit latently. As Andrew S. Curran documents, Demanet plagiarized Maupertuis's 1745 *Physical Venus,* twisting it to his purposes.[26] Demanet first approaches Blackness via an analogy with the darkening of white dough in breadmaking, tacitly making Black people into consumables (2:211). But soon he undertakes, rather ineptly, a chemical explanation: "The air is full of an infinity of intangible corpuscles endlessly emanating from the womb of the Earth & which are in continual & very quick motion, notwithstanding what we receive from sweating: they pierce us, penetrate us & mix in our blood. These corpuscles are nitrous, sulfurous, or metallic, depending on the place" (2:237, with near verbatim echoes in 232, 239, 286). Fast-acting chemical-metallic corpuscles were never part of the classic thermometabolic theory of Blackness. As evidence, Demanet indicates that locals living near mines in France "have a tan complexion [teint brun]. . . . They are more than brown [basanés]" (2:238). Untroubled by differences between tanning, soot, and phylogeny, he makes a second puzzling claim: White and Black people are fungible into each other.

> On the isle of Gorée, where a third of the inhabitants originate from the Frenchmen who passed through, & who, in the fashion of Negroes, allied themselves with Negresses, whose children display through the different gradations of their color the constant process of physical causation upon the skin of inhabitants of the Torrid Zone, in each generation, until the complete metamorphosis of whites into blacks which occurs more slowly, & of blacks into whites which occurs more rapidly—for to get [parvenir] from white to black takes four & even five generations, & to pass [passer] from black to white only three. (2:316)

This passage exemplifies the routine conflation, found in many premodern chroniclers of skin color, between mixed-race reproduction (phylogeny) and individual mutation (ontogeny). Maupertuis's own equivocation on the topic opened the way (see chapter 2). The big question with Demanet is why, in order to propone the colonization of Africa and the enslavement of Africans, he so insists on their latent whiteness and fungibility with white people.

The answer lies in his perverse theory of Africa. He posits the continent as a giant motherlode of "nitrous, sulfurous, or metallic" ore so potent that it toxifies aboriginally white Africans by blackening. Although he never mentions the blackening property of silver nitrate on white peoples, it seems very likely that this compound represents his concealed paradigm. Demanet's black toxification has two corollaries, the first of which is his most chilling statement: "The African seems to be a machine that can be assembled and disassembled spring by spring, like soft wax to which we can give whatever figure we want" (*Nouvelle histoire de l'Afrique françoise*, 2:1, cited by Miller, *Blank Darkness*, 3; Curran, *Anatomy of Blackness*, 119). That is a foundational concept for Fred Moten's black apparatus: Black peoples considered as objects, parts, or automatons.[27] Demanet's candid clause "to which we can give whatever figure we want" directly links ontological racism to visual mediation and reproduction. Achille Mbembe glosses this passage as Blackness evincing raw materiality and malleable objectification but also visual distortions among the white Enlightenment.[28] The second corollary is that slavery and conquest are therapeutic. By removing polluted Black Africans to plantations while digging up the minerals that poison them, enslavers would restore the continent to geophysical normalcy, progressively ridding Africans of their chemical-metallic poison, making them healthy—that is, white—again.

This detoxification thesis requires Demanet to delve into physiological processes within the infamous Malpighian layer of skin: "[The corpus reticulum] is a small velvety cover upon which light's globules find no resistance, and in the meantime penetrate it & lose their momentum; if instead they found some hardness they would be reflected & produce in our eyes enough of a violent motion to make a white pass for [passer pour] black" (*Nouvelle histoire de l'Afrique françoise,* 2:276–77). The first part of this statement conforms to Hooke's and Isaac Newton's notion that chromatic blackness results from light's arrest in microstructures of black matter. The second part—sheer nonsense—exhibits Demanet's Black phobia. He fails to notice that he meant to say that the hypothetical "violent motion" of light reflected outward would make a Black person pass for white, not the reverse. But science serves him only as a veneer legitimizing his enslaving enterprise, as his book's misleading subtitle attests: *Enhanced with Maps & Astronomical and Geographic Observations.* It contains not a single reference to astronomy.

The reason we bother with Demanet's pitiful constructs is their disproportionate influence. Because of them, Guillaume-Thomas Raynal and Denis Diderot changed the explanation of Blackness in their antislavery monument, *History of the Two Indies,* between the 1770 and the 1780 editions, adopting verbatim Demanet's "nitrous, sulfurous, and metallic" nonsense.[29] In the 1770s, taking Demanet as authoritative source, économistes and physiocrates proposed moving the plantation system from the Americas to Africa to eliminate the slave trade—a supposedly progressive idea shared by British abolitionists Granville Sharp and William Wilberforce (Røge, *Economistes,* 97).

Neither Tiphaigne nor Demanet, eliciting different fictional versions of Africa, came up with the idea of photography. Yet together they inscribed race and racism into the two halves of future photopicturing technology: the chemical fixation of images for the first and optical-metallic blackening for the second.

Enter Photochemistry: Light Becomes Matter

In terms reminiscent of Demanet, Jean Senebier professed that "[my book] makes us see that those corpuscles, which hit our eyes & rejoice our souls through the spectacle of NATURE, contribute to the maintenance and dissolution of parts of this spectacle by combining with them."[30] Light is no longer an abstract principle or just an aid to visibility: It changes matter. That is the physical condition of possibility of photography. Senebier may be credited with launching modern photochemistry with his four-volume study *Physico-Chemical Memoirs Upon the Influence of Sunlight in Modifying Beings of the Three Realms of Nature & All Those in the Vegetal Realm* (1782). Named city librarian of Geneva in 1773, he researched plant growth and botanical chemistry under the tutelage of naturalist Charles Bonnet and geologist Horace Bénédict de Saussure, contributing to the elucidation of photosynthesis together with Dutch chemist Jan Ingenhousz.[31] The first two volumes of his opus concern debates about light, phlogiston (oxygen), dephlogisticated air (carbon dioxide), and plant growth. In the third volume, tackling animals and minerals, Senebier observes that "it is evident that man's skin bears the impressions of light," fugitively so for white people like peasant women whose "complexion, burnt in the countryside" later "dons a lily-whiteness in the city" (Senebier, *Mémoires physicochymiques,* 3:172, 174). He comments ever so briefly on skin color: "I believe that the different color of peoples around the globe is due to the combined action of heat & light. The looser the Malpighi layer, the more it favors the action of light. This is what happens in the burning hot areas of Africa. At least, this is what Europeans experience there, soon losing their whiteness. After a few generations they would likely become as black as these unfortunate Africans whom they believe they have the right to enslave" (3:175–76). Like Demanet and most Enlightenment thinkers, Senebier posits that skin color has an unseen physiological basis, and he conflates ontogenetic and phylogenic racial shifts.[32] Yet he also argues on the basis of skin color shifting that enslavement by white people is illegitimate since they too can become Black. This provocative spin proceeds from his general conclusion that, across all animal species, color variations tend unidirectionally toward blackening.[33] Demanet's and Senebier's simplistic models of mineral and photochemical blackening overtook more discerning analyses by contemporary anatomists like Petrus Camper, who demonstrated that Blackness has no physiological reality. In 1768, after dissecting the corpses of Black, white, and biracial persons, Camper declared about the Malpighian layer: "When this second layer is completely without color, then we are very white and pale: that is to say, we are white Moors, or rather; we are people similar to Blacks in every way except that we have this middle layer less tanned."[34] That is the simple scientific fact that the Enlightenment—and nineteenth-century scientific racism in its wake—could not admit. Armchair naturalists affirmed counterfactually that the organs of Black persons, from sperm and blood to brain, were black or tinted and that Black people transplanted to Europe turned white (Curran, *Anatomy of Blackness,* 120–28).[35] The most racist advocates like Cornelius de Pauw proponed the eradication of "black sperm" by eugenically breeding Black women with white men—unsurprisingly, just what the plantation machine enabled. In this respect, Senebier's paradigm of photochemical blackening refocused the thermometabolic theory of skin color to its surface alone and, increasingly, to the direct action of light. This partially depathologized Black bodies, although the fast-acting model of Demanet reinforces the framework of "affectability" theorized by Denise Ferreira da Silva, making nonwhite people more susceptible to materiality and thus less susceptible to reason.[36]

Senebier's careful research on photosensitive compounds opens the era of modern photochemistry. His book cites the classic literature on silver compounds by Cesare Beccaria, Johann Friedrich Meyer, Johann Heinrich Schulze, and Carl Wilhelm Scheele, as well as Joseph Priestley—with whom he corresponded (Senebier, *Mémoires physico-chymiques,* 3:192).[37] Senebier established three determinant facts for the history of photography: that only light, not heat, blackens silver salts; that the blue end of the spectrum is more photoreactive; and that lenses accelerate reactivity. “This change of color is due only to the impression of light,” he writes, and “reflected and refracted light produces the same effects” (3:194, 198). He gauged prismatic colors by using a heliostat, “a mirror that turns with the sun, and always keeps the sunray in place” (3:198–99). He timed darkening from fifteen seconds for violet rays to twenty minutes for red rays, a result surprising enough he mentions it twice (3:199–200, 315). His experiments not only circumscribed photosensitivity as a field of research—rather than a mere side effect of medication—they also established the basic pre-photographic setup comprising: a camera obscura; a plate treated with silver nitrate; a lens accelerating photochemical reactions; attention to timed exposure; and a focus on the sensitive blue end of the spectrum—a technical refinement William Henry Fox Talbot and Louis Daguerre rediscovered fifty years later. As for the heliostat developed by Dutch mathematician Willem 's Gravesande in the 1740s, it became a central apparatus for investigations of the wave theory of light, photochemical imaging, and precinema (see chapters 4, 6, and 7).

The one apparently missing component is chemical fixation. Paradoxically, however, fixation is everywhere in Senebier's rhetoric, since his leading claim is that light changes matter: “This light that our eyes alone can seize up [saisir], is fixed [fixée], accumulated, more or less entwined in all the bodies around us” (Senebier, *Mémoires physico-chymiques,* 3:247). Fixation is also the dynamic motor of life: “This matter that light is, launched six thousand years ago, would serve only to hit our retina, and paint bodies on it? Can it have no other effects? . . . It seems that I see it animating vegetation [il me semble la voir animer la végétation]. . . . Without it, the Earth . . . would present but horrid crevices, bald stones, sterile ground, & the repulsive idea of dead matter, an inanimate mass” (3:301–2). Visualizing photochemical reactions as “animating” matter may have precluded Senebier from delving into their fixation of photochemical imaging. This is suggested by his book on scientific observation, which he defines as "a fine and quick touching [tact] that moves the soul, focusing [fixe] it first on those parts of objects the most apt to illuminate them."[38] The verb fixer (to fix) means both "to focus on" and "to affix" in French, and Senebier's prose plays across both meanings. The privileged domain for observing observation in his treatise was astronomy, particularly William Herschel's polyvalent dynamic practices, which he knew in surprising detail.[39] This brings Senebier to ponder the visual perception of motion: "A circle can appear either oval, or as a straight line, like Saturn's ring in certain circumstances. A body moved with a certain speed shows a continuous line, although it occupies parts of this curve only in succession. When we rotate a piece of burning coal at a certain speed, we see a flaming circular line" (Senebier, *Essai,* 1:173). The phenomenon had long been known, and Senebier explains that the eye's "nervous fibers are moved in certain circumstances as though the objects were actually acting upon them," because "the permanence of the impression may last longer than the permanence of the object producing it" (1:174). Senebier thus takes vision to be a durational phenomenon occurring between the eye and the brain, in contradistinction to the myth of retinal persistence, whereby motion can be perceived only as a series of static visual images. Bringing together optics and chemistry, light and visual motion, photoimaging, and the ever-present obsession with Black skin, Senebier's work began the crystallization of the photocinema matrix at the hinge between natural philosophy and nineteenth-century science.

Nature's Pictures: Photoimaging Hieroglyphs

While he produced test images via stencils and screens in his investigations of photosensitivity, Senebier had no interest in producing specific or verisimilar pictures. His approach to imaging conforms to the model of automatic hieroglyphs of nature outlined in the introduction and at the start of this chapter. Such imprints of spontaneous patterns expressly served the purpose of making visible forces that could not be directly observed. They too were test images of forces in action—slices of kinetic phenomena—amounting to visual and aesthetic ciphers of transcendent Nature. But they were not reproductions of the visible world.[40]

As mentioned in the introduction, physicist and astronomer Georg Christoph Lichtenberg publicized such natural hieroglyphs in the 1770s.[41] Working with his electrophorus, a powerful Leyden jar, he noticed that dust stuck to it (electrostatically) in remarkable patterns:

> At times, there were almost countless stars, galaxies, and larger suns. . . . Splendid little branches formed, similar to those produced by the frost on windowpanes; and small clouds in the most varied forms as well as some figures of a special shape could be seen. . . . If I carefully wiped the dust with a feather or hare's paw, I nevertheless could not prevent the figures that had been destroyed shortly before from effectively reappearing again anew and in a more beautiful form. I therefore covered a piece of black paper with an adhesive substance, placed it on the figures and pressed softly. I thereby managed to create some impressions of these figures.[42]

The first resemblance of these "projectiones," as Lichtenberg called them in Latin, is with astronomical objects, suggesting they partook of macrocosmic structures. Indeed, proponents of Naturphilosophie actively sought to materialize the higher graphology of the macrocosm in its nonhuman script.[43] As Antje Pfannkuchen astutely notes: "It is almost uncanny how closely this process seems to resemble the processes of early photography—the effect of light projections onto a sensitive surface."[44] Lichtenberg thought so as well, albeit in passing, since such trifling experiments did not carry the yield of his projections' standing to reveal the architectonic of the universe (see the introduction). He also sought to differentiate hieroglyphic projections: "Figures created by positive electricity differ from those produced by negative current like the Sun from the Moon" (Lichtenberg, *Novi Commentarii,* 387). He clearly hoped astronomy and electricity could be synthesized. I will return to how Lichtenberg's positive/negative opposition migrated to silhouetting, racial discourses, light studies, and, ultimately, photography.

German Romantics and idealists like Johann Gottfried von Herder, Novalis, and Johann Wolfgang von Goethe dreamed of reconciling nature with philosophical thought by producing or

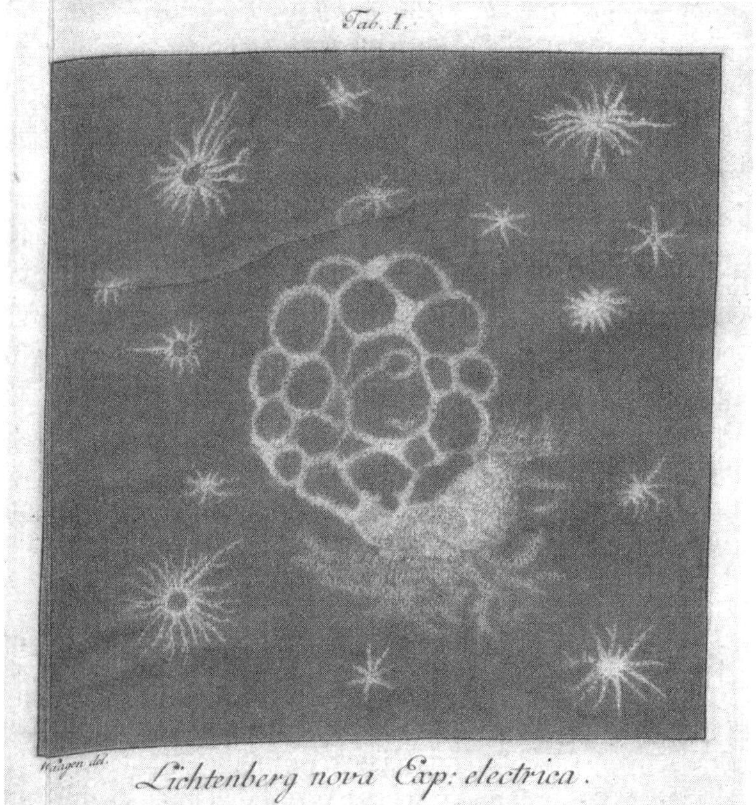

Figure 3.1. **Electrostatic dust pattern. Georg Christoph Lichtenberg, *De Novam Methodo Naturam Ac Motum Fluidi Electrici* (Göttingen, Germany: Dieterich, 1778), plate 1. Courtesy of Münchener DigitalisierungsZentrum.**

developing a universal language made of nature's ciphered scripts that would circumvent the mechanical mathesis of Western science. They tended to associate (super)natural traces with older Eastern cultures from Egypt to India, according to a symbolics of civilizational youth associated with the east–west movement of the Sun. The fascination for cultural hieroglyphics as closer to nature has a long Orientalist history. It surfaced in Athanasius Kircher's Eurocentric proposal to unify the West Indies and East Indies through a common script—as if their being connected by the same geographic name justified their colonization. The hieroglyphic impulse was always related to ideologies of nonwhite subjection as eighteenth-century scholars like William Warburton make plain when positing that nonalphabetical writing betrays civilizational underdevelopment.[45]

The fervor for supposedly scientific hieroglyphs rebounded in the 1780s when experimental philosopher and music-lover Ernst Florens Friedrich Chladni published *Discoveries in the Theory of Sound* (1787). Inspired by his friend Lichtenberg, he placed fine sand on metal plates and rods, substituting vibration to Lichtenberg's electrification. The strangely symmetrical figures generated when he struck the plates with a violin bow comforted proponents of the grand unified theory of forces.[46] "The very first figure that presented itself to my eyes, on the above-mentioned round plate, resembled a star with ten or twelve rays," Chladni writes, echoing Lichtenberg's astronomical paradigm.[47] Lichtenberg was well read in Herschelian astronomy and was (rightly) convinced that meteors were nonterrestrial objects—another type of hieroglyph from beyond Earth.[48] Chladni shared that opinion and in 1794 published a work justifying Lichtenberg against the doxa that meteors came from volcanic eruptions, demonstrating instead that ferrous meteors could not have a telluric origin.[49]

The 1802 publication of Chladni's full theory in *Die Akustik* not only launched acoustics but brought attention to the phenomena of wave motion, confirming Thomas Young's related insights that led him to restate the wave theory of light (see chapter 4).[50] What made Chladni's sound figures remarkable was that "the different vibratory movements of a sonorous plate" shaped the sand kinetically through "different appearances" (Chladni, *Traité d'acoustique,* vii). Electrical figures, sound figures, and meteorites were congruent imaging concretions of the kinemorphic Herschelian cosmos. In 1803, Chladni's friend Johann Wilhelm Ritter suggested placing "moist silver oxide, moist horn silver," on his vibrating plates, hoping to produce photosonographs.[51] That photoimaging is an apt term for this entire class of patterns is confirmed by another disciple of Naturphilosophie: naturalist, anatomist, and Romantic holist Lorenz Oken. He was the first to use the word Photographie in 1826 to denote "visual

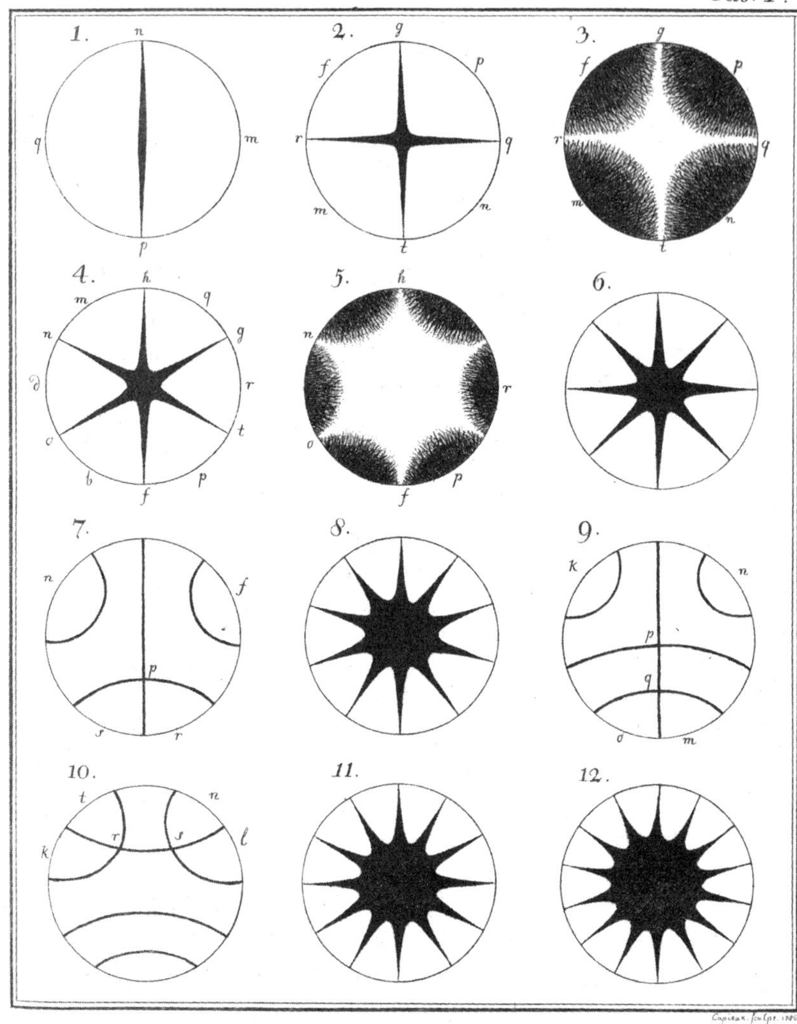

Figure 3.2. **Schemas of sand patterns on vibrating plates. Ernst Chladni, *Entdeckungen über die Theorie des Klanges* (Leipzig, Germany: bey Weidmanns Erben und Reich, 1787), plate 1. Courtesy of ETH-Bibliothek Zürich.**

apparitions [Gesichtserscheinungen]" like ocular images and hallucinations (studied by his friend Johannes Müller) classified among forms of "natural writing [Naturbeschreibung]."[52] Photoimaging as natural writing within the mystical branch of natural philosophy was foundational for pre-photographic thought. It also segued directly with the reemergence of time-graphing machines in the early nineteenth century, which yielded working models of moving pictures by the 1860s (see chapter 6).

Black Silhouetting

The most public technology of hieroglyphic photoimaging was silhouetting. The fad of silhouette drawings and cutouts, known as "profiles," "shades," and "black profile portraits," arose across Europe during the Seven Years' War as a cheap alternative to costly portrait painting.[53] It piggybacked on new printing technics such as the mezzotint, which started with saturated ink from which elements of composition were progressively delineated—a "black

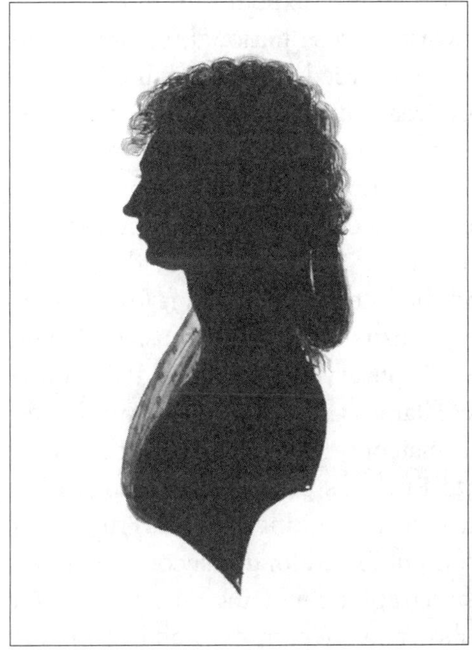

Figure 3.3. **Silhouette of Caroline Hershel (ca. 1768), MS, Gunther 36, fol. 146r, inv. 11894. Copyright History of Science Museum, University of Oxford.**

manner" according to William Hogarth in his 1753 *The Analysis of Beauty.*[54] The terms *shade,* meaning "nuance," and *backpainting,* for mezzotints on backlit glass, point to a new approach to imaging and picturing based on light projection and screens with high black-and-white contrasts.[55]

The most important astronomical event of the eighteenth century contributed to the higher standing of silhouetting: the twin transits of Venus in 1761 and 1769. These global events occurred during the Seven Years' War for the first and in its aftermath for the second—in the new geopolitical and racial context outlined at the beginning of this chapter. This is an important conjuncture for photocinema that deserves fleshing out. Timing exactly the few minutes it takes for the silhouetted dot of Venus to glide across the face of the Sun was expected to provide the dimensions of the solar system, improving navigational astronomy, and hence maritime supremacy. Despite the war, France and England—who had planned this event since 1724—guaranteed safe passage for astronomers of the other camp.[56] The 1761 campaign involved hundreds of observers in Europe and America and dozens of expeditions to East Asia. In activating knowledge networks across national, colonial, and navy infrastructures, the event reinforced the cohesion of the astronomical community.[57] As Andrea Wulf writes: "The transit projects revealed the importance of international communication and collaboration. Never before had scientists and thinkers banded together on such a global scale—not even war, national interests or adverse conditions could stop them. The intensity of their commitment was unparalleled and the international ties it fostered remained in place long after the transits" (*Chasing Venus,* 205). The second transit of 1769 involved 250 observers at 130 worldwide locations. The famed expeditions of James Cook and Louis-Antoine de Bougainville were funded for transit observation, bringing the South Pacific and its inhabitants into Europe's purview.[58] While British astronomers tended to produce curt scientific reports, French astronomers stranded on location published longer accounts mixing astronomy, journaling, and ethnographic reporting.[59] Legentil de La Galaisière, for instance, was shown an elegant method of computing lunar eclipses by a Tamil astronomer from Pondicherry whom he calls “my Master [mon Maître]” unironically.[60] Such firsthand accounts disproved armchair historians like Voltaire who opined that astronomical science on the Indian subcontinent had disappeared.

The Venus transits deeply transformed visual and media culture, while generating a new sense of the globe’s visual connectedness.

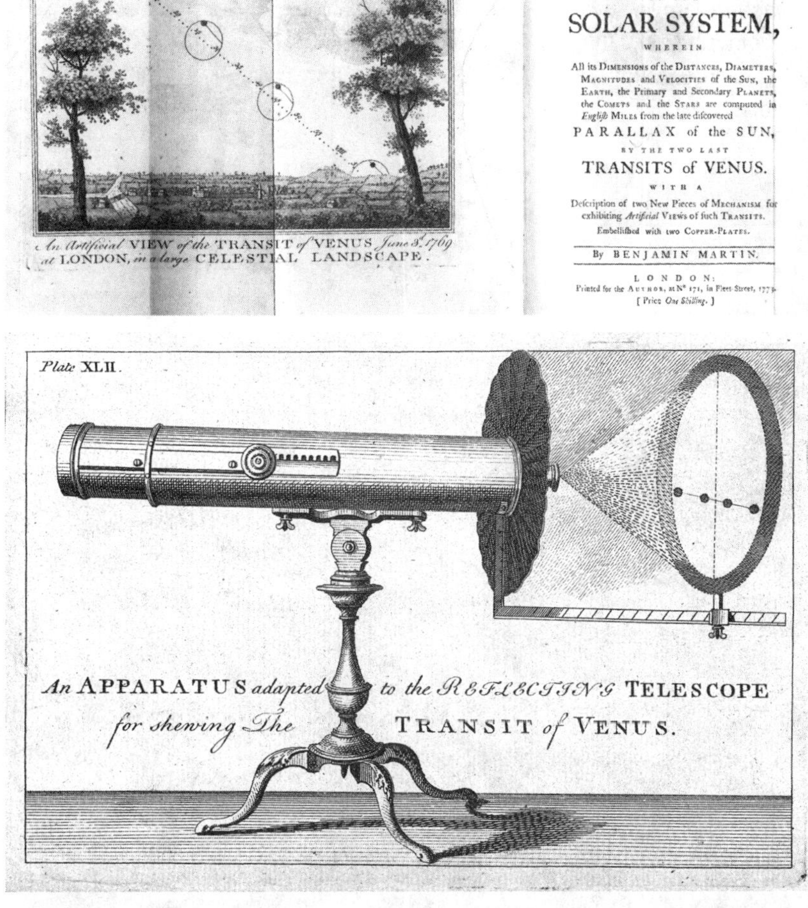

INSTITUTIONS
OF ASTRONOMICAL
CALCULATIONS;
CONTAINING A
SURVEY
OF THE
SOLAR SYSTEM,
WHEREIN
All its DIMENSIONS of the DISTANCES, DIAMETERS, MAGNITUDES and VELOCITIES of the SUN, the EARTH, the Primary and Secondary PLANETS, the COMETS and the STARS are computed in *English* MILES from the late discovered
PARALLAX of the SUN,
BY THE TWO LAST
TRANSITS of VENUS.
WITH A
Description of two New Pieces of MECHANISM for exhibiting *Artificial* VIEWS of such TRANSITS.
Embellished with two COPPER-PLATES.

By BENJAMIN MARTIN.

LONDON:
Printed for the AUTHOR, at No 171, in Fleet-Street, 177[illegible].
[Price *One Shilling.*]

Figure 3.4. **Projection telescope for the 1761 Venus transit and illustration of an artificial transit show, 1761. Courtesy of the Wellcome Library, University of London, London, UK.**

Figure 3.5. ***Right,*** **Black-drop effect. Charles Green and James Cook, "Observations at King George's Island,"** ***Philosophical Transactions of the Royal Society*** **61 (December 31, 1771);** ***below,*** **W. Hirst, "Account of Several Phenomena,"** ***Philosophical Transactions of the Royal Society*** **59 (December 31, 1769). Courtesy of the Royal Society.**

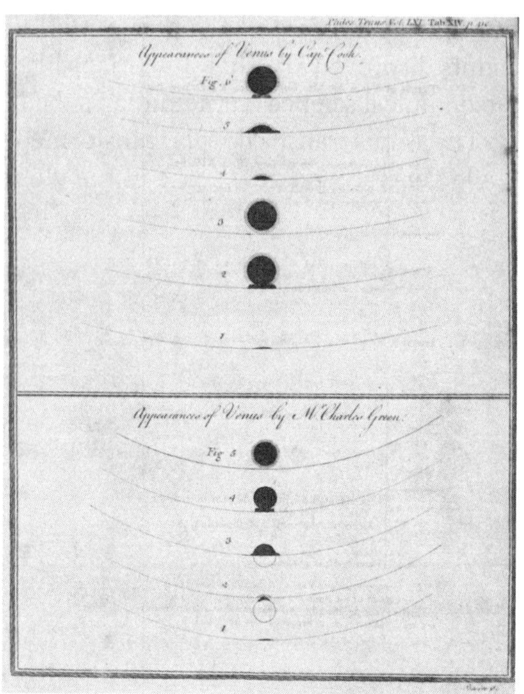

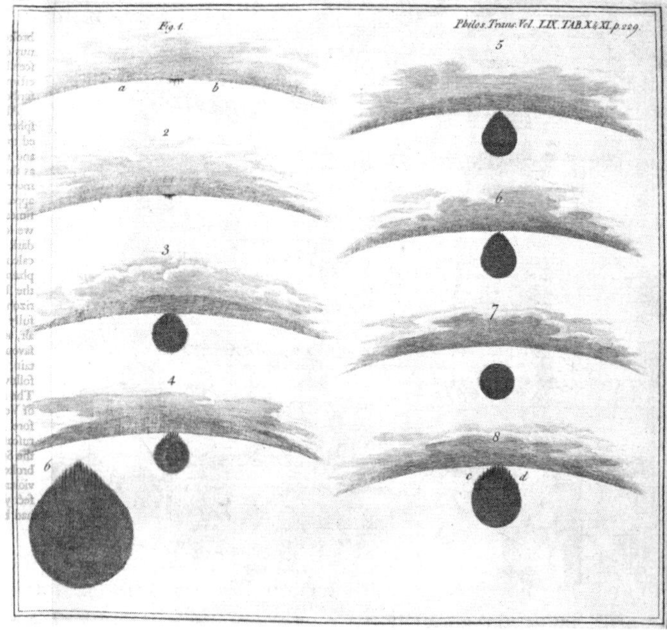

A slew of pamphlets, conferences, plays, and caricatures sensitized urban populations to astronomy. In London, where it was not viewable, a simulated artificial transit was built, "a seven-and-a-half by five-foot depiction of the sky over London on the day of the transit, including a clock-type mechanism that moved a model of Venus across a painted sun" (Wulf, *Chasing Venus,* 187). Specialized transit devices like projector-telescopes brought further attention to the kinematic nature of celestial phenomena and to moving projections on screen.

The motion of the black silhouette of Venus across the solar disk was largely responsible for the scientific failure of transit observations. Not only was it difficult to coordinate time recordings at faraway locations because of unreliable longitude, but when the black dot reached the edge of the solar disk a strange optical phenomenon distorted the moment of contact: the so-called black-drop effect. As Jimena Canales shows, this problem precipitated the use of photography for the next paired transits of Venus in 1874 and 1882, occasioning the development of Jules Janssen's photographic revolver (see chapter 6).[61] Moreover, during transits and solar eclipses, Mercury, Venus, or the Moon turn into black bodies; this natural photonegative inversion was long glossed by alchemy in racial terms.[62] In fact, the black-drop effect shares a deep rhetorical and epistemic connection with one-drop rules from the antebellum South. Both mobilize the phobia of black/Black impurity, and both expressions came into usage simultaneously in the 1830s.[63]

Anti-Blackness was woven into human silhouetting through its main proponent, Johann Kaspar Lavater. The inceptor of physiognomy, he commercialized his own silhouetting machines, an apparatus overlooked in the development of photocinema.[64] It was improved upon by musician Gilles-Louis Chrétien with his 1786 physionotrace. Chrétien's setup enabled the drawing of a full-size profile while an articulated pantograph simultaneously produced a small-scale version used to etch a copper plate for reprinting minisilhouettes or cartes de visite—early selfies.[65] Around 1800, Chrétien's device was sold in the United States by artist and naturalist Charles Willson Peale. His enslaved assistant Moses Williams

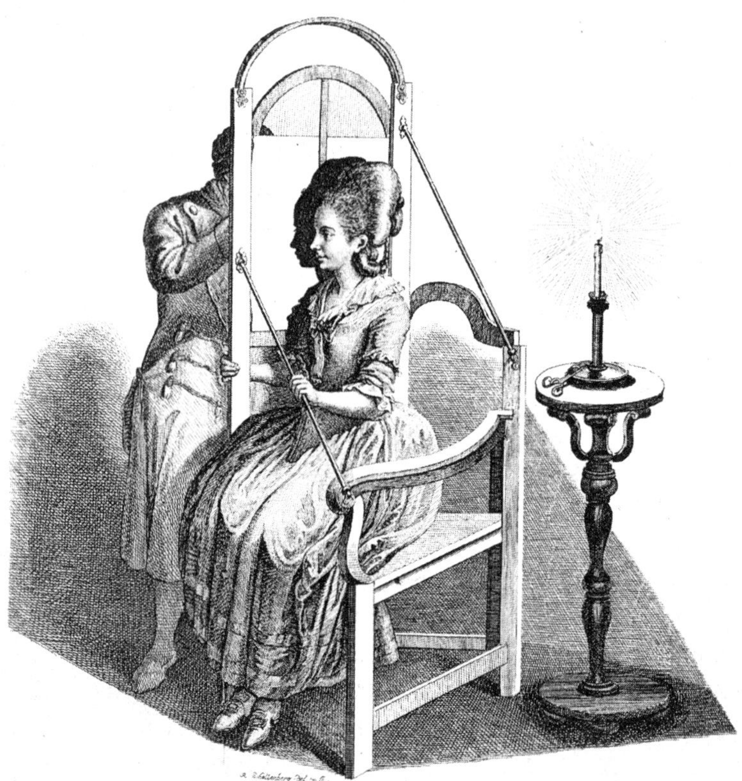

Figure 3.6. **Johann Rudolph Schellenberg, *Sure and Practical Machine to Draw Silhouettes,* circa 1778–1783. In Johann Kaspar Lavater, *L'Art de connaître les hommes par la physionomie* (Paris: Depelafoi, 1807), plate 456.**

became among the best artists of the new media and with his earnings paid for his own manumission in 1804.[66]

Lavater's theory of physiognomy rested on silhouetting (Schattenbild). Published between 1775 and 1778, its founding claim, according to John B. Lyon, was that "external, physical features are readable manifestations of inner, spiritual qualities."[67] Reading bodily contours enabled human interiority to be visualized. In practice, there were multiple limitations to silhouetted reproductions: "If the light stands at a proper distance, if the face falls on a clean surface—is parallel enough with this surface," then it yields "the truest and most faithful image." But Lavater adds, "It is nothing positive, it is only something negative, only the outline of half of the face."[68] As we saw, Lichtenberg too invoked positive/negative electrical poles (proposed by Benjamin Franklin) for imaging: This illustrates the deep transduction across electricity, vision, and life force within Naturphilosophie. Lavater acknowledged the composite character of a silhouette outline, which combines "a series of moments that never coexist in nature" since "in nature there is no stationary point—movement, everything eternal movement" (Lavater, *Physiognomische Fragmente,* 3:45, quoted in Lyon, "Science of Sciences," 268).

Lavater's comments point to structural tensions within the matrix of photocinema. On the one hand, a silhouette is an "immediate imprint of nature," discursively close to photoimaging and later portrait photography (Lavater, *Physiognomische Fragmente,* 2:90, quoted in Lyon, "'Science of Sciences,'" 262). On the other hand, the inherence of movement in bodies makes silhouetting a simulacrum at best, signaling a major hurdle in the automatic picturing of the visible. Silhouetting spectacles in the 1780s leveraged motion, like the ombres chinoises (Chinese shadows) shows in the Palais-Royal in Paris, exhibiting moving shadows behind a screen with the same Orientalism as much photoimaging productions (Vigarello, *Silhouette,* 27). In the same years, Louis Carrogis Carmontelle displayed full-size rolling canvas panoramas at a nearby locale, showing elegant peoples in profile seemingly walking amid colorful parks.[69]

For Barbara Maria Stafford, Lavater's physiognomic theory belongs to Winckelmannian aesthetics affirming the cosmetic supremacy of Greek sculpture's depiction of (ostensibly) white male bodies.[70] This white bent translates into Lavater's systematic pejoration of chromatic blackness and racial Blackness. He contends that the profile of Black peoples' heads indexes a lack of intellectual capacities, extending his anti-Blackness to birthmarks objectifying moral flaws and mixed-race bodies typifying faulty reproduction—another crucial intersection of visual and racial reproduction (Stafford, "'Peculiar Marks,'" 189–90). In a particularly vicious circle,

Lavater argues that because of their cosmetic "prejudice . . . Negroes lost . . . the natural sentiment of the beautiful."[71] Like for Demanet, blaming the victim serves to conceal limitless racism under a veneer of scientific-sounding fatuity.

While the Enlightenment by and large swallowed such nonsense hook, line, and sinker, Lichtenberg was incensed. An abolitionist and the bearer of a congenital malformation, he published an anonymous pamphlet in 1778, "On Physiognomy, Against Physiognomists," denouncing Lavater for his utter lack of scientific rationale and protocol. "But where are the experiments, the facts?" he protested (quoted in Lavater, *Essays on Physiognomy,* 2:279). Lavater asserted the impossibility that "in the head of a Moor, with flattened nose, eyes protruding from the head, lips so fleshy and round that hardly reveal the teeth, the planets could be tracked and a beam of light split [into its components]" (quoted in Bindman, *Ape to Apollo,* 112). Lichtenberg countered: "Why not the soul of Newton in the head of a negro?" (quoted in Lavater, *Essays on Physiognomy,* 2:274). In response, Lavater produced no evidence: "It is not in the nature of things, not in the relation of cause and effect, that virtue should look like vice, or wisdom like foolishness" (2:278). There are few clearer acknowledgments that looking white was inherently normative for reason.

According to Victor I. Stoichita, Lavater opposed filling the inside of silhouettes in black because "the silhouettes must be precise, we must distance ourselves from the black arts [Schwarzkunst]," an expression conflating occult and racial meanings.[72] On the screen of silhouetting machines, however, all people looked Black—a rare and striking intimation of universalism through Blackness. For the abolitionist movement, this universal silhouetting became a critical didactic tool, as Asma Naeem shows. She comments on the infamous cutout view of the slaving ship *Brookes* published in 1788. It displayed captive Africans stacked in the hold like merchandise, exposing "the magnitude of the brutality from the cumulative effect of the graphic patterning" while emphasizing the sheer dehumanization of "the silhouette form and its various structural operations of erasure, compression, and legibility."[73] The 1787 Wedgwood profile cameo of a kneeling, enchained Black man sought to personalize such mass carceral silhouetting. Yet just as in nefarious want ads of American colonial newspapers tracking fugitive individuals with generic Black silhouettes, thereby facilitating misidentification and poaching, the cameo is a stereotype, another just-innovated kind of reprographics—that is, profiling in the contemporary racist sense.[74]

Charles's Photochemical Silhouetting

The first unfixed photographs were photochemical portrait silhouettes made by Jacques Charles in the 1780s. In his famous 1839 speech to the French Parliament presenting Daguerre's invention, François Arago stated that "Charles, our compatriot, would use in his lectures an impregnated paper to create silhouettes by the action of light."[75] Arago repeated this account in 1850, suggesting it was well considered.[76] The fullest description of this photo-silhouetting work appeared in 1874 with an illustration showing Charles's setup. Its author, Gaston Tissandier, notes that the illustration shows the start of the experiment, with a black silhouette against a white

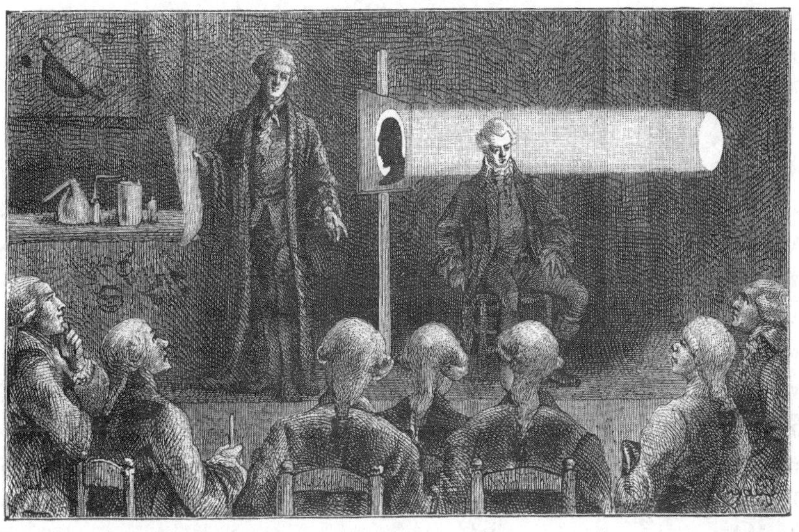

Figure 3.7. **Charles's photo-silhouetting in the 1780s. Gaston Tissandier, *Les Merveilles de la photographie* (Paris: Hachette, 1874), 11. Courtesy of La Bibliothèque Nationale de France.**

background. When the subject moves away, "it is his shadow, now seen in black, that will appear white," while the white background has blackened.[77]

In 1903, R. B. Litchfield, a descendant of the Wedgwood-Darwin families, undertook to debunk Arago's claim and place Thomas Wedgwood as the sole inceptor of photography.[78] Subsequent historians followed him unquestioningly. An examination of Charles's work, however, strongly confirms he had the technical capabilities and motivation to produce pre-photographic silhouettes. In the late 1770s, Charles became a public lecturer and experimenter in physics and chemistry, giving two sets of lectures from 1781 to 1783 and again from 1784 to 1792.[79] Experimenting with gases, he built the first hydrogen balloon, which he flew in 1783, making him an instant celebrity. Granted an apartment in the Louvre in 1786, he brought with him his famed trove of hundreds of the finest scientific instruments ever built. In 1792, revolutionaries let him continue his residence in exchange for ceding the instruments to the French Republic upon his death. Some entered the collection of the Conservatoire National des Arts et Métiers, where dozens still exist, notably several portable camera obscuras of his design.[80] According to Friedrich Johann Lorenz Meyer, a German tourist who visited him in 1796, Charles set up a person-sized camera obscura with periscopic mirrors projecting on a tabletop the image of people walking in the Cour Carrée below. Meyer indicates that Charles cohabited with a woman who assisted him with teaching and demonstrations (her identity is unknown).[81] In 1804, Charles married the twenty-two-year-old Julie-Françoise Bouchaud des Hérettes, whose family owned plantations of sugar, coffee, and indigo in the Gonaïves area of Saint-Domingue, which they fled after the Haitian Revolution. In Paris, the Bouchaud family petitioned the revolutionary government for assistance as refugee planters, and we can only conjecture that Charles was aligned with the enslaver planter class opposing abolition.[82] Charles was elected to the Académie des Sciences and became the librarian of the three national French academies (the Institut de France), though paradoxically, few documents by him exist apart from his course notes and anonymous articles.[83]

Charles figures in media history for his megascope, which Laurent Mannoni describes as a large magic lantern projecting the image of an object or a painting.[84] He asserts that this apparatus was invented by Leonhard Euler in the 1750s and only renamed by Charles. Mannoni in fact confuses two different setups. In 1784, Charles described "an instrument that many amateurs know, to which I have given the name of megascope." With it, "one can exhibit persons and any kind of objects. It contains a solar microscope, a camera obscura and a magic lantern. I am determined to magnify only through distances, and I use lenses with a very long focus." He adds, "The most cumbersome is to throw enough light on the object."[85] Charles expressly mentions "persons" and a solar microscope, while Mannoni describes only "a small platform" and "a paraffin lamp" (*Great Art,* 131–33). Mannoni overlooks the fact that in early nineteenth-century Parisian scientific circles, Charles was considered a leading expert in optical and meteorological instrument design. He improved thermometers, hydrometers, and goniometers and trained a whole generation of experimenters and instrument-makers, including the intermediary through whom Niépce and Daguerre met: Charles Chevalier (see chapter 4). In his lecture, Charles demonstrated the use of the heliostat of 's Gravesande (which he improved): "a parallactic clock moving with the body of the mirror, following the direction of the sun," and able to "still the sun for two hours without change."[86] With a solar microscope and a heliostat, "the sun residing in space" becomes "a torrent of light coming out of a lens [foyer]," and calling it "an artificial candle [une bougie artificielle]," he affirmed that "the image will have a strong intensity" and thus could project silhouettes.[87] When he described Charles's megascope in 1874, Tissandier himself worked at the Conservatoire National des Arts et Métiers, where he had firsthand access to Charles's instruments, including the megascope.[88] Hence, both Charles and Tissandier knew experimentally the amount of illumination required to produce photochemical silhouettes. The physicist Étienne-Louis Malus confirmed that he witnessed Charles using his heliostat with a camera obscura during his public lectures.[89] In sum, Charles's megascope may be described as a modular setup with a solar microscope, heliostat, and a portable camera obscura or a magic lantern, any of which could be used in combination.[90]

The notebooks of Charles's courses confirm that he had the motivation, technical know-how, and scientific and philosophical curiosity to conduct photochemical experiments with camera obscuras.[91] He describes experiments using silver salts, including "a solution of silver nitrate deposed on a plane of glass" reacting with copper.[92] He certainly knew the photosensitive properties of silver nitrate and Senebier's experiments with a heliostat and a camera obscura. His notebooks specify the use of portable camera obscuras for both optical experiments and artistic and topographical drafting.[93] The projection of light rays seems of particular interest, as he explains in vivid language: "You see that the first thing to do in painting is to draw in one's mind with an imaginary pencil [un crayon imaginaire] the image that pencils emanating from exterior objects would trace on the canvas [l'image que traceraient sur la toile des crayons émanés des objets extérieurs]."[94] Sketching here amounts to hallucinating an image on canvas and letting imaginary light rays flow into one's eyes and retracing them into the image. The polysemy of *pencil* meaning, in both English and French, "a writing instrument" and "a thin ray of light" informs Charles's instruction. But what is most important is that here Charles is visualizing light rays bouncing from objects to trace their image by themselves on a canvas, a physical adumbration of photography. After mentioning how he uses an "optique [box]" together with "a camera obscura," he adds: "If through some impossible art one could instantly fix [fixer sur le champ] on a canvas this admirable illusion, the most beautiful tableau would result."[95] Given Charles's interest in generating, projecting, drawing, and fixing images from the camera obscura, combined with his familiarity with silver compounds and the role of the megascope in silhouette-making, we must conclude that he conducted proto-photographic experiments prior to 1784—as Arago always insisted.[96] As we will see in chapter 4, Arago was undoubtedly the most knowledgeable experimentalist in pre-photography.

This chapter presented developments of the matrix of photocinema around the paradigm of photoimaging—imprints of natural forces bearing hieroglyphic patterns—between the 1760s and 1780s, within the context of the aftermath of the Seven Years' War and enslaved peoples' revolts in the Caribbean. These developments include the procrustean fiction about photography sited in Africa (1760), a racist theory of Black skin caused by nitrous and metallic toxification (1767), electrostatic and sonic images (1770–1780s), the emergence of photosensitivity and the protoapparatus of photography (1782), silhouetting, its tracing apparatus, and racist entailments (1778), and photochemical silhouetting made in a megascope (1780s). While photoimaging was the proximal antecedent to photography, we must emphasize that it was only very marginally driven by the aim of reproducing the visible world in fixed images. Rather, it aspired to obtain spontaneous visual imprints from kinetic nature to render visible transcendental signs, cosmic forces, and past historical events. Finally, as Black skin was increasingly explained via photosensitivity, while abolition movements amplified, Blackness and anti-Blackness remained, respectively, an enduring topic and an ever-present prejudice in the matrix of photocinema.

4

Photology

Black Light, the Wave Theory of Light, and Pre-Photography

This chapter makes four major interventions in the history of pre-photography between Jacques Charles's photoimaging silhouettes in the 1780s and Nicéphore Niépce's photographic experimentation beginning in 1816 (see chapter 5). First, it proposes that natural philosophers' research on light induced photography much more directly than previously thought. Second, it shows how photological blackness—the discovery of black and invisible components in light—played a decisive role in the turn of physical optics toward photochemical applications. Third, it argues that photological blackness helped overturn the epistemic equation of light and racial whiteness, enabling the slow process of depathologizing Black skin and in some ways contributing to abolition. And finally, it demonstrates how research on the wave theory of light (WTL)—developed and then abandoned by British natural philosophers—was subsequently taken up by François Arago and involved the very same Parisian instrument-makers who subsequently assisted Niépce, Louis Daguerre, and William Henry Fox Talbot.

Late Enlightenment Photochemistry and Black Skin

Modern photochemistry, launched in the 1770s by the Swedish chemist Carl Wilhelm Scheele and then mainstreamed by Jean Senebier, was a pan-European affair in which Black skin remained an ever-present reference.[1] In 1795, James Watt, Thomas Wedgwood, and Thomas Beddoes made plans to create the Pneumatic Institution, a clinic treating patients with ailments ranging from consumption and breast cancer to depression, using various combinations of gases.[2] It opened in 1798 in Bristol, England's principal port for the transatlantic slave trade, and ran for a short time. It employed a young chemist, Humphry Davy, who had just developed a laughing gas. The institute's director was Beddoes, who had received an MD from Oxford and would have been named professor of chemistry there but for his penchant for the French Revolution and the new chemistry of Antoine Lavoisier—both perceived as anti-British. Beddoes lectured against slavery and collaborated with Samuel Taylor Coleridge's abolitionist newspaper in the early 1790s.[3] It was Beddoes who introduced Coleridge to German Idealism, and to Wedgwood as well.[4]

Beddoes was well versed in photochemistry. In 1786, he translated a book of Scheele's experiments referencing light-sensitive silver compounds.[5] In 1796 he reviewed *An Essay on Combustion with a View to a New Art of Dying and Painting* by chemist Elizabeth Fulhame for *The Monthly Review* (Stansfield, *Thomas Beddoes,* 109). Fulhame presented catalytic methods for depositing metals on cloth and paper, including "small films of reduced silver" made from silver nitrate. She references Scheele's photochemical experiments from another English translation directed by Joseph Priestley.[6] As a medical doctor, chemist, and German translator, Beddoes oversaw experimental therapeutic applications at the Pneumatic Institution. Early in his career, Beddoes treated a free Black man who came to him. "At Oxford in 1790," he writes, "I had proposed to a distressed negro, to try to whiten part of his skin with oxygenated marine acid air [hydrochloric acid]. He was to exhibit the appearance, if it should be curious, for the relief of his family." The Black patient had "ulcerations" between his fingers, and the treatment caused him "severe pain." Beddoes concludes: "The back of his fingers had acquired an appearance as if white lead paint had been laid upon them, but this did not prove permanent."[7] It is unclear what "relief" was sought from exactly what distress; Beddoes's veiled words do hint at a young man suffering from internalized racism.[8] As Beddoes had flayed and blistered his own fingers to observe the action of various gases, his aggressive treatment was not unusual.

Well publicized in medical literature, the attempted cure was notoriously taken as further evidence that "the black colour of negroes depends upon a black pigment, situated in this substance [rete mucosum]," not found in white skin.[9] Beddoes also used silver nitrate medicinally, treating a white child's hand to cure excessive perspiration—an equally painful treatment.[10] Among books Beddoes reviewed for *The Monthly Review* was *Medicine Informed by the Physical Sciences* (1791) by French chemist Antoine-François Fourcroy (Stansfield, *Thomas Beddoes,* 256). Fourcroy mentions the case of a priest near Hamburg, Germany, who absorbed "nitric silver dissolution" for a liver ailment and whose skin became "almost entirely black." Silver nitrate remained a widely used topical ointment through the nineteenth century for hair ailments, acne, impetigo, cauterization, color whitening, and tattoo removal, and even conditions like epilepsy.[11] An authority on skin diseases indicates in the 1820s that silver nitrate produces "a tanned hue of the skin analogous to that of *mulattoes,*" adding that a patient he treated with silver nitrate was "usually taken at first to be a mulatto."[12]

Skin color anomalies were of particular interest for natural philosophers like Pierre-Louis Moreau de Maupertuis and Georges-Louis Leclerc, count de Buffon, and in the 1790s unexplained color mutations were sensationalized as both medical puzzles and public exhibitions; this signaled their heightened stakes for the racialized order.[13] In 1795, London MD William Charles Wells, whose research focused on physiological optics, examined a white woman who displayed patches of very dark skin from birth.[14] Wells acknowledges monogenism, by then widely accepted: "Blackness of the skin in negroes is no proof of their forming a different species of men from the white race" (Wells, "Account of a Female," 431). After warning that the supposed "deformity of [Black peoples'] features" is only due to "our [e.g., white people's] notions of beauty," he adds: "Their present appearance may possibly be regarded not only as a sign, but as a cause of their degraded condition, by preventing, in some unknown way, the proper development of their mental faculties; for the African negroes have in all ages been slaves" (438, 439). While Wells echoes the victim-blaming of Johann Kaspar Lavater, he shifts anti-Blackness from skin and features to mental and civilizational underdevelopment—the hallmark of nineteenth-century scientific racism.[15]

Interestingly, Wells indicates that "Sir Everard Home," who examined the woman with him, opined with clear prejudice that "the dark arm smelt more strongly than the white," which Wells did not confirm (Wells, "Account of a Female," 429, 430). Wells further conjectures "from observations lately made on two negroes, that the action of the sun tends rather to diminish than augment the colour of their race" (431). As "both of those persons were born in European settlements," it is possible that the two Black men on whom Home experimented two years later (see introduction) were the same individuals (431).

What seems clear from all these cases is that new photochemical studies of silver nitrate in the 1790s piggybacked on its former dermatological applications to redirect the etiology of Black skin. Edward Bancroft, the author of an influential reference work on color-making, stated in 1794 that "silver nitrate also gives the skin a black colour, which cannot be effaced, but by a removal or change of the skin itself." He adds: "The blackness of the negro child is found, by observation, to be considerably hastened by early exposure to strong light, which seems to favor the absorption, or combination of oxygene; an effect which is not surprising, since, by many of Mr. Sennebier's experiments, the light was found to act in this way through coverings of greater thickness than those which oppose its access to the reticular membrane in negroes."[16] This new photological thesis of Black skin cut both ways. On the one hand, it depathologized Blackness through an established and superficial natural phenomenon. On the other hand, it added an unseeable physiological difference potentially related to "the development of mental faculties." However, these supposedly scientific debates were overdetermined by the context of 1760s Caribbean rebellions by enslaved peoples, especially the 1791 Haitian Revolution, which had unprecedented repercussions on black-and-white racial rhetoric and the philosophy of history.[17] Let us note that this black-and-white approach to skin color forestalled other approaches, such as Thomas Clarkson's gradation model and Martin Delany's prescient 1850s theory of quantitative pigmentation.[18]

Black-Making Rays

Determinant for this study was locating William Herschel's notes on "black-making rays" in the Royal Greenwich Observatory Archives. To my knowledge, these mysterious rays have never been commented on. Their story begins in 1800 when William Herschel discovered infrared or "calorific rays" after experiencing a warm sensation around his eyes when looking at red-colored stars in the eyepiece of his telescope. The relationship between heat and light stood at the center of physics and chemistry in the last two decades of the eighteenth century, and the only published research of Thomas Wedgwood was in that critical area.[19] Herschel placed thermometers in a camera obscura under a light beam reflected from a solar microscope and refracted through a prism. He found that the hottest area laid outside the visible spectrum beyond red, confirming that optical rays were the cause since they reflected and refracted like visible light. In 1801, Johann Wilhelm Ritter, a polymath from the Jena circle around Friedrich Wilhelm Joseph von Schelling, Johann Wolfgang von Goethe, and Scheele, conjectured that another variety of "invisible rays" lay at the other end of the spectrum—given the Jena circle's shared belief in the polarity of natural forces. Exposing paper imbued with silver chloride to the area past the blue end of the spectrum, he found that it darkened faster than in the most reactive area of blue established by Senebier.[20]

After his own discovery, Herschel sought a new theory of light. His idea was based on "modifications of light"—how light's trajectory alters at the contact of matter. For white light, he wrote, the signature deviation is reflection on a mirrored surface, while for decomposed color rays it is refraction through glass. The question Herschel pondered was what ray corresponded to flexion—that is, the bending of rays at the edge of objects:

> When light passes by an opaque body at a certain distance it is bent from its rectilinear course towards the body. This modification of light is well known and has generally been denoted very properly by the name of inflection.
>
> This has been proved by different authors but most of the experiments they have given are fallacious. The unexceptionable one is that an opaque globe when exposed to the unconfined rays of the sun, the solar penumbra being properly allowed for, will cast a shadow which is less than it would have been if light had not been inflected toward the body*
>
> *See the experiments of M. Marat published in 1780 and those of G. W. I in 1799.[21]

This important passage deserves a careful gloss, starting with Herschel's surprising reference to Jean-Paul Marat. Elsewhere in his notes, Herschel confirms that "a work called *Découvertes sur la lumière* par M. Marat, contains likewise several experiments which, had they been properly understood by the author, would have laid open very different views to him from those he believed to see in them" ("Modifications of Light," folio 14).[22] Before turning to politics, Marat had been a physics experimenter and lecturer competing with Charles, with whom he had a run-in in 1783.[23] Born in Geneva, Marat moved to Bordeaux as a teen to tutor the children of Pierre-Paul Nairac, a trader of enslaved people.[24] In his twenties he moved to England, obtaining an MD from the University of St Andrews before returning to France as doctor to the guard of future King Charles X. Despite having no training in mathematics, Marat acquired a strong reputation as an experimenter in natural philosophy.[25]

In *Physical Research on Fire* (1780), Marat claimed to have discovered the underlying substance of heat, which he called the "igneous fluid," immodestly comparing his discovery to that of electricity and Isaac Newton's theory of light.[26] His claim rests on a visual phenomenon he carefully observed: convection wisps of air rising from heated objects. To visualize them properly, he employed a solar microscope in a camera obscura (a "helioscope") to silhouette objects placed on rollers against a movable screen and locate "the place where the image appears most distinctly" (Marat, *Recherches physiques,* 196–97).[27] His book is illustrated with fine drawings by "Madme Ponce," the engraver Marguerite Hémery Ponce who worked for the Comte d'Artois, Marat's employer.[28] These drawings feature silhouettes of airflow arabesques—combining silhouetting and hieroglyphs—which Marat interprets as imaging the yet unseen fluid of heat. He declared that a flame starts only when its "shadow has entirely crossed" the "bright band [raie lumineuse]" of igneous fluid surrounding it (27). He believed he had solved the enigma of combustion through the diffraction of rays: "Light rays constantly bend at the circumference of all bodies whose sphere of attraction they traverse," he stated (196). In a complementary monograph also from 1780 titled *Discoveries by M. Marat on Light,* he examined more closely that "bright band [raie lumineuse]."[29] Projecting light beams at blades and small holes in his camera obscura setup, he observed that the light band appeared within the shadow

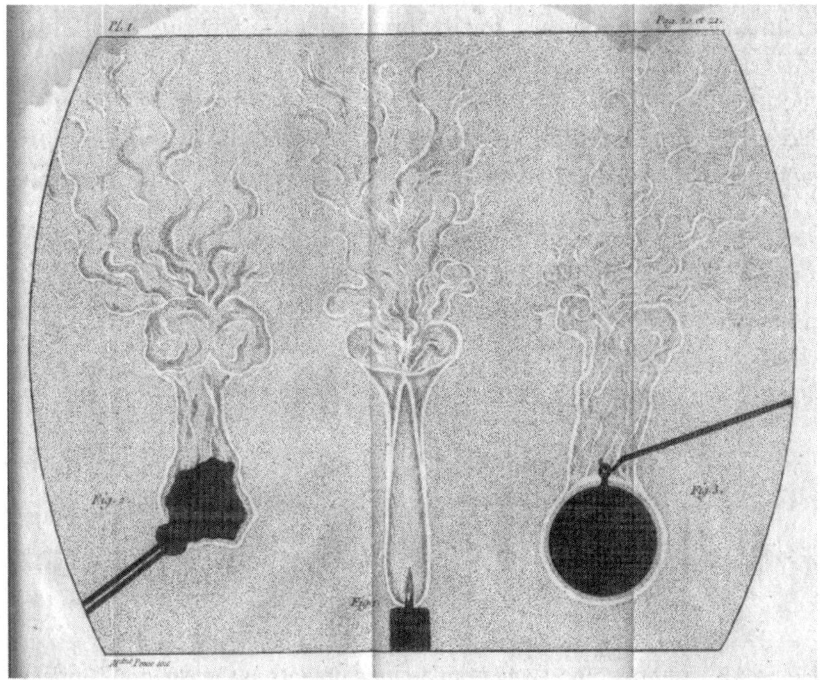

Figure 4.1. **Heat convection patterns. Illustration by Marguerite Émery in Jean-Paul Marat, *Recherches physiques sur le feu* (Paris: Jombert, 1780). Courtesy of La Bibliothèque Nationale de France Gallica.**

area, concluding that these "rays . . . are thus mainly attracted by the edges" (3). With an even smaller hole, "you will see the shadow of the [hole's] edge surrounded with a bright aureole outside, darker midway, dark inside, and ever darker as it nears [the center] of the shaded area" (3–4). The result was confounding. It was as if light exchanged places with darkness when passing through the hole.

Newton thought that light rays deflect away from bodies. But the innovative rack focus in Marat's setup enabled him to observe that the opposite was true: Light is attracted by matter. In an inspired experiment, Marat showed that rays bending around a small sphere converge into a small "luminous point" at the center of its shadow cone (*Découvertes*, 3–4, 7fn1, 10). Forty-two years later, this experiment, known as the Poisson Spot, was reproduced by François Arago and Augustin-Jean Fresnel, providing decisive proof that light is a wave. As Herschel noted, however, many of Marat's experiments were hasty and shoddy, leading him to false and vainglorious claims. Marat concluded, for instance, that the igneous fluid invalidated gravitation and that Newtonian optics was wholly counterfactual. The subtitle of his book on light, *Resulting from a Series of New Experiments Made Numerous Times Under the Eyes of Commissioners from the Academy of Sciences,* was a plain exaggeration. The

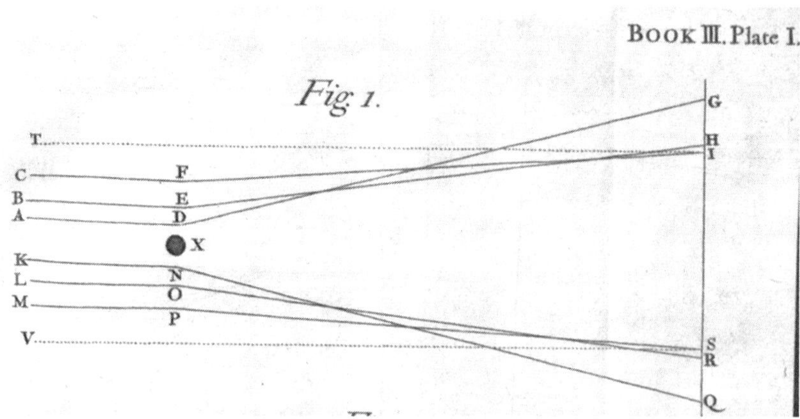

Figure 4.2. **Light bending away from opaque objects. Isaac Newton, *Opticks,* 3 vols. (London: Samuel Smith & Benjamin Walford, 1704), 3:139. Marat observed the opposite: Ray N ends in G and ray D in Q. Courtesy of ETH-Bibliothek Zürich.**

commission's head examiner—Marie-Jean-Antoine-Nicolas de Caritat, marquis de Condorcet—required inclusion in the monograph of a warning that Marat's experiments "do not seem to prove what the author imagines he has established" (iv).

Separating the wheat from the chaff, Herschel confirmed experimentally that light does bend toward matter (although he oddly mistakenly stated that Newton thought so too). His hunch was that invisible rays—infrared and perhaps ultraviolet—represented a new kind of light ray whose proper motion was deflection:

> The novelty of black-making rays . . . will induce us to pause before we admit them; but has not each modification its particular properties? Reflection will not separate red-making from green-making rays, but refraction will do this. Neither reflection nor refraction, it might be said, will separate black-making rays from others whereas it seems that deflection will bring on their separation.
>
> On the present occasion I must remark that this is not the first instance I have had of the appearance of black-making rays; and though hitherto I have always endeavored to evade such ideas as deceptions, I might for the future be less scrupulous. (Herschel, "Modifications of Light," 10–11)

Herschel stayed publicly mum about his black-making rays theory for one simple reason: At the height of the Napoleonic Wars, British jingoism was so intense that any invocation of recent French science—a fortiori the work of Newton-denier Marat—was anathema. As we will see, Thomas Young was forced to cease research on the wave theory of light in 1804 for the same reason. The story of black-making rays does not end there, however. We return to it later in this chapter since in 1839 it occasioned a letter from John Herschel to François Arago in the context of the emergence of photography.

Black Light

Invisible rays and their linkage to both heat and photochemistry made the nature of light central to physics circa 1800, against the backdrop of the oxygen/phlogiston controversy.[30] In quick succession, two other forms of blackness-in-light were found. William

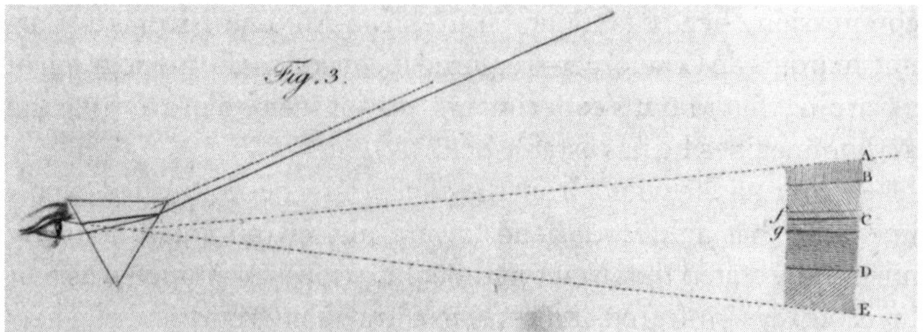

Figure 4.3. **Black lines in the spectrum. William Hyde Wollaston, "A Method of Examining Refractive and Dispersive Powers, by Prismatic Reflection,"** ***Philosophical Transactions of the Royal Society*** **92 (1802): 380. Courtesy of the Royal Society.**

Hyde Wollaston, an MD and chemist studying light refraction, published a paper in 1802 stating that a "very narrow pencil of light . . . admitted into a dark room," after decomposing through a prism into the color spectrum, showed "other distinct dark lines . . . that might be mistaken for the boundary of these colors." These black lines (absorption lines) had never been noticed before. In a footnote, he adds that he also detected "invisible rays" beyond violet—independently of Ritter and using silver chloride as well—finding "that the blackness extended not only through the space occupied by the violet, but to an equal degree, and to about an equal distance, beyond the visible spectrum."[31]

In the same 1802 issue of the *Philosophical Transactions of the Royal Society,* Thomas Young published "On the Theory of Light and Colours," a momentous paper solving at once two enormous problems by linking them. Young was a prodigy who learned a dozen languages and digested Newton's *Principia* and *Opticks* by age seventeen. At fourteen, he had resolved to "abstaining from the produce of the labor of slaves," and the banker David Barclay later paid for the manumission of thirty enslaved persons at the urging of Young, who tutored his son.[32] He was elected to the Royal Society at twenty-one after publishing a paper proposing that the eye lens is a muscle. In 1794, he had a meeting with the Herschels at their observatory in Slough, England.[33] In 1796, after defending his MD thesis on the forty-seven sounds the human mouth can articulate, he traveled to Germany. On the way, he stumbled on two Englishmen on their grand European tour: Thomas Wedgwood and John Leslie, a specialist of heat science. In Weimar, Germany, Johann Gottfried von Herder eagerly awaited his arrival to discuss universal phonetics (Robinson, *Last Man,* 52). Fascinated by the hieroglyphic patterns of sound and light, and a key actor in the decipherment of Egyptian hieroglyphs, Young bridged the spirit of German Naturphilosophie and modern physics.

"On the Theory of Light and Colours" suggests that the eye has three distinct receptor cells for yellow, red, and blue, with other colors resulting from mixing. The larger proposal on which he had been at work is that light is a wave. With music as analogy, he both outlined the mathematical grounding for the WTL and chose the right frame for visualizing unseeable light waves: interferences.[34] Before Young, it was thought that two soundwaves with different ratios (frequencies) remained separate in a musical chord. Young argued instead that they must combine, since the same particles of air can hardly vibrate at two frequencies at once. He extrapolated that the same occurred in light and proposed three ways for visualizing interferences. The first was a ripple tank, a water container with a transparent bottom illuminated from below and projecting ripple patterns on a 45-degree mirror. It showed that water waves combine their crests and hollows, and the same should be expected of light waves. Water wave interferences were known in Europe since 1678 but had been understood long before by Vietnamese fishermen who connected complex estuary tide patterns to the lunar cycle.[35] Using that precedent, Young conceptualized his second visualizing method: the famous two-slit experiment splitting a light beam into two in a camera obscura and projecting the image of their interferences on a screen. In 1803, to verify that the phenomenon was not an optical illusion, he devised a third method: replacing the screen with "a strip of paper dipped in a solution of nitrate of silver," on which "portions of three dark rings" were imprinted. While Charles, Wedgwood, and Henry Peter Brougham all produced fugitive photochemical images, they did not describe a single one in detail. Young's print is thus the first photochemical image ever described.[36]

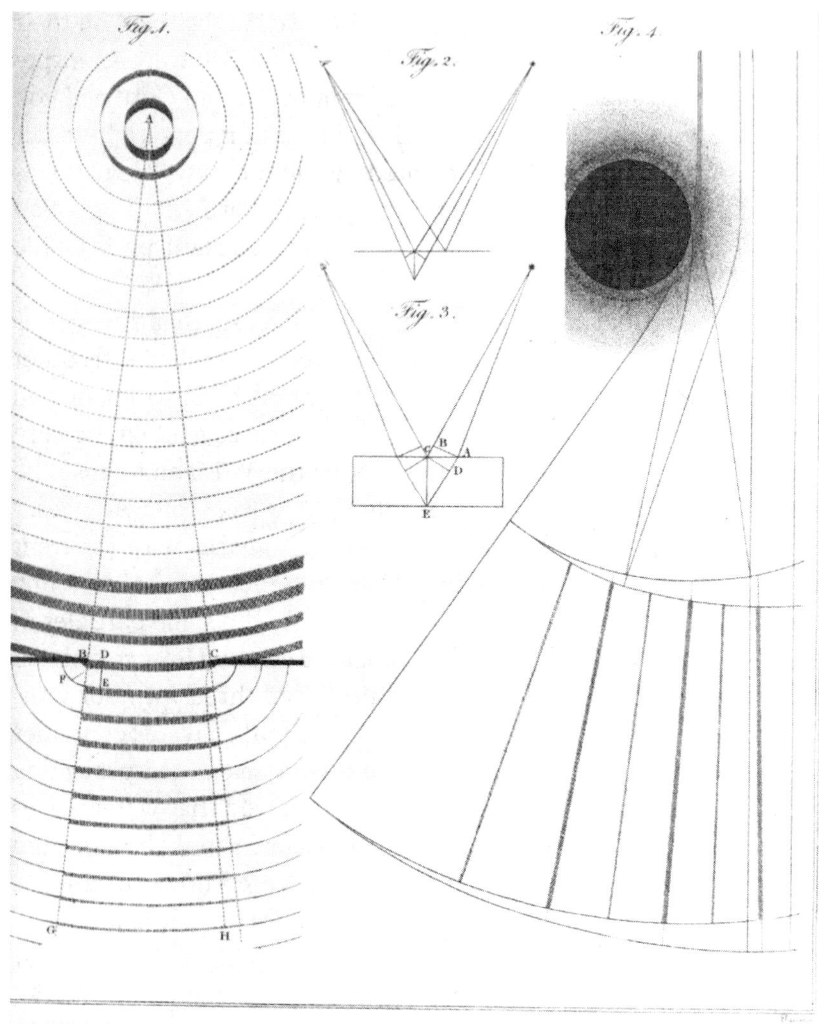

Figure 4.4. **Diffraction patterns. Thomas Young, "On the Theory of Light and Colour," *Philosophical Transactions of the Royal Society* 92 (1802), plate 1, 48. Courtesy of the Royal Society.**

In his 1801 paper, Young spelled out the larger philosophical consequence of crests and hollows of light waves overlapping. In "Corollary IV. Of Blackness," he stated that any "substance can become positively black" at the places where waves cancel each other when interference patterns are projected on it.[37] This corollary expresses

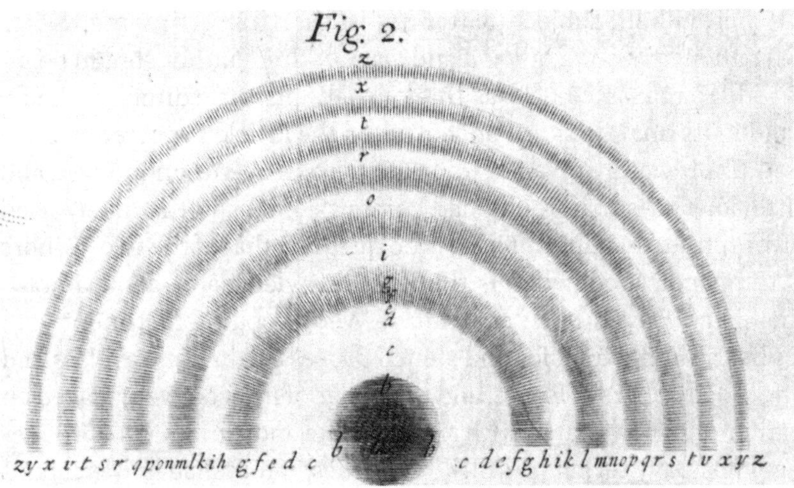

Figure 4.5. **Newton's rings. Isaac Newton, *Opticks,* 3 vols. (London: Samuel Smith & Benjamin Walford, 1704), 2:49. Young's 1803 photochemical prints showed portions of three such rings. Courtesy of ETH-Bibliothek Zürich.**

a radical idea that I believe is connected to Young's antiracist stance: Blackness can result from light added to light. The word *positively* is key since it undoes the century-old preconception that both chromatic blackness and racial Blackness are a lack, a negative—the sheer absence of light or whiteness.

Recontextualizing Thomas Wedgwood's Photochemical Dabbling

To sum up this chapter until now, in the wake of William Herschel's discovery of invisible "caloric rays," British physical optics led by Wollaston and Young evidenced three new kinds of species of black light: absorption lines (1801), ultraviolet (1801), and interferences fringes (1802). The last two were ascertained by photochemical blackening. This is the proper frame within which to reconsider the purportedly original source of photography: Humphry Davy's famous 1802 article.

The title is worth citing in full: "An Account of a Method of Copying Paintings Upon Glass, and of Making Profiles, by the Agency of Light Upon Nitrate of Silver. Invented by T. Wedgwood, Esq. With Observations by Humphry Davy."[38] What jumps out immediately is a split in both subject matter and authorship: art reprographics and silhouetting; Wedgwood and Davy. A third author should be invoked, Young, since he was the journal's physics editor and had a hand in its final version. Indeed, when the article appeared in June 1802, Davy was involved in replicating experiments on infrared and ultraviolet rays that Young had commissioned and that likely used silver nitrate imaging.[39] There is no question that of the two authors of the paper, Wedgwood is the least knowledgeable about photochemistry. Davy's terse account of Wedgwood's experiments describes a simple transfer and stencil process. Paintings on glass and "the woody fibers of leaves, and the wings of insects" were placed on leather or paper treated with silver nitrate and illuminated, producing what Davy terms "profiles," "outlines," and "shades" ("Account of a Method," 169, 167, 168). Davy indicates that using "a camera obscura" was "the first object of Mr. Wedgwood," after "a friend" (169) told him about silver nitrate, but the images Wedgwood produced proved too faint to register (169).

Davy then describes his own experiments using "a solar microscope" in a camera obscura on "small objects" to make images on "prepared paper" held at "a small distance from the lens" ("Account of a Method," 169). Like other experienced photologists, Davy makes full use of Senebier's setup, most notably a convex lens. Davy compares the effects of silver chloride and silver nitrate, the first acting faster but insoluble in water, the latter acting more slowly and being soluble. He hopes that a means might be found for "destroying the compound," thus "preventing the unshaded parts of the delineation from being coloured by exposure," thereby fixing the image (170). Importantly, this last suggestion is not attributed to Wedgwood. Since the paper is couched as a tribute to his dabbling (and now ill) friend, if Wedgwood had used a lens, different compounds, or entertained the possibility of fixation, Davy would have certainly credited him.

Photography historians have conjectured about the identity of the unnamed "friend," and there is a plethora of possibilities. Young, Wollaston, and Davy are the obvious first choices. But he could be any of the associates and assistants in the workshop of Josiah Wedgwood who were knowledgeable in photochemistry: William

Bentley, James Keir, William Lewis, and head of research Alexander Chisholm. Older members of the Lunar Society funded by Wedgwood's father represent a third avenue: Erasmus Darwin, Leslie, Priestley, Watt, and Beddoes. Any of them was more familiar with photochemistry than Thomas Wedgwood.[40] A notorious letter from Watt to Josiah Wedgwood mentions "silver pictures," which the latter had sent the former, and it has been wrongly taken as evidence for Thomas Wedgwood's photoimaging.[41] Yet all the actors above knew better than to confuse whitish-gray silver salt compounds with "silver" proper. The Wedgwood factory was experimenting at the time with silver plating, as Alan Barnes shows, so Watt's "silver pictures" were almost certainly silver-plating samples.[42] My overall point is not to diminish Thomas Wedgwood's contributions but rather to contextualize them within collective photochemical imaging experiments in the early 1800s spearheaded by Wollaston, Young, and Davy as part of innovative investigations in physical optics.

Wedgwood's family circle was very much interested in both hieroglyphic imaging and the camera obscura. After reading about Priestley's work in chemistry and optics, Josiah Wedgwood Sr. wrote the following to his partner Bentley in 1779 regarding the education of his two sons: "If visible images could be made of these bodies, their unions, & changes, it would make the study pleasanter to them, & the painted images could be easier stored up in their memory & perhaps with more precision than the ideas alone without the assistance of such painted images."[43]

In 1786, Robert Waring Darwin published an essay on "ocular spectra" that investigated negative afterimages and "retinal persistence."[44] The bulk of his research is thought to have been coauthored by his father Erasmus Darwin (Thomas Wedgwood's uncle-in-law), who was convinced that optical images directly shaped mental images and ideas. Introducing his 1795 summa of natural philosophy, Erasmus Darwin figures his book itself as a camera obscura, writing: "Gentle Reader! / LO, here a CAMERA OBSCURA is presented to thy view, in which are lights and shades dancing on a whited canvas, and magnified into apparent life!"[45] In the circle dominated by Erasmus Darwin, artificial image-making was discussed together with optical processes underlying perception, imagination, and cognition. When Beddoes argued in 1794 against Darwin's thesis that the genesis of mental images begins with ocular spectra, Thomas Wedgwood took the side of his uncle (Barnes, "Negative and Positive Images," 246–47). As both Barnes and Francis Doherty document, Thomas Wedgwood debated models of vision, perception, and imagination with his close friend Coleridge, who sided with Beddoes (Barnes, "Negative and Positive Images").[46] Thomas Wedgwood proponed a mechanistic model of experience centered on vision where serial perceptual images continuously imprint the mind. Coleridge opted for a model of perceptual experiences reinterpreted by revisualization and re-creation—that is, poetic in the original sense of image-making (poieîn). For Thomas Wedgwood, by contrast, visual perception was a self-registering apparatus (Doherty, "Tom Wedgwood," 309). Direct impressions, for Wedgwood, are complemented by extrapolated visualization: "The idea of the invisible part of the globe instantaneously blends with the perception of that which is visible, and they jointly form my notion of the globe. . . . Thus a standard visual idea of every object is formed, which instantly blends with every fugitive perception, and corrects it."[47] Thomas Wedgwood inquired about retinal impressions in a letter, mentioning "his own attempts at drawing the different positions of the wings of birds in flight, which would 'coalesce' into the impression of smooth movement," in Barnes's words ("Negative and Positive Images," 255). For his brother Josiah Wedgwood Jr. writing in 1800, Thomas Wedgwood's general philosophical agenda in the years when he dabbled in photochemical experiments was "no less than Time, Space, and Motion" (cited in Litchfield, *Tom Wedgwood,* 207). This befits a protocinematographic approach to vision rather more than a pre-photographic one, as Matthew C. Hunter keenly proposes.[48]

An opium user, Coleridge favored the creative genesis of visual impressions, "the rising up of Spectra in the eye," as he puts it in a letter.[49] Inspired by his readings of German Idealism, he made imagination the central faculty as he insisted to Thomas Wedgwood in 1803: "William Hazlitt is a thinking, observant, original man, of great power as a Painter of Character-Portraits, and far more in the manner of the old Painters than any living Artist, but the objects must be before him; he has no imaginative memory."[50] When he fashioned his influential poetics a dozen years later in *Biographia Literaria,* Coleridge drew an even sharper contrast between simple mimesis and creative imagination. The former, which he calls "fancy," is "a sort of mental camera obscura manufactured at the printing office, which *pro tempore* fixes, reflects, and transmits the moving phantasms of one man's delirium." Pure imagination, by contrast, "is *creation* rather than *painting,* or if painting, yet such, and with such co-presence of the whole picture flashed at once upon the eye, as the sun paints in a camera obscura."[51] Coleridge rejects the kind of animated visualization proponed by Erasmus Darwin and Thomas Wedgwood in favor of a "flash" poetics closer to a photographic snapshot. Interestingly, the camera obscura appears on both sides of Coleridge's models of imaging, suggesting a wider conceptual currency of photocinema formations by around 1815.

French Physical Optics: From the Wave Theory of Light to Pre-Photography

The remarkable research in physical optics and the WTL produced in England ended with a whimper with the short-lived Treaty of Amiens between France and England in 1802–1803. In October 1801, during treaty negotiations, Napoleon Bonaparte obtained approval from England to send an expeditionary force of over twenty thousand troops to recapture Saint-Domingue from formerly enslaved fighters led by Toussaint Louverture.[52] In 1802, as England returned Martinique, Tobago, and Saint Lucia to France, Napoleon passed a secret law confirming that "slavery will be maintained" and "the trade of blacks and their importation in the above-mentioned colonies, will take place according to laws and regulations prior to 1789."[53] Decrees restricting entry to France of Black people and other people of color (1802) and forbidding marriage on French soil between Black people and white people (1803) were passed as well.[54]

As Napoleon crowned himself emperor (1804), the two pro-Napoleonian leaders of French science, astronomer Pierre-Simon, marquis de Laplace and chemist Claude-Louis Berthollet, dictated a strict agenda centered on mechanics, light corpuscles, and celestial bodies. Laplace headed physical sciences due to the prestige of his *Exposition of the System of the World* (1796), the first secular cosmology based on a similar nebular hypothesis as Immanuel Kant's and William Herschel's.[55] French scientific research at the beginning of the nineteenth century reflected a combined allegiance to Napoleonic rule, universal reason, and expansionist foreign policy. Within this agenda, optics was strongly promoted as a theoretical litmus test for the unification of physics and mathematics into a universal corpuscular theory. But there was a very pragmatic reason as well: the continental blockade. Cut off from its colonies and from England's leading industries, Napoleonic France had to boost very quickly all areas of fundamental and applied research, starting with lens-grade production without England's superior and proprietary crown-glass.[56]

In 1806, Laplace tasked mathematician and astronomer Jean-Baptiste Biot with investigating the refraction of light in gases. Biot was aided by a young astronomer, François Arago.[57] After attending École Polytechnique for two years, Arago was named secretary astronomer at the Paris Observatory in 1805—even though in 1804 he had led a protest at the school against Napoleon, whom he detested.[58] In 1806, Arago published a paper on the speed of light before being sent to Spain in 1807 to finish the geodesic survey of the meridian from which the meter was to be computed.[59] When Napoleon invaded Spain in 1808, Arago became, de facto, a spy. He underwent a year of perilous captures and spectacular escapes from Spain to Morocco and Algeria before returning to Paris in 1809. Reincarnating the Maupertuis-like figure of the astronomer turned adventurer, Arago became an overnight sensation. Over the next decade, he progressively overtook Laplace as the leader of French physics, not through brilliant theories or major discoveries but because he was a keen experimenter and teamwork leader with an encyclopedic knowledge of astronomy, optics, electromagnetism, and meteorology. Unlike his older colleagues, he was an anglophile who strongly favored transnational collaboration, notably with Young, John Herschel, Adolphe Quetelet, and Alexander von Humboldt. A proponent of free speech and free education who admired England's constitutional monarchy, he embraced republicanism in the

1830s. Elected to Parliament, he pushed unsuccessfully for so-called universal suffrage (albeit limited then to male property-owners), became an opponent of the July Monarchy, and was a leader of the revolutions of 1848, during which he oversaw the abolition of slavery in French colonies (see chapter 5).

When Arago was named secretary of the Académie des Sciences in 1830, it signaled that the central wager of his scientific career—that the wave model of light has a better explanatory power than corpuscular and emissive theories—was won. Knowing Young's work closely, he adopted the WTL around 1810 and systematically recruited junior researchers who could assist in its proof, notably a transportation engineer named Augustin-Jean Fresnel.[60] Prior to joining Arago in 1814, Fresnel had submitted a soda-making process to the committee on new innovations in 1811. Commissioners Louis-Jacques Thenard and Joseph-Louis Gay-Lussac forwarded it to the arbiter in chemistry at the Académie des Sciences, Nicolas-Louis Vauquelin, who never read it. Fresnel was only told that his process was not economical. Disappointed, he pored over scientific journals, stumbled upon debates about the nature of light, and retooled his career. This minor episode is worth mentioning because in spring 1811, the Niépce brothers followed the exact same path. They devised an indigo ersatz process to compensate for the loss of Saint-Domingue's production. Thenard and Gay-Lussac reviewed the process, turning it down on similar uneconomical grounds in 1813.[61] Looking for another area of innovation, they turned to the print and reprographic sector and then to pre-photography.[62] In other words, the WTL and Niépce's heliography got their respective contingent start from the same industrial context: the French metropole bereft of its stolen Caribbean labor.

In 1814, Arago tasked Fresnel with researching the deviation of light rays at the periphery of objects—the very phenomenon studied by Marat and William Herschel that led Young to focus on light interferences. With a solar microscope projecting a light ray through a camera obscura onto thin wires, Fresnel noted in 1815: "Since intercepting the light from one side of the wire makes the internal fringes disappear, the concurrence of the rays that arrive from both sides is therefore necessary to produce them." Fresnel, who could not consult Young's work for lack of English (unlike Arago), rediscovered interference fringes (Buchwald, *Rise of the Wave Theory of Light,* 117–19). His 1816 memoir reexplaining diffraction phenomena concludes that they "confirm the system that considers light as vibrations of a particular fluid."[63] The emissionist camp headed by Biot and Laplace set up a prize to adjudicate "the nature of these motions" taking place in "the diffracted bands that form and propagate outside the shadow of bodies" as well as "within the shadow proper"—again, the very terms used by Marat and William Herschel (170). After Fresnel received the prize in 1819, Siméon-Denis Poisson, an emissionist, worked out a damning mathematical objection from Fresnel's own theory: If light was projected at an opaque disk of a certain size, according to Fresnel's equations a white spot should appear smack in the middle of its umbra. Since that was palpably absurd, so was the theory. An experiment was ceremonially set up with Poisson, Biot, Arago, Fresnel, and others present, and a white spot indeed became visible in the middle of the shadow as predicted. This was what Marat had described in 1780 and what, in part, led William Herschel to search for black-making rays.

The testing apparatus for that experiment was constructed by Arago himself, as Fresnel indicates in "On Light" (1821), a key document bridging the WTL and pre-photography.[64] When Fresnel began his darkroom experiments in 1815, it was also Arago who had suggested the use of a solar microscope (Fresnel, "Mémoire sur la diffraction de la lumière," 236). To eliminate uncertainty regarding the effect of light's diffraction at the edges of bodies, Fresnel had developed the so-called double-mirror experiment in early 1816, a spin-off of Young's double-slit experiment—again at the urging of Arago. In that experiment, a ray of light was bounced onto two adjacent mirrors at a slight angle to make their reflections interfere (Buchwald, *Rise of the Wave Theory of Light,* 137). In 1821, Fresnel used a heliostat to still the sunbeam and measure the distance between fringes, verifying that starlight produces fringes as well. He pointed out that light as "a certain mode of vibration of a universal fluid" exerts a chemical action that should be regarded less as a combination of "molecules" than as the rearrangement of the structure of matter—a continuation of Senebier's insight (Fresnel, "De La Lumière," 10, 116, 135).

A postscriptum hastily inserted at the end of the volume containing "On Light" is crucial for pre-photography. It was added because Fresnel became belatedly aware of an experiment Arago had conducted: "By projecting on freshly prepared silver chloride the fringes produced by the interference of two pencils of light reflected from two mirrors at a slight angle between them, Mr. Arago has noticed that [the fringes] traced black lines equally spaced and separated by white intervals."[65] Depending on the placement of the photosensitive paper within the area of interference, the "same rays" would blacken the silver chloride at certain distances but not others, providing material proof that the waves added up or canceled each other. Fresnel specifies that a heliostat must be used to counter the Sun's motion, that the exposure should be at least ten minutes, and that a semicylindrical lens should be used as Arago suggested (Fresnel, "Post-Scriptum," 537–39). This camera obscura "apparatus [appareil]" that combined a specified lens,

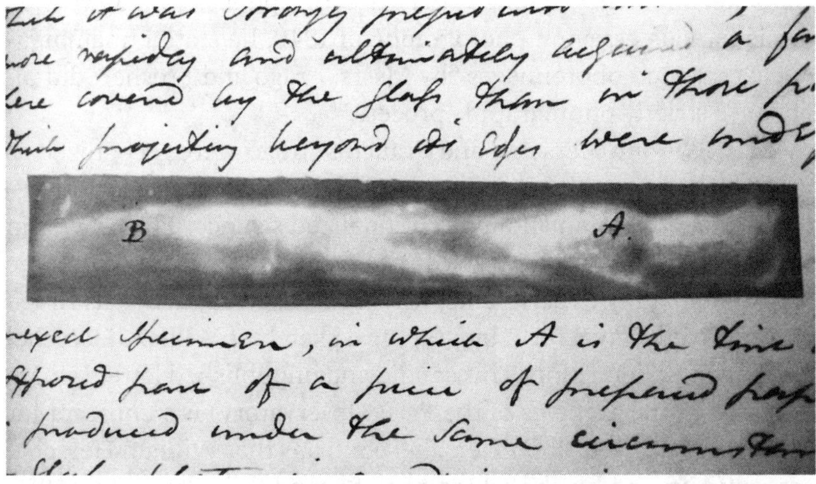

Figure 4.6. **Photographic paper strip, experiment with exposure time. John Herschel, "Note of the Art of Photography, or the Application of the Chemical Rays of Light to the Purpose of Pictorial Representation," unpublished draft, March 1839. Abstract in *Proceedings of the Royal Society of London* 4, no. 37 (1839): 132–33. Courtesy of St John's College Library, Papers of Sir John Herschel, James 510', Cambridge University.**

a silver chloride covered "plate," and a precise exposure time produced a series of photochemical prints that imaged and visualized a 3D field of light interferences. It was a great deal more sophisticated than the setups with which Niépce was dabbling at the time. Arago's photoimages showed a series of parallel black striations in a narrow band in the middle of the white plate, with some prints showing less striation when the plate was closer or farther from the mirrors. The iterative process between photochemical prints, modifications of the setup, then new prints improving the sharpness of the bands places Arago's experiments among similar trial-and-error practices as experiments by Niépce, Daguerre, and Talbot. As for the absence of fixation, the reason is simple: The prints do not matter, only the description of how they can be replicated. Fresnel's detailed instructions indeed aim to enable the exact reproduction of the experimental setup rather than the exact reproduction of what it images.

Dated August 1821, these experiments have not been sufficiently recognized in the accepted prehistory of photography.[66] Yet John Herschel knew they belonged to it. In the unpublished 1839 version of his famous essay on photography of 1840, he stated unambiguously that such photoimages "by Mssrs. Arago and Fresnel" did pioneer "a strictly photographic process."[67]

By 1839, John Herschel and François Arago were recognized as the leading authorities in photology and they respected each other's commitment to open and internationalized science. This is why, in summer 1839, the former disclosed to the latter his father's quixotic black-making ray experiments, which I alluded to earlier, as Arago was involved in writing a biographical sketch of William Herschel and had queried his son. This candid and unpublished letter (which I located in the archives of the Paris Observatory) is significant for three reasons. First, John Herschel confirms that William Herschel actively pursued black-making rays. Second, it is dated July 1839, when England was in a diplomatic rift with France for its support of Muḥammad ʿAlī of Egypt. And third, at that very time, Talbot, whom John Herschel had assisted, was publicly challenging Daguerre, whom Arago had championed, over the invention of photography—a word John Herschel had just coined.

Dated "Slough, July 1–5, 1839," it reads:

> The analysis of the solar rays was always a very favorite object of [William Herschel's] pursuit, and his detection of the calorific rays beyond the visible spectrum is well known to every photologist. But there was another branch of photology which led him into many and laborious experiments. . . . The shadows of objects in clear sunshine are marked, according to his observations (which my body may verify) by two phenomena—1st a bright edge or border, wholly without the shadow, more strongly illuminated than the space far exterior to it—and 2nd, a band or fringe within the shadow, darker than the shadow itself. I speak of shadows not as seen in darkened chambers and as cast by objects of small dimensions—but in the open sunshine and from large objects. Of these phenomena the theory of diffraction renders a satisfactory account. But that theory was unknown to him, and the phenomena, being studied under the circumstances above mentioned could never have sufficed for the formation of a distinct theory. I consider it therefore not a little remarkable that these phenomena, so studied, should have led him to a conclusion he considered too strange and too bold to publish. Viz.: that there are in the solar rays some which have the reverse property to illuminating & to which he used to give the name of black-making rays! To such rays, inflected into the shadows according to Newton's theory of inflection (of which he was always an advocate) he ascribed the blackest at the inner edge of the shadow—and to their absence, the bright fringe exterior to it. This power of illumination and obscuration which he thus attributed as inherent qualities to rays of different species we now, in the theory of interferences admit, as properties of the positive and negative phases of the undulations constituting one and the same ray. I beg you to observe that it is now for the first time that I make mention of this curious point in my father's scientific history, and that, if the nature of the work you are engaged in, leads you into any account of his scientific or rather intellectual character you are at liberty to mention it, on my authority. I would not trust the mention of it to any one else than you, however.[68]

This letter attests to John Herschel's unease at the possible revelation of William Herschel's black-making rays conjecture, fearing it might tarnish his scientific reputation. Yet he trusts Arago—and Arago alone—to make the call. More broadly, the letter demonstrates the conceptual contiguity between photology, interference phenomena and the WTL, black-and-white rhetoric—"positive and negative phases of the undulations"—and photography.

French Photochemical Research, 1802–1820

Photography historians have not queried whether and how photochemical experiments by Thomas Wedgwood, Davy, and Young disseminated to France. A cursory foray into the archives shows that they were quickly and profusely reported on in the French scientific press. Berthollet reported on Wedgwood's experiments as soon as they were published in 1802, and in an 1803 textbook on chemistry he referenced William Herschel's calorific rays and Senebier's photochemical experiments.[69] Another report on Wedgwood surfaced in 1807, one by Biot in 1811, and another in an 1812 translation—more are likely to be found.[70] This marked interest is connected with a strong uptick in studies of metallic compound photochemistry over the years 1808–1820 in *Annales de chimie,* the main journal for the field. In the 1809 introduction to the first edition in French of Thomas Thomson's *A System of Chemistry,* Berthollet relates the experiments of Scheele, Ritter, and William Herschel.[71] The same year, chemist Jacques-Étienne Bérard wrote an article on tin muriate and its photosensitive properties.[72] In 1811, Étienne-Louis Malus, while theorizing polarization, gave a poor review of Goethe's 1810 *Theory of Colors,* with the exception of the appendix by Thomas Johann Seebeck describing how to obtain silver chloride images of the solar spectrum.[73] In 1813, Berthollet, Jean-Antoine Chaptal, and Biot reviewed Bérard's set of publications, supporting his claims that the analysis of the effects of light on metallic compounds was now a central direction for optical research.[74] Bérard's results were published only later in 1817. His apparatus follows the standard setup with heliostat, darkroom, prism, and "paper treated with silver chloride," while its prism came from "the superb cabinet of Mr. Charles," suggesting that Charles himself may have been involved.[75]

Arago knew all these developments firsthand and was therefore among the most knowledgeable photochemists of the period.

Neither John Herschel nor Arago invented photography, even though the former suggested in 1839 that the latter did in 1821. Yet both had the requisite optical, photochemical, and instrumental know-how; this is why Daguerre chose Arago as his champion in 1838. As soon as he heard of the daguerreotype, John Herschel retro-engineered photographic processes in a few days, offering improvements on the paper process within months.[76] Why neither of them pursued fixed photographic processes earlier is not hard to guess. Their focus was the fast-moving and sprawling field of physical optics, in which a unifying theory seemed just around the corner. Both were committed to transparent science, criticizing Joseph von Fraunhofer in 1824 for keeping his superior glassmaking process a trade secret. Niépce, Daguerre, and Talbot, however, shared Fraunhofer's commercial proprietary secrecy.

The earliest photochemical imaging experiments by Nicéphore Niépce date from 1816, neatly coinciding with the apex of photochemistry research in France. Yet Niépce was sufficiently unfamiliar with optics and photochemistry that when reporting on his first photosensitive print to his brother Claude, he marveled both at the camera obscura's top-down inversion and the fact that the farm aviary he shot from his window appeared in photonegative. The brothers nonetheless caught on quickly. A few months later, Claude recommended "a solution of iron muriate" about which "he had read" (Bonnet and Marignier, *Niépce,* 1:407–8). The source is likely the 1813 issue of the *Annales de chimie* mentioning Bérard's experiments with silver oxide photosensitivity and an article by Gay-Lussac on iron muriate. Nicéphore soon indicated he just read about guaiac resin dissolved in alcohol turning green when exposed to light, a reaction described in Thomson's 1809 French edition of *System of Chemistry,* with a dedicated section on photochemistry. The book includes a sizable section on indigo, explaining why he would be familiar with it (Bonnet and Marignier, *Niépce,* 1:407–8).[77] While the Niépce brothers suggested that their original insight about photography came from the time they were conscripted and stationed in Sardinia in 1797, they set out to devise a workable photographic process only in 1816 at the exact apex of French photochemical research. It is therefore reasonable to assume that the

Niépce brothers were more aware of contemporaneous photochemistry research than they let on. The overlooked intermediaries between pre-photographic bricoleurs and scientists were Parisian instrument-makers, whom I examine after a brief but important detour through Talbot.

Talbot's Internship with Arago at the Paris Observatory

Photography historians have consistently downgraded or overlooked the role of physical optics research in the emergence of working photography. A case in point is Talbot's apprenticeship with Arago in 1825. After graduating from Cambridge in 1821, Talbot dabbled in chemistry, physics, and archaeology but began considering a career in astronomy.[78] His notebooks of 1821 and 1822 are replete with astronomical observations, comet coordinates, computations of ellipses and parallax, and advanced algebra—an ad hoc training program.[79] By 1822–1823, he knew Fresnel's work on interferences, explored chromatic aberration, and made plans for constructing a photometer and a heliostat.[80] In 1824–1825 he traveled to Paris and spent two weeks in March 1825 interning directly with Arago at the Paris Observatory. Talbot's travel journals collect bits of Arago's opinions, teachings, hypotheses, past research, and current investigations. For example, Arago explained to him why the constant speed of light among stars moving in different directions disproves the emission theory of light.[81] In sum, it was a one-on-one seminar with the leading specialist in astronomy, optics, light, and photoimaging. Talbot does not mention photochemistry, yet he indicates: "Hook's *Micrographia* [Arago] mentioned as a work too little known: he says the same explanation of the coloured rings is there to be found which Young afterwards imagined."[82] Young, we recall, made photochemical images of these diffraction rings in 1803. Talbot's journal indicates that interference fringes and the WTL were topics he had discussed with Arago; there is little reason why Arago would not have shared with him his 1821 photochemical prints of interference fringes that confirmed the WTL.

Larry J. Schaaf, the leading expert on Talbot, conjectures that the latter's interest in photochemistry dates only from 1831, after he (and Charles Babbage) witnessed experiments by John Herschel on platinum muriate exposed to sunlight. Schaaf trusts Talbot's statement in *The Pencil of Nature* that failing to draw with a camera lucida at Lake Como in 1833 convinced him to turn to the camera obscura (Schaaf, *Out of the Shadows,* 36–37). Neither conjecture appears tenable. In early November 1827, John Herschel personally mailed Talbot his essay on "Light," which became a standard in British optics for decades and marks John Herschel's final conversion to the WTL.[83] The essay states clearly: "Thus, a set of fringes formed by the interference of two solar pencils with a common origin, being kept very steadily projected for a long time on one and the same part of a sheet of paper rubbed with muriate of silver, a series of black lines became traced on it, the intervals of which were smaller than those of the dark and luminous fringes formed by homogeneous violet light."[84] This refers to Arago's 1821 photochemical prints of interference fringes. Talbot certainly read Herschel's essay very closely, and if he had not already learned of these experiments from Arago himself, he would have in John Herschel's essay in 1827.[85] As for the camera obscura, Talbot's notebooks contradict his own statement about the 1833 date. One entry from summer 1829, about equipment for a mountain trek, mentions "shoes-gun-sextant-cam. lucida & obscura. English flora. 2 lorgnoles."[86] Neither Niépce nor Talbot, despite their claims to the contrary, worked in a vacuum outside of physical optics.

The Missing Link: Parisian Instrument-Makers

The inceptors of working photography—Niépce, Daguerre, Talbot—and astronomers and physicists at French research institutions depended heavily on an intermediary community that has gone largely unrecognized: instrument-makers. In large European cities in the late eighteenth and early nineteenth centuries, industrial, scientific, and educational needs for precision apparatuses caused a growth in specialized workshops producing new instruments.[87] In Paris they concentrated around the Seine in the Latin Quarter, where the continental system as well as new research schools and institutions boosted the density and quality of their output from 1800 to 1820. By 1825, French commercial optics matched leading British firms and Fraunhofer's lens-making process.[88]

Not only were instrument-making ventures highly concentrated and competitive, they were often familial establishments spinning up from or merging with each other. Physicist Jean Nicolas Pierre Hachette describes a microscope made by Charles Chevalier in 1825 as "a convex prism similar to that of the camera obscura which M. Vincent Chevalier made in 1819. . . . This prism, as M. Fresnel put it nicely in his report on the microscope of M. Selligue, serves both as mirror and magnifier. As for the diaphragms . . . we must in truth say that they were known and appreciated by the late M. Charles, as well as those who took the courses on optics from this excellent professor, among whom we can cite MM. Baillif, Dumotiez uncle and nephew."[89] This passage evidences intensive and reciprocal interactions between instrument-makers and scientists who commissioned, reviewed, and used their instruments.[90] It also shows the pivotal role of Jacques Charles in training the Parisian instrument-making community. Conversely, employees at instrument shops often ran workshops for students or served as préparateurs (technical assistants) in course demonstrations and experiments (Blondel, "Electrical Instruments," 164). The imbrication was so complete that catalogs of instrument-makers were referenced in or even printed within leading European scientific journals.[91] When international scientists visited Parisian instrument-makers in the early decades of the nineteenth century, they sampled specialized devices and gathered information about the latest innovations and theoretical advances. Alessandro Volta, Michael Faraday, and Davy, for instance, all visited the Dumotiez firm in the early 1800s, while Talbot stopped at the Lerebours shop every time he came to Paris (Brenni, "19th-Century Scientific Instrument Advertising," 508).

I want to focus on two instrument-makers germane to this study: Paul Gustave Froment and Vincent Chevalier. Froment graduated from École Polytechnique, where he had worked with Arago before constructing optical instruments and investigating photosensitive compounds. He made photochemical contact prints of leaves, feathers, and other semitranslucid objects, succeeding in "fixing" them in 1836 independently of Daguerre and Talbot.[92] When Arago publicized the process of Daguerre, Froment went home and made a photochemical image the same day.[93] Froment subsequently built a telegraph with a disk keyboard producing tracings on a clock-driven "strip of paper unreeling at uniform speed," electrical wires for a telescope eyepiece for Arago, a chronograph, the official replicas of the meter, the wind turbine for the rotating mirror in Armand-Hippolyte-Louis Fizeau and Jean-Bernard-Léon Foucault's apparatus measuring the speed of light, and Foucault's famous pendulum (Laussédat, *Notice biographique sur Gustave Froment,* 14, 17–18, 20, 25). This array of devices, parenthetically, evidences the common formations of photocinema from the 1830s to the 1850s (see chapter 6).

Vincent Chevalier was the hinge figure in the implementation of photography: He worked directly with Arago, Charles, Niépce, Daguerre, and Talbot. In 1823, Chevalier released a meniscus-prism portable camera obscura that artists—including Daguerre—considered the best available. In the early 1820s, Vincent Chevalier and his father Charles Chevalier, together with several scientists including Jacques Charles, worked to procure flint-glass from England and devise new technics for making achromatic lenses.[94] After confirming in a letter to Niépce in December 1825 that "your discovery . . . is of major importance," in 1826 Vincent Chevalier suggested to Daguerre that he should meet Niépce since both were working on photochemical picturing (Bonnet and Marignier, *Niépce,* 1:733–34; Chevalier, *Étude,* 21). At that time, the Chevaliers were collaborating with Giovanni Battista Amici and Arago on optical lens design and assembly for telescopes. As for Talbot, it was Charles Chevalier who provided Talbot with optical components and camera obscuras (Chevalier, *Étude,* 146). These cursory indications of interactions between pre-photographers, astronomy and light physics researchers, and instrument-makers likely represent the tip of the iceberg. The tight interweaving of these three communities is still to be accounted for in the siloed historiographies of photography and cinema.

5

Selenography

The Moon, Slavery, and the Dark Side of Photography

J'ai saisi la lumière au passage et je l'ai enchaînée! J'ai forcé le soleil à me peindre des tableaux. [I have seized light in its path and chained it! I forced the Sun to paint canvases for me.]
—Attributed to LOUIS DAGUERRE by Charles Chevalier, *Guide du photographe*

I have seized the fleeting light and imprisoned it! I have forced the sun to paint pictures for me!
—LOUIS DAGUERRE, as translated by Helmut Gernsheim and Alison Gernsheim, *L. J. M. Daguerre*

I have captured the light and arrested its flight! The sun itself shall draw my pictures!
—LOUIS DAGUERRE, as translated by Roger Watson and Helen Rappaport, *Capturing the Light*

What is startling in Louis Daguerre's epochal, albeit attributed, statement about achieving working photography—and its translations into English—is how the rhetoric of fugitivity, capture, coercion, and indeed enslavement takes precedence over any claim about reproduction.[1] It is as if the true miracle was submitting light to forced labor. Daguerre's words exemplify Fred Moten's "black apparatus"—the structural entanglement of anti-Blackness in the development of audiovisual media.[2] Accordingly, this chapter examines the formations of race and Blackness subtending the historical emergence of photography—its "dark side," as it were, which indeed involves the Moon.

There is a surprisingly close parallel between halting advances in pre-photographic research and the sputtering progress of abolition in France and England. Pre-photography runs from Nicéphore Niépce's 1816 experiments and William Henry Fox Talbot's dabbling in the mid-1830s to Daguerre's perfecting of the daguerreotype by 1838. The delegitimization of slavery followed from England's 1811 Slave Trade Felony Act and 1833 Slavery Abolition Act and France's 1848 abolition. Both countries were also interconnected. The collapse of Franco-British entente in 1840 over colonial geopolitics—when France threw its support to Muḥammad ʿAlī of Egypt to counter British interests—set back French abolition efforts for years, since the latter heavily depended on the British-led international abolition movement.[3] That 1840 spat fueled jingoistic jabs between French and British newspapers regarding the true inventor of photography—Daguerre or Talbot. Entwined geopolitically, photography and abolition also shared a procedural equivocation concerning instantaneity. While many white abolitionists favored incrementalism with compensations for enslavers, Black advocates insisted on immediate emancipation. On the side of photography, while Niépce was content with reprography as the target application because of long exposure times, in 1826 Daguerre convinced him to reduce exposure to a few minutes to enhance photography's polyvalence.

But these correlations would hold little meaning were it not for the role of François Arago in the finalization of both photography and abolition. Daguerre sought his assistance and advocacy in 1838, well aware of his position as the leader of French physical optics and photochemistry. Ten years later, during the revolutions of 1848, of which he was one of the leaders, Arago fast-tracked immediate abolition and signed it into law as the acting minister of the navy and the colonies. Coincidentally, the British official who brought the gradualist Slavery Abolition Act into law in 1833, Lord Henry Peter

Brougham, was among the earliest experimenters in photochemical imaging. This chapter unpacks the extensive connective tissue between ending slavery—by force or law—and bringing about near-instantaneous photography.

Between Sun and Moon

While Daguerre undertook to domesticate sunlight as his ghostwriter—a job the French language renders with the N-word—we will focus on the role of the Moon in the passage from pre-photography to photography.[4] In the long duration of photocinema, the Moon was always the primeval picture show. Moving across the starry vault, it waxes and wanes, moves closer or farther from Earth, which alters its apparent size, and glides across the Sun during eclipses, becoming black. When crossing the Earth's umbra, it turns orange to brown, and under various atmospheric conditions looks silvery, yellow, or nearly gray and white. Its tidal lock on our planet means that the same portion of its surface seems to be looking back at us, like a face that can take on virtually any color.

According to media historians, the word *photography* in its current sense was coined four times between 1834 and 1840.[5] In actuality, the German word Photographie dates from 1826, when it denoted visual hallucinations (see chapter 3), and around 1830 a second meaning arose in French: the scientific study of light.[6] This is why, in February 1839, the German astronomer Johann Heinrich von Mädler renamed Daguerre's process die Photographie, rejecting Niépce's term *heliography* as scientifically incorrect since light from all celestial bodies will register on sensitive plates.[7] Mädler had just completed *Mappa Selenographica* (1834–1836), the first high-magnification cartography of the lunar surface, giving it the tangible feel of an inhabitable world.[8] Interestingly, in 1792, Thomas Wedgwood tried taking the temperature of moonlight using a lens with a highly sensitive thermometer.[9]

The first mention of Daguerre's photographic research work appeared in print anonymously in 1835. In September 1836, it was commented on at length by the well-informed architect Alphonse Eugène Hubert. He voiced doubts that Daguerre obtained anything more than a "night album" of unfixed photosensitive prints, insisting

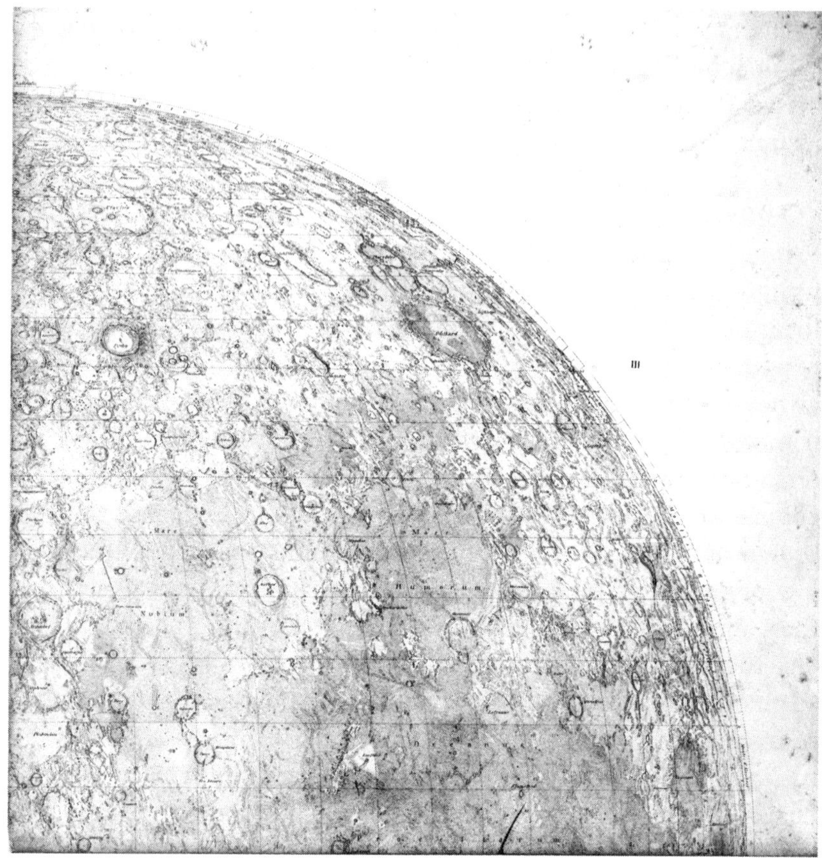

Figure 5.1. **Moon map. Wilhelm Beer and Johannes Heinrich Mädler, *Mappa Selenographica* (Berlin: S. Schropp, 1836), plate III. Courtesy of ETH-Bibliothek Zürich.**

that they were viewable only by "moonlight," since daylight would erase them. He continues: "Here is why the moon finds itself involved in this affair: M. Arago . . . said during his lecture three weeks ago that, 'of all known substances, silver chloride [changes] color the most strongly and rapidly through the action of light, and yet, if exposed for a [long] time not to [direct moonlight but moonlight focused by a very large lens, a sheet] of this chemical compound does not lose any of its natural whiteness.'"[10] Hubert states that he too had conducted photographic experiments "seven or eight years ago" (circa 1828–1829), adding that, due to the long exposure time, objects he shot were placed on a clockwork-driven contraption to prevent shadow-blurring. Hubert's remarks demonstrate an advanced knowledge of photochemistry and optics, explaining why Daguerre hired him as a collaborator in 1837.

Daguerre understood early on that photography could succeed as near-instantaneous imaging technology only by rendering grayscale. Attention to light's gradations had made his Diorama shows popular in the 1820s. These picture shows displayed landscapes painted on several stacked semitranslucent surfaces that light sources illuminated from above in succession, giving the overall impression of seeing a landscape illuminated from morning to night—from sunlight to moonshine. They belong more to the archaeology of cinema than that of photography. Among the plates that Niépce left behind during his trip to England in 1827–1828, one was a gift to Francis Bauer of Kew. It is titled *Le Clair de Lune* (Moonlight). It depicts the ivy-covered vaults of a ruined abbey lit by the Moon. As Stephen Pinson documents, this photograph is perplexing because it reproduces an engraved sketch made by Daguerre himself for the set of an Orientalist play adapted from the Old Testament.[11] Researchers who analyzed its chemical composition consider it the finest among Niépce's early production. Pinson conjectures that Daguerre asked Niépce to reproduce his chiaroscuro artwork to test heliography's capacity to render grayscale prior to entering into an association with him.[12]

Arago too thought moonlight was the true testing ground for photography. After Daguerre first approached him in 1838, Arago presented him with the challenge of photographing the Moon. He writes: "At the request of the academicians above-mentioned Mr. Daguerre projected the image of the Moon, formed at the focus of a common lens, upon one of his screens, and it left a perceptible white imprint. When a commission of the Académie composed of Mr. Laplace, Malus and Arago made a similar experiment with silver chloride, we obtained no appreciable effect. Perhaps exposure to light was not long enough. In any case, Mr. Daguerre was the first to produce a sensible chemical modification with luminous rays from our satellite."[13] This comment reveals an overlooked episode in the history of pre-photography. Since Étienne-Louis Malus died in 1812,

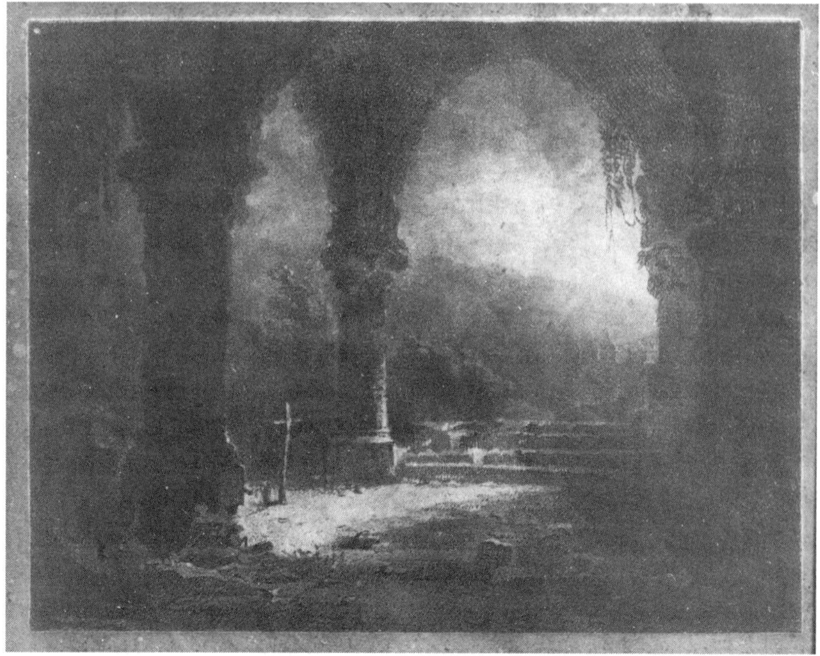

Figure 5.2. **Nicéphore Niépce, *Le Clair de Lune,* 1827. Contact print. Original photograph is very faint, partly due to deterioration. Copyright Victoria and Albert Museum.**

this photochemical experiment took place prior to that year, likely in 1811 when Arago was investigating the polarization of moonlight.[14] It represents the earliest known attempt at photo-picturing a specific object: the Moon. According to Hubert, Arago made another experiment with silver chloride around 1835, which is why he opted to assess the sensitivity of Daguerre's process with moonlight. In March 1840, using a heliostat, astronomer John William Draper produced the first known photograph of the Moon from the roof of the City University of New York. In a lecture of 1848, Arago concluded that "we can very easily obtain photographic images of our satellite, as I had predicted already in 1840." Then he added the following, without segue: "One cannot find . . . proof that the blackening of skin cannot be attributed to a direct action of lunar light."[15] This odd quip ostensibly addresses beliefs from antiquity addressed in his talk. But delivered in 1848—at the very time Arago had empowered Victor

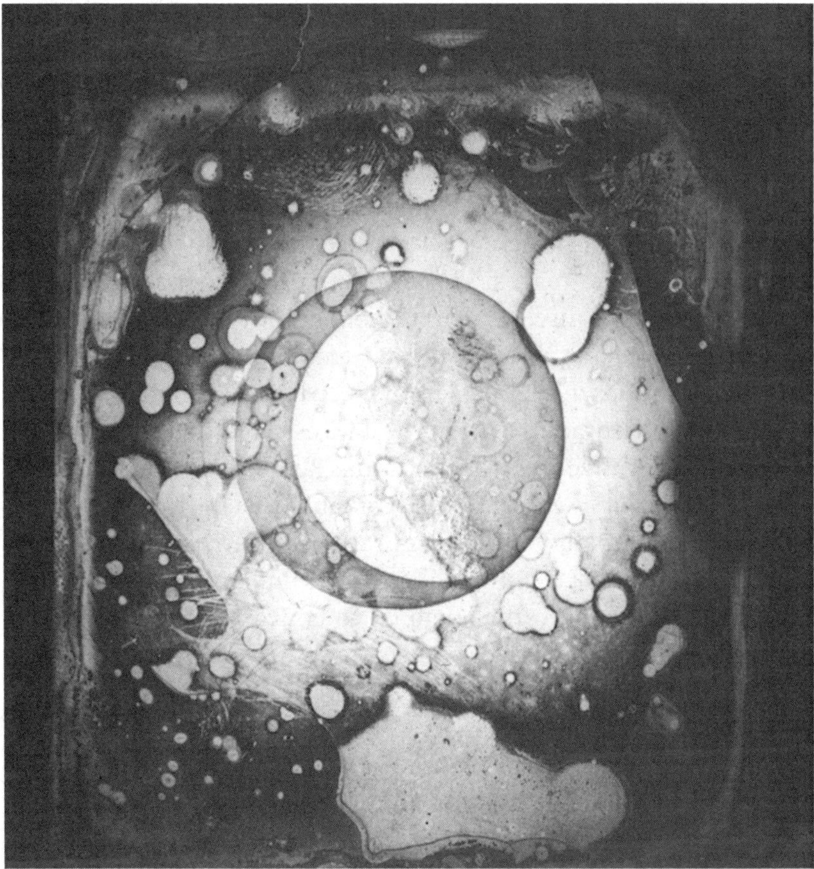

Figure 5.3. **First photograph of the Moon. J. W. Draper, 1840. Provided by New York University Special Collections.**

Schoelcher to draft immediate abolition legislation—the quip testifies to the constancy with which Black skin acted as a revelator of photography.

Photoimaging Technics, Black Skin, and Black-and-White Rhetoric

Recent scholarship explores linkages between race and early photography. Tanya Sheehan finds that in nineteenth-century photography, black-and-white contrast in "the medium serves as ready metaphor for racial difference."[16] Alessandra Raengo points to recent studies showing how nineteenth- and early twentieth-century photographs reinforced race as a "visualizable fact" that "further sutured race to the body," leading to "an investment in the indexicality of the photographic image facilitated by its analogy with the black body."[17] Descriptive comments on light values in pre-photography and early photography deploy indeed conspicuous racial valences, attached to both the difference and the convertibility between positive and negative images. In December 1829, Niépce stated, for instance, that "the discovery of . . . heliography consists in spontaneously reproducing through the action of light, with value gradients [dégradations des teintes] from black to white, images received in a camera obscura."[18] He does not address whether his prints are positives or negatives for a good reason: Researchers suspect—with deterioration complicating the assessment—that his tin heliographs were only marginally positive and rather somewhere in between. In 1836, Hubert used a photochemical commonplace when stating that photography's challenge is "to convert in the camera obscura lit areas into shadows, and shadows into lit areas."[19] By 1839, Arago celebrated the daguerreotype for doing just the opposite: "On the screens of Mr. Daguerre, the drawing and the object are exactly alike: white corresponds to white, half-tint to half-tint, black to black." By contrast, other experimenters (like Talbot) were stuck with "white reproduced as black, and reciprocally."[20] In his 1840 article on photography, John Herschel celebrated Talbot's photonegative-to-paper-positive process making reproduction easier, adding: "To avoid much circumlocution, it may be allowed me to employ the terms positive and negative, to express respectively, pictures in which the lights and shades are as in nature, or as in the original model, and in which they are the opposite, i.e. light representing shade, and shade light" ("On the Chemical Action of the Rays of the Solar Spectrum," 3). As we saw in chapter 3, Georg Christoph Lichtenberg adapted Benjamin Franklin's positive and negative electrical polarity to his electrical "projections" in the 1770s, and so did Johann Kaspar Lavater for his anti-Black physiognomic theory of silhouetting. John Herschel bolstered the in-built racial valence of positive/negative imaging in 1840 when remarking that on photonegatives "fair women transformed into negresses."[21] This belies an identification of positive natural representations with whiteness and negative representations—connoted as counternatural—with Blackness.

Certainly, black-and-white chromatic rhetoric in racialized visual culture predated photography. Let us examine two case studies. In 1816, just as Niépce began experimenting, a Haitian mixed-race political thinker who identified as Black emphatically deconstructed centuries of binary racist thinking. Sickened by the recurrence of polygenic arguments, he wrote:

> It is the most absurd reasoning to deny the identicalness of the human species. . . . After having proven the sameness of negroes and whites, I should still need to prove the sameness of Africans and negroes, and probably also the sameness of Haytians with the former; as for me, being born of an African woman, I consider myself very much identified [très-identifié] with Africans; yet . . . I should still need to demonstrate whether the peoples from the South of Europe form a particular species with the peoples of the North; whether sameness exists between the French and the Laps; and the Spanish and the Russians. What miserable sophisms! What puerile constructs![22]

The author was King Henry Christophe's political adviser Pompée Valentin Vastey, among the most influential antiracist diasporic Black intellectuals at the start of the nineteenth century.[23] The 1805 Haitian Constitution defined all its citizens as Black regardless of their color—that is, suspending the divisive taxonomies of the Code Noir. Vastey extrapolated this juridical clause into a critical project for his 1814 book *The Colonial System Unveiled.* In it, he debunks white enslavers' anti-Black discourse, denounces France's reluctance to outlaw the slave trade as England did, and sketches a detailed indictment of white Europe for crimes of slavery and conquest. Well read in medicine and chemistry, Vastey refers pointedly to Thomas Beddoes's 1790s experiment applying "muriatic acid" to lighten the skin of a Black patient (see chapter 4). He proposes a reverse process: "Without being a chemist, I hold the secret of *blackening* a white person by simple immersion."[24] This sarcastic barb sends up the only right of enslaved people—being baptized and thus saved—by alluding to photochemical blackening as the photonegative of supposed white benevolence. Vastey's political project is "to make the *shadow of the white man* disappear" (Vastey, *Le Système,* 92–93). This is a subtle formulation implying that the proslavery Enlightenment eclipsed access of Black subjectivity to the light of reason, exercising obscurantism willfully. Vastey likely leverages the black light discoveries of physical optics in 1800–1802 to debunk the false equation of whiteness with reason, invoking a higher reason: "What white person, from any nation, would be so ungenerous as not to applaud the design animating us, and not join us?" (96).

In his follow-up 1816 work, Vastey went one step further. Invoking Georges-Louis Leclerc, count de Buffon's notion of "prototype"—that is, the base type for a species' subsequent variations—he argued that if Black people are more primitive than white people, as Enlightenment thought propones, from a biblical perspective it means that they are closer to the prototype that God made in his image, which also entails that God is Black (Vastey, *Réflexions,* 8–10). Racist history is rewritten in photonegative. Vastey shared with abolitionist thinkers like Constantin-François de Chasseboeuf, count de Volney, Mungo Park, Henri Grégoire, J.-C.-L. Simonde de Sismondi, and later Martin Delany the belief that Greek culture came from Egypt and that Egyptians were Black. He wrote: "It is from this primitive hearth/focal point [foyer], says M. Lesage, from which most certainly the spark of antiquity was issued, which in subsequent centuries engendered the whole mass of light/enlightenment [toute la masse de lumière] which today illuminates [éclaire] Europe" (34). Invoking the symbolic lexicon of fire, lens optics, the Enlightenment, and illumination, Vastey suggested that Western civilization originated in black light. While William Hyde Wollaston had located a few black lines in the spectrum in 1802, by 1815 Joseph von Fraunhofer had observed and imaged over five hundred black absorption lines.[25] Light was increasingly black.

In his 1816 book, Vastey mentions Jacques-Henri Bernardin de Saint-Pierre as an ally in undoing anti-Blackness. A friend of Marie-Jean-Antoine-Nicolas de Caritat, marquis de Condorcet within the Society of the Friends of Truth, Bernardin was a radical abolitionist. Famous for the maudlin Rousseauist bestseller *Paul et Virginie,*

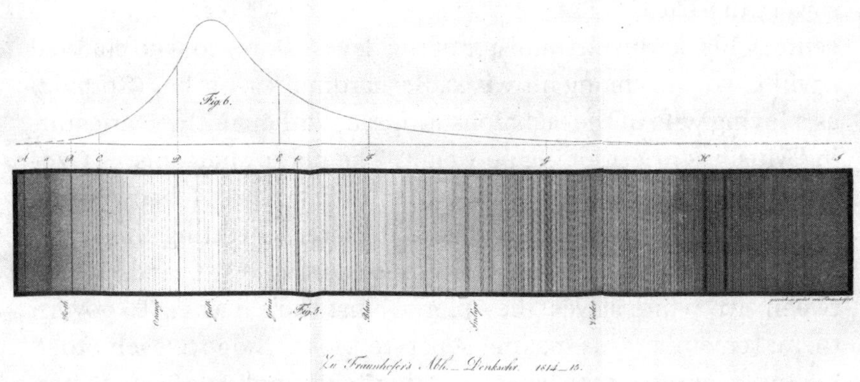

Figure 5.4. **Drawing of spectroscopic lines. J. von Fraunhofer, "Bestimmung des Brechungs- und Farbenzerstreuungs-Vermögens verschiedener Glasarten, in Bezug auf die Vervollkommnung achromatischer Fernröhe," in *Denkschriften der Königlichen Akademie der Wissenschaften zu München für die Jahre 1814 und 1815,* vol. 5 (1817), 226. Courtesy of ETH-Bibliothek Zürich.**

his true lifework was a metaphysical synthesis of natural philosophy based on a system of correspondences or "harmonies" between "souls" and "natural powers," whose combinations account for everything in the universe. One soul called "celestial" has "solar" and "aerial" powers, while a fundamental harmony is "soli-lunar," amalgamating the Sun and Moon.[26] In his unfinished summa *Harmonies of Nature,* which displays deep familiarity with Herschelian cosmology, we find a fictional coda titled "Empsaël; an Episode, or Dialogue, Illustrative of Human Harmonies" (1815).[27]

Mixing prose and dramatic dialogue, this text leverages a rhetoric of black-and-white inversion to denounce the absurdity of slavery. Arguments against abolition or for gradual abolition with compensation rested on enslavers' propaganda that slavery was benevolent and humane. Bernardin assails this premise in the foreword: "I thought that nothing was more apt to make one feel the weakness of the reasons with which the white inhabitants of our islands in America justify the slavery of blacks than to put these very reasons in the mouth of a black man from the Barbary coast towards some inhabitant of our islands having himself fallen into slavery in Africa."[28] The play is loosely based on a real seventeenth-century Black Muslim minister of the dey of Morocco who counted a white woman among his wives. Bernardin presents her (Zoraïde) as a loving wife of the righteous Empsael without either caricaturing Muslims or critiquing polygamy. The play's antagonist is Ozorio, the now enslaved former owner of Empsael. "I know white people," Empsael's Black overseer declares, inverting the terms of anti-Blackness, "as soon as there is the slightest friendship between two white slaves, they plot against their master. To govern them, remember this maxim: separate those who love each other, put together those who hate each other" (Bernardin de Saint-Pierre, *Empsael et Zoraïde,* 39). This was of course a structural containment feature of the "plantation machine."[29] Later, an imam echoes hypocritical Christian benevolence, again in photonegative: "The only thing missing to this white man, to be perfect, is to be black," and "We should not despise Zoraïde because she is white. God gave her a soul as he did to you and me" (47, 49). Bernardin casually catalogs anti-Black violence in his satire: "Whites are made to serve blacks. In fact, there is no better mount than white men. Donkeys are too slow, and our Arabian horses too speedy. But with white slaves you go fast and stop whenever you want" (65). He is nonetheless careful to let Empsael speak of the psychic trauma he's endured as a Black person: "Men of your country who form respectful, sweet, and obliging feelings at your contact because you are white, experience in my presence feelings of contempt, hatred, and ferociousness, because I am black. They have no reason other than the color of my skin, for, had you been black like me, Zoraïde, even though you are the best among creatures, they would have hated you as they hate me, and had I been white like them, even if I were as perfidious a scoundrel as they are, they would have respected me as one of their own" (148–49). The rapid succession of pronominal markers—*you, me, they*—together with chiasmic racial markers—*white, black* and *black, white*—foregrounds white prejudice from the side of Black subjectivity. These works of Vastey and Bernardin, leveraging prephotonegative discursivity to confound anti-Blackness, disclose critical intersections between the long emergence of photocinema and the implementation of emancipation.

"Abolition and Astronomy": Blackness and Photocinematic Hyperpresence in the Great Moon Hoax

A salient illustration of such intersections is the 1835 Great Moon Hoax reprising seventeenth-century motifs (see chapter 1) of Moon and Earth mirroring each other while locked in a master-to-subaltern relationship. The episode occurred in the context of heightened anxiety in the United States about the foreseeable end of slavery. In August 1835, while the astronomically savvy awaited the return of Halley's Comet (a paying telescope was installed near Central Park in New York City), the one-year-old abolitionist newspaper *The New York Sun* released a fictional story in installments relayed from the imaginary *Edinburgh Journal of Science.*[30] It was the brainchild of Richard Adams Locke, a British radical polymath who had fled England after publishing a history of the Polish revolution found subversive by the Crown. At seventeen he had penned "a poem, in six cantos, of nearly a thousand lines each, entitled 'The Universe Restored' which illustrated the theory of the alternate destruction and reproduction of all things throughout the universe of space."[31] A central feature of post-Kantian kinemorphic cosmology, cyclical cosmogony embodied the threat of secular naturalism for nineteenth-century Anglo-American Protestantism.

Later called the "Moon Hoax," Locke's "Great Astronomical Discoveries, Lately Made by Sir John Herschel, L.L.D., F.R.S, &c, at the Cape of Good Hope" was published in installments in August 1835. The spoof describes what Herschel supposedly observed on the Moon with a powerful new telescope he invented. Locke depicts lunar vegetation, goatlike animals, and two species of inhabitants resembling hybrids of humans and bats. Hotly debated, each installment sent *The New York Sun*'s sales through the roof. The story was covered by the European press and figures among the first global media phenomena. A vivid reaction came from Edgar Allan Poe, whose "Hans Phaall—A Tale" had appeared in June 1835. He believed that "the idea of *Telescopic* discoveries in the moon, his original intent before sending a balloon observer, was his."[32] Having liberally plagiarized John Herschel as well as Abraham Rees's *Cyclopaedia* in his short story, Poe hardly had a leg to stand on (Goodman,

Sun and the Moon, 160–61). Within a month the story was debunked, forcing Locke to justify his intention. He fell back on antislavery sarcasm: "We are curious to know whether *Lynch Law* exists amongst our lunar neighbors, or whether they have not yet arrived at this degree of *refinement*!" He ultimately argued that "abolition and astronomy being the only matters of exciting interest on the tapis," his newspaper had sought to tamp down the virulence of the former with the dreaminess of the latter (Locke quoted in Goodman, *Sun and the Moon,* 220–21).[33]

In truth, the convergence of abolition and astronomy in the United States began on February 12, 1831, when an annular eclipse cut a sickle-shaped swath from New England to Louisiana, linking the abolitionist Eastern Seaboard to the enslaving South. As the first solar eclipse in the United States since 1811, news of its occurrence was broadly disseminated. Abolitionists took it as a divine sign of emancipation: "The oppressed and enslaved of every country, Hayti and Virginia as well as France and Poland, have a right to assert their 'natural and inalienable rights' whenever and wherever they can," *The Massachusetts Journal* enthusiastically claimed in 1831.[34] An enslaved Virginian man envisioned the eclipse as manifesting the cosmic struggle between whiteness and blackness: "I had a vision—and I saw white spirits and black spirits engaged in battle, and the sun was darkened—the thunder rolled in the Heavens, and blood flowed in streams."[35] His name was Nat Turner. After the rebellion he led failed and he was arrested, his antiracist and mystical confessions transformed emancipation debates in antebellum America.[36] The wake of the Turner affair surfaced, for instance, in the 1834 Tappan Riots of Manhattan when white people hounded abolitionists and killed hundreds of African Americans because of a rumor that forced intermarriage had become a tenet of the abolitionist movement.[37] Locke hoped the Moon Hoax would distract the New York populace from the past year's murderous fake news.

His tale begins by painstakingly explaining the improvement in optical scale achieved by Herschel's twenty-four-foot mirror telescope—a size well beyond mirror-making technology of the time.[38] The telescope combined "artificial light" from a "hydro-oxygen" lamp with a solar microscope magnifying the image to project it "on the floor or on the wall of the apartment" with "a diameter of nearly fifty feet" (Griggs, *Celebrated "Moon Story,"* 63, 69).[39] The telescope was mounted on a clock-driven mechanism enabling observers to "detain the object upon the field of view for any period" (72). This design had been famously enacted in 1825 by Fraunhofer for the new meridian telescope at Dorpat, Estonia. Locke stated that Herschel changed the lens of the eyepiece to progressively heighten magnification, intensifying the sense of cinematic telepresence in his account. Lunar trees became visible "for a period of ten minutes" and "were followed by a level green plain" after which the observers "immediately perceived that we had been insensibly descending, as it were, a mountainous district" (73). Of course, lens changes can only produce an axial zoom effect, but Locke skillfully dovetails credible and incredible optics to generate a ubiquitous Oculus-like perception of the lunar surface. As a herd of unicorn goats appears into view, Locke writes: "The mimicry of its movements upon our white painted canvas was as faithful and luminous as that of animals within a few yards of a camera obscura, when seen pictured against its tympan [i.e., glass screen]. Frequently, when attempting to put our fingers upon its beard, it would suddenly bound away into oblivion, as if conscious of our earthly impertinence" (80). Accentuating moving image hyperpresence and haptic perception, this passage reveals Locke's familiarity with screen immersion projected from a camera obscura. Soon, humanlike creatures come into view, "four feet in height" and "covered, except on the face, with short and glossy copper-colored hair," with "wings composed of a thin membrane, without hair" (95). Their faces "of a yellowish flesh-color, [were] a slight improvement upon that of a large orang-outan, being more open and intelligent in [their] expression," and their mouths were "very prominent" with "lips far more human than those of any species of the simian genus" (95–96). This description of Lunarians as human–animal hybrids scarcely conceals racist stigmatization. Indeed, the telescope locates a second group of humanlike inhabitants of "a larger stature than the former specimens, less dark in color, and in *every respect* an improved variety of the race" (107–8). Locke's tale thus appears to be but another example of astroracialization transparently rehearsing anti-Blackness on the Moon. The

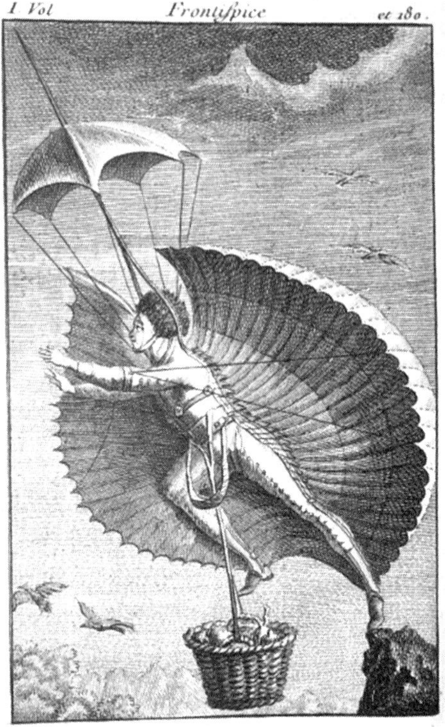

Figure 5.5. **Illustration for Restif de la Bretonne, *La Découverte australe par un homme-volant, ou le Dédale francais,* 2 vols. [The Austral discovery] (Leipzig, Germany: n.p, 1781), 6. Courtesy of La Bibliothèque Nationale de France.**

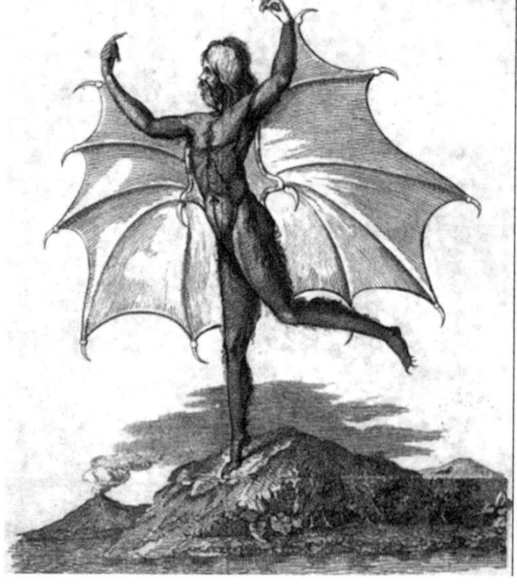

Figure 5.6. **Illustration of "Man-Bat" for "The Moon Hoax" in the Italian version. Leopoldo Galluzzo, *Altre scoverte fatte nella luna dal Sigr. Herschel* (Napoli, Italy: L. Gatti e Dura, 1836).**

fact that both races have dark skin, and that the "improved variety" built pyramids—hinting at Black Egyptian culture—does little to compensate for his traffic in racist stereotypes. Nor does his conclusion that a "universal state of amity among all classes of lunar creatures" reigns (109).[40]

During the whole affair—of which he heard with some delay—the real John Herschel resided in Cape Town, completing the laborious task entrusted by his late father of cataloging the southern skies.[41] He'd arrived in late 1833 when colonial administrators debated the time frame and logistics of freeing enslaved Khoisan, !Kung, and Xhosa peoples subsequent to the abolition act. As Elizabeth Green Musselman notes, among his first sights in South Africa was the taxidermized remains of a Khoisan woman kept by a local physician as a specimen of a "Venus Hottentot."[42] Herschel interacted with "coolies" hired for his astronomical work and described "Abdul" in a letter as "a fine Sultan-looking fellow" with "a noble intelligent good-natured black countenance" in contrast with "Thom," who was but "a low-looking thicklipped ugly Negro" (Herschel quoted in Musselman, "Swords into Ploughshares," 425). This purely visual racial hierarchy relies on just about the same stereotypes as Locke's. In a letter from Cape Town, Herschel starkly transduced visual racialization to the Moon itself: "The Moon at full—as it rises it presents a round, dull blotchy human face, with broad nose sulky mouth and standing perpendicularly has just the effect of some preternatural being—Demon—or god—of some barbarous nation looking down on its African territory & sniffing with sullen pleasure the scent of some bloody rite or looking down on the whole region as a scene of carnage agreeable to his nature & will. The European face is quite lost, by the reversal of its position" (425). The man in the Moon of the Northern Hemisphere appears transfigured from the antipode from a tacitly white face into the racialized mien of a cannibalistic African divinity—a photonegative. "The European face is quite lost, by the reversal of its position," Herschel fessed up, speaking about the Moon, his own loss of face, and the small white community surrounded with Black Indigenous people. Musselman argues that Herschel endeavored with local British representatives to dampen armed conflict between freed Khoisan peoples and

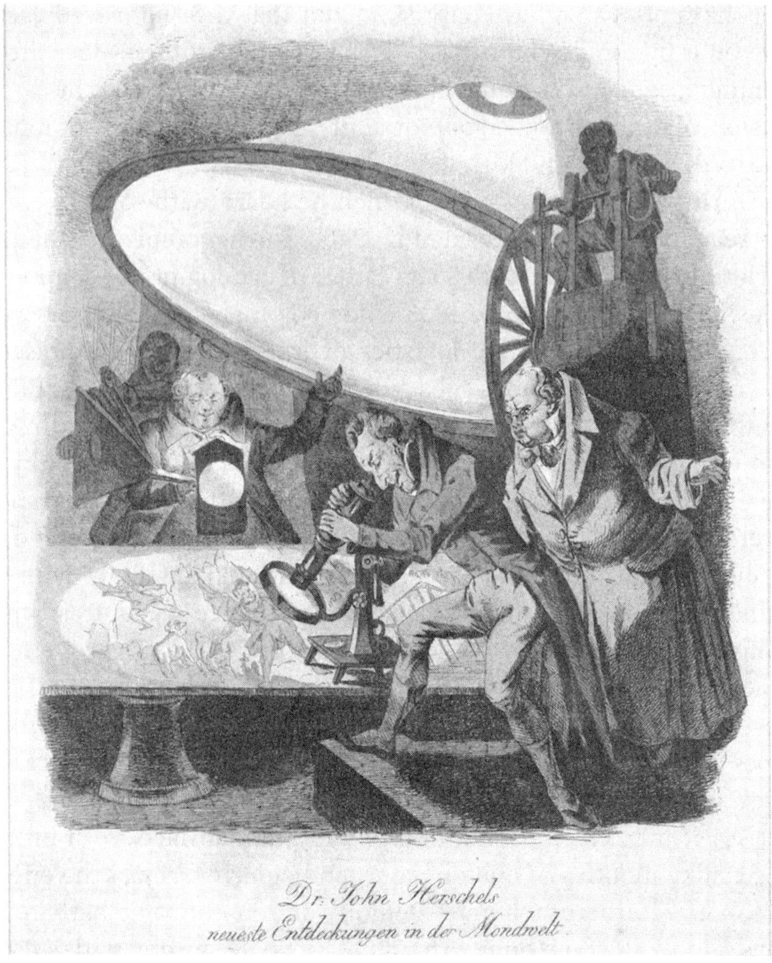

Figure 5.7. **"The Newest Discoveries of Dr. John Herschel in the Moon." The attendant manning the telescope (*top right*) may be Black. German print circa 1835. Courtesy of Cooper Hewitt Gallery, museum purchase through gift of the Estate of David Wolfe Bishop, 1957-162-11.**

Afrikaners and British troops, especially after a military massacre in December 1834. He vowed to work toward erasing "the humiliating distinction between master and slave" through education and social initiatives (429–30).[43] That distinction proves hard to overcome in his own words.

In 1852, *New York Sun* reporter William N. Griggs gave the Moon

Hoax a second life in book form. In his commentary, he makes technical observations worth citing at length for their photocinematic insightfulness:

> It will be seen, on reperusing [Locke's] description of the new Herschel telescope, that [Herschel] magnified the shadow or "focal object" of his mammoth lens, as projected upon a receiving screen, or tympan, like that of a camera obscure . . . and in the same manner that the solar picture in a daguerreotype may be indefinitely magnified, developed, and rendered more exquisitely distinct, by means either of that or any other magnifying instrument. In fact, the optical process suggested in this part of the "Moon Story," with some slight modifications, and so far as its mere magnifying and "distinctifying" functions are concerned, remains unexplored. . . . Indeed, it is . . . an anticipation, to no small extent, of the daguerreotype discovery, for it teaches the important principle, now fully verified, that focal objects, whether permanently fixed, or merely transient, after being received on any surface, may be further magnified, and rendered, at the same time, more distinct, when exposed to additional or artificial light. The realization of this fact, in relation to the telescopic image, was a desideratum in optical astronomy worthy of the profoundest research. (*Celebrated "Moon Story,"* 29)

What Griggs's halting and flowery language suggests is that the tale was prescient of how a high-resolution daguerreotype plate lends itself to progressive optical magnification, revealing more and more details, as if new images could flow from the single original plate. In so doing, Griggs embeds the cinematic purview of Locke's account within the daguerreotype—an oblique confirmation of the polyvalence of the photocinema as a matrix.

Pre-Photography and Abolition

Among the overlooked early precursors of photography was Henry Peter Brougham, who spearheaded the passage of emancipation legislation in 1833 as lord chancellor. In his posthumously published autobiography, Brougham claimed that in the summer of 1795 he submitted a draft paper to Charles Blagden, editor of the *Philosophical Transactions of the Royal Society of London,* where he described "having observed the effect of a small hole in the window-shutter of a darkened room, when a view is formed on white paper of the external objects, I had suggested that if that view if [*sic*] formed, not on paper, but on ivory rubbed with nitrate of silver, the picture would become permanent. . . . Now this is the origin of photography."[44] Helmut Gernsheim dismissed this claim as a "myth" but offered no justification for his assessment.[45] When Brougham attended the University of Edinburgh, he took chemistry classes with Joseph Black and counted Thomas Young as a fellow student. Brougham revered Black, who considered himself a disciple of Carl Wilhelm Scheele, and it is likely from Black that both Young and Brougham were trained in photochemistry (Brougham, *Life and Times of Henry,* 66). Edinburgh at that time was a hotbed of abolitionist thought—especially among medical doctors and chemists all too aware of the reliance of Scotland on Caribbean enslaving industries for its wealth.[46] Still a student, Brougham published two youthful articles on optics in the *Philosophical Transactions,* in 1796 and 1797, about the "flexion, or the bending of the rays in their passage by bodies," a nodal topic for the wave theory of light (WTL) as we saw throughout chapter 4.[47] Brougham experimented in a dark room with a pinhole and a prism to observe patterns of diffraction generated by interposing thin objects (blades, pins, holes), also using mirrors and putting some objects in motion. In 1853, he revisited these early experiments, sending two new essays to the *Philosophical Transactions* on "interference fringes" and the WTL, but the journal declined publication.[48]

Early surviving letters between Blagden and Brougham tend to confirm Brougham's version of events. After receipt of Brougham's first paper draft in 1795, Blagden sent back comments to Brougham, who responded in October 1795: "The Newtonian philosophy having now given way (in its turn) to the wonderful discoveries of modern chemistry and this induced me to add many of the queries which connect the two sciences together." With these words, Brougham explained the draft's disquisitions he proposed to take out, to which Blagden assented in February 1796.[49] These disquisitions must have concerned photochemistry, the clearest intersection of optics and chemistry, which Blagden must have judged beyond the paper's scope. Brougham's two articles multiply approximate, vainglorious, and confused hypotheses (akin in this to Jean-Paul Marat's claims). Occasionally, an inspired proposal pops up, such as the use of "an inclined mirror" to produce "flexions"—the idea Arago and Augustin-Jean Fresnel used in their twin mirror setup.

Brougham soon left natural philosophy behind to become a lawyer. He advocated for social causes like the democratization of education and in 1802 cofounded *The Edinburgh Review.* In 1803, he mounted an intense jingoistic attack against his former comrade Thomas Young, indicting his work on the WTL as anti-Newtonian and pro-French. His campaign succeeded and put an abrupt end to Young's research in physical optics. It is reasonable to assume that Brougham felt that Young, who made no bones about belittling Brougham's scientific achievements, cheated him out of his own ideas about interferences and perhaps photoimaging too, which were certainly earlier (but not of the same stature) than Young's.[50]

In 1803, Brougham published *An Inquiry into the Colonial Policy of the European Powers,* critiquing slavery from moral and realpolitik perspectives. He nonetheless called enslaved and free Black people, Haitian rebels, and Africans alike "savages" incapable of "industry."[51] Brougham turned into a dogged reformist and democratizer advocating for stigmatized populations, including workers and women, later playing a key role in the rise of the popular astronomy culture of the 1830s.[52] Starting in the 1810s, he made the abolition of slavery his signature mission, working on curbing the slave trade and pushing antislavery legislation for two decades, progressively amending his anti-Black sentiments. Elected to the House of Lords, then named chancellor, he finally passed the Slavery Abolition Act in 1833. It was a gradualist measure deferring full emancipation until 1840 and compensating enslavers for their economic losses—not enslaved people.

Brougham's 1795–1796 experiments with photochemical imaging, together with Arago's similar research in 1811 and 1821, suggest a tantalizing correlation between their pre-photographic work and their abolition legislation. As mentioned in the introduction, however, that correlation is dubious and likely weak, albeit not inexistent. A third unacknowledged proto-photographic experimenter, astronomer and anatomist John William Draper, allows us to probe it further. Originally from Lancashire, England, he was in the first class to attend University College London in 1829—a secular institution founded by James Mill and Brougham himself. After moving to the United States and receiving an MD, Draper was appointed head of chemistry in 1839 at New York University's planned medical school. Between 1834 and 1837, he conducted photochemical research in the hope of clarifying the relationship between visible light, chemical light (ultraviolet), and thermal light (infrared).[53] In 1834, he made the first attempt at photoimaging Fraunhofer's black "fixed lines of the spectrum" using "silver bromide."[54] In 1837, he replicated Arago and Fresnel's photochemical imaging of interference fringe patterns that confirmed the WTL: "The conclusion to be drawn from this result possesses no common interest . . . that light consists of undulations of an elastic medium."[55] Draper made sketches of the photoimaging prints showing interferences both via Newton rings and intersecting light waves forming a pointed oval (Draper, "Experiments on Solar Light," 44).[56]

He also found in 1837 that silver bromide could not register the light of the Moon—the third failed attempt at photographing the Moon. In 1842, he succeeded in making daguerreotypes of both spectroscopic lines of sunlight and interference fringes (Draper, "Experiments on Solar Light," 115–16; Hyde, "John William Draper," 1727). He also noticed that silver compounds do not react to refracted light the same way as the human eye, understanding at about the same time as Daguerre that photography required lenses leaning toward the blue end of the spectrum. Draper's theoretical and empirical understanding of physical optics, photochemistry, and pre-photography was comparable only to that of John Herschel and Arago at the time. His overlooked work confirms the thesis that physical optics and the testing of the WTL were central to the development of photography. After learning of the daguerreotype, Draper quickly worked out a new paper process and produced the first photographic portrait in 1840: that of a white woman who was his assistant, her face covered with a thin layer of flour enhancing contrast. Over the next few years, Draper believed he discovered a new kind of ray that he called "tithonic," bridging the natural philosophy of William Herschel's "black-making rays" in the late 1790s with Thomas Edison's infamous experimental discovery of the "etheric force" in the 1870s.[57] Around the time of the Civil War, his appointment as dean of New York University's medical school led him to enter national debates about abolition—which he favored. After emancipation, nonetheless, refocusing his research on dynamic physiology, he became a central proponent of the new scientific racism connecting human phenotypes and craniology to civilizational attainments. I examine this work in chapter 6 because it parallels that of physiologist Étienne-Jules Marey as factoring in the emergence of precinema. As to the correlation between pre-photography and abolition, what Draper confirms as an astronomer is that photologists like Brougham and Arago (and, before them, Pierre-Louis Moreau de Maupertuis, David Rittenhouse, and Condorcet) seemed prone to engage with the optical aspects of racial difference, which may have influenced their favoring abolition. But that did not prevent most of them from adopting racist and especially anti-Black stances.

Photography and Abolition: Frederick Douglass

During the short-lived revolutions of 1848, as soon as he was named minister of the navy and colonies in late February, Arago declared that abolition was integral to the revolution's call for liberty. He informed colonial governors that immediate emancipation was forthcoming.[58] In March, he named Victor Schoelcher head of the Commission for the Abolition of Slavery, charged with drafting a law to be ratified by the National Assembly. By April, however, opposition by enslavers and delays with electing the assembly convinced Arago to adopt Schoelcher's draft abolition without further delays by executive decree. Arago and eleven members of the provisional government signed it into law.

Arago's overall views on race were divergent, especially when it came to the Arab Muslim populations of the Maghreb, which came under French control after 1830. While he explained in his memoirs that he owed his life to Muslim sailors who refused to give him up to a force dispatched by the dey of Algiers in 1809, as a French elected official he voiced anti-Arab and anti-Muslim sentiments.[59]

Raised in a liberal centrist family with ten siblings, Arago progressively embraced republicanism and democratic rights in the 1830s and 1840s.[60] His younger brother Étienne was close to Schoelcher after the latter turned toward immediatism in the early 1840s. A radical socialist and Carbonari, Étienne turned to journalism and theater before becoming a leader of the 1830 July Revolution.[61] In 1836, he collaborated in a vaudeville act titled "Paris in the Comet"—leveraging popular excitement over the 1834 comet—which included a cameo played by "a man half-black, half-white, African on one side, European on the other," dramatizing the plight of mixed-race peoples. This showed—like the Great Moon Hoax a year later—how astronomy lent itself to racial commentary.[62] A close friend of the Arago brothers was Alexandre Dumas, the leading mixed-race figure in 1830s France and the prime target of newspapers controlled by the enslaver lobby. A third brother, Jacques Arago, gave international antislavery efforts higher visibility. A member of a circumterrestrial scientific expedition from 1817 to 1820, Jacques published *Voyage Around the World* upon his return. This four-volume account of his travels turned into a bestseller by 1823 when it was translated into English, in part because its ethnotourism denounced slavery graphically from firsthand observation in Brazil, the Caribbean, and the Southern United States.[63] Documenting Pacific Islander culture, some of Jacques's drawings are now considered a primary source of information for historians and Native activists, although Jacques exoticized and exploited Native women.[64] The fourth brother, Jean Arago, was an army soldier who fled France and joined the Mexican War of Independence in 1817, taking the side of Antonio López de Santa Anna and ending as a general in the corps of engineers. The Arago brothers certainly counted among the most prorevolutionary and antiracist families in early nineteenth-century France.

When Frederick Douglass heard of the revolution of 1848 in France, he wrote an editorial in *The North Star* entitled "France" on April 28, 1848—not yet apprised of the emancipation decree signed the day before:

> Thanks to steam navigation and electric wire, we may almost hear the words uttered, and see the deeds done, as they transpire. A revolution

> now cannot be confined to the place or the people where it may commence, but flashes with lightning speed from heart to heart, from land to land, till it has traversed the globe, compelling all the members of our common brotherhood at once, to pass judgment upon its merits. The revolution of France, like a bolt of living thunder, has aroused the world from its stupor.
>
> . . .
>
> There are only two classes in this country who are in a position sincerely to sympathise with France in her present glorious struggle in behalf of liberty, and these are the negroes and Abolitionists.[65]

Douglass was aware of Arago's abolition program prior to the decree and took the revolution in France as a global event that would hopefully recharge the momentum of abolition in the United States. The instantaneity rhetoric of "lightning speed" and "bolt of living thunder" "travers[ing] the globe" combines revolutionary energy, new technics of photography and the telegraph, and, of course, immediatism. Celebrating the burgeoning African American press, Douglass declared in January 1848, "Facts are facts: white is not black, and black is not white," a justification for an independent Black press and something of a final rejoinder to the black-and-white rhetoric crisscrossing race and pre- and early photography.[66]

Douglass's now well-studied approach to photography aimed at undoing the racial and racist rhetoric that caricatured and mischaracterized Black experience without giving African Americans the right to self-represent. He made his own self-portraiture into an activist weapon, posing for hundreds of photographs, most often sporting an uncompromising demeanor as if to command the recognition of Black dignity.[67] In a famous 1863 lecture on photography, "Pictures and Progress," Douglass wrote: "Daguerre, by simple but all abounding sunlight has converted the planet into a picture gallery. . . . Men of all conditions may see themselves as others see them."[68] For Douglass, the power of the daguerreotype came from sunlight at last put in the service of the global equality of representation—an objective form of photoimaging issued from our nearest star in the cosmos. Henry Louis Gates Jr. keenly analyzes the chiasmic mastery with which Douglass leveraged photography to recast at once the black/white binary and the power of self-representation within the horizon of abolition.[69] For Gates, the technical gaze of photography served first "to *erase* the astonishingly large storehouse of racist stereotypes," to replace it with the opportunity of "visualizing ourselves *doing* an action and reflecting upon it as we do it, rendering the subjective 'objective,' giving it form" (Gates, "Frederick Douglass's Camera Obscura," 46, 59). In this purview, photography is more an apparatus of visualization than vision, an emancipative instrument for reconstructing Black sovereignty to come, not just memorializing one's likeness.

Commenting on "Pictures and Progress," Ginger Hill notes that this "perceptual constitution of interiority" for African Americans was construed by Douglass through what he calls "thought pictures."[70] These visualizations represent for Hill a "universal vernacular" enabling anyone regardless of their level of instruction "to internally imagine forms" and develop an "object-seeking drive" that could foster a sense of agency toward the goal of changing the world (Hill, "'Rightly Viewed,'" 55). Douglass writes that "rightly viewed, the whole soul of man is a sort of picture gallery[,] a grand panorama, in which the great *facts* of the universe, the *tracings* of *time* and *things* of eternity are painted" ("Pictures and Progress," cited in Hill, "'Rightly Viewed,'" 42). These thought-pictures correlate not to photographs but rather to photoimaging as spontaneous imprints from nature, unbiased by prejudiced culture, especially the gamut of white calibration. Thought-pictures together with photographic portraits confound fictional and phobic racist representations disseminated by cheap reprography technologies such as stereotyping in the first part of the nineteenth century. But thought-pictures cannot be static since they form a virtual reserve of future representations and actions, while they also bear the marks and movements of history. These "*tracings* of *time,*" then, are more akin to the self-traced graphs at the origin of cinema.

6

The Graphic Method
Time-Tracing, Colonial Supremacy, and Astrophotography

This universal language . . . exists for science. . . . The graph comprises all the signs of the natural representation of objects, their shape, and their changes of state.
—ÉTIENNE-JULES MAREY, "Du mouvement dans les fonctions de la vie" (my translation)

Reframing Photography as a Time-Tracing Technology

If in Frederick Douglass's hopeful perspective (see chapter 5), photography's "*tracings* of *time*" indexed Black and global emancipation, for Étienne-Jules Marey they represented a new "universal" tool for science and Western positivism. In the French-accented story of how cinema was implemented, Marey's graphic method functions as the hinge paradigm.[1] *Graphic method* is his proprietary term for analog apparatuses recording time or motion in visual and measurable traces from the mid-1860s. At the dawn of the Darwinian era, Marey promoted his method as a revolutionary innovation for physiological research on inner and outer body functions, from pulse to locomotion and animal flight. For scholars of modernity, it crystallized the rise of time-picturing culture and a decisive break with centuries of static representation. Its application to photography directly ushered in cinema.[2]

As the story goes, inspired by Eadweard Muybridge's multiple-camera sequences of animal locomotion from 1877, Marey opted for a single-camera with multiple exposures on a single plate. He initially called this adaptation of the graphic method "photochronography"—I'll return to this crucial term—before adopting *chronophotography* in 1886.[3] In 1888, he replaced the single plate with a light-sensitive paper strip on which each exposure was separate, producing the first bona fide pictures of motion. Meeting Marey at the International Exposition of 1889 in Paris, Thomas Edison was shown his flexible-strip camera and soon jettisoned the cylindrical chronophotographic setup he had been working on in favor of celluloid (Braun, *Picturing Time,* 151–53). The Muybridge–Marey–Edison axis of chronophotography forms the core of the accepted history of precinema.

This chapter and the next argue that this story gives short shrift to longer technical developments and truncates crucial historical contexts through which sequential photographic recording was introduced and adopted. I focus in this chapter on the genealogy of self-recording instrumentation, its applications for atmospheric research and astrophotography, and its intersections with the study of temporality in human vision. All these strands were deployed prior to Marey as part of the competitive imperialist ambitions of nineteenth-century Western state science and technology that informed Marey's physiological research as well.

Self-Tracing Instruments from the Seventeenth Century to Marey

The earliest time-tracing apparatuses appear to have been contemporaneous with the arrival of the telescope. Anselmus de Boodt, a naturalist and draftsman from Bruges, Belgium, is credited with an odometer-and-compass apparatus with punch-hole registration on a paper strip around 1610. It was likely devised within the new logic of engineering compendia known as the "theater of machines," in which simple devices were experimentally combined, often for aspirational applications.[4] Yet until the well-publicized construction of a pendulum clock by Christiaan Huygens in 1657, time-tracing technology stalled. In the 1660s, Christopher Wren designed a weather clock with paper-and-pencil registration on both cylinder and disk: Robert Hooke is said to have built a prototype after this design in 1678–1679 with a punch-hole recording system.[5] Another similar apparatus was constructed by Louis Léon Pajot d'Ons-en-Bray, who gathered one of the finest collections of scientific instruments and "devices of wonder" in the eighteenth century, including a scrolling panorama box.[6] In 1734, d'Ons-en-Bray published an illustrated article on a clock-driven anemometer that traced wind speed on a gridded paper cylinder and wind direction on a soot-covered cylinder. This is the first self-tracing instrument reliably known to have been built and used.[7] Tremor-recording devices were constructed following the 1755 earthquake that devastated Lisbon and the deadly 1783 Calabria earthquakes, with both sand-tracing and ink-brush pendulum setups.[8] Nonetheless, it is fair to say that from the 1600s to the late 1700s, self-recording machines remained marginal and fell short of real-world applications.

In 1795, one of the founders of the Royal Society of Edinburgh, Alexander Keith, built a weather station with a recording cylinder thermometer. His description contains a novel insight:

> And as the pencil rises or falls by heat and cold, it will mark the degrees on the scale of the cylinder; and the cylinder being constantly revolving, the division for each day will successively be marked by the pencil, which will leave a trace, describing an undulated line. . . . These papers, when taken off and bound together, will make a complete register of the temperature for the year; or, if they are pasted to one another . . . the variations of heat and cold, during the year, may all be seen and compared by one glance of the eye.[9]

This passage exhibits the same imperative of visualizing and quantifying duration that informed Jacques Barbeu-Dubourg's 1756 chronographic machine. It too favored the cylinder over disks, plates, pendulums, and hole-punching systems.[10] Thomas Young certainly knew Keith's weather recorder (he was at Edinburgh University in 1795) and provided the first general account of self-tracing technology in an 1807 lecture given at the Royal Institution. He describes a "chronometer . . . for measuring small portions of time" consisting

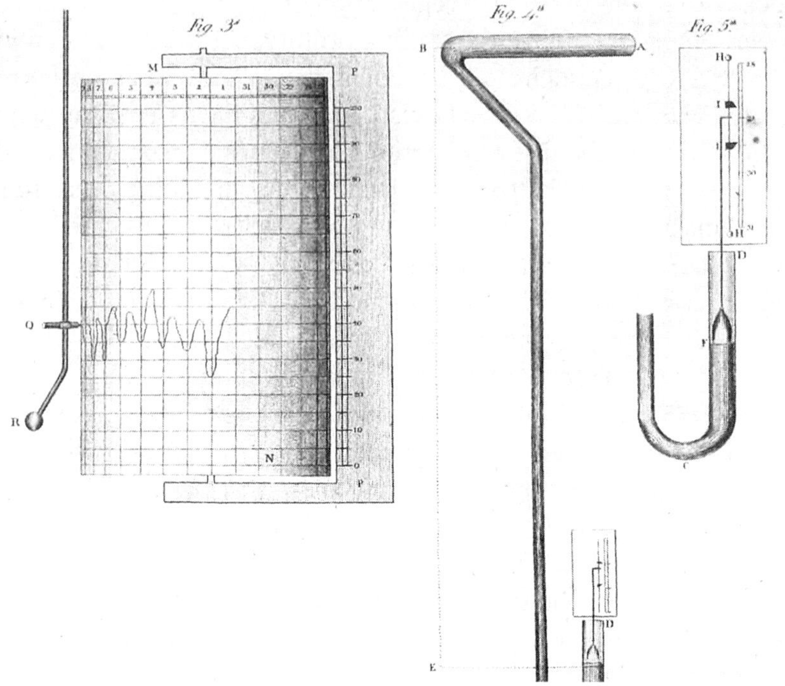

Figure 6.1. **Self-recording thermometer. Alexander Keith, *Transactions of the Royal Society of Edinburgh* 4, no. 2 (1798): 208. Courtesy of the Royal Society of Edinburgh.**

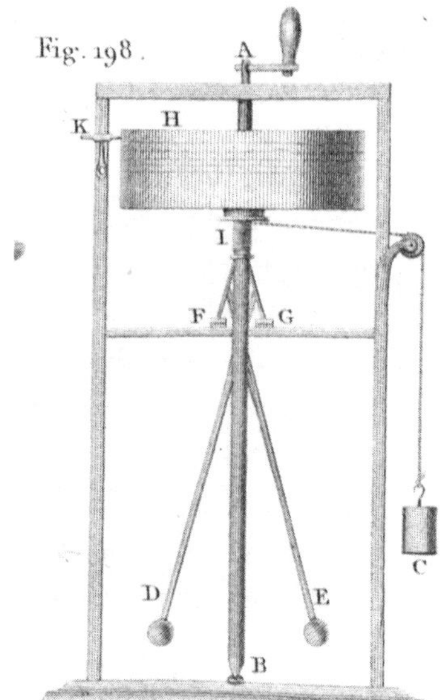

Figure 6.2. **Weight-driven self-recording cylinder, "chronometer." Thomas Young, *A Course of Lectures on Natural Philosophy and the Mechanical Arts*, 2 vols. (London: Joseph Johnson, 1807), 772, plate XV, figure 198. Courtesy of ETH-Bibliothek Zürich.**

of a weight-activated, revolving and descending cylinder on which a fixed needle traced the vibrations of an object or tuning fork. The cylinder's "surface, being smooth, may be covered either with paper or with wax, and a pencil or a point of metal may be pressed against it by a fine spring, so as to describe always a spiral on the barrel." Young expressly calls it a "chronometer" that can graph "the motion of any other body."[11] Importantly, this apparatus aimed either at tracing continuous durations or registering quantifiable variations. This double function split into two types of graphic recording setups by the mid-nineteenth century, which Marey's graphic method straddled. Young's chronometer applied to the recording of sound inspired the prototypes of Charles Cros's and Edison's cylinder phonograph designs, with reversible recording and playing functions, both in 1877. However, Camille Flammarion's cinema apparatus of 1867, the telechronoscope, had preceded these audio applications. Flammarion replaced the wax in Young's chronometer with miniature photographs arrayed in a helix around the cylinder. William Kennedy Laurie Dickson and Edison adopted the same design for their 1888 kinetoscope (see chapter 7).

Young's chronometer bespeaks a new valence of time-tracing technicity at the start of the nineteenth century. Durations became both longer in theory and smaller in practice. The age of Earth was pushed back to several millions, then tens of millions of years by the 1830s, while at the opposite end the second was broken down. Swiss clockmaker Abraham-Louis Breguet, who worked in the Île de la Cité in Paris from the 1770s through the Revolution and Empire, was the chief horological and aesthetic innovator. His self-winding perpetual motion clock of 1780, his 1801 tourbillon mechanism anachronistically named after René Descartes's vortex theory, and the addition of "moon-tip" hands and sun-and-moon dials in thinned-out pocket watches all invoked astronomical durations to vouchsafe portable timekeepers' precision. Breguet came from the same upwardly mobile class of petit bourgeois technician-scientists as his close friend Jean-Paul Marat, whose sister Anne-Marie worked with Breguet. Both émigrés and anglophiles from Neuchâtel, Switzerland, they saved each other's lives during the Revolution despite their diverging political allegiances.[12] Breguet's craftsmanship made him among the instrument-makers most prized by the Paris Observatory. In September 1813, François Arago named him official timekeeper of that institution; meeting notes from 1819 indicate that Breguet had "brought a useful amelioration to the mechanism he has imagined for splitting a second into ten equal parts."[13] Among Breguet's apprentices was Louis Moinet, his right-hand assistant after 1811. An amateur astronomer, in 1816 Moinet built a chronometer (compteur de tierces) with a precision of one-sixtieth of a second, which he adapted to telescope eyepieces to improve the recording of celestial coordinates.[14]

In propounding his graphic method, Marey is rather succinct about this long tradition of self-recording instruments. A footnote from an 1867 lecture indicates that he learned that history from the grandson of Breguet, Louis-François-Clément Breguet, the engineer who built Marey's first sphygmograph in 1859. L.-F.-C. Breguet knew the history of self-tracing instruments from d'Ons-en-Bray to Young, and Marey points in particular to the up-and-down motion of Young's cylinder, thanks to which "the graph . . . inscribes itself in the form of a helix, which can be very long."[15] The construction and use of self-recording cylindrical apparatuses took off in the first decades of the nineteenth century, with an early model built in 1808 in Germany by Johann Albert Eytelwein, followed by French

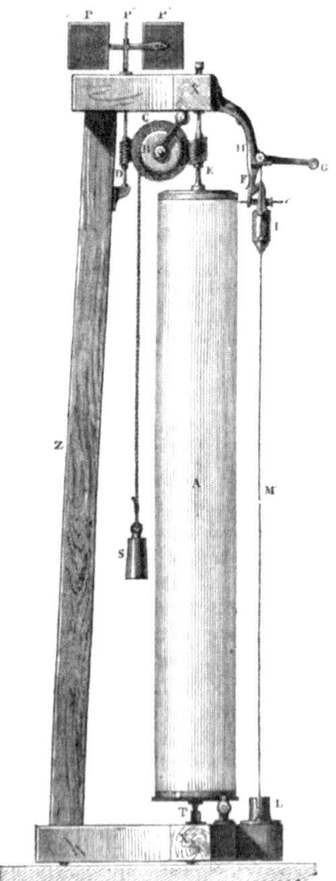

Figure 6.3. **Chronometer modeled after Morin, 1829. [Étienne-Jules] Marey, "De La Production du mouvement chez les animaux,"** ***Revue des cours scientifiques de la France et de l'étranger*** **14 (March 2, 1867): 213. Courtesy of La Bibliothèque Nationale de France Gallica.**

military engineers endeavoring to quantify the speed, friction, and forces of propelled gun shells, illustrating the continued closeness of photocinema prototechnologies with military and colonial power.[16] Working for the War Ministry in the late 1820s, engineer Arthur Jules Morin developed a vertical cylinder machine tracing the parabolic curves of falling bodies that he too called "a chronometer."[17] Marey provides an illustration for it in an 1866 article, while stating in another essay that it was "the first among recording machines"—a nationalist exaggeration.[18]

Electrification made cylinder self-recording devices among the most polyvalent new instruments for research and industrial applications in the second half of the nineteenth century. British polymath Charles Wheatstone designed and built the first electrical cylinder recording machines in the early 1840s. Growing up in his father's musical instrument business, Wheatstone, like Young, worked across acoustics, optics, horology, and electricity—waveform industrial arts. In 1834, he devised an ingenious setup to time the speed of electricity in a copper wire and was recognized as among the best experimental scientists of England. He expressly cites Young's cylinder tracing chronometer as his inspiration.[19] Wheatstone is on record as having explained the principle of his "chronoscope" to astronomer Adolphe Quetelet in 1840, which later helped invalidate L.-F.-C. Breguet's 1845 nationalistic claim of priority for its invention.

There were two main types of cylinder recording machines based on the same setup: an electrical circuit turning on and off an electromagnet connected both to a clock and the rotating cylinder equipped with a graphing stylus.[20] The interval chronoscope served to record a precise duration for applications in mechanics, ballistics, nerve signal research, and synchronization. The other type, a tracing chronograph, aimed at imaging a continuous variable phenomenon as a graphic curve, with applications for navigation, meteorology, physiology, and power engines. The three terms—*chronometer, chronograph,* and *chronoscope*—remained interchangeable in practice. Graphic electro-chronometers of both kinds were especially tied to geophysical and astronomical research because of the new electromagnetic paradigm. Multiple innovations around electricity from the 1810s to the 1830s (batteries, electromagnets, conduction, production, relays, etc.) led to a boom in electrical technologies such as the telegraph, which came into use after 1837, with a patent by Wheatstone and William Fothergill Cooke. Telegraphic electrification and natural disturbances in telegraphic transmission soon evinced the idea that the Earth was a giant electrical object: the "theory of the Earth circuit."[21] The dream that communication could take place directly through Earth's electromagnetic field, resulting in a single panhuman "body electric" (to echo Walt Whitman's 1855 poem), was reinforced by the laying of submarine cables in the 1850s, before a powerful solar magnetic storm destroyed many telegraph lines in 1859. Quetelet commented in 1840 that electricity in telegraphic wires could transmit "signals with the speed of thought, since in the span of one second they could go around the globe six or seven times."[22] Admiring Wheatstone's self-recording telegraphic weather stations mounted on balloons or lowered down mining shafts, the popularizer François-Napoléon-Marie Moigno exclaimed in 1849: "Here the imagination is truly awed. The depths of space and the abyss are now accessible. You put an inert instrument there, and space and the abyss take it upon themselves to send you instantaneously the indications of atmospheric pressure, temperature, and humidity you wanted, which arrive as if by magic in your laboratory. . . . Yesteryear it was light that became for us an astounding drawing artist, today it is the whole of nature that paints itself before our eyes."[23] Self-tracing instruments were thus central for the mid-nineteenth-century technocratic project of making all aspects of the natural world visible. But Moigno suggested also that chronographic recording technology was a conceptual expansion of photography—that is, in retrospect, an intermediary step from photography to cinema. That is the reason why Marey coined

Figure 6.4. (*Top*) **Cylinder actinograph holding both strip and disk sensitive plates. (*Below*) thermographic strips (top three) and photographic strips (bottom two) recording heat and light. John F. Herschel, "On the Chemical Action of the Rays of the Solar Spectrum on Preparations of Silver and Other Substances, Both Metallic and Non-Metallic, and on Some Photographic Processes," *Philosophical Transactions of the Royal Society of London* 130 (1840): 50, 54. Courtesy of the Royal Society.**

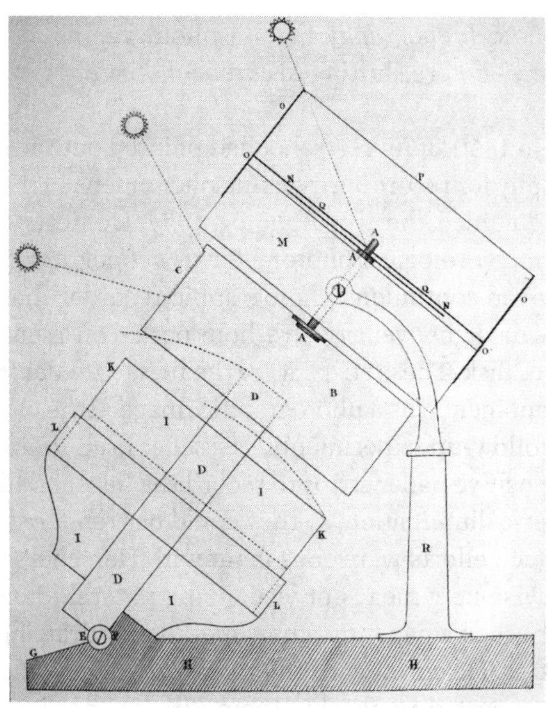

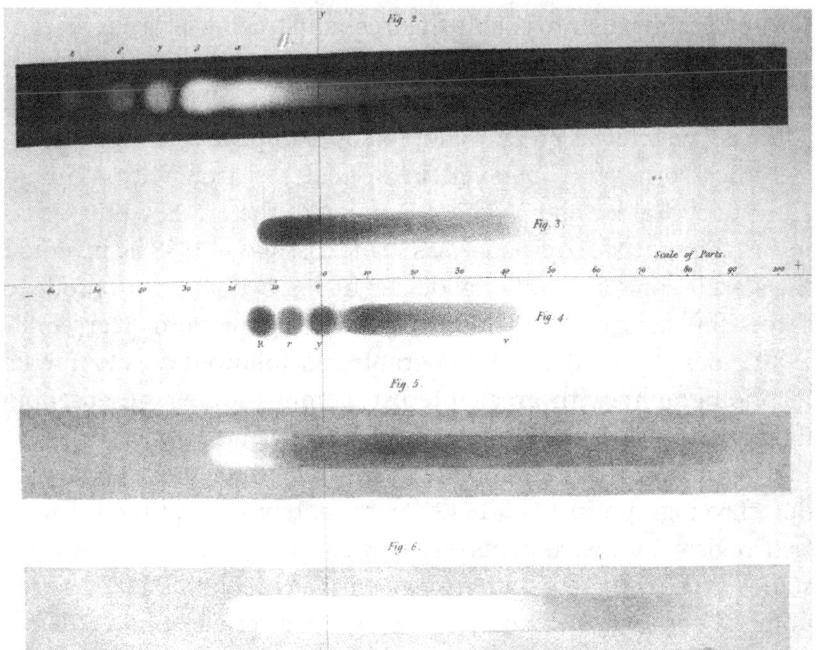

Fig. 2.

Fig. 3.

Fig. 4.

Fig. 5.

Fig. 6.

the word *photochronography* first—a photographic application of chronography—before shifting to *chronophotography,* the picturing of time.

Already in 1840, John Herschel had pointed out the capabilities of photography for recording dynamic phenomena in the very essay in which he coined the word *photography.* He describes "a self-registering meteorological photometer or *actinograph,*" a cylindrical clock-driven continuous photographic recorder that registered variations of daylight over a twelve-hour period on a sensitive paper strip or paper disk. These strips were the first to render visible a durational phenomenon as a photographic image—true chronophotographs. In follow-up experiments, Herschel used thermosensitive and photosensitive paper strips to record the heat and light spectra of atmospheric illumination, so they could be "rendered sensible to the eye."[24] Such efforts were consonant with Herschel's broader attempt to devise new means of visualizing natural phenomena. In 1833, he published a paper on a new method for drawing the orbits of double stars. He considered this "process . . . essentially graphical," and it consisted in plotting the positions of binary stars over time on graph paper to enable the freehand tracing of "a curve . . . of large and graceful sinuosity," which represented their respective elliptical orbits. In 1849, he refined what he then called his "graphical process," which was quickly adopted by European astronomers.[25]

Wheatstone was involved in optical research with William Henry Fox Talbot and Michael Faraday in the 1830s while working on the spectroscopic analyses of metals, and in 1838 he invented the stereoscope, a sensational device fusing two images to produce three-dimensional visual perception. He knew John Herschel's 1840 clock-driven drum actinograph and followed developments in photography with great interest, commissioning stereoscopic daguerreotypes from French physicist Armand-Hippolyte-Louis Fizeau in 1842.[26] Wheatstone built his first paper-recording cylinder chronograph in 1842–1843 for "a meteorological record with 'self-registering instruments on a new construction,'" which was installed at the new Kew station located in the decommissioned astronomical observatory.[27] Just thirteen years after Nicéphore Niépce came to Kew, "self-registering instruments" were deployed there to image graphically the variations of atmospheric temperature, pressure, electricity, humidity, and wind speed.

By the mid-1850s, electrically driven cylinder-recordings were used in dozens of applications and described and illustrated in scientific and popular publications.[28] They acquired a particular urgency in the United States. To become a full partner with Europe in world affairs, the country needed key data for its global linkage: synchronized time and exact transatlantic distance. Calculating the longitude of American locations compared to the Greenwich and Paris meridians became an urgent priority for the US Coast Survey. A Boston clockmaker and amateur astronomer tackled that issue while working unpaid at Harvard: William Cranch Bond. In September 1848, with his son George Phillips Bond, he discovered a new satellite of Saturn—the first major discovery in the solar system since William Herschel found Saturn's Mimas in 1797. The new Saturnian moon, which he named Hyperion, was simultaneously discovered in England by William Lassell, yet the two sets of coordinates could not be compared for lack of longitude reconciliation, depreciating Bond's discovery. With other American astronomers, Bond worked to remedy the situation throughout the 1840s by shipping chronometers back and forth to the Greenwich Observatory—116 in thirty-four crossings in 1848 alone—to compute longitude.[29] In 1849, drum chronographs were used to register the transit of a star at the meridian of several telegraphically linked observatories in New York, Cambridge, Massachusetts, and Philadelphia, comparing their recordings to solar and sidereal clocks to establish respective longitudes (Holden, *Memorial,* 239–42). Synchronization remained problematic because the rotary motion of the chronographs was irregular due to the clocks' escapement mechanisms, occasioning asynchronies. The problem was solved by Bond, helped by his two clock-making sons George and Richard, with a "spring-governor" chronograph that achieved near-perfect rotary continuity in 1850 (243–46). The Bonds' so-called American method of electromagnetic paper-drum chronography, linking astronomical observatories by telegraph, became the most reliable means of coordinating the longitude and time of distant locales.[30]

From this quick survey of self-tracing cylinder instrumentation, we can draw three conclusions. First, astronomer John Herschel's 1840 actinograph attests that photography was entangled with the recording of duration from its very beginning. By 1860, Herschel envisioned "the stereoscopic representation of scenes in action" using photographic shots taken at intervals of "a tenth of a second"—a prototype of 3D cinema.[31] Second, the development of the self-registering electromagnetic chronoscope/chronograph cylinder by Wheatstone in 1842 was directly influenced by Young's chronometer and Herschel's actinograph. Third, two innovations in astronomy—Herschel's development of a "graphical process" between 1833 and 1849, and the Bonds' American method correcting the uneven rotation of electro-chronographic cylinders by 1851—prepared Marey's vaunted graphic method, the first theoretically and the second technically. The initial apparatus Marey perfected in 1859, the sphygmograph, was a portable clock-driven device tracing human pulse on a soot-covered "small plate of glass or metal."[32] Better informed about chronographic technologies, in the early 1860s he adopted the cylinder chronograph as his main operational setup.

Visual Duration and Ocular Hieroglyphs

An important factor behind the emergence of time-tracing technologies in the 1840–1850s was the development of temporal research in vision studies. It is significant for understanding late developments of photocinema for three reasons. First, it further complicates the simplistic paradigm that Marey's chronophotography just added time to photography across a conceptual and technological void of forty years. Second, vision research showed that human eyes are neither instantaneous nor passive optical receptors; they are coproducers of inherently dynamic visual images, and instrumentation was devised to simulate such dynamic imaging. And third, the class of images produced by human vision and its simulators had a distinct family resemblance with the earlier class of hieroglyphic imprints (see chapter 4).

Robert Darwin, Erasmus Darwin, Samuel Taylor Coleridge, and Johann Wolfgang von Goethe were all fascinated by afterimages and other ocular spectra between the 1780s and the 1810s because their ambiguous status—partly phenomenal and partly subjective—fueled

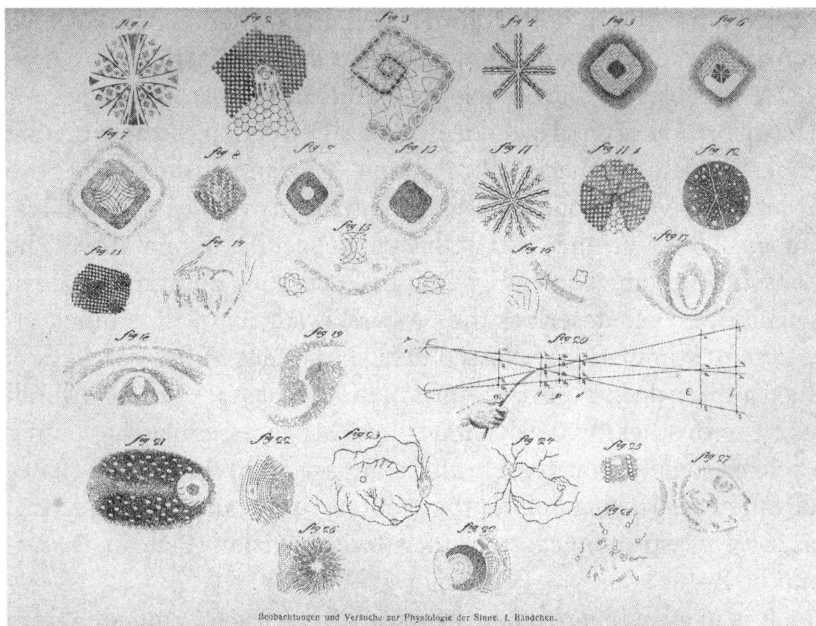

Figure 6.5. **Intraocular images produced by pressure, electricity, motion, etc. Johann Purkinje, *Beiträge zur Kenntnis des Sehens in subjektiver Hinsicht* (Prague: Calve, 1819), 178. Courtesy of ETH-Bibliothek Zürich.**

the quest for metaphysical bonds between humans and the physical world (see chapter 4). In 1819, Czech anatomist Jan Evangelista Purkinje published his dissertation about experiments on "vision in its subjective aspects," meaning visual phenomena endemic to the eyes. Purkinje produced and analyzed instances of afterimages, pressure images, galvanic images, entoptic images (of blood vessels), peripheral vision, double vision, unfocalized sight, floaters, and visual deformations due to motions of the eyes or the body. He collected them into a new category of visual patterns that disclosed hidden physiological functions of the human visual apparatus.[33] Purkinje showed that human eyes produced streams of automatic images that were kinemorphic and nonmimetic.

In 1828, Joseph Antoine Ferdinand Plateau wrote his PhD dissertation "On Some Properties of the Impressions Produced by Light on the Organ of Sight," investigating photosensitive processes within the human eye. His director was astronomer Adolphe Quetelet, who corresponded with both John Herschel and Arago and played an outsized role in the adoption of graphs as visualization tools.[34] In 1824, Quetelet read an article by Peter Mark Roget puzzling over the distortion of carriage wheel spokes in rotation, suggesting that topic for Plateau's thesis. Like Purkinje, Plateau transformed the eye from a passive photographic-like organ into a complex psychophysiological medium endowed with its own peculiar temporality: "The sensations produced in us by light have a certain duration," Plateau concluded.[35] He describes the process as starting with a quick increase of stimulation, followed by a short stage of full perception, then a sharp decline of visual information. He associated this overall curve with other known dynamic physical processes like the cooling cycle or sonic resonance. He also compared it to the path of "igneous meteors leaving behind them a long luminous trail," injecting, as it were, astronomical trajectories within vision (Plateau, *Dissertation,* 17–18).

It is in a complementary theory of afterimage phenomena from 1834 that Plateau coined the expression "persistence of impressions" in the retina.[36] Synthesizing prior research, he shows that natural vision and afterimages form colors in opposite ways and formulates the following law: "*In all cases when natural colors produce* WHITE *by their combination, afterimage colors of the same hues produce the opposite of white,* BLACK" (Plateau, *Essai d'une Théorie générale,* 49). He then redefines afterimage vision as "*negative vision*" by contrast with positive natural vision (58–59), and it is likely from this essay that John Herschel developed his own ideas of positive and negative images (see chapter 5). When natural vision is exposed to the motion of a lit object, Plateau affirms that a complex "oscillation" of positive and negative impressions occurs (60). On this basis, he offers a concluding definition: "The interval elapsing between the instant when the retina is removed from the action of a colored object, and that when the impression starts taking a negative state constitute what we mean by PERSISTENCE OF IMPRESSIONS ON THE RETINA; and the negative phases of the impression constitute the phenomenon of accidental colors [afterimages]" (64). Plateau does not posit, interestingly, that the perception of visual motion devolves from positive impressions melding with one another; quite the contrary, he documents visual experiments where positive and negative impressions mutate into each other with sequential oscillations (61).

The research of Purkinje and Plateau weakened the camera obscura model of vision. While Jonathan Crary famously argues in a Foucauldian vein that this took place in the 1820s when "the physiology and temporality of the human body" came to the fore, Crary leaves unexamined the role of motion and duration in vision.[37] Yet, accounting for these new dimensions of sight led vision researchers in the wake of Purkinje and Plateau to investigate visual and ophthalmic temporal subprocesses not just by generating ophthalmic imaging but by constructing devices able to produce, simulate, and test such images. The stroboscopic disks and the rotating phenakistoscope drum devised quasi-simultaneously by Plateau and Simon von Stampfer (who also worked in astronomy) in the early 1830s were no mere philosophical toys; they were kinemorphic imaging simulators. Plateau's most intriguing device was the anorthoscope, two spinning disks with cutout portions spinning in opposite directions that generated a stable pattern. Plateau commented that "in the mist of the sort of gauze produced by the motion of both lines," a paradoxically static image appeared that he called "the flying heart" (*Dissertation,* 20). While Niépce and Louis Daguerre were wrestling with parasitical motion in long-exposure photography, a new species of image emerged that was neither static nor in motion, blurring the lines between the two traditionally antagonistic categories of imaging.

For vision researchers, the new duration of simulated imaging became a key to understanding human vision.[38] In 1825, John Herschel's musings on the topic led to the invention of the thaumatrope, a small device fusing recto-verso afterimages by quickly flipping between them.[39] The question of visual motion synthesis, as observed in afterimage trails generated by a whirled branch with a burning tip—a perennial source of puzzlement since antiquity—came to the fore.[40] In December 1830, electrophysicist Michael Faraday published an article about experiments with spinning wheels that created both static and moving stroboscopic images. His conclusions indicated that visual motion was still difficult to conceptualize and,

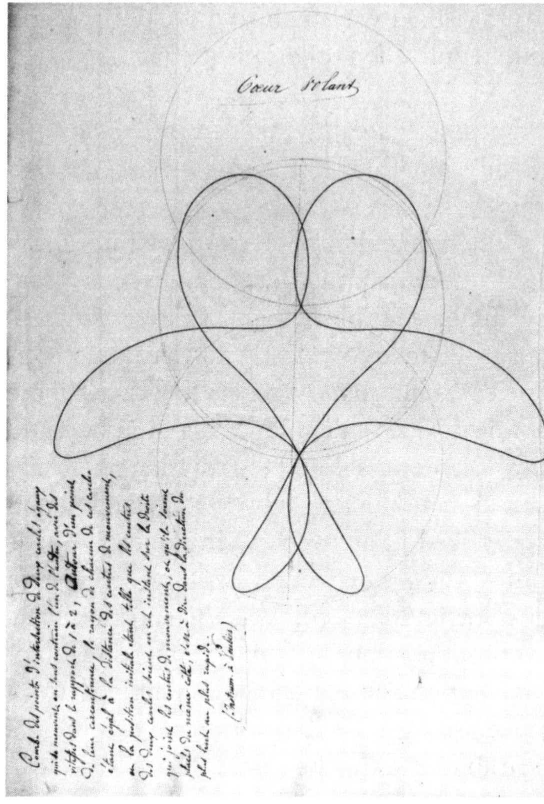

Figure 6.6. **Joseph Plateau, *Flying Heart*, anorthoscopic pattern, 1828. Courtesy of Ghent University Museum.**

indeed, visualize: “The eye has the power, as is well known, of retaining visual impressions for a sensible period of time; and in this way, recurring actions, made sufficiently near to each other, are perceptibly connected, and made to appear as a continued impression.”[41] The preconception of retinal persistence is partly overcome here through the “connection” between discrete “impressions.” But the resulting “continued impression” is qualified by the expression “made to appear,” which still suggests an illusion or artifice. Faraday’s description of visual motion, in other words, cannot quite bridge static and moving images; it remains stroboscopic.

A year later in the same journal, Wheatstone provided a detailed account of Purkinje’s work while synthesizing new research on the “physiology of vision” on the Continent by “Müller, Plateau, etc.,” still “entirely unnoticed in this country.”[42] In his account on vision

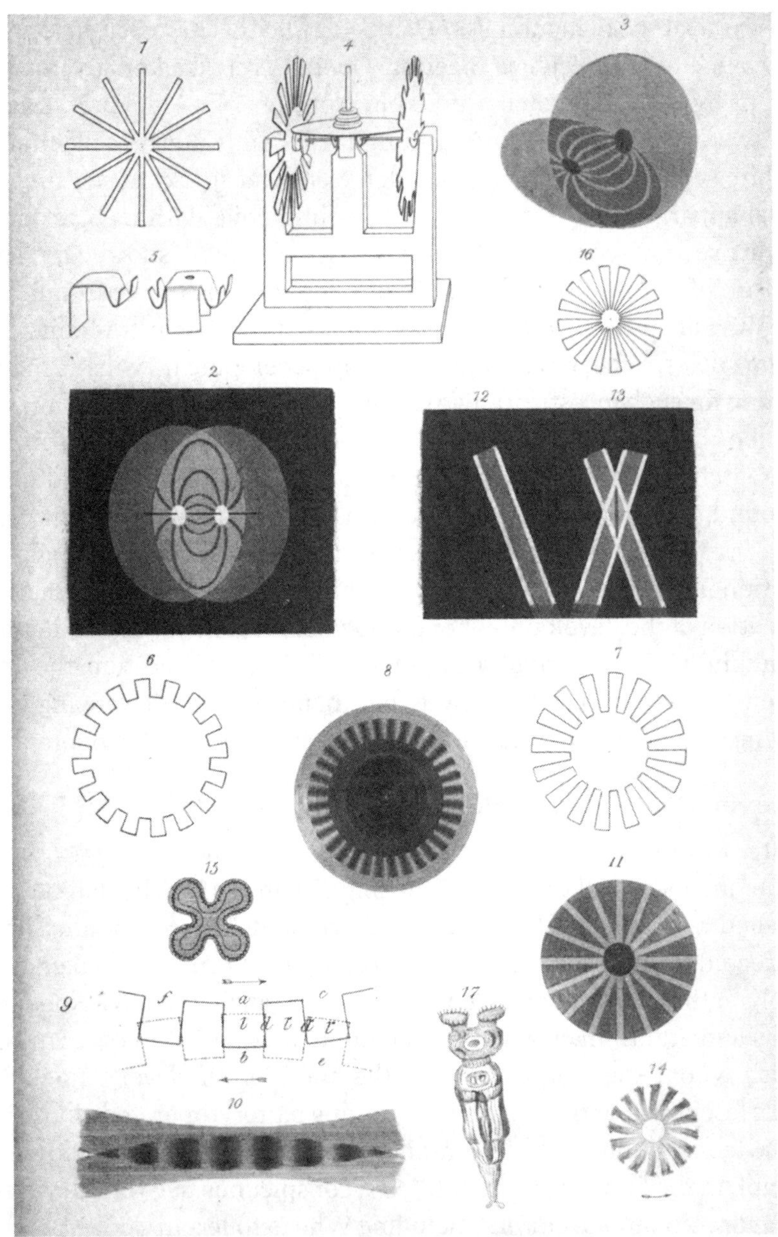

Figure 6.7. **Spinning wheels and stroboscopic patterns produced with them. Note the pattern resembling interference fringes (lower left). Michael Faraday, "On a Peculiar Class of Optical Deceptions,"** ***Journal of the Royal Institution*** **1 (1831): plate 3, 639. Courtesy of the Royal Institution.**

research at the inaugural 1833 Cambridge British Association for the Advancement of Science meeting, Quetelet reported on an experiment by Wheatstone conducted in front of John Herschel, David Brewster, and others. While a spinning disk with alternate black and white sectors looked gray, a sudden electrical spark caused the visual apparatus to perceive the disk as immobile with its black and white sectors separated.[43] This amusing experiment showed the opposite of the traditional view: Visual motion was native to human sight, and static vision merely its interruption. As Chitra Ramalingam shows, Wheatstone was central in developing new instrumentation for such investigations, working closely with both Faraday and Talbot in 1833–1834. Ramalingam summarizes Wheatstone's main research hypothesis on durational phenomena in various mediums (sound, vision, timekeeping, etc.) this way: "A dynamic event was made to leave behind a fixed trace on a sensitive surface, through its action in time."[44] This polyvalent formula represents a keen encapsulation of the development of photocinema in the 1830s and 1840s, combining the tail end of the hieroglyphic imprint tradition, the implementation of photography, experiments with static-moving imaging simulators, and the rise of time-tracing electro-chronographs.

Moving-Plate Chronophotography in the 1840s

After the Kew Observatory was repurposed as a meteorological station and electrical instrument testing site in 1842, Wheatstone installed a bank of "self-registering instruments" there. Although he directed the effort, the station was run by an instrument-maker and polymath who has not received his due: Francis Ronalds. Ronalds was a liberal thinker whose sister Emily befriended Robert Owen, with whom she worked toward the abolition of slavery. Ronalds was fascinated with electricity, inventing battery-operated clocks in 1815 before building a thirteen-kilometer-long working electric telegraph in the family garden in 1816—a conspicuous network of wires that drew many spectators, including Wheatstone and Cooke.[45] Only in 1868 was Ronalds recognized as the precursor of the telegraph (Ronalds, *Sir Francis Ronalds,* 141–49, 162). He developed telescope mounts and perspective-tracing machines, publishing detailed accounts and precise drawings of his new instruments (101–9). Among these were clock-driven self-tracing devices recording atmospheric electricity, designed as early as 1815. These machines traced a spiral groove on a horizontal disk covered with a layer of resin softened at the contact of a thin electrified spindle, making Ronalds a key innovator in self-recording instrumentation (133). He had a lifelong interest in imaging and used a camera lucida for drawing, and he constructed tracing instruments for perspective, elevation, geometrical curves, etc. An excerpt from his "ideas book" dated 1814–1829 describes a "chemical camera": "Place any substance or infusion upon the paper or other surface receiving the image which by the action of light would *stain* the paper . . . illuminate the object as strongly as possible by means of lenses in any number or any size. . . . If this were practicable we should obtain far better mechanical *painters* than human ones of light & shade" (214). Although he did not follow through at the time, as early as 1841 he came up with the idea of putting photographic plates in motion to trace the continuous variations of indices of instruments.[46] By 1845, he collaborated with Henry Collen on a prototype. Collen was a London portrait painter and art teacher to future Queen Victoria who worked with Talbot on calotype photography in 1841. In 1842, with his connection at Westminster, Collen was asked to photograph the Treaty of Nanjing ending the Opium Wars—the first political document and international treatise reproduced by photography.[47] Although Collen sought to take credit for the invention of moving-plate self-recording, Ronalds was the inceptor. He describes his project in an article of 1847 as: "self-registering, photographically, the variations of the declination magnet and the thermometer which were made previously to *the use of good achromatic lenses, for projecting, upon photographic paper, a sharp image, magnified to any required degree, of that part of the instrument whose motions are to be registered.*"[48] In such devices, an Argand light illuminates the instrument's indicator (a needle or mercury column) to imprint its image on a vertical photographic plate driven by clockwork and gravity, creating a twelve-hour chronographic record of the continuous variation of current, magnetism, or pressure.

In the same 1847 issue of the *Philosophical Transactions* where Ronalds published his essay on self-registering instruments,

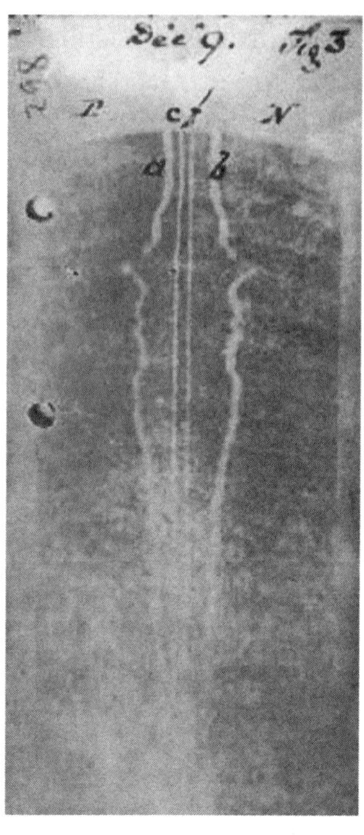

Figure 6.8. **Photographed index of a variation, F. Ronalds (1845), RGO 6/701 298. Courtesy of Royal Greenwich Observatory. (Reproduced in Beverley F. Ronalds, "The Beginnings of Continuous Scientific Recording Using Photography: Sir Francis Ronalds' Contribution,"** ***European Society for the History of Photograph,*** **2016, 2, figure 2, http://www.eshph.org/wp-content/uploads/2016/05/ronalds_camera.pdf.)**

Charles Brooke published a description of a similar process he had developed for the Greenwich Observatory "On the Automatic Registration of Magnetometers, and Other Meteorological Instruments, by Photography," with the difference that it used photographic paper on a cylinder and a different caching system.[49] The simultaneous appearance of both papers suggests that the Royal Society regarded their inventions as independent.[50] Because of the faintness and fugitivity of photographic traces on paper, Brooke resorted to retracing them with ink. Ronalds initially used paper calotypes between glass plates, but in 1849 at the urging of John Herschel, he turned to daguerreotypes with a better resolution. In the words of Beverley F. Ronalds: "Ronalds was the first to develop and document a successful 'movie camera,' complete with optical system, to capture the continuous modulation of natural phenomena using photography. His initial model was built in 1845 and original photographic curves from that year survive" (*Sir Francis Ronalds,* 496). Although short of recording visual motion proper, Ronalds's moving-plate setups and Brooke's rotating cylinder devices were certainly chronophotographic prototypes—the latter certainly derived from John Herschel's 1840 actinograph.

Marey, we should emphasize, was well informed of these developments. He stated as much when his research took its first turn toward chronophotography in July 1876, admitting that "for many

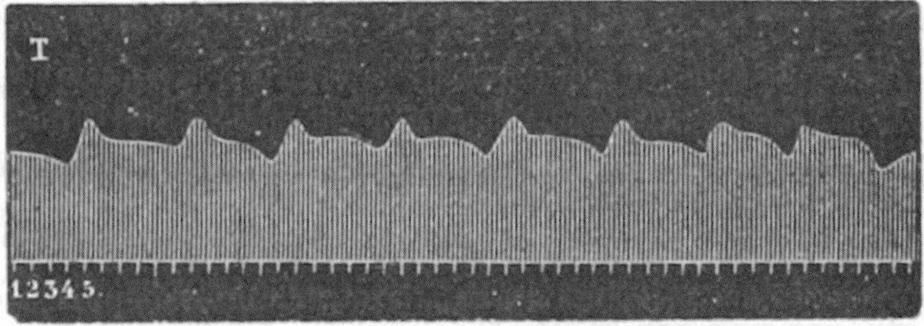

Fig. 2.

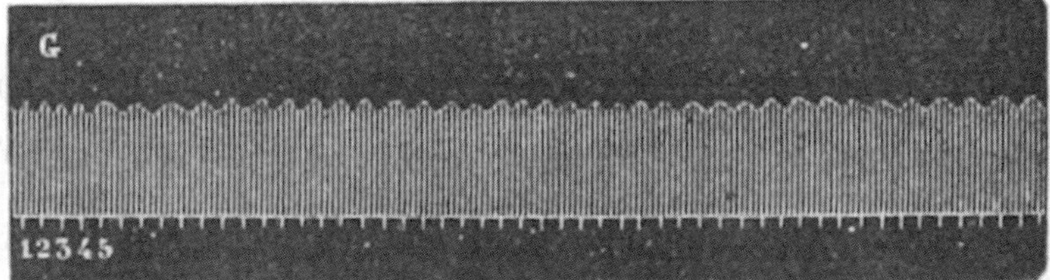

Figure 6.9. **Moving-plate photographs of mercury column. Étienne-Jules Marey, "Inscription photographique des indications de l'électromètre de Lippmann,"** ***Comptes Rendus Hebdomadaires des Séances de l'Académie des Sciences*** **83, no. 4 (1876): 280. Courtesy of La Bibliothèque Nationale de France Gallica.**

years, the variations of a thermometer have been photographed in this way at Greenwich." Using a thin mercury column to gauge cardiac pressure at small intervals, Marey decided to forgo the photonegative approach and instead light the mercury column against a black background, as "the luminous image travels the entire length of the photographic plate." He concluded his contribution cryptically: "We cannot enter into any detail of the signification of these curves that open up a new domain for the graphic method."[51] His famous monograph on the graphic method was published two years later in 1878, but only in 1884 did he publish an addendum about the use of photography.[52] The continuous capture of indices in 1876, however, was not the first time he pondered photography; what opened the way to graphic applications in 1874 was astrophotography.

Astronomy and Positivist Hegemony in the Nineteenth Century

While in the eighteenth and early nineteenth centuries astronomers had often been at the forefront of antiracism, from Marie-Jean-Antoine-Nicolas de Caritat, marquis de Condorcet and Benjamin Banneker to Arago, in the second half of the nineteenth century physical scientists largely subscribed to positivist views on civilizational development and nonwhite racial degeneracy. In 1866, when three French navy steamboats reached the walls of Seoul, a Korean official asked why the French had come. "He was told the only purpose was the observation of a lunar eclipse which, in fact, was to occur within a few days. He did not seem satisfied with that answer."[53] The Korean official's suspicions were well founded. Astronomy had become an integral cog in the colonial apparatus of Western powers. Observation campaigns in the nineteenth century were routinely used as alibis for colonial penetration. As Alex Soojung-Kim Pang shows in the case of India, military support for astronomical expeditions to control visual disturbances in the surroundings of observation sites turned into blatant displays of colonial might.[54] Astronomical instrumentation and observation in colonized lands served as tools of imperial consolidation as well as displays of civilizational superiority aimed at colonized peoples.[55] This global, transnational, and colonial framework, which accompanied the birth of astrophotography as a central technology for modern astrophysics, shadows the emergence of the graphic method.

The politicization of astronomy as a component of global control heightened during the Napoleonic Wars. Henri de Saint-Simon is emblematic in this regard. After fighting with colonists in the American Revolutionary War, he trained as an engineer back in France, soon turning to land speculation and entrepreneurship. He then became the new voice of science leveraged for globalization in a prophetic, autocratic, and colonial perspective. In 1803, he proposed a "Newton" prize to be awarded by the Royal Society through a vote by international men and women of science in the fields of mathematics, physics, chemistry, physiology, literature, painting, and music: "The committee of the twenty-one elected by humanity will be known as the Newton Council; it will represent me on Earth; it will split humanity in four divisions to be called British, French, German and Italian. . . . Every person, wherever they live on the globe, will be bound to one of these divisions."[56] This globalist European hegemony piggybacked on Naturphilosophie holism by invoking the bonds between human and cosmic history: "The mechanism of man and the mechanism of the universe are the same with the following differences: The universe is a mechanism endowed with perpetual motion as motor. The mechanism of man being moved by a derived motion is of limited duration."[57] His 1808 work closes off with the famous diagram "Figurative System of All Human Knowledge," prefiguring the fad of textual-visual nomenclatures of knowledge by the likes of Jeremy Bentham and André-Marie Ampère in the wake of the 1815 Vienna Congress. In an 1810 text, he exhorted his readers: "Bring yourself, in thought, back to the epoch of the formation of the globe, then descend along centuries by observing the progress of the human spirit, and you will clearly see the means to be employed for accelerating its perfection" (Enfantin, *Oeuvres de Saint-Simon et d'Enfantin,* 16:89). Diagrammatic thought and the kinemorphic visualization of cosmic history combine to shore up the new historicity. By 1813, he addressed himself directly to Napoleon Bonaparte in *Work on Universal Gravitation, Means of Forcing the British to Recognize the Independence of Flags.* This composite pamphlet proposes a "European parliament" that, following Napoleon ending his occupation of European countries, would promote political equality for all Europeans, including women.[58] In exchange, England would rescind its 1807 law enabling the British Navy to board any ship suspected of engaging in the slave trade—a policy the French planter lobby and Saint-Simon himself berated as a violation of national sovereignty (Saint-Simon, *Oeuvres choisies,* 2:167–74). The first part of the title illustrates Saint-Simon's driving idea that gravitation should become the universal principle of secular knowledge binding science, politics, and peace: "The idea of universal gravitation must serve as basis to the new philosophical theory, and the new political system of Europe must be a consequence of the new philosophy." This is what he called "the positive system," an expression that originated the notion and term of positivism made famous by his disciple Auguste Comte (2:174, 210).

By the 1840s, European historiography, anthropology, political theory, and astronomy concurred in making whiteness the civilizational vector of global destiny. One of the bestsellers of scientific vulgarization in England and the United States was Robert Chambers's *Vestiges of the Natural History of Creation* (1844)—an amphibological title asserting all at once the power of the deity and the autonomy of nature. Under the guise of astronomy's view from on high on all matters scientific, the book recycles polygenism and crude anti-Blackness. "The Negro alone is here unaccounted for; and of that race it may fairly be said, that it is the one most likely to have had an independent origin, seeing that it is a type so peculiar in an inveterate black colour, and so mean in development," Chambers proponed, adding that, "in the Caucasian or Indo-European family alone has the primitive organization been improved upon. The Mongolian, Malay, American, and Negro, comprehending five-sixths of mankind, are degenerate."[59] Such gratuitous claims of degeneracy—found in many astronomy books at mid-century—justified colonial conquest as deliverance through regeneration.[60]

For astronomer, physiologist, and early photoimagist John William Draper as well, the natural history of the cosmos directly informed Western hegemony (see chapter 5). In 1856, he published *Human Physiology, Statical and Dynamical,* tackling physiology on the model of "Astronomy and Chemistry" to make it a "Positive Science."[61] His treatise recasts human evolution as a natural play of physical and chemical forces between human bodies and air, water, matter, and light—a pre-Darwinian mechanical framework. It was during the questions and answers following Draper's 1860 lecture at Oxford on Europe's epistemic development—reinterpreted through social Darwinism—that William Wilberforce (apocryphally) quipped that Thomas Henry Huxley proponed human descent from monkeys.[62]

In his *Human Physiology,* Draper sought a middle position between the proslavery polygenism of Louis Agassiz and Josiah Clark Nott and the traditional monogenism of James Cowles Prichard.[63]

"The human race," Draper asserts, must not be seen as made up of "varieties, much less of distinct species, but rather as offering numberless representations of the different forms which an ideal type can be made to assume under exposure to different conditions." This malleable type materializes into races through a "plastic power," defined as "the capability of metamorphosis or transmutation from form to form" over "several centuries" (Draper, *Human Physiology*, 565–66). He contrasts this plastic power arranging living matter with a "totally distinct agency, the sunlight," which contributes to organic matter (459). The point is that, lacking Charles Darwin's trove of biological observations, he relies purely on visualization through explicitly kinemorphic and photoimaging insights to simulate the unseen diversification of races. Human metamorphosis for him rests primarily on "complexion" as a factor of sunlight and "the form of the skull" dictated by the "condition of development of the brain" judged optimal in the "Indo-European race" (573–74). His compromise formation presents white supremacy as Indo-European intelligence morphing the braincase from the inside out. He conjectures flippantly that Blackness results from "degenerating haematin" in the liver, overloading the skin with a high "percentage of iron" that causes the "misshaping" of Black peoples' heads—an echo of Jean-Baptiste Demanet's metal-toxification theory of Blackness (592). His monogenism is thus just as racist and antiscientific as the polygenism of Johann Kaspar Lavater or Chambers. "What a contrast between the astronomer, of whom the human race may justly be proud," he exclaims referring to Isaac Newton, "and the Australian savage portrait Dr. Prichard has furnished," whose "features" cannot "acquit him of the charge of cannibalism" (564–65). His central claim, simply put, is that "universal history is only a chapter in physiology" (611). On that basis, Draper redefines white people as optimal plastic incarnations of the ideal human type.

This equation of history and physiology rests on little reliable scientific data: It is wholly informed by optics. It is, in fact, as a photochemist, spectroscopist, and astronomer that Draper theorizes phenotypical variations of skin and skull shape. A striking passage from another book written at the end of the Civil War illustrates the point, with clear relevance for media prehistory:

> If the life of a man could be prolonged through many centuries, and he were to occupy it in making a journey over the earth from the Arctic to the Antarctic Circle, though he might have been perfectly white at first, his complexion would in succession pass through every degree of darkness, and by the time he had reached the equator, towards the middle of his life, he would be perfectly black. Continuing his journey, his color would lighten as he proceeded, and on his reaching the Antarctic he would become pale again, all these changes occurring without any loss of his personal identity. Moreover, in this progress, supposing that his mode of life, as regards food and comfort, was such as natural conditions suggest, even his skull would vary, and with it his *intellectual powers*. . . . If, in his career, children were born to him, they would be of every shade of color and of every form of skull.[64]

This visualization scenario of racial morphing synthesizes his two-prong theory of race: skin photosensitivity and skull kinemorphism—that is, photography and protocinema. Let us notice that while he formerly asserted that white intelligence increased the braincase volume (a fiction of craniometry, as Stephen Jay Gould shows), here he advances the opposite thesis: that position on the globe alone shapes skulls.[65] Either way, within his astronomical purview, species of static and dynamic vision are necessary and sufficient rationales for explaining racial variations of the human species.[66]

Although Darwin's framework was meant to dispel such gratuitous conjectures, the issue of visualization shows up in Darwin's perplexity regarding the vector responsible for speciation and variation—what the often-elided full title of *On the Origin of Species* formulates as *The Preservation of Favoured Races*. This vector for Darwin is "the mystery of mysteries—as it has been called by one of our greatest philosophers."[67] That philosopher is John Herschel, who, together with Alexander von Humboldt, inspired Darwin's scientific avocation.[68] John Herschel wrote this quip to Charles Lyell in a letter from February 1836, a few months before Darwin, on his way to South America, visited him in Cape Town. Darwin discovered John Herschel's letter in 1839, jotting in a notebook: "Herschel calls the appearance of species, the mystery of mysteries. &

has grand passage upon problem! Hurrah.–'intermediate causes'" (Eldridge, *Eternal Ephemera,* 30). The challenge of Darwin's theory is how to properly visualize an extraordinary number of interactions and generations over time and space from tiny windows on extant and fossil species in order to reconstruct their overall sequential developments. Darwin posits that "an interminable number of intermediate forms must have existed, linking together all the species in each group by gradations as fine as our present varieties" (*On the Origin of Species,* 462). That focus on intermediate states reprises John Herschel's highlighting of gradual processes of causation formulated in his 1830 *Preliminary Discourse on the Study of Natural Philosophy,* an influential work propounding the visualization of changes within temporal processes that cannot be directly observed—or whose sequence is so "instantaneous that the interval cannot be perceived."[69] For John Herschel, intermediate forms were placeholders for unseen gaps and unseeable mutations in kinemorphic continua. Interestingly, in the same book he mentions Thomas Young's 1807 cylinder-chronometer design that might "permit us to appreciate intervals to the nicety of the hundredth, or even the thousandth part of a single second" (John Herschel, *Preliminary Discourse,* 355). John Herschel's intermediate moments, we can then surmise, triangulated a new temporal model of visualization through his father's kinemorphic cosmology, the long duration development of living species, and self-tracing instrumentation—all part of his new graphical process in approaching duration.

This leads us back to Marey. With an MD in human physiology, Marey pioneered the same new "dynamic physiology" as that espoused by Draper, and he too contrasted the old "static" physiology with its innovative "dynamic" improvement.[70] In 1867, Marey replaced his mentor, the anti-Darwinian and creationist anatomist Marie-Jean-Pierre Flourens, as the Chair of Natural History of Organized Bodies at the Collège de France. In his inaugural lecture, Marey emplaced his graphic method within contemporary science and the overall history of scientific knowledge.[71] "Allow me to retrace in a quick overview [retracer dans un rapide coup d'oeil] the principal phases of the evolution of science," he declared, adding that he could not "unfold for your eyes this entire historical picture" but only suggest the overall vector of its unseeable movement (Marey, "Évolution historique des sciences," 257). He begins with how eighteenth-century taxonomy divided humans and animals into "families," "tribes," and "species," carefully eschewing the term *race* (257).[72] Then he moves on to anatomy, embryogenesis, physiology, and, ultimately, studies of physiological functions. To anchor this epistemic evolution, Marey, like Draper, turned for analogy to "the science which dominates and contains all others, that of the universe" (260). Taxonomy, he infers, corresponds to the classification of cosmic bodies into stars and planets, descriptive anatomy is akin to planetary geography, structural anatomy to geophysics, embryogenesis to cosmology, and physiology corresponding to meteorology and oceanography—the life-sustaining motions of water, air, and heat. Together with marquee names like Georges-Louis Leclerc, count de Buffon, Georges Cuvier, and Johannes Müller, Marey mentions lesser-known lights, including Jean Senebier and Purkinje, locating his own expertise as a synthesis of physical and biological sciences. Echoing Condorcet's historical vector, he insists that "the course of Progress accelerates ceaselessly" toward "new conquests," especially now that science can rely on the graphic method as a new universal language (260). He concluded that the road into the future "is nonetheless traced visibly," a final wink at his graphic method (261).

While Marey said little about race, the idea of Western science developing a "universal language" through graphs has strong racial implications for Draper. The latter concluded his 1856 overview of world historical "social mechanics" by stating that white Europeans succeeded as a "race" because their physiological transformation yielded "an analytical mental character," endowed with "a capability of indefinitely modifying our state" (Draper, *Human Physiology,* 635). This capability relied on a single technic: "A high psychical condition demands as its essential, both in the individual and in the race, a mechanism of registry" (637). While this ostensibly refers to alphabetic writing—as superior to ideographic or syllabic systems—Draper had certainly in mind self-graphing instruments representing the apex of science technology. In other words, the graphic method of Marey and the "mechanism of registry" of

Draper partake of the same positivist vector of human evolution in which whiteness is the favored race because it alone is universal.

Solar Photography in Colonial Context

Given the premium bestowed on the macrocosm in confirming positivist visualizations of human history, it is no surprise that astronomy was among the privileged fields of application for photography—once Daguerre and Draper demonstrated the feasibility of photographing the Moon. The leading British astronomer George Biddell Airy declared in 1857 that "in due time we may make astronomy self-tracing," a signal confirmation that photography was already thought of as just one among other "self-tracing" technics.[73] The proximal motivation for astrophotography, however, was the nature of the Sun. On September 25, 1841, a large solar magnetic burst was detected at astronomical/meteorological observatories. Drum-recording electro-chronographs were subsequently installed at meteorological stations to monitor such magnetic outbursts, which threatened burgeoning telegraphic networks and electromagnetic machines.[74] In 1843, an amateur astronomer named Samuel Heinrich Schwabe published the results of twenty years of sunspot observations he had conducted in the hope of demonstrating that one of these spots was a new planet. What he found instead is that sunspots follow an eleven-year cycle, reviving curiosity about the source of solar energy and its relation to light, heat, and magnetism. On July 16, 1850, John Adams Whipple and George Phillips Bond succeeded in obtaining the "first-ever daguerreotype of a star other than the Sun," Vega.[75] In the article announcing this achievement, Bond pointed out two remarkable facts: Light had taken twenty years to arrive from Vega, and it acted the same way on the photosensitive plate as the light of the Sun. This was the first concrete evidence that the Sun was a star and, conversely, that stars must have roughly the same chemical composition as the Sun. Investigations of solar physics brought attention back to a phenomenon that, for its awe-inspiring grandeur, had remained but an oddity: total solar eclipses. At the moment of totality when the Moon blocks out the Sun's disk, the outer solar layers called the corona can be observed directly. But totality is viewable only for a few minutes, and only in thin swaths across the globe, making access to such global locations an absolute requisite.

The main precursor of astrophotography was British astronomer Warren De la Rue. For my purpose, I will focus on a lesser-known French actor, Aimé Laussedat, because his work directly prepared that of Jules Janssen and his 1874 photographic revolver. Trained in astronomy and geodesy at École Polytechnique—whose uniformed students were army officers—Laussedat embraced photography early on as a polyvalent tool of visualization. While conducting a topographical survey in the Pyrenees in 1846, he noted that with his theodolite "each of my stations was a point of view so that what I projected on my horizontal paper were visual rays."[76] This pioneered the use of photography for three-dimensional mapping. Assisted by Paul Gustave Froment (at the suggestion of Arago), Laussedat subsequently built a device using a camera lucida for directly transducing drawings into relief measurements (Laussedat, "Les applications de la perspective au lever des plans," 8fn2). After military cartographers colonizing Abyssinia complained of unreliable mapping technics, Laussedat came up with new ways of triangulating photography for cartography. In the 1850s, he participated in an expedition to the Maghreb to extend the measurement of the meridian begun by Jean-Baptiste Biot and Arago. The expedition was part of the strategic agenda by the War Ministry to link Algeria and Morocco to the metropole astronomically in order to make them tighter possessions of France.[77] Laussedat also helped develop military photographic surveillance, experimenting with "instant photography" from trains, balloons, and even kites as part of what he called "the art of reconnoitering."[78] One of his photographic setups combined a camera lucida and a field telescope to reshoot a small portion of a larger photograph in a zoom effect.[79] His work in photographic instrumentation and astronomy was integral to France's colonial conquests in the last third of the nineteenth century.

The three-points-of-view photographic method for cartography that he finalized in 1851 was called "metrophotography" and "topophotography."[80] It was not adopted in France, but Prussian military scientists quickly learned of and improved on it, explaining in part why their maps of France during the Franco-German

War of 1870–1871 proved finer than those of the French high command. Laussedat subsequently taught astronomy at École Polytechnique and in 1857 built a teaching observatory for the school. It was around that time that he began applying photography to astronomical observation, particularly eclipses (*Notice sur les travaux,* 6).

The total solar eclipse across the Mediterranean in 1860 was the first great test for astrophotography. England mounted a large expedition to Spain led by De la Rue, with major astronomers such as Otto Wilhelm von Struve and Airy and other scientists interested in photography such as Francis Galton. Vatican astronomer Pietro Angelo Secchi planned to travel to a different observation site in Spain. At the last minute, the French Ministry of the Navy assented to dispatch Laussedat in an expedition to Batna in Algeria so France would not be left behind. The common aim was investigating the nature of solar protuberances, as well as the mysterious red spots detected during 1842's totality by Francis Baily—the so-called Baily's beads. It was unclear whether either phenomenon was an optical aberration or a physical event—or the latter deformed by the former. Laussedat used wet and dry collodion plates to photograph the eclipse but missed totality because of a technical failure. De la Rue made thirty-five wet collodion plates and Secchi fourteen dry collodion photographs during totality. Some astronomers saw the beads and others did not, but the results regarding protuberances were conclusive: Since they were impressed on plates just before the Moon disk entirely covered the Sun, they belonged to the latter; and since the same protuberance patterns were seen on plates from different stations, they were real physical phenomena.[81]

De la Rue used a huge clock-driven solar telescope from Kew called a photo-heliograph—a final irony considering Niépce's unsuccessful 1827 trip to Kew with his heliographic plates. As for Laussedat and his colleague Aimé Girard, they only brought a small reflector telescope that was not clock-driven. Laussedat, however, by then a professor at the Conservatoire National des Arts et Métiers, had procured the signal instrument of French optical physics since Senebier: a heliostat.[82] While De la Rue's machine tracked the Sun directly, Laussedat affixed the camera to the eyepiece of the fixed horizontal telescope aimed at the heliostat that itself tracked the Sun.[83] Even though his photographs during totality failed, Laussedat documented the aspect he prized most, the serial kinematics of the phenomenon: "Juxtaposed in the order in which they had been obtained, [the twelve plates] reproduced in the most striking fashion the gradual path of the moon's disk in front of that of the sun," he wrote, formulating an early definition of *chronophotography* (Laussedat, *Lunette,* 7). De la Rue used an efficient chute system of plate replacement to obtain successive shots, but he was not interested in sequencing the eclipse. An admirer of Wheatstone, what he most sought to obtain were slightly spaced shots producing stereophotographs. Curiously, both Secchi and De la Rue obtained similarly "defective" plates: They show three different phases of a protuberance impressed on the same plate at a few seconds' intervals because of a shock given to the telescope. Accidental quasi-chronophotographs.

In his official report of the Batna eclipse expedition to the Académie des Sciences, Laussedat described local Maghrebi spectators within the purview of colonial control. They are first mentioned in relation to a spectacular phenomenon occurring only during total eclipses: interference fringes projected as shimmers from obstacles such as leaves. "The gatherings of Arabs rendered the appearance of [fringes] all the more striking that these dark lines coursed upon their white garment," he recounted (Laussedat et al., "Rapport," 996). Dark-skinned colonized peoples with their white djellabas were turned into observational screens. Addressing the impact of the eclipse on "animated beings," Laussedat described the reaction of animals in the same breath as that of the locals. "We could not neglect the effect produced on races so different from ours," he commented, pointing out that the apparent calm men displayed was "obviously a matter of not showing themselves inferiors." This acknowledgment of resistance to power differentials within a colonial setting is countered by his next indication that in Constantine a "renowned marabout hostile to France" was pummeled with stones by local women for having predicted that there would be no eclipse. Women figure here as reliable allies to the conquerors, with Laussedat explaining that after banging pots to ward off evil, they ululated when the sun reappeared, in the same manner that

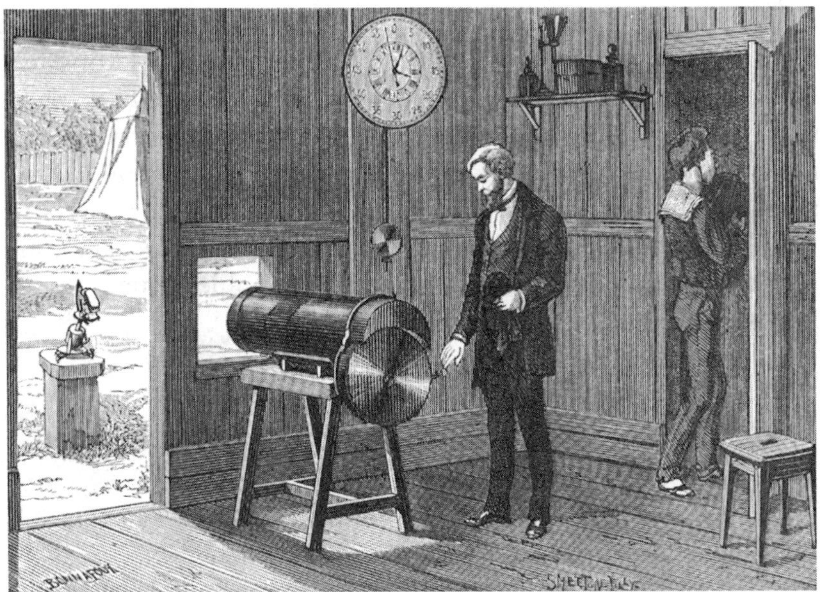

Figure 6.10. **Jules Janssen's horizontal camera telescope assembly with heliostat. Camille Flammarion, "Le Passage de Vénus," *La Nature* 3 (1875): 357. Courtesy of La Bibliothèque Nationale de France Gallica.**

"Maronite women salute French soldiers at every halt of our glorious flag" (Laussedat et al., "Rapport," 998–99). Left out of histories of astrophotography, such comments bespeak the active reinforcement of white supremacy by European scientists imagining and imaging the cosmos.[84]

This chapter has shown that chronophotography was the end development of a long-held concern with tracing not just time or animal bodies in motion but the physical forces shaping celestial bodies, including all levels of our world—from the microcosm of the human eye to global earthquakes, planetary atmospheric data, magnetic solar storms, and the protuberances of our closest star. On April 7, 1876, astronomer Jules Janssen presented his revolving camera attached to a horizontal telescope to the French Photographic Society, suggesting that sequential shots could be used to study "physiological mechanics related to walking, flight and other animal movements."[85] Marey scholars take this well-known astronomical provenance of chronophotography as a neutral technical adaptation. Yet tracing technology devised to account for the macrocosm was never part of a disinterested enterprise. As Marey's and Draper's work in dynamic physiology shows, that framework easily segued with post-Darwinian racist universalism aiming at ruling the nonwhite world. It is that racial animus behind photographic chronography that filmmaker Jordan Peele foregrounds in *Nope* (2022) while recovering the figure of the African American jockey concealed in one of Muybridge's chronophotographic sequences and long elided by the history of media.

7

Flammarion's Telechronoscope

The End of Natural History and the Beginning of Cinema

> The [Edison] kinetoscope, we are told, has recently been made to run backwards, and the effects of this way of running it are truly marvelous. In his remarkable romance, "Lumen," the imaginative French astronomer Flammarion conceives of spiritual beings who, by travelling forward on a ray of light, see, with the keen vision of the spirit, all that the ray of light carried from the beginning of creation.
>
> —*St. Louis Post Dispatch,* 1896

For this commentator, it was not possible to write about Thomas Edison's kinetoscope in 1896 without referring back to Camille Flammarion's novella *Lumen.*[1] Though it had appeared in English twenty-three years before that—and before cinema itself—it still represented an explicit benchmark for film techniques.[2] While *Lumen* has been commented on in passing as prescient of cinema, this chapter shows why that astronomical tale, contextualized within Flammarion's broader concerns, should be considered the origin of projection cinema.[3] The chapter makes five claims about Flammarion's role in cinema history. First, Flammarion integrated astronomical kinemorphic visualization with photoimaging in a self-recording setup that constitutes a theoretically complete working apparatus. Second, as a close acquaintance of Nadar, Charles Cros, Étienne-Jules Marey, and Jules Janssen, his thought was pivotal in the development of precinema. Third, having devised three different fictive cinematic setups (1867, 1889, 1894) and built a cylinder photographic motion actinometer (1873), he was a precursor of the cinema apparatus proper. Fourth, in 1897–1898 he directed and exhibited animated shorts and should be counted among the originators of animation cinema. Finally, as an intellectual who was at once an astronomer, a writer and popularizer, a historian, and a republican activist, Flammarion was familiar with most of the sources of the matrix of photocinema that I have examined in this book. Yet it is as a believer in parascientific ideas that he incepted cinema, by combining rearguard natural philosophy with state-of-the-art technoscience. The racial discourses coextensive with his astronomical cinema reflect this deep ambiguity, at once pro- and antipositivist.

Camille Flammarion

Born on a small farm in Northern Burgundy, France, Flammarion credited his Catholic mother with encouraging his early passion for astronomy. In his memoir, he links this passion with a primal horror of death, which manifested in a fascination for fossils as a form of afterlife but also in his abhorrence of militarism and wars.[4] He was eleven when François Arago died in 1853, and he was struck by the eulogy given in church by his local priest praising Arago as an astronomer, a republican, and a believer—perspectives Flammarion had thought incompatible. In 1856, Flammarion's father lost his farm and was hired as a menial worker at the Adrien Tournachon Jeune & Cie photographic factory in Paris run by Nadar. Flammarion's training in astronomy thus grew in parallel with photography's profound transformation of visual culture and the beginnings of astrophotography. Working as an apprentice silverware engraver to complement the meager income of his parents, he took night classes. With other penniless students seeking knowledge capital, he organized a free academy where he gave lectures in the sciences, compiling them at fifteen under the lofty title *Universal Cosmogony*.[5] With the help of the doctor treating him for exhaustion (!) in 1858, he secured a position of calculator at the Paris Observatory. After Arago's death, the observatory was headed by Urbain-Jean-Joseph Le Verrier, a staunch supporter of the Second Empire who had canceled Arago's public lecturing and lorded it over the staff (Flammarion, *Mémoires,* 132–35).

In 1862, Flammarion's first published book, *The Plurality of Inhabited Worlds,* updating seventeenth-century conjectures about extraterrestrials, became an instant bestseller translated into a dozen languages. Le Verrier took it as an affront against real science and promptly fired him (Flammarion, *Mémoires,* 153–55). Mixing rigorous cosmology and spiritism, the book was panned by both the positivist and the Catholic press, while the more liberal cultural wing saw it as a manifesto of freethinking. Victor Hugo dispatched: "Your studies are my studies. Yes, let us dig into infinity" (quoted in Flammarion, *Mémoires,* 213–17). Like Hugo, Flammarion believed in the transmigration of souls and subscribed to the thought of Allan Kardec and later Helena Blavatsky.[6] By the early 1870s, Flammarion stood among the leading cultural figures of the Third Republic. He incarnated the synthesis of innovative vulgarization with advanced science and spiritual aspirations and presented with literary panache for the edification of freethinking masses.[7]

Lumen and the Inception of Cinema

According to Flammarion, the idea of *Lumen* came to him in 1865 while mulling over the time it takes distant starlight to reach Earth, a topic he'd just written about. As mentioned in chapter 6, estimations of the size of the universe increased exponentially over the nineteenth century, which meant that images received by telescopes showed stars and galaxies as they had been dozens of million years ago. That uncanny simultancity between the present of observation and the past of observed objects boggled the minds of the likes of Hugo, who wrote: "The sky we see is not present; it is past. The today of the sky is unknown to us; all we have in front of our eyes is Yesterday, a Yesterday which, for some stars, goes back thousands of years. . . . The stars which a three-meter telescope catches now no longer existed perhaps by the time of Charlemagne, and the stars observed in a six-meter telescope right now had perhaps vanished already by the time of the Trojan Wars."[8] There are two components to such realizations. One was the curious tangibility of the deep past of history received as light in the present within astronomers' eyes and on photographic plates. The other was more unsettling. The current state of the cosmos was strictly unseeable and unknowable; humans lived in cosmic epistemological darkness. This anxiety resonated with the thermodynamics of Rudolf Clausius, especially his 1865 concept of entropy, stipulating that the universe trends toward disorder and energy loss, with perfect stillness at absolute zero temperature as an end scenario. This tragic horizon of cosmogony redoubled anxieties about the "heat death" of the Sun, not to mention the death of God.[9] Until the arrival of the Big Bang theory in the 1920s, the nebular hypothesis explained the local formation of planetary systems and galaxies but not the overall structure or fate of the universe (see chapter 3). It is within that cosmological hiatus that Flammarion wrote *Lumen.*

Flammarion's goal was to offer a salve, at once fictive and scientifically sound, to entropic fears. *Lumen* follows the Dantean genre of travel to the beyond modernized by Humphry Davy's 1830 *Consolations in Travel* (a book Flammarion translated into French). It is structured as a conversation between a dead man named Lumen (Light) and his living friend Quaerens (the Seeker), whom he instructs on matters of the afterlife. It is like awakening from a dream, Lumen declares, as "called by the future and the past, the spirit seeks all at once to regain possession of itself and seize the fugitive impressions of the vanished dream—with their procession of tableaus and events, still passing before it" (Flammarion, *Récits de l'infini,* 5). The afterlife is immediately photocinematic. It enables ubiquitous macrocosmic visualizations, as a further passage indicates:

> Instead of seeing the stars in the sky as you are seeing them from Earth, I could clearly distinguish the worlds gravitating around them; and, oddly, when I no longer wanted to see the star so as to examine these worlds unconstrained, it would disappear from my vision. . . . Moreover, when my vision focused on a particular world, I could distinguish details of its surface, its continents and seas, clouds and rivers, and while

> it did not seem to get visibly larger to my eyes as when we use a telescope, I succeeded through a particular intensity of concentration of sight in my soul to see the object on which it concentrated, such as a town or the countryside . . . as distinctly as if I had been in a balloon. (18–19)

There are direct echoes of Johannes Kepler, Bernard Le Bovier, sieur de Fontenelle, Thomas Wright, Immanuel Kant, and the Great Moon Hoax—sources Flammarion commented on in *The Plurality of Inhabited Worlds.* The manipulable field of vision Lumen describes—with close-ups and fast-moving tracking shots—is that of the Oculus, which it likely inspired. Lumen asks Quaerens to "imagine refracting telescopes which, through a succession of lenses and an arrangement of diaphragms can make worlds successively closer and isolate from view the illuminating source" or else "a multitude of eyes" like "those of insects" (21). Flammarion defamiliarizes readers from known apparatuses and regimes of vision to acculturate them to transcalar visualization across space-time. Lumen then recounts being transported after death to an airborne purview over Paris. Thinking time had gone by since his death, he believed he was seeing the Paris of the future until he began witnessing the events of the French Revolution in real time. What was going on? That is the heuristic puzzle driving the novella.

Deducing that he is currently located in the Capella star system, seventy-two light-years away from Earth (the estimate of the time), Lumen suddenly understands that he is seeing earthly events occurring in 1793, since their light-images have just now reached the Capella system. He explains: "A light ray would be a sort of mail bringing us rather than written news the photography or even more rigorously, *the very aspect* of the country from which it came. . . . Hence there is a surprising transformation of the past into the present . . . [as] each aspect is followed by another, and so on successively; and it is like a series of undulations bearing the past of the worlds and made present for observers" (Flammarion, *Récits de l'infini,* 43, 45). Lumen can move to, and view at will, any part and time of the universe. As he tries explaining to Quaerens that this ubiquity follows "the laws of perspective," the latter cuts in to say, "You mean, of politics?" To which Lumen retorts, "No, of perspective (although both are very much alike), since, seeing great men from the sky, I judge them otherwise than they appear to the common men" (92–93). Flammarion's Oculus view on history is thus inherently critical, Lumen stating, for instance, that "Napoleon has willfully caused, to satisfy his personal ambition, the death of five million men," a bold revisionist assessment in Second Empire France (138). As he moves farther away, Lumen views the continuous history of Earth in reverse, from the Battle of Waterloo back to the nebular formation of the solar system (97–98). This reversal of time's arrow back to historical then cosmological depths was the brainchild of Nicolas-Edme Restif de la Bretonne's 1802 novelistic saga, one of Flammarion's key inspirations.[10]

As Quaerens cannot quite wrap his head around where Lumen is or when his "present" is occurring, Lumen expands the simile of photography, explaining that he can "find again the light rays gone in earlier years and bearing with them the photography of these years" (Flammarion, *Récits de l'infini,* 106). He analogizes light with "a series of terrestrial photographs staggered on the same line at intervals" so that "in a light ray, or better, in a jet of light composed of a series of distinct and juxtaposed images we have the fluidic inscription of the history of the Earth" (107, 108). The indication of "distinct and juxtaposed" photographs demonstrates that Flammarion carefully thought out the technical conditions of possibilities for the visual synthesis of motion. To Quaerens's objection that clouds and night would curtail access to a total view of history, Lumen responds that nonvisible rays like infrared traverse such obstacles (125–30). After this long didactic preamble, Flammarion reaches his technical goal: the detailed description of a photographic apparatus for projecting motion imaging.

> The image of a celestial body traversing dark abysses is in an analogous condition to the image of a person or object a photographer brought into his *camera obscura.* It is not impossible that these images meet in such vast spaces a dark celestial body (celestial mechanics has noted the existence of several), of a particular condition, whose surface

> (perhaps made of iodine, if we believe spectral analysis) would be sensitized [sensibilisée] and capable of fixing on itself the image of a faraway world. Hence terrestrial events would come to paint themselves on a dark globe. And if this globe turns on itself like other celestial bodies, it will present successively its different zones to the terrestrial image and will thus take the continuous photograph [photographie continue] of successive events. Moreover, descending or ascending according to a line perpendicular to its equator, the line on which the images are reproduced would describe not a circle but a spiral, and, after the first rotation concluded, the new images would not coincide with the older ones and not superimpose on them but would follow above or underneath. Imagination could now suppose that this world is not spherical but cylindrical, thus seeing in space the indestructible column around which the great events of terrestrial history would engrave and roll themselves. (135–37)

Astronomical verisimilitude clearly breaks down in favor of describing a working cinema apparatus. Pierre-Simon, marquis de Laplace theorized the existence of dark stars (akin to black holes), but no serious astronomer ever proposed cylindrical or photosensitive celestial bodies.[11] Flammarion does not specify a shutter mechanism for splitting light rays into "distinct and juxtaposed images" or a process for their spontaneous arrangement into a spiral. But technical feasibility, as we will see, was entirely within his reach.

The original design Edison proposed for his kinetograph fifteen years later was exactly the same: microphotographs arranged in a spiral around a cylinder. Flammarion's level of technicity sets *Lumen* apart from earlier tales of cosmic visualization, like Felix Eberty's 1846 *The Stars and the Earth,* which deploys a similar premise of light allowing a voyage through the past via a "microscope of time."[12] Perhaps Flammarion knew of Eberty's book when he states: "This process cannot rigorously be called a microscope, but rather a *chronoscope,* or chrono-tele-scope (to see time from afar)" (Flammarion, *Récits de l'infini,* 228). I want to emphasize the importance of the chronoscope as an intuition pump for cinema. While Eberty rekindles the Christian myth of an all-seeing divinity, *Lumen* dispenses with a godhead, turning instead to other intelligent beings and the transmigration of souls with a concomitant antipositivist decentering of "Man."

Flammarion as Technical Inceptor of Cinema

Flammarion's conjectural cinema apparatus has a clearly different valence than prior technical speculations like Charles François Tiphaigne de la Roche's 1760 photochemical canvas or the Great Moon Hoax's filmlike telescope. That is because, through his own readings and practice, as well as contacts with key technicians of precinema, he possessed the technological knowledge to envision a workable motion picture setup. By 1867, he had befriended established personalities like Hugo and Nadar but also up-and-coming writers and scientists including Jules Verne, Cros, Janssen, and Marey. All of them attended Flammarion's famous Wednesday evening salon, an ideal venue for cross-pollinating debates and precinema speculations.

Benoît Turquety analyzes precinema in the 1860s through the notion of distinctive problem. Invoking Gaston Bachelard and Georges Canguilhem, he shows that individual practitioners worked from specific technical problems that were never quite the same, though they may seem so a posteriori.[13] Eadweard Muybridge sought to establish a physical fact to win a bet; Marey aimed to represent physiological functions as quantifiable continua; Edison transduced the cylinder phonograph into the kinetograph for profit, and so on. Turquety closely scrutinizes the patents of two early technicians of motion-imaging apparatuses—Louis Ducos du Hauron (1861) and Charles Cros (1867)—to reframe their genesis. While Ducos du Hauron deployed a technically unrealistic design—hundreds of cameras in a grid whose plates are woven into a large canvas strip that is scanned in zigzags—Cros was content to explain the "general" principles of motion (and color) photography combining rotating microphotographs in the phenakistoscope (Turquety, *Inventing Cinema,* 131, 141–46). Hence, while both claimed the feasibility of recording and projecting a "moving scene [scène mouvementée]" (Ducos du Hauron) and "moving scenes [scènes mouvementées]" (Cros), their projects entailed significant conceptual and technical differences.

Ducos du Hauron and Cros nonetheless presumed that visual motion perception was due to retinal persistence and took place within "the eyes" of observers (Turquety, *Inventing Cinema,* 119). For both, visual motion was only approximated by serial photographs. Flammarion's astronomical model radically contrasts with this eighteenth-century preconception: It presupposes instead that visual motion perception and its technological re-presentation are coextensive. There is not, on the one side, streaming light with an infinite blur of overlapping images and, on the other side, machines mimicking human vision's intermittent sampling. For Flammarion, light is a kinemorphic imaging flow to begin with. It follows that his telechronoscope does not take the reproduction of visual motion as its distinct problem, since it is no problem at all. What Flammarion tackles instead is how to render visible the imaging flows born by light rays. This (astro)physical realism of Flammarion's approach to moving images sets him apart from all other precursors. Although the fictional telechronoscope is couched as a mind experiment rather than as an engineering proposal, its setup rests on advanced optical and mechanical know-how that Flammarion had secured by 1867 in five particular areas I examine in turn.

The first is magic lantern projection. In spring 1866, following Arago's example, he started giving free astronomy conferences at the Association Polytechnique. To make these lectures more vivid to working-class audiences, he collaborated with Alfred Molteni, the scion of a well-known optical instrument-maker, to produce a set of thirty astronomical magic lantern slides.[14] Flammarion claims that this collaboration with Molteni was single-handedly responsible for the fad of scientific slide projections over the following decades (*Mémoires,* 345–46). Whatever the case, serial and especially mechanical astronomical slides for nineteenth-century educational magic lantern shows were a central contribution to animation technology.

The second component is spectroscopy, the study of the light spectrum decomposed by a prism, which was revolutionized by photography in the 1850s and 1860s. In January 1866, Flammarion began contributing to *Le Siècle,* the semiofficial newspaper of the liberal anticlerical opposition. His first article was titled and

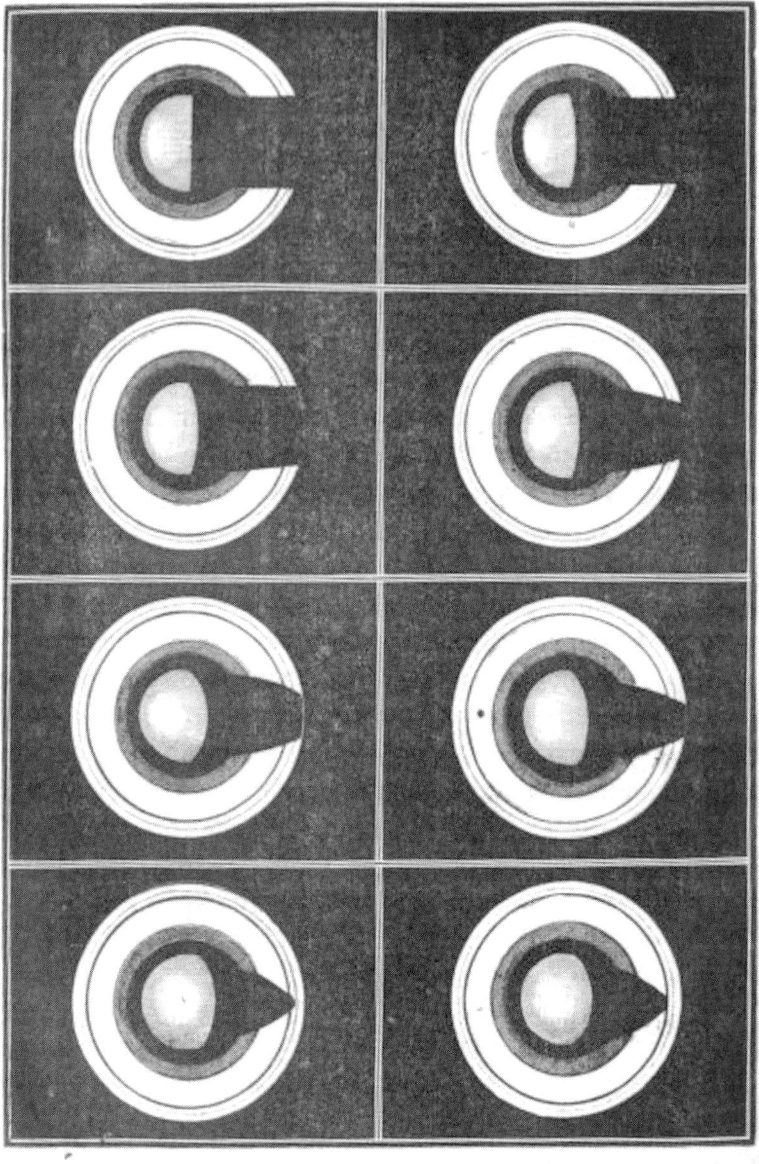

Figure 7.1. **Saturn's shadow cast on its ring; this is the kind of animation effect of serial and mechanical lantern slides. Camille Flammarion, *Les Terres du ciel* (Paris: Marpon & Flammarion, 1877), 704. Courtesy of La Bibliothèque Nationale de France Gallica.**

addressed "The Chemical Composition of Celestial Bodies Revealed by the Analysis of Their Light."[15] He explains how Gustav Kirchhoff and Robert Bunsen solved the mysterious bands discovered by William Hyde Wollaston and Joseph von Fraunhofer by determining that each represents the visual signature of a chemical element present in or traversed by the light source. During the 1860s and 1870s, photographic spectrographs became the main tool of burgeoning astrophysics. Let us note that spectral lines are unseeable by human vision without a prism, just like moving-image streams without a camera obscura.

The third component informing the telechronoscope is Flammarion's personal experience as a balloonist with mobile airborne points of view. Balloonists were the first to witness the smooth, kinemorphic, and truly cinematic unfolding of our three-dimensional visual continuum. In 1867, mischievously picking the day of the Ascension, Flammarion took his first balloon ride, writing enthusiastically: "You rise up slowly, majestically into space. This is already a first, unique, wholly new and very singular sensation. The motion taking us up is completely unnoticeable; for us the balloon seems immobile, it is Earth that lowers itself" (*Mémoires,* 375). The lack of kinesthetic motion cues for the observer creates the illusion of a spontaneous transformation of the visual field, reinforcing the sensorial import of kinemorphosis.

The fourth technical component is Flammarion's deep knowledge of both theoretical and instrumental optics. In 1867, he published (under the rebus-like pseudonym of Fulgence Marion) a popular treatise on optics describing human vision, the behavior of light, the history of vision science, optical instrumentation, and all the main devices producing visual motion effects, from Robertson's phantasmagoria to Joseph Antoine Ferdinand Plateau's phenakistoscope.[16] Hence, while drafting *Lumen,* Flammarion had the entire field of optics and visual instrumentation at his immediate recall.

The fifth and determinant component of his cinema setup is the application of the cylinder to photography. In 1849, Plateau and Charles Wheatstone recommended the use of stereoscopic photographs with the phenakistoscope, and several technicians like Jules Duboscq with his 1852 Bioscope followed their suggestion.[17]

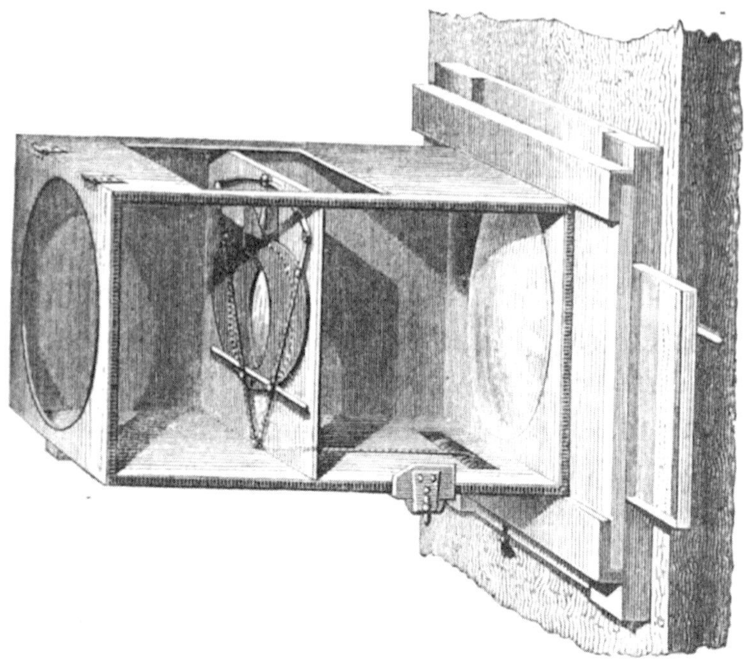

Figure 7.2. **Robertson's Fantascope with its cat-eye diaphragm system. Camille Flammarion, *L'Optique* (Paris: Hachette, 1867). Courtesy of La Bibliothèque Nationale de France Gallica.**

Yet all technicians, down to Muybridge and his 1880 Zoopraxiscope, placed photographs either on a disk or on the inner surface of a drum with slits or mirrors. Flammarion's use of the cylinder's outer surface with photographs arrayed in a tight spiral enabled a much longer sequence to be recorded and played. That design originated with John Herschel's 1840 actinograph combined with the helicoidal trace of electro-chronoscopes—hence the name *telechronoscope.* While drafting *Lumen,* Flammarion was working on a photographic cylinder recording device he called a "photometer," which he asked a clockmaker for the French Navy, Louis-Joseph Lecoq, to build in 1867 for use in a balloon.[18] It is described in Flammarion's 1872 book *The Atmosphere*: "Nitrated paper can be used as an impressionable substance. A clockwork mechanism activates, in a copper casing, a cylinder around which is rolled a band of sensitized paper. The case is placed on a table; on its upper part is a small

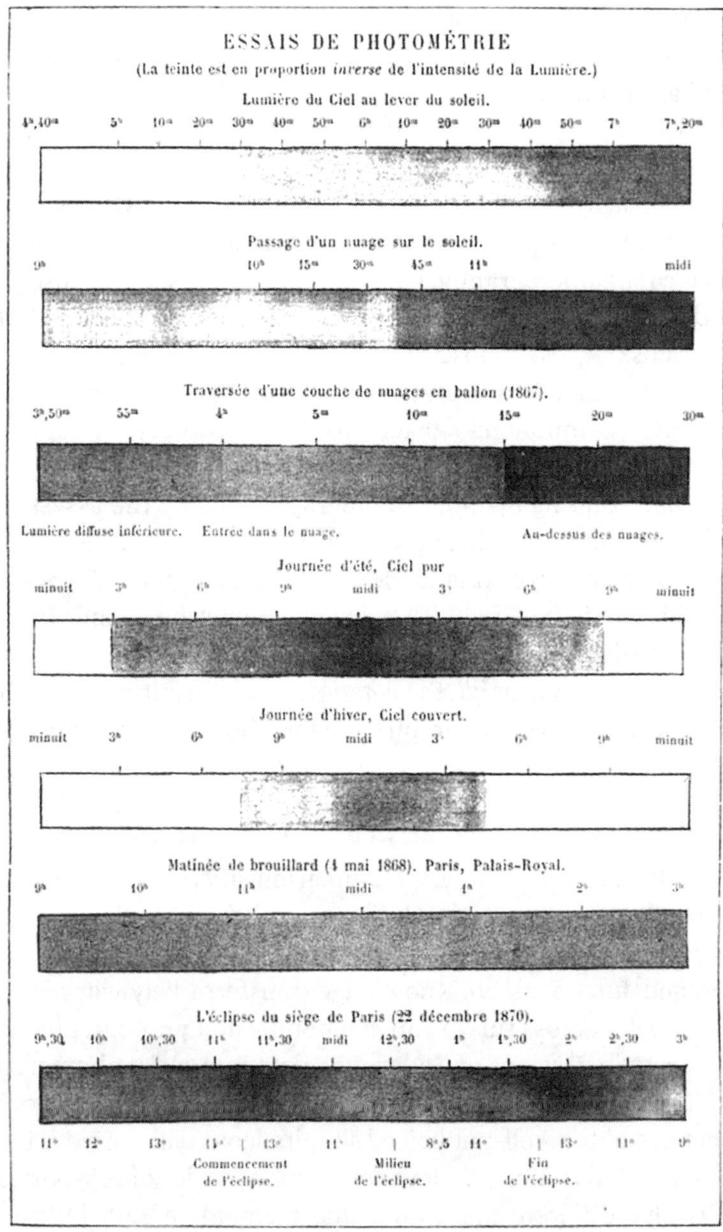

Figure 7.3. **Photometric prints using a chronographic cylinder; made from an air balloon by Flammarion. Camille Flammarion, *L'Atmosphère: Description des grands phénomènes de la nature* (Paris: Hachette, 1872), 281. Courtesy of La Bibliothèque Nationale de France Gallica.**

window, an aperture through which light passes and whose width is calculated based on the diameter of the cylinder. The latter turns around a central axis, either in one hour for delicate and quick observations, or in twelve hours. Passing underneath the window, the prepared paper is impressed proportionally to the light intensity acting upon it" (Flammarion, *L'Atmosphère,* 280). In 1870, Flammarion presented that photometer to the Académie des Sciences and showed a long photographic strip taken during a solar eclipse.[19] He reproduced part of that strip in *The Atmosphere* together with other photograms.[20] These strips accentuate the resemblance between his "photometer" and John Herschel's "actinograph" (see chapter 6).[21]

All five components taken together—projection, spectrophotography, surround aerial vision, optical and photographic technology, and rotating cylinder photography—justify the assessment that Flammarion's telechronoscope is no mere figment but a bona fide prototype of a working model for a cylinder cinema projection apparatus. In his 1867 book *L'Optique,* Flammarion spends considerable attention on shutter mechanisms, confirming he was aware of the need to synchronize the rotation and intermittent immobilization of each microphotograph to enable the fluid projection of visual motion.

The Precinema Club: Nadar, Cros, Janssen, and Marey

Around 1870, already famous, Flammarion stood at the center of a close nexus of precinema technicians and thinkers that included photographer Nadar, poet and inventor Charles Cros, Étienne-Jules Marey, and Jules Janssen. Knowledge transfers likely worked multidirectionally across this group. Ballooning and photography were notorious twin passions of Nadar, who patented aerial photography in 1858. He and Flammarion became close friends and ballooning advocates, staging well-publicized simultaneous balloon rides in the spring of 1867.[22] In 1865, Nadar shot a famous series of self-portraits from twelve different angles forming a complete 360-degree sequence that could be animated in a phenakistoscope. The Czech researcher Jan Evangelista Purkinje did the same that year, placing twelve photographic frames on a disk in his "kinesiscope."[23] In 1870, Nadar took a sequence of photographs of Flammarion shaving his

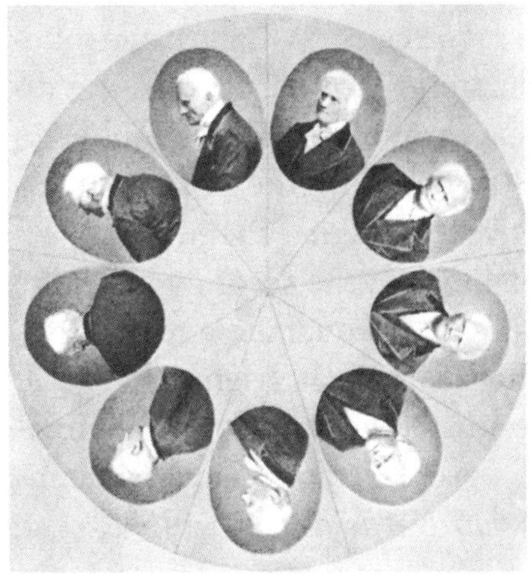

Figure 7.4. **Kinesiscope disk self-portrait by Jan Evangelista Purkinje, circa 1865. Courtesy of the National Technical Museum Collection, Prague. Photo credit Petr Kliment.**

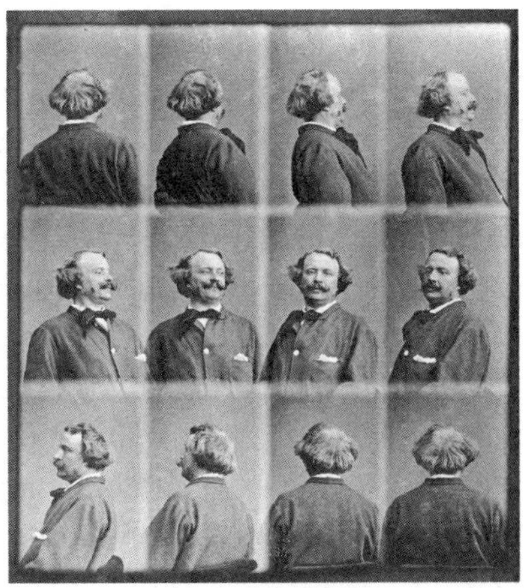

Figure 7.5. **Revolving self-portrait by Nadar, 1861–1867. Prints and Photographic Department, EO-15 (1)-PET FOL. Courtesy of La Bibliothèque Nationale de France.**

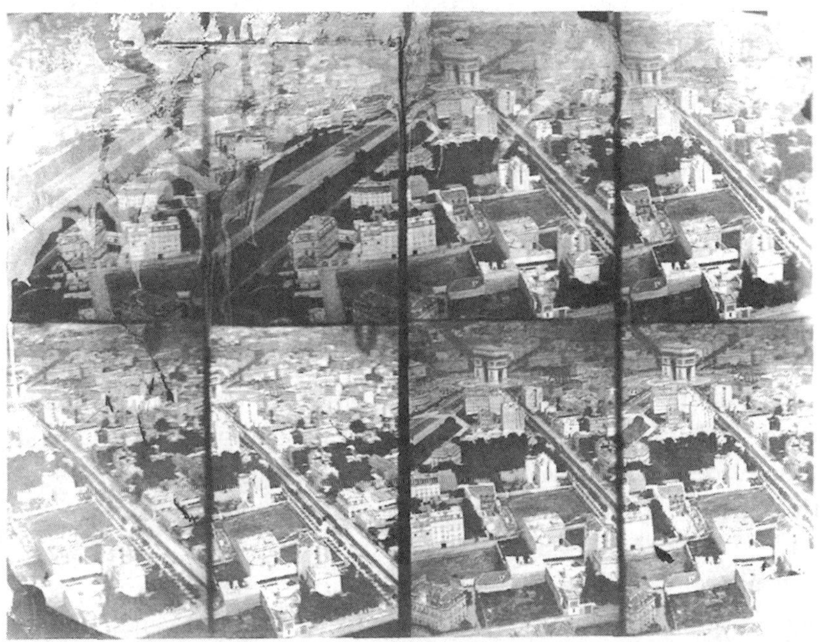

Figure 7.6. **Serial aerial photographs of Paris from air balloon by Nadar, 1868. PHO1991-2-168. Courtesy of Fonds Félix Nadar, Collection Marie-Thérèse et André Jammes, Musée d'Orsay, Paris, France.**

beard and mustache, ending with a smooth face—a remarkable time-lapse experiment that could be animated as well. It was likely a direct homage to Flammarion's interest in animated photography (La Cotardière, *Camille Flammarion,* 130–31). One of the closest friends of Nadar's was Désiré van Monckhoven, a Belgian chemist who became an authority in photographic optics in the second half of the nineteenth century. He was an amateur astronomer, and, in 1892, Nadar referred to him as "among the [likes of] Janssen . . . and that incredible Marey" for his inventiveness, in particular "his enlargement apparatuses with heliostats," a process van Monckhoven initially published in 1867 (Nadar, *When I Was a Photographer,* 122, 127).[24]

In 1900, Janssen wrote to Flammarion on a private matter that "the telescopes of friendship often produce anamorphs," attesting to the optics-centric complicity they shared.[25] The two met in 1873 around preparations for the 1874 Venus transit, about which Flammarion wrote several articles. Janssen was trained as a colonial astronomer who made his mark in expeditions to Peru and India in the 1860s. In 1868 in Madras, he observed a new spectroscopic line in the Sun's chromosphere that did not correspond to any known chemical element. Joseph Norman Lockyer observed the same line a few months later, and in 1871 he confirmed the discovery of the first extraterrestrial chemical element: helium.[26]

Janssen plays a key role in the history of cinema thanks to his design for a photographic revolver with a heliostat. It was the first automated serial-photograph apparatus according to Françoise Launay and Peter D. Hingley, and it directly inspired Marey's application of chronophotography to physiological research.[27] On February 17, 1873, Janssen presented his revolving photographic disk design to the French Commission of the Transit of Venus, admitting he had paid little heed to photography until then. According to an October 1873 quip by British astronomer George Biddell Airy—who appropriated Janssen's original device for his own expedition—Janssen had "not the least idea of mechanics" (Launay and Hingley, "Jules Janssen's 'Revolver Photographique,'" 64). The burning question is then where Janssen derived his breakthrough components:

a disk plate exposed at one-second intervals and rotated by a clockwork drive equipped with an intermittent electrical shutter.

To obviate the black-drop effect of the previous Venus transits, as well as variable reaction times by observers, astronomer Hervé Faye began campaigning in 1870 for photography for the upcoming transits of 1874 and 1882.[28] In a presentation to the Académie des Sciences, Faye championed the heliostat setup Laussedat had experimented with during the 1860 total solar eclipse (see chapter 6). He argued it was superior to clock-driven equatorial telescopes and allowed "to multiply almost indefinitely these plates and measurements," to which Flammarion publicly acquiesced.[29] Faye cites a letter from Laussedat that refers to articles by Warren De la Rue, Major Tennant, and Richard A. Proctor on transit observation sites. The mention of Proctor is significant because he was about to publish *Other Worlds than Ours,* a book reprising the multiple-world hypothesis together with Flammarion's conceit of a cosmic observer witnessing the photographic archive of Earth's history.[30] Proctor envisioned an observer with a total telescopic vision of the universe, endowing him with "powers of locomotion commensurate with his wonderful powers of vision," another instance of the Oculus. He expands on Flammarion's framework by noting that because Earth moves through space, "millions of eyes" would be needed for recording a total archive: "The whole history of the earth, so far as light could render it, would have been in a moment of time presented before the myriad-eyed sphere." Proctor aligns with Eberty's divine omniscient gaze and mentions the Battle of Waterloo in reverse motion, lifting the episode from *Lumen*'s 1867 publication (Proctor, *Other Worlds,* 319–29; Flammarion, "Lumen, les paradoxes de la science" [May 1867]). Proctor's emulation of *Lumen* is a critical piece of evidence demonstrating that international organizers of the 1874 Venus transit, well aware that it was a crucial test for astrophotography requiring both "a large number of pictures" and "the comparison of successive pictures," were keenly aware of Flammarion's fictional cinema apparatus (Proctor, "On the Application of Photography," 64).

The first optical manufacturer Janssen approached in 1873 was Eugène Deschiens, among the most respected astronomical and electrical instrument-makers of Paris at the time.[31] In 1866, Deschiens had collaborated on the construction of the "photobioscope" of Henry Cook and Gaetano Bonelli. It was a compound phenakistoscope with "two series of pictures placed on a glass disk" that "enable[d] viewing stereoscopic photographs in motion" and might reproduce "all imaginable movements shot on the fly [pris au vol]."[32] It makes sense that Janssen chose Deschiens (likely on Flammarion's advice), although their relationship quickly soured. Janssen turned to his previous collaborator Antoine Rédier for the final design of the photographic revolver in 1874.[33]

The last member of the precinema group was Charles Cros, a remarkable media inventor and respected writer and poet who devised numerous self-recording devices, worked on electrical cylinder telegraphic systems in 1866–1867, and drafted projects for motion and color photographic systems.[34] Among Cros's recurring obsessions was a means of communication with other planets, a topic on which Flammarion invited him to lecture in 1869. Cros presented his light-coding device for exchanging signals with the planet Venus during the transit, and Cros and Flammarion would undoubtedly have discussed their respective fascination for animated photography and kinemorphosis. In a treatise on perception simulation, Cros explicitly considered the human biosensorial apparatus to be kinemorphic: "The perception of motion results from a succession of morphic [morphiques] impressions," he writes.[35] In 1872, he published "An Interastral Drama," in the same journal where Flammarion's *Lumen* appeared five years earlier.[36] That short story tells of a male Earthling and a female Venusian, both children of astronomer fathers, who fall in love through telescopes and communicate in secret:

> They sought to vanquish the distance separating them by exchanging the most complete traces of their beings. They sent each other their photographic likenesses in sufficient series for the reproduction of relief and motion.
>
> When no observation was possible, Glaux [the Earthling] would shut himself in a room to reproduce on smoke or floating dust the moving

> image of his beloved—an impalpable image solely made of light. He also made of it a still likeness with plastic substances.
>
> Then they imagined sending each other the sound of their voice, their speech, their songs. All of these were recorded in curves and reproduced within an electrical apparatus using a diapason. (Cros, "Un Drame interastral," 240)

After three years of multisensory sexting, the virtual lovers take their own lives, while "all of Glaux's photographs, photosculptures, and phonographs [phonographies]" are placed in a secret archive (241). Incidentally, this is the first mention of the word *phonograph(y)* to denote the automatic recording of sound, rather than its prior usage of phonetic transcription of words. As is well established, in 1877 Cros published the description for a cylinder phonograph apparatus, a few months before Edison.[37]

In sum, it is fair to say that, prior to Muybridge's and Marey's turn to chronophotography in the late 1870s, Flammarion, Nadar, Cros, and Janssen worked intensely and collaboratively on precinematic

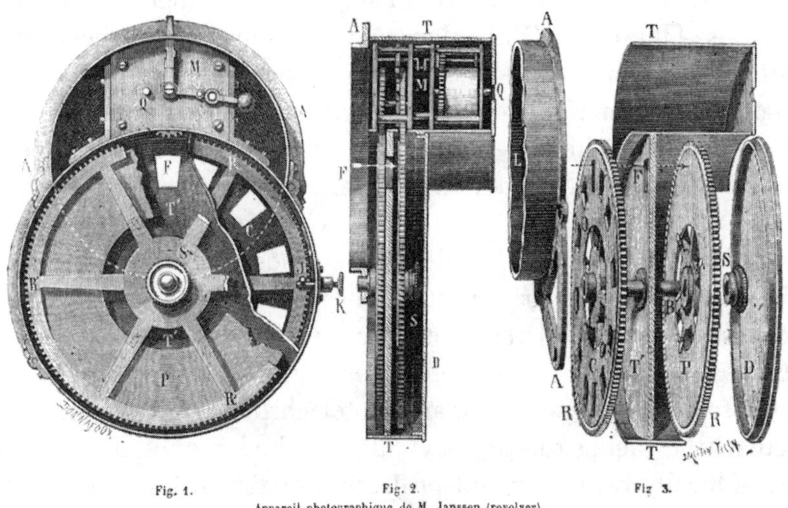

Figure 7.7. **Engraving of Janssen's revolving camera for the first article describing it. Camille Flammarion, *La Nature* 3, no. 1 (1875): 357. Courtesy of La Bibliothèque Nationale de France Gallica.**

animated photography for astronomical and aerial applications in a way that qualifies this foursome as collective innovators of cinema. It was Flammarion, moreover, who penned the authoritative description of Janssen's photographic revolver for the periodical *La Nature* in 1875, and he seemed better suited to explain how it functioned than Janssen himself.[38] Flammarion writes of Janssen's instrument that it aims "to catch on the spot and record, at the very moment they are occurring, the successive and useful phases of the phenomenon" (Flammarion, "Le Passage de Vénus," 357). This is exactly what his telechronoscope ambitioned: "It will take in this way the continuous photograph of successive events" (Flammarion, *Récits de l'infini,* 136). We must conclude that Flammarion's astronomical cylinder motion-recorder photographic prototype design was key to Janssen's sudden application of rapid-sequence photography to the observation of the 1874 Venus transit.

Flammarion and Edison

Within current media history, the emergence of cinema apparatuses is envisioned as an application of sequential photography for the analysis of human and animal motion. The subsequent crucial step ostensibly taken in 1887–1888 by Edison and his chief kinetograph engineer William Kennedy Laurie Dickson, followed by Marey and Georges Demenÿ in 1889–1890, was to reverse the process to project the synthesis of photographed motion.[39] Flammarion's telechronoscope inverts this narrative. It takes the synthesis of serial photographic imaging as aboriginal to the cosmos, placing synthesis as phenomenologically prior to its analysis in discrete chronophotographs. As mentioned earlier, together with John Herschel's 1840 actinograph and his own photometer, both using nonintermittent photosensitive strips, Flammarion's telechronoscope has the particularity of being the only cylinder method proposed for photographically recording and projecting motion prior to Edison's kinetograph/kinetoscope.

The question might then be raised whether influence or transfer occurred from Flammarion to Edison. Here is how the latter describes his new machine in a caveat for the US Patent Office on October 15, 1888:

> My invention relates to an instrument which is intended to do for the eye what the phonograph does for the ear, that is to record and reproduce views of things and objects in motion, and the instrument is designed to be in such form as to be cheap, practical, and convenient. I call the apparatus a Kinetoscope. When the instrument is used in recording motions it may be called a kinetograph, but when used for subsequent reproduction, which will be its most common use to the public, it is properly called a kinetoscope. The principal feature of the invention consists in continuously photographing a series of pictures at slight intervals, not less than eight per second. These pictures are photographed in a continuous spiral line on a cylinder or plate in the same way that sound is recorded on the phonograph. The cylinder is provided with an escapement which keeps it at rest at the instant the chemical action of photographing takes place on it and between the operations of photographing it is advanced in rotation a single step at a time, this motion taking place while the light is cut off by a rapidly vibrating shutter. . . . For reproducing the photographic record, I substitute for the photographing instrument a microscope, and when the instrument is revolved the continuous series of photographs passes above the eye with such rapidity as to produce on the eye the impression of a continuous scene in motion which occurs in the same manner as those originally recorded.[40]

The kinetoscope uses "a collodion or soft film," and the exchangeable photographic apparatus or microscope (*M* in Figure 7.8) is mounted on an arm synchronized with the axle of the cylinder, while the shutter is vibrated between two magnets (*F* and *G* in Figure 7.8). Flammarion's telechronoscope and the kinetograph/kinetoscope share three key operative features: sequential microphotographs on the outer surface of a cylinder, the helicoid arrangement of microphotographs, and the lateral reading of the helix of microphotographs. Edison's light-focusing photographic/microscope mechanism is a fourth feature not so much absent in the cosmic chronoscope as implicit, given Flammarion's knowledge of optical apparatuses. Edison adds another feature not found in Flammarion: "By using very large transparent shells the pictures may be projected on a screen

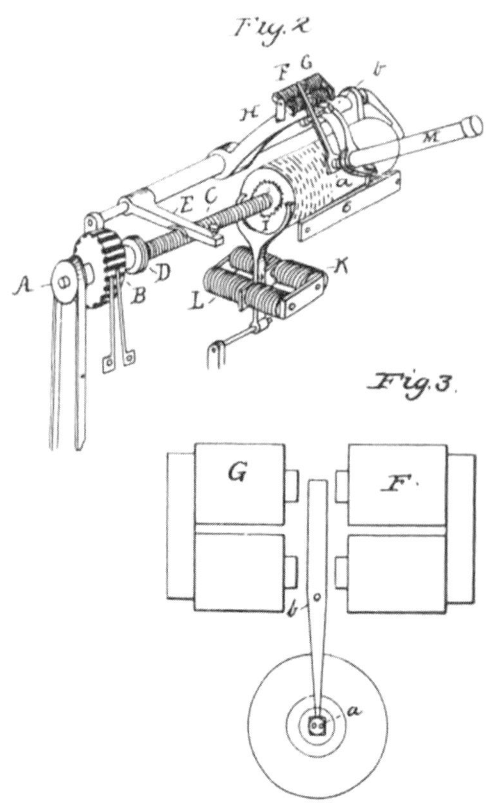

Figure 7.8. **Drawing of the Kinetograph for US Patent Office Caveat, October 15, 1888. Thomas Alva Edison, QM001348, Thomas A. Edison Papers Digital Project, accessed June 18, 2025, https://edisondigital.rutgers.edu/document/QM001348.**

as is done in the enlargement of micro-photographs. . . . The source of light will be placed inside the cylinder" (Edison, "Patent Caveat," 353). Edison thus envisioned a glass cylinder rotating and sliding across a lamp whose light beam traverses the successive microphotographs magnified by a lens to project them on a screen.

There are so many channels potentially linking Edison to Flammarion's *Lumen* that the question seems less *whether* Edison learned of the telechronoscope than *when* and *how.* These channels include the following: Dickson and his sister Antonia were raised in France in the 1860s, and Antonia was a scientific writer and translator from French while Dickson was the main engineer for the kinetoscope; self-recording cylinder telegraphy, specifically Edison's knowledge of the model developed by Charles Cros in 1867; Edison's lasting interest in astronomy (see his invention of the tasimeter for measuring stellar heat); Theosophy (both Flammarion and Edison were in the orbit of Helena Blavatsky); Edison and Charles Batchelor's fascination for unknown cosmic forces such as the etheric force;[41] the name and subsequent productive misunderstanding by caricaturist George du Maurier in 1877 regarding Edison's sound-amplifying machine, "the chronophonoscope"; Cros's 1877 cylinder phonograph, of which Edison was clearly aware; international expos (Edison's representatives are said to have hired Flammarion for the 1881 Paris International Exposition of Electricity); and, of course, a most likely direct encounter by Edison of Flammarion's book or reviews of it, either in English or in French.[42] I have found no smoking gun in Edison's archives (now coming online), but this should come as no surprise. Edison was wary of patent claims and infringement laws and did not hesitate to alter or suppress documents when it suited him. Though absence of proof is proof of nothing, we are left with two equally striking alternatives: either Edison discovered the cylinder setup idea in *Lumen,* in which case cinema as we know it comes from Flammarion, or Edison did not know *Lumen,* in which case the protoapparatus for working cinema—prior to celluloid strip technology after 1888—was invented twice, twenty years apart.

In either alternative, let us insist that the phonograph should no longer be considered the paradigmatic setup for time-based audiovisual media. Cros made electrical cylindrical apparatuses a standard for media design prior to the phonograph, notably for a self-tracing cylinder music machine (1866) and telegraph (1867).[43] In the case of Edison, historians have followed his vaunted explanatory schema for the 1888 kinetoscope as trying "to do for the eye what the phonograph does for the ear," as indicated in his patent text. Yet in that chain of media, it was the telescope that came first. In 1878—ten years before that consecrated formula—Edison described a microphone capturing and amplifying sound at a distance: "TELEPHONOSCOPE This little instrument is to the ear what the telescope is to the eye. As the eye receives and transmits the vibrations of the ether or, in other words, the light, so the ear receives and transmits the vibrations of the air, set in motion by some disturbance. . . . Mr. Edison proposes to invent something which can be concealed and connected to the ear."[44] Modern audiovisual media designs did not originate from sound only to migrate to vision in some telic evolution paralleling the immemorial switch from orality to writing. The telescope was the paradigm. Indeed, Edison's coinage of *telephonoscope* may well have copied and remediated for sound Flammarion's *telechronoscope.*

Flammarion as Cinema Thinker and Animation Pioneer

No sooner had Edison and Dickson implemented the cylinder cinema than Flammarion devised a second-generation cinema apparatus in his novel *Uranie* (1889).[45] It reprises the space travel genre of *Lumen* but with a female guide, in a more transparent retracing of Flammarion's own intellectual trajectory. The plot follows a young astronomer under the thumb of a ruthless Jean-Joseph Le Verrier, who falls into a daydream triggered by his fascination for the female figure of Urania atop a mantle clock at the Paris Observatory. Coming alive, Urania takes him across deep space to a planet populated by tiny androgynous dragonfly-like beings. "Their eyes are superior to your best telescopes," the celestial muse quips, adding, "For printed matter they have the direct photography of events and the phonetic fixation of speech itself" (Flammarion, *Uranie,* 18–19). Urania explains that astronomy and the discovery of extraterrestrial intelligence will achieve world peace, and to illustrate the point she reaches back into the past as though merely "changing microtelescopic eyepieces [objectifs micro-télescopiques]" (46). The second part of the novel jumps forward to 1867 with the narrator's friend George Spero and his fiancée, just after the Paris "Universal Exposition" where cylinder chronographs and photographic technology intersected (57). Spero is a second doppelgänger of Flammarion, an astronomer obsessed with death and the transmigration of souls. He shares this passion with his Norwegian fiancée, but as they go ballooning to watch an aurora borealis, they crash and die. Soon after, the narrator communicates with their souls through a hypnotist who tells him they now live on Mars where they "exchanged *sexes*" (136). Long developments on psychic communication with the dead follow, citing the fashionable work of the moment: Edmund Gurney and Frederic W. H. Myers, *Phantasms of the Living*

(1886). The narrator is ultimately transported to Mars, inhabited by talking plants and fantastical creatures—but everything dissolves as in a dream, and he is back on Earth. Spero then reappears, passing as male though "really" female, but he is only a 3D filmic hologram: "They [Martians] have invented, among other things, a kind of telephotographic apparatus [appareil téléphotographique] in which a spool of fabric constantly receives, by unfolding, the image of our world and fixes it durably. An immense museum dedicated to the planets of the solar system preserves in a chronological order all these photographic images forever fixed. The whole history of the Earth is found there" (214).

In 1894, Flammarion devised a third cinema apparatus in his dystopic *The End of the World.*[46] A docufiction, the book is premised on a comet whose orbit, discovered by a woman mathematician, will cross Earth's path. Martians warn Earth by sending a "photophonic message" to an astronomical observatory in India—which is now postcolonial and independent from Great Britain. Martians also send a live-cast communication via a "telephonoscope"—that is, a "projection apparatus" showing "hieroglyphs" all at once on a "plate," a "mirror," and a "curtain" (Flammarion, *La Fin du monde,* 131–32).

Given his decades-long interest for cinema technology, it is not surprising that after the Lumière Cinématographe was unveiled in December 1895, Flammarion quickly adapted the new media for astronomy. In December 1897, he presented to the Société Astronomique de France the following project: "Through the cinématographe, however, a terrestrial globe may be photographed revolving on itself, seemingly isolated in space against the dark background of a starry sky, tilted on its axis and seen from all points of the equator as well as the pole. We can thereby behold an image of the Earth as we would see it from the Moon, for instance, and see our planet slowly and majestically rotating in a uniform and calm motion."[47] At last, the enduring visualization of rotating Earth seen from a lunar point of view would be materialized.

With the help of an artist painting the globe (Hippolyte Berteaux), an engineer designing a rotating machine with an invisible

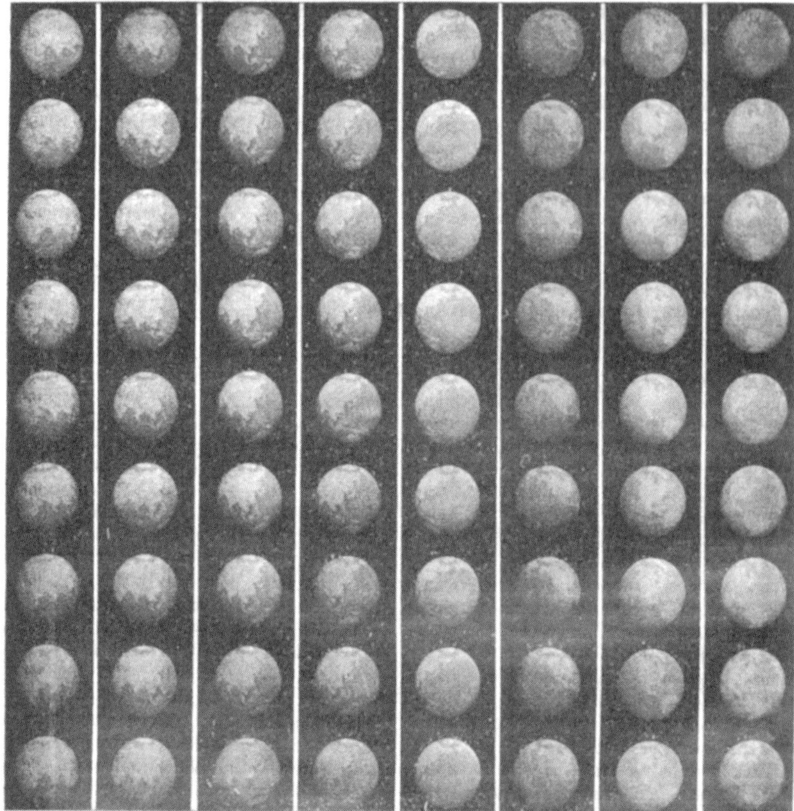

Figure 7.9. **Reproduction of filmstrip by Eugène Pirou for Flammarion's animation film. L. Reverchon, "Le Kosmokinétographe," *Cosmos* 693 (May 7, 1898): 588. Courtesy of La Bibliothèque Nationale de France Gallica.**

cam (M. Chateau), and a camera operator filming the rotating globe (Eugène Pirou), Flammarion directed this simulation movie. A piece of the actual filmstrip was reproduced in an issue of *Cosmos* of May 1898.[48] Danielle Chaperon states that the film was never shown, but this is not quite correct.[49] A correspondent from the *Los Angeles Herald* in Paris witnessed one of the shows on February 15, 1898, and gave a detailed account. There were at least two films. One, lasting two minutes, is described as "a picture of the earth as seen by the inhabitants of the moon, if there be any," and was thus likely the animation picture I examined. The correspondent describes a second

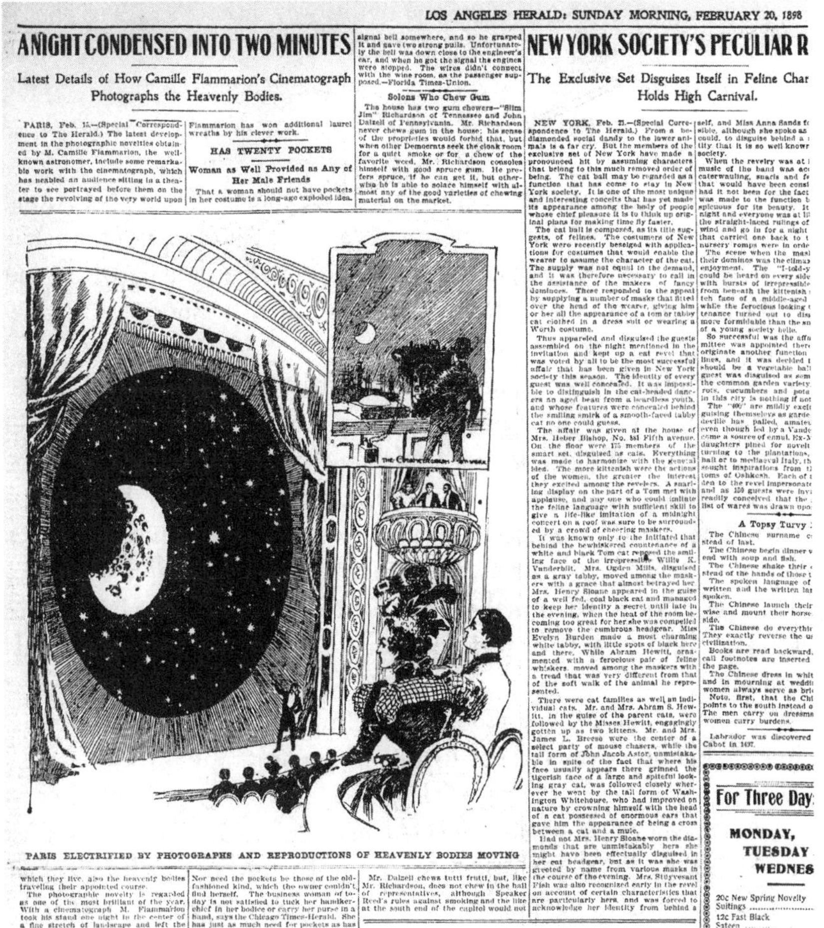

LOS ANGELES HERALD: SUNDAY MORNING, FEBRUARY 20, 1898

A NIGHT CONDENSED INTO TWO MINUTES

Latest Details of How Camille Flammarion's Cinematograph Photographs the Heavenly Bodies.

PARIS, Feb. 15.—(Special Correspondence to The Herald.) The latest developments in the photographic novelties obtained by M. Camille Flammarion, the well-known astronomer, include some remarkable work with the cinematograph, which has enabled an audience sitting in a theater to see portrayed before them on the stage the revolving of the very world upon which they live, also the heavenly bodies travelling their appointed course.

The photographic novelty is regarded as one of the most brilliant of the year. With a cinematograph M. Flammarion took his stand one night in the center of a fine stretch of landscape and left the

Flammarion has won additional laurel wreaths by his clever work.

HAS TWENTY POCKETS

Woman as Well Provided as Any of Her Male Friends

That a woman should not have pockets in her costume is a long-ago exploded idea. Nor need the pockets be those of the old-fashioned kind, which the owner couldn't find herself. The business woman of today is not satisfied to tuck her handkerchief in her bodice or carry her purse in a hand, says the Chicago Times-Herald. She has just as much need for pockets as has

signal bell somewhere, and so he grasped it and gave two strong pulls. Unfortunately the bell was down close to the engineer's ear, and when he got the signal the engines were stopped. The wires didn't connect with the wine room, as the passenger supposed.—Florida Times-Union.

Solons Who Chew Gum

The house has two gum chewers—"Slim Jim" Richardson of Tennessee and John Dalzell of Pennsylvania. Mr. Richardson never chews gum in the house; his sense of the proprieties would forbid that, but when other Democrats seek the cloak room for a quiet smoke or for a chew of the favorite weed, Mr. Richardson consoles himself with good spruce gum. He prefers spruce, if he can get it, but otherwise he is able to solace himself with almost any of the good varieties of chewing material on the market.

Mr. Dalzell chews tutti frutti, but, like Mr. Richardson, does not chew in the hall of representatives, although Speaker Reed's rules against smoking and the like at the south end of the capitol would not

PARIS ELECTRIFIED BY PHOTOGRAPHS AND REPRODUCTIONS OF HEAVENLY BODIES MOVING

NEW YORK SOCIETY'S PECULIAR R

The Exclusive Set Disguises Itself in Feline Char Holds High Carnival.

NEW YORK, Feb. 21.—(Special Correspondence to The Herald.) From a bediamonded social dandy to the lower animals is a far cry. But the members of the exclusive set of New York have made a pronounced hit by assuming characters that belong to this much removed order of being. The cat ball may be regarded as a function that has come to stay in New York society. It is one of the most unique and interesting conceits that has yet made its appearance among the body of people whose chief pleasure it is to think up original plans for making time fly faster.

The cat ball is composed, as its title suggests, of felines. The costumers of New York were recently besieged with applications for costumes that would enable the wearer to assume the character of the cat. The supply was not equal to the demand, and it was therefore necessary to call in the assistance of the makers of fancy dominoes. These responded to the appeal by supplying a number of masks that fitted over the head of the wearer, giving him or her all the appearance of a tom or tabby cat clothed in a dress suit or wearing a Worth costume.

Thus appareled and disguised the guests assembled on the night mentioned in the invitation and kept up a cat revel that was voted by all to be the most successful affair that has been given in New York society this season. The identity of every guest was well concealed. It was impossible to distinguish in the cat-headed dancers an aged beau from a beardless youth, and whose features were concealed behind the smiling smirk of a smooth-faced tabby cat no one could guess.

The affair was given at the house of Mrs. Heber Bishop, No. 881 Fifth avenue. On the floor were 175 members of the smart set, disguised as cats. Everything was made to harmonize with the general idea. The more kittenish were the actions of the women, the greater the interest they excited among the revelers. A snarling display on the part of a Tom met with applause, and any one who could imitate the feline language with sufficient skill to give a life-like imitation of a midnight concert on a roof was sure to be surrounded by a crowd of cheering maskers.

It was known only to the initiated that behind the bewhiskered countenance of a white and black Tom cat reposed the smiling face of the irrepressible Willie K. Vanderbilt. Mrs. Ogden Mills, disguised as a gray tabby, moved among the maskers with a grace that almost betrayed her. Mrs. Henry Sloane appeared in the guise of a well fed, coal black cat and managed to keep her identity a secret until late in the evening, when the heat of the room becoming too great for her she was compelled to remove the cumbrous headgear. Miss Evelyn Burden made a most charming white tabby, with little spots of black here and there. While Abram Hewitt, ornamented with a ferocious pair of feline whiskers, moved among the maskers with a tread that was very different from that of the soft walk of the animal he represented.

There were cat families as well as individual cats. Mr. and Mrs. Abram S. Hewitt, in the guise of the parent cats, were followed by the Misses Hewitt, engagingly gotten up as two kittens. Mr. and Mrs. James L. Breese were the center of a select party of mouse chasers, while the tall form of John Jacob Astor, unmistakable in spite of the fact that where his face usually appears there grinned the tigerish face of a large and spiteful looking gray cat, was followed closely wherever he went by the tall form of Washington Whitehouse, who had improved on nature by crowning himself with the head of a cat possessed of enormous ears that gave him the appearance of being a cross between a cat and a mule.

Had not Mrs. Henry Sloane worn the diamonds that are unmistakably hers she might have been effectually disguised in her cat headgear, but as it was she was greeted by name from various masks in the course of the evening. Mrs. Stuyvesant Fish was also recognized early in the revel on account of certain characteristics that are particularly hers, and was forced to acknowledge her identity from behind a

For Three Day

MONDAY,
TUESDAY
WEDNES

Figure 7.10. **Illustration of Flammarion's simulation film of an eclipse with illustration of stop-action filming of a real eclipse. Anon. "A Night Condensed into Two Minutes,"** ***Los Angeles Herald: Sunday Morning,*** **February 28, 1898, 17.**

live-action film condensing an entire night of astronomical observation into two minutes by way of stop-action astrophotography:

> In order to make the consecutive pictures that would enable him to portray the scenes of the heavens at various stages of the night, [Flammarion] took thousands of proofs on the same film, and made a number

> of proofs on different nights, and in this way made a series of photographs showing the gradual going down of the sun, the coming out of the stars, the rising of the moon, its motions during the night, and the entire movements of the ever-changing astronomical bodies from darkness to dawn.
>
> The flying stars that shot mysteriously across the firmament during the night were all faithfully portrayed, and the whole scene of the star-lit heavens transferred to the film, ending with the breaking of day and the chasing away of the stars by the rising sun in the morning.[50]

Chaperon provides the scenario of a third film, which is more like an entire program with a travel journey shown in various episodes—from a seaside at night to the Andromeda galaxy and back (Chaperon, "Le Cinématographe astronomique," 58). Through much of 1898, Flammarion worked on a complex show of astronomical films meant to be projected at the Cosmorama building planned for the 1900 Exposition Universelle in Paris. Nothing came of it, but the grandiose space journey program Chaperon describes fits that millennial occasion.

When *Lumen* was republished in English in 1897 in the era of cinema, Flammarion added the following paragraph:

> Already your terrestrial scientific knowledge enables you to take instantaneous photographs of the successive aspects of rapid phenomena, such as lightning, a meteor, the waves of the sea, a volcanic eruption, the fall of a building, and to make them pass before you graduated in accordance with their effect on the retina. Similarly, you can, on the contrary, photograph the pollen of a flower, through each stage of expansion to its completion in the fruit, or the development of a child from its birth to maturity, and project these phases upon a screen, depicting in a few seconds the life of a man, or a tree.[51]

Such a comment is prescient of the way high-speed cinematography and accelerated stop-action began altering human perception and knowledge of space-time. These new techniques were in fact at the very heart of the cinema of attraction and, subsequently, the experimentalists of the first French avant-garde of cinema in the 1920s.[52]

Popular Science and Race in Flammarion's Pancosmic History

Flammarion exemplifies the new professional class of late nineteenth-century best-selling astronomer-popularizers, together with Agnes Mary Clerke in the United States and Proctor in England. Unlike them, early on he developed a passion for the occult shared by intellectuals and mass culture alike, as a reaction against Weberian rationalization and modernization.[53] Flammarion was a radical vitalist who rejected empirical approaches making mind and soul epiphenomena of the brain. He favored instead a pancosmic panpsychism—the belief that the human soul is but one facet of a fluidic energy animating the entire cosmos, leading to metempsychosis after death. William James—who knew Flammarion through the Society for Psychical Research—Alfred North Whitehead, William Crookes, and Henri Bergson, among many others, shared such convictions. Importantly, Flammarion's panpsychism was interpreted by Black diasporic thinkers as inherently emancipatory. Haitian intellectual and politician Louis-Joseph Janvier wrote in 1882 that "for us, mulattoes of Haiti, the preponderant authority in philosophy as in astronomy is Flammarion" (quoted in Flammarion, *Mémoires,* 296fn).[54] By presenting the soul as independent from the body and capable of migrating to other envelopes beyond the human phenotypical spectrum, panpsychism de-essentialized race. In his magisterial retort to Arthur de Gobineau's anti-Black Aryan theory, Haitian philosopher Anténor Firmin also paid homage to Flammarion's spiritualism as an alternative to the psychological materialism of white scientific racism.[55] Among nineteenth-century African American thinkers as well, panpsychism was invoked as an area of scientific inquiry circumventing biological racism.[56]

Flammarion's own views on race cover a wide spectrum in his published writings. In *Imaginary Worlds and Real Worlds* (1865) he reviewed what I call "astro-ethnography," the makeup of conjectural inhabitants of other planets. He mentioned Georges Cuvier's description of putative Venusians as "midway between the Orang Utang and the Kaffir [Black African]" and Martians "resembling our negroes" while pointing to earlier commentators envisioning

Venusians as "akin to the Black peoples of our Africa."[57] Without unilaterally condemning their anti-Blackness, Flammarion argued that such analogies were nonsensical given the vastly different physical conditions (gravity, atmosphere, light) on other planets. He calls for a Copernican revolution in thinking about extraterrestrials. Rather than projecting human races on space aliens, he posits that all intelligent life-forms constitute a continuum within which there is no justification to privilege humanity: "Amid such a variety [of possible life-forms on other planets], how can we maintain the idea of a universality of type, how can we maintain the universality of an organism whose first character is to mold itself after a requisite form, to place itself in unison with the ambient harmony, to be eminently plastic, in order to be out of place nowhere, in no system?" (Flammarion, *Mondes imaginaires,* 121). Flammarion's racial thinking is fundamentally qualified by his relativizing humanoid centrality through the plasticity and diversity of macrocosmic sentient life-forms. In *Lumen,* when asked by Quaerens, "What people are you taking as typical of the degree of intelligence on Earth?" Lumen answers unexpectedly: "The Arab people. They are capable of producing Keplers, Newtons, Galileos, Archimedes, Euclids and d'Alemberts" (Flammarion, *Récits de l'infini,* 159).[58] In "The Story of a Comet," added to *Lumen* in 1873, civilizational developments are seen through the eyes of a comet orbiting Earth at long intervals and gendered as a female gaze (since une comète is feminine in French). It flies by our planet at three-thousand-year intervals to take stock of humanity's progress, like a camera-equipped probe sent by a more advanced civilization. As the comet passes over ancient Egypt, the female voice indicates that "the celestial observer had not yet, in truth, glanced upon the white race among humans though she noted nonetheless great progress in the ways things appeared" (309). In a later orbit, the comet notes that "the ancestors of the Toltecs" built an advanced culture in the city-state of "Tenochtitlan," while "the Celts" remained steeped in "natural primitive life." In other words, non-Europeans developed urban cultures while white peoples were still "savages" (315–17). Such comments show Flammarion's reliance on archaeological research to debunk Gobineau-like white supremacy. As for phrenology and craniometry, Flammarion dismisses them in another work in terms reminiscent of Georg Christoph Lichtenberg: "The Caucasian brain is oval, the Mongol brain round and the negro brain elongated—but in what way is the human spirit associated to granulated or cylindric fibers? What have notions of justice and injustice to do with carbonic acid?"[59] Such arguments secured respect from Black diasporic intellectuals, despite racist barbs and anti-Black clichés unfortunately popping up in his prose.[60]

Flammarion's worldview is composite in a way that challenges ours. On the one hand, he was trained by and beholden to positivist science, from whence his relative antiracism sprang. Firmin subtitled his masterpiece *Positive Anthropology* within the same purview of true science as critique. On the other hand, Flammarion's writings as a popularizer occasionally traffic in Eurocentric, colonialist, and racist clichés of a kind that his friend Jules Verne's novels reflect more starkly and shamelessly. Yet what ultimately commits Flammarion's thought to a horizon of gender and racial equality is his view of history in which material and civilizational progress synonymous with white supremacist purviews are de-emphasized via a forward-and-backward model of macrocosmic temporality. For Flammarion, metempsychosis links past and future through the same soul energy, merely shedding material envelopes. And for him, the past is never dead, primitive, or to be overcome; it remains present and animated, albeit optically distant.

The telechronoscope thus opens perspectives for rethinking Western historicity. While the arc of photocinema followed a protracted history of poisonous racism as part of progress, Flammarion's telechronoscope displays, technically and conceptually, a tenuous but tangible potion: a nontelic horizon of justice committed to a sense that history is ever alive—always right here, with us, and always in the future too.

Conclusion

The Matrix of Photocinema and the Moral Universe

As stated in the introduction, the thesis put forward in this study is that astronomical and cosmological visualizations generated new modes of imaging from the seventeenth to the nineteenth century, which gradually coalesced into photocinema. Integral to such visualizations were accounts of racial differentiation and Blackness, which linked Earth to the cosmos and photochemistry to skin color. Such a sweeping and transhistorical argument comes with obvious pitfalls. Michel Foucault notably warns us against conflating similar concepts that are distant in time and place ("discursive formations") since they function very differently within the episteme of each period.[1] Also, given the necessary selectiveness of the three centuries' worth of ideas, instruments, texts, and historical hinges analyzed herein, there is a chance of overlooked counterevidence or bias confirmation. The argument itself may appear too broad and hubristic, while recycling the temptation of grand narratives from which critical humanities and media archaeology have distanced themselves. These are valid concerns. The findings in this study confirm each other and exhibit convergences over long periods of time, but I do not claim that they are exhaustive.

Bearing these limitations in mind, this conclusion offers justifications for proponing such an overarching thesis against the grain of the scale of today's humanities research. It also sketches out

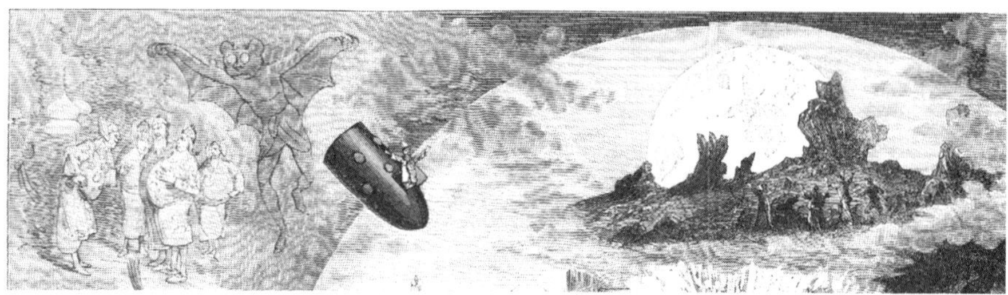

Figure C.1. **Detail of poster for Jacques Offenbach's 1875 operetta *A Trip to the Moon*. The "photographer" with a lens protruding from his belly is at left, facing a group of Orientalized figures, under a flying bat-Selenite. Auguste ["Sweeton"] Tilly, *Illustrated Sporting and Dramatic News* 4, no. 90 (November 13, 1875): 153.**

how this study can open new frameworks for intersections of astronomy and race in the history of movies. Finally, reading two stories of W. E. B. Du Bois, we ponder a recurring feature permeating this study: intertwinements between protocinematic forms and our modern idea of racialized history—particularly from the purview of the Black intellectual tradition.

Global Justice and Polymathy

This study began as a work of media archaeology focused on astronomical culture, until I realized that what that meant in the seventeenth and eighteenth centuries was not at all the same as today. Well into the development of this book, I realized that what had begun as a work of media archaeology had morphed into something else. At its best, media archaeology puts in question the disciplinary contours of its objects—media. But it has not been proactive at addressing how race figures in their inception. The reigning presumption is that race entered only through representations within constituted media. In other words, in current media archaeology, race is unseeable. To a large extent, this is also true for media theory. Take Roland Barthes's *Camera Lucida* (1980). It was canonized for thirty years in media studies until Shawn Michelle Smith demonstrated the pivotal role of racist and antiracist discourse within Barthes's notion of photographic punctum.[2] My intent, however, had not been to race media archaeology—quite the opposite. I proceeded to set aside the references to race I came across in my corpus as being beyond the scope of this study, as the chaste expression goes, following media archaeology's premise. But then I came across Susan Buck-Morss's luminous injunction that "disciplinary boundaries allow counterevidence to belong to someone else's story" and her concomitant call for our "loyalty to the idea of a universal humanity," to the exact extent that it has historically been betrayed by its white inceptors.[3]

As a result, this book committed to cross-disciplinarity or, rather, critical polymathy. As Siegfried Zielinski, Jussi Parikka, and other media archaeologists show, early media thinking was inherently polymathic.[4] Moreover, Black diasporic thinkers and thinkers of color like Édouard Glissant, Sylvia Wynter, Fred Moten, Arjun Appadurai, Dipesh Chakrabarty, Achille Mbembe, Lisa Lowe, and Denise Ferreira da Silva (among many others) have taught us to examine racialization critically across disciplines, at long durations, and at the scale of the planet.[5] This is the purview of racial and colonial reparations. For Olúfẹ́mi O. Táíwò, that perspective entails a "worldmaking project" in which the acknowledgment of five centuries of white supremacy over the globe is a necessary propaedeutic step for reconstructive practices honed on racial injustice and justice to come.[6] What I find striking in Táíwò's work is its reliance on envisioning history by making visible the "structure and motion" of enslaved and free peoples over centuries, the unequal distribution and reproduction of their dis/advantages, and the field of forces generated by historical flows of goods. He foregrounds "nested scale" and an expanded awareness of "real space-time" to counter Rawlsian approaches that he calls "a 'snapshot view' of distributive justice," limited to analyzing discrete places and times (Táíwò, *Reconsidering Reparations,* 20, 33, 74). In this endeavor to reframe reparative justice, retracing the origins of photocinema becomes more than an academic exercise. It helps us contextualize the relationship Táíwò uncovers between history seen as mere snapshots and history rethought as a kinemorphic "trajectory . . . in the unfolding of a process . . . about today, about yesterday, and about the narrative arc that unites them" (85). In this sense, the origins of photocinema outlined in the present study partake of a larger model of racialized historicity that still subtends the temporality of our world system. In the last section, I return to that model and the temporal purview of Táíwò's constructive reparations.[7]

The Beginnings of Cinema at the End of Indigenous Rule

The findings of this study can help us understand nonintuitive connections between astronomy and race in early moving pictures. Cinema as an artful medium arguably began with Georges Méliès's *A Trip to the Moon* in 1902. Relying on colorized frames, trick shots (stop action), féerie sets, and tableau staging, it follows five white males' journey to the Moon, where they encounter Lunarians. The thin plot has little ambition beyond showcasing the technical wizardry of the cinema of attractions.

The movie was inspired not directly by Jules Verne's popular 1865 novel *From the Earth to the Moon* but by *A Trip to the Moon,* an 1875 derivative operetta by Jacques Offenbach. It centers on a scientist named Microscope, who takes his king Vlan and retinue to the Moon. There they meet blue Selenites, their king Cosmos, and his counselor Cactus. "How backward they are on the Moon," Vlan remarks as Cosmos mounts a dromedary—a transparent Orientalist cliché.[8] Male Selenites sell females they find displeasing, and the third act centers on the public auction of a lunar princess, one of the bidders being "a slave merchant." One character is a Selenite photographer who displays insect-like characteristics, Orientalized clothing, a hooked "Semitic" nose, and an accordion-camera body (see Figure C.3). Other Selenites have bat-like features that were influenced by 1835 Great Moon Hoax illustrations (see Figure C.2), while the operetta's moonscape sets imitate "lunar landscapes from Flammarion" (Vanloo et al., *Le Voyage dans la Lune,* 132, iv).

The success of Offenbach's lunar fairy show, with its overt racism and primitivism, was widely emulated. In 1901, a fair attraction called "Trip to the Moon" was shown at the Buffalo Pan-American Exposition, while H. G. Wells published *The First Men in the Moon.*[9] Méliès leveraged the success of this turn-of-the-century lunar revival.

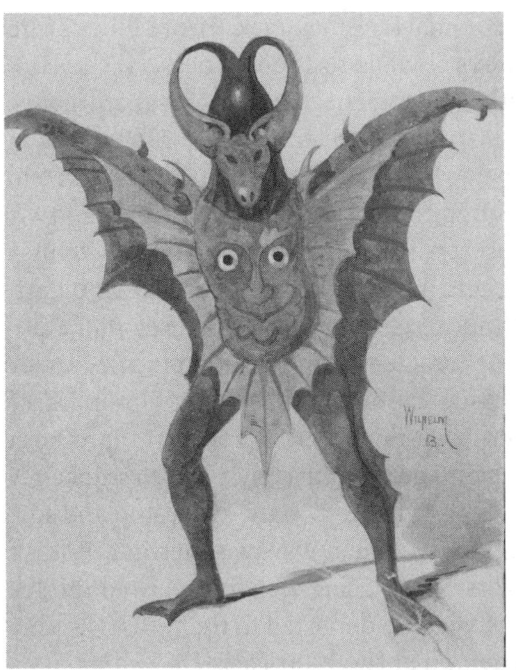

Figure C.2. **Wilhelm, Selenite costume (1898) for Jacques Offenbach's *Trip to the Moon*. Courtesy of Victoria and Albert Museum.**

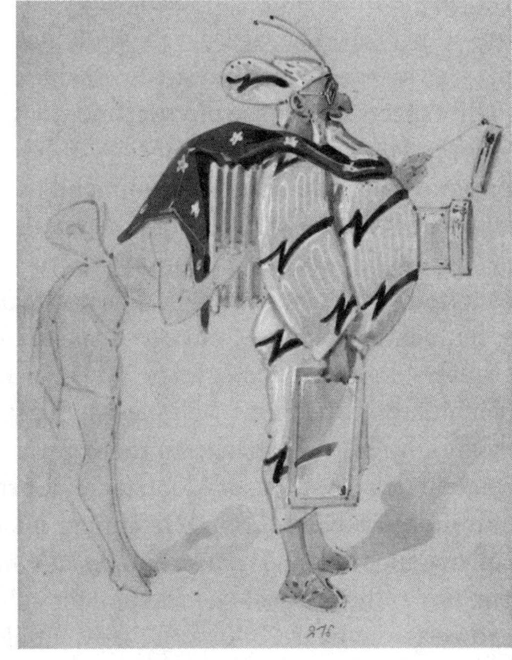

Figure C.3. **Alfred Grévin, *Photographe,* 1875. Watercolor. Collection Albert Vizentini, vol. 3, libretto of Offenbach's *Trip to the Moon,* call number Brown M.Cab.2.31 v.2 pt.1, Allen A. Brown Collection of Music, Boston Public Library.**

Recent critics note the colonial racism at the core of Méliès's film but not the proximal context obvious to French viewers: the conquest of Madagascar.[10] With near-total hegemony across continents, Western powers in the 1890s turned to strategic island nations in the Pacific and Indian Oceans: Madagascar for France, Hawai'i and the Philippines for the United States, and federated Australia for the British Empire. The lobster-like costumes of Méliès's Selenites barely conceal the movie's anti-Indigenous, anti-African, and anti-Islamic stance (the king's house is adorned with crescents). Selenites bear the long lances characteristic of depictions of islander Native people in Western visual culture. The white explorers carry no weapons, only umbrellas that nonetheless transform into both shields and ray guns that disintegrate Native people into smoke for a laugh.[11] A Selenite who has piggybacked on the spaceship and survived the ocean splash is paraded like a war prisoner in a Roman triumph. For French viewers, that closing vignette recalled the 112 Merina and Malagasy Native people deported to the "ethnographic zoo" of the Madagascar pavilion at the 1900 Paris Exposition Universelle, which expressly celebrated France's final victory. A description of the Madagascar pavilion makes this clear: "Indigenous peoples in motion in the gardens provided animation and local color to this spectacle, whose picturesque was enhanced by the presence of several detachments of Malagasy militiamen and scouts. . . . At the center of the Madagascar exhibit, and part of its very body as a felicitous complement, is located the panorama of the taking of Antananarivo, with a series of dioramas picturing various episodes of the conquest."[12] Méliès's movie falls back on the exoticism and racism of seventeenth-century Moon travel tales, but with two notable differences.[13] As a work of colonial propaganda at the height of the Scramble for Africa, the movie no longer depicts Selenites as culturally or technologically advanced. To the contrary, recycling seventeenth-century visualizations of Moon travel for the screen becomes a way of training viewers through a familiar imaginary and couching the cinema apparatus itself as a supposedly innocuous new visualization tool rather than as the weapon for colonialism that it is. Méliès had certainly heard of or watched Camille Flammarion's 1898 astronomical animated shorts, but in his *A Trip to the Moon* he merely

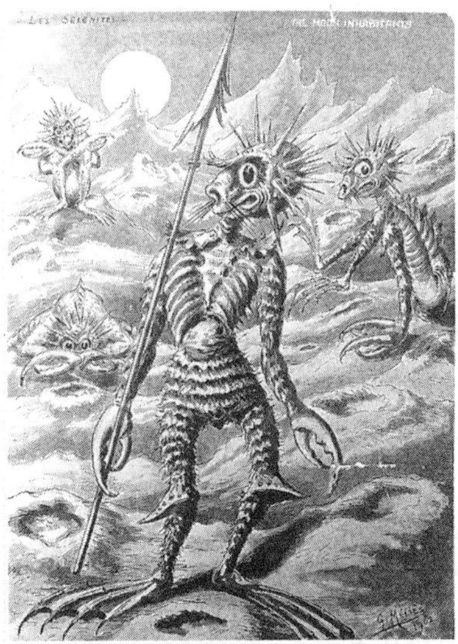

Figure C.4. **Georges Méliès, watercolor and ink, "Selenites," 1902 (public domain).**

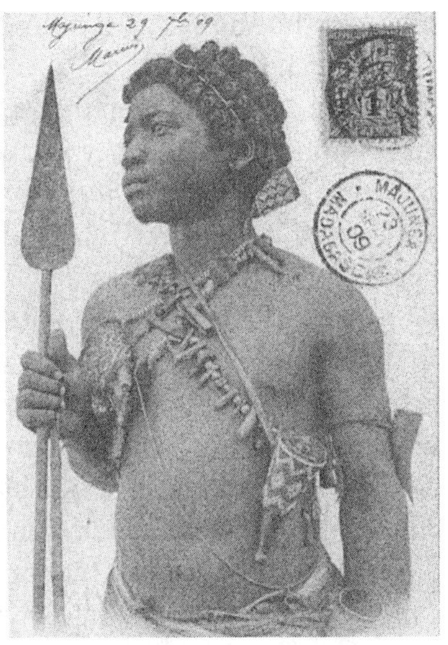

Figure C.5. **Postcard, "Malagasy Types: Tanosy Warrior," 1909.**

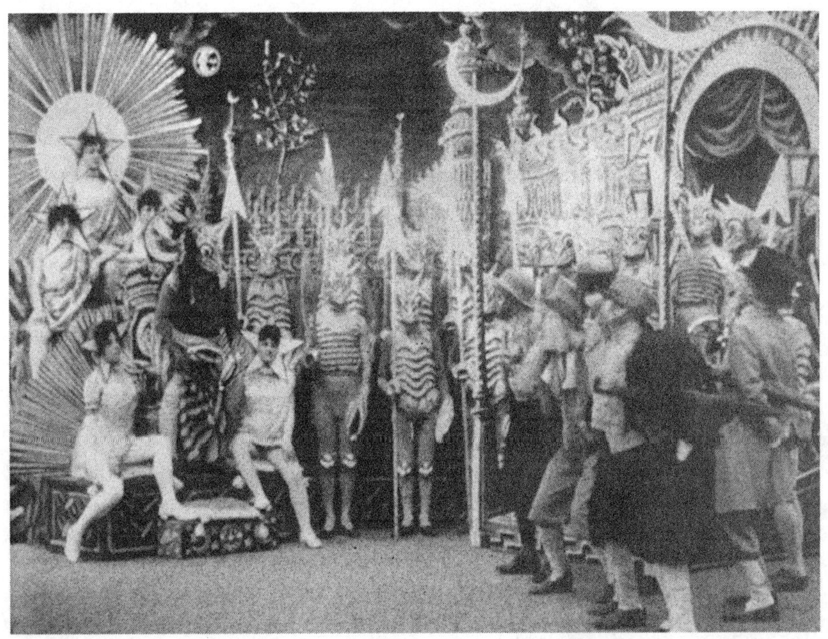

Figure C.6. **Still from *Voyage dans la lune,* dir. Georges Méliès (Star Film, 1902).**

sends up the animist astronomical context from which Flammarion devised cinema.

A few films attempted to revive the antiracist and antihegemonic potential of the matrix of photocinema, such as Jean Renoir's subversive 1927 film *Charleston Parade*.[14] It takes place in a war-devastated 2028 Paris, where the sole survivor is a white woman played by Renoir's then-wife Catherine Hessling. She has devolved into a so-called primitive state and is accompanied by a pet ape (played by Renoir himself), whom she frees from bondage at the beginning of the film. Action begins when atop her hut—an advertising column—an African astronaut lands his shiny spacecraft. He is played in blackface by African American vaudeville performer Johnny Hudgins, a former member of the Harlem Chocolate Dandies.[15] But it is she, as a white "primitive," who teaches him the Charleston, an ironic twist reviving the discursive use of photonegative inversion for antiracist purposes. Henry Louis Gates Jr. rightly reads the film as satirizing colonial conquest and anti-Black clichés, especially since the astronaut's map shows "Europa Deserta."[16] The film's key sequence crosscuts between Hessling and Hudgins dancing "at" each other in medium shots, then medium close-ups, and finally slow motion. The back-and-forth crosscutting between their closely dancing bodies and excited faces suggests intercourse. It makes visible the miscegenation that cannot be shown. At the end of the film, he rescues her from European savagery, and both fly back to Africa—the phantasmatic origin of photographic and televisual technologies in *Giphantie*.[17] Curiously, the Black astronaut's hand-cranked map system reprises the earliest prototype of two-reel devices: Jacques Barbeu-Dubourg's 1753 chronographic machine. Through *Charleston Parade*'s astronautical send-up of the colonial fiction of L'Afrique française, and its embrace of interracial love, the anti-Black origins of photocinema return in palimpsest as avant-garde critique.

A few decades earlier, W. E. B. Du Bois penned a plot similarly leveraging miscegenation in his short story titled "The Comet."[18] Jim, a Black bank employee, and Julia, the white daughter of a banker, are the sole survivors of a cataclysmic comet that wiped out New York

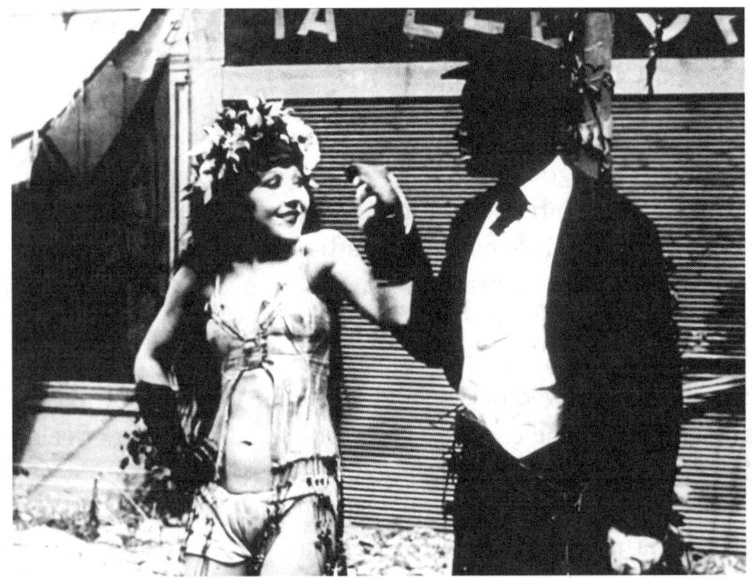

Figure C.7. **Still from *Charleston Parade*, dir. Jean Renoir (Néo-Film, 1927).**

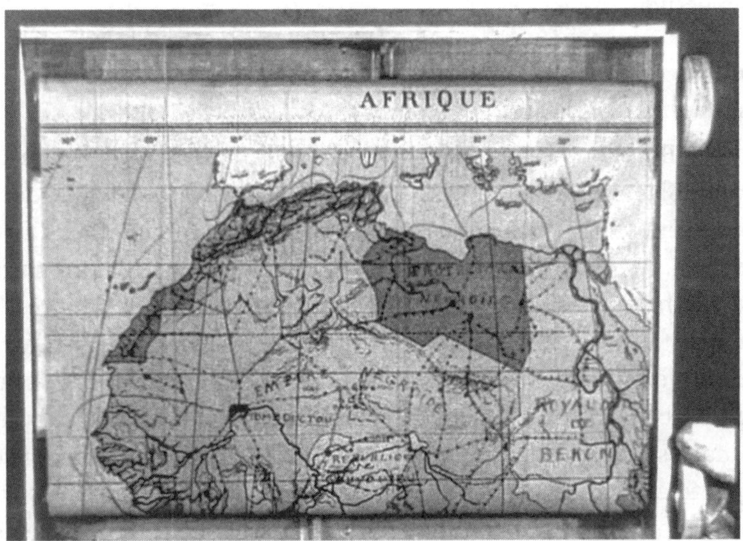

Figure C.8. **The Black astronaut's gloved hand turning dials to take his spacecraft from Africa to Paris. Still from *Charleston Parade*, dir. Jean Renoir (Néo-Film, 1927).**

City. When they encounter each other, he is at the wheel of a luxury automobile: "Of all the sorts of men she had pictured as coming to her rescue she had not dreamed of one like him" (Du Bois, "Comet," 259). They look for her father and other survivors, accessing the telephone exchange to send an open call across the world, but it is left unanswered. Intimacy builds and they are on the brink of having sex when her white fiancé and father reappear ex machina. The fiancé wastes no time fantasizing that Jim raped Julia, calling for his lynching. The story ends with the return of Jim's Black wife, holding their dead son. While Jim's life was preserved by the bank's basement vault, Julia owed hers to a "dark room" where she was "developing pictures of the comet" (260). The fated collision of celestial bodies stands here in direct relation to the taboo of sex between interracial bodies. The dark vault and the dark room signal the two extremes of the camera obscura: exploitation crystallized into white wealth and snapshots of a comet as ephemeral as breaches in the color line. Significantly, for both Du Bois and Renoir, only at the end of history can anti-Blackness be rescinded—from an astronomical perspective.

Backward Motion as Forward Thinking: Cinema and the Machining of History

Both Du Bois and Renoir take white positivist teleology as predicated on anti-Blackness. As mentioned earlier, the chronological order of the present study does not celebrate the arrival of cinema as a culmination. Indeed, the technical inception of cinema for Flammarion resulted from retrospection—how to access the past in its present, albeit distant, visibility. It was meant neither as an apparatus for or evidence of progress nor as a media of reproduction. The 1753 chronographic machine of Barbeu-Dubourg and the 1760 photo canvases of Charles François Tiphaigne de la Roche had similar aims of retrospective access rather than reproduction. This is the case as well with an apparatus that cinema archaeologists consider the least ambiguous antecedent to moving pictures: Robertson's *Fantasmagorie* shows, which started in Paris after the end of the Reign of Terror.[19] In the wake of the American, French, and Haitian Revolutions, the

Hegelian and then positivist structure of historicity took the form of universal recapitulation in which progressive stages overcome the past. Progress served not only to leave the past behind but also to justify and overwrite its enormous human cost. The matrix of photocinema, in this respect, is rather ambiguous. While the telescope and the first combinations of photography and telescopes arose within explicitly military and racist contexts, photoimaging and the history machines of Barbeu-Dubourg, Tiphaigne de la Roche, Restif de la Bretonne, and Flammarion developed a backward-forward temporality blunting the telos of the conquests of progress. Similarly, for Táíwò, "bending the arc of the moral universe" by "join[ing] actions up across time and space—even with those we have never met and may never know of," and doing so by invoking as well "the moral perspective of the ancestor," represent the proper mode of visualizing how to start carrying out the work of global reparations (Táíwò, *Reconsidering Reparations,* 200–01).

Flammarion's telechronoscope proposed more literally that past history could be filmically imaged in the future so that the past also lies in the future. That paradoxical temporality remained subjacent within the development of photocinema. As Shawn Michelle Smith puts it: "Photographs move physically as material objects (or as digital information viewed on physical platforms). . . . If the photograph is emblematic of the way the past persists in the present, it also foreshadows how fragments of the present will punctuate a future moment."[20] It was Du Bois again who anticipated the potential of cinema for making visible a counterhegemonic historiography. In his short story "The Princess Steel," written between 1908 and 1910, Du Bois restaged double consciousness by deploying cinema as a tool of historical visualization and repair.[21] A Black sociology professor from Pittsburgh named Johnson has invented the "megascope," an apparatus capable of replaying, as virtual reality, two centuries of unrecorded African American history. It is made of a glass sphere described as "a scintillating captive star" in which the diagrammatic "curves" and "counter-curves" encoding structural racism are projected (Du Bois, "Princess Steel," 823). A single white couple responds to Johnson's public invitation to watch the film. Their ears and eyes plugged into the megascope, they watch the virtual reality footage of how Pittsburgh derived its steelmaking wealth. The film depicts a captive African princess whose hair is plucked by white "Over-Men" to make steel. Johnson calls their undisputed power a "Zeit-Geist," so ingrained that "we vaguely identify it with the universe," an echo of the historical simultaneity of celestial mechanics and slave codes in the 1680s (823). The incarcerated African princess embodies at once the origins of enslaved African Americans and Pittsburgh's Black lumpenproletariat in the era of segregation. The white couple grows uneasy and, unwilling to watch the film to the end, untethers themselves and leaves without a word. The story breaks at this point, as if white people's refusal to acknowledge Black history broke the film. But Du Bois's point is also that the archive of Black enslavement, dehumanization, and social subalternity, though unrecorded, persists within history, and cinema might be able to partially rematerialize it on screen.

"The Princess Steel" leveraged Du Bois's lifelong interest in visual and visualization media, from telescope observation and Étienne L. Trouvelot's astronomical illustrations to socioeconomic diagrams, photos, and film.[22] It is very possible that he read Flammarion's *Lumen* in his student days. For the 1900 Exposition Universelle in Paris, he organized an exhibit titled "The American Negro" displaying hundreds of photographs of African Americans from all walks of life, offering a critical sociological portrait through longitudinal data. This gave white fairgoers an unfiltered glimpse of two centuries of Black American culture—the very aim of Johnson's megascope.[23]

The newly invented cinema apparatus was the star of the 1900 Exposition Universelle in Paris, with another booth dedicated to the history of chronophotography, organized by Étienne-Jules Marey. Among various kinds of film technologies exhibited was a color film projector called the "*chromo-mégascope,*" Du Bois's likely proximal source for Johnson's machine.[24] The original "mégascope," of course, was that of Jacques-Alexandre-César Charles in the 1780s (see chapter 3). The chromo-megascope's introduction of color to cinema suggested a polysemy not lost on Du Bois. The new kinds of

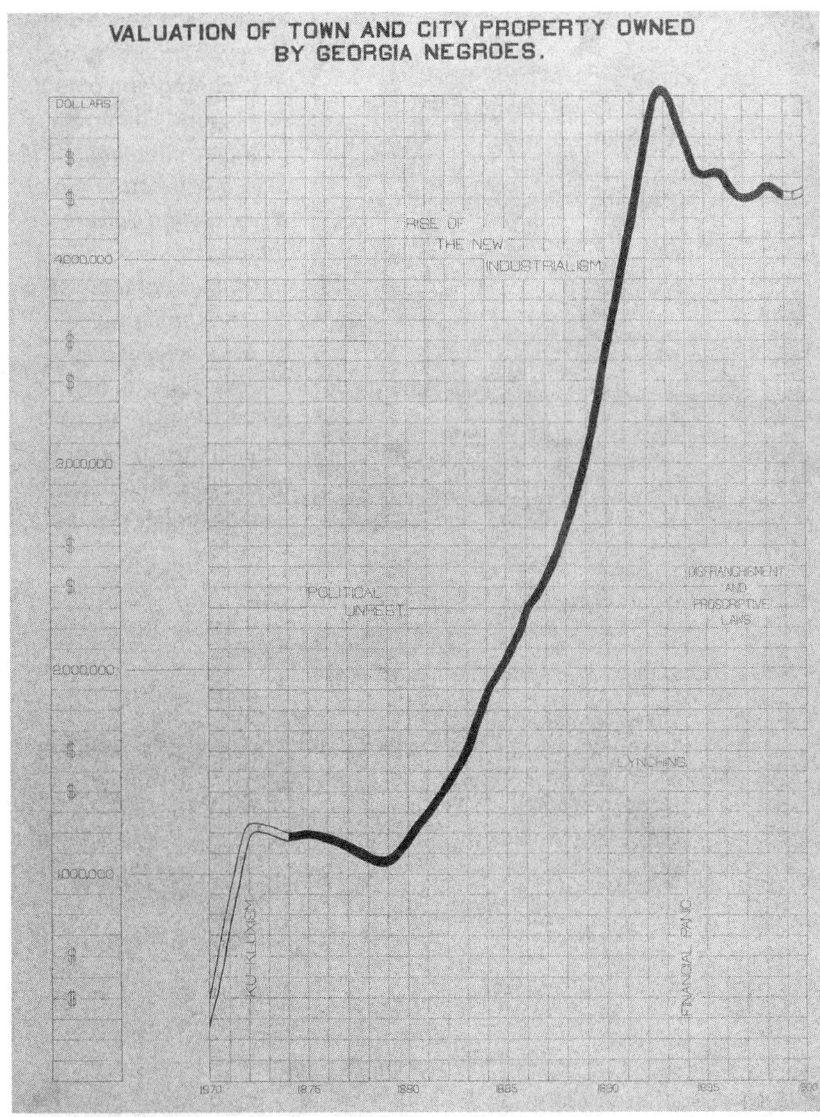

Figure C.9. **W. E. B. Du Bois and students of Atlanta University, "Valuation of Town and City Property Owned by Georgia Negroes," 1900. Ink and watercolor on board, 71 × 56 cm (27 15/16 × 22 1/16 in.). Library of Congress Prints and Photographs Division.**

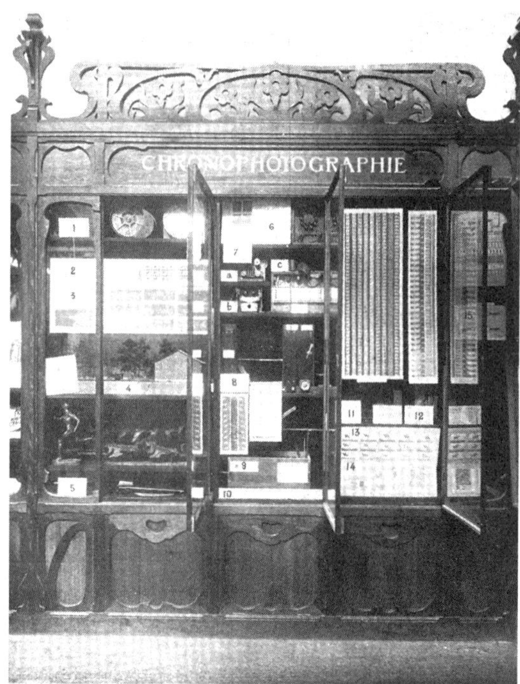

Figure C.10. **Étienne-Jules Marey, "Chronophotography," photograph of 1900 Paris World Fair booth, in** ***Musée centennal de la classe 12 (photographie) à l'exposition universelle internationale de 1900 à Paris: Métrographie et Chronophotographie,*** **by A. Laussédat and Étienne-Jules Marey (Saint-Cloud, France: Belin, 1900), 10; courtesy of La Bibliothèque Nationale de France Gallica.**

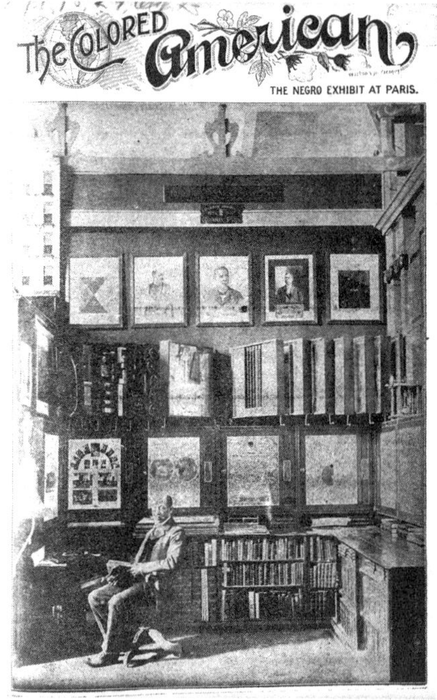

Figure C.11. **W. E. B. Du Bois, "The American Negro," photograph of 1900 Paris World Fair booth, from W. E. B. Du Bois, "The American Negro" exhibition, cover of** ***The Colored American*** **(November 3, 1900); courtesy of the Library of Congress.**

movies African American and Black diaspora filmmakers have undertaken to make over the last decade generically partake of Johnson's unseeable movie.[25] That is, they endeavor to make visible the unrecorded history of racial injustice—bending the arc of the moral universe.

Notes

Introduction

1. Only in the wake of photography in the 1850s did thorough pictorial realism emerge with Gustave Courbet and his followers (Marnin Young, *Realism in the Age of Impressionism: Painting and the Politics of Time* [New Haven, CT: Yale University Press, 2015]). For Lorraine Daston and Peter L. Galison, the notion of an objective world surfaced similarly with photography (*Objectivity* [Princeton, NJ: Princeton University Press, 2007]).

2. See Siegfried Zielinski, *Deep Time of the Media: Toward an Archaeology of Hearing and Seeing by Technical Means,* trans. Gloria Custance (Cambridge, MA: MIT Press, 2006).

3. See, for instance, Benjamin Schmidt, *Inventing Exoticism: Geography, Globalism, and Europe's Early Modern World* (Philadelphia: University of Pennsylvania Press, 2015); Ann Marie Plane, *Dreams and the Invisible World in Colonial New England: Indians, Colonists, and the Seventeenth Century* (Philadelphia: University of Pennsylvania Press, 2014).

4. See Steve Shapin, *The Scientific Revolution* (Chicago: University of Chicago Press, 1996).

5. Stephanie Smallwood, *Saltwater Slavery: A Middle Passage from Africa to American Diaspora* (Cambridge, MA: Harvard University Press, 2007); Christopher Miller, *The French Atlantic Triangle: Literature and Culture of the Slave Trade* (Durham, NC: Duke University Press, 2008); Thomas McCarthy, *Race, Empire, and the Idea of Human Development* (Cambridge, MA: Cambridge University Press, 2009); Manisha Sinha, *The Slave's Cause: A History of Abolition* (New Haven, CT: Yale University Press, 2016).

6. Italian poet Alessandro Allegri illustrates this nonpresentism in a 1607 text (just prior to the telescope) by comparing "glasses" and "texts"—that is,

prosthetic vision and envisioning. Allegri argues that "if the former let you look at many things, with the latter you may learn an infinite number; if the former reveal distant things, the latter show you bygone ones. . . . With glasses we see no more than present things, but with texts, we can even learn the future." Alessandro Allegri, *Seconda parte delle rime piacevoli* (Verona: Bartolamio Merlo dalle Donne, 1607), fol. B2v–B3, cited in Eileen Reeves, *Evening News: Optics, Astronomy, and Journalism in Early Modern Europe* (Philadelphia: University of Pennsylvania Press, 2014), 18.

7. For this hegemonic imperative, see, for instance, Daniel J. Cook, "Leibniz on 'Advancing Toward a Greater Culture,'" *Studia Leibnitiana* 50, no. 2 (2018): 163–79.

8. See David Cahan, ed., *From Natural Philosophy to the Sciences: Writing the History of Nineteenth Century Science* (Chicago: University of Chicago Press, 2003); Matthew C. Hunter, *Wicked Intelligence: Visual Art and the Science of Experiment in Restoration London* (Chicago: University of Chicago Press, 2013).

9. Mechanical objectivity is the signature pictorial priority of post-photography nineteenth-century science according to Daston and Galison (*Objectivity*).

10. David Philip Miller, "The Story of '*Scientist*: The Story of a Word,'" *Annals of Science* 74, no. 4 (2017): 255–61.

11. For crossovers between science, imaging, and metaphysics, see Robert M. Brain, Robert S. Cohen, and Ole Knudsen, eds., *Hans Christian Ørsted and the Romantic Legacy in Science* (Dordrecht, Netherlands: Springer, 2007); John Tresch, *The Romantic Machine: Utopian Science and Technology After Napoleon* (Chicago: University of Chicago Press, 2014).

12. *Visualizing* encompasses what Svetlana Alpers calls "picturing," which itself exceeds visual art representations per se via cultural discourse, experimentation, and theorization (*The Art of Describing: Dutch Art in the Seventeenth Century* [Chicago: University of Chicago Press, 1983]). For visualization as an overlooked practice in visual culture, see Klaus Hentschel, *Visual Cultures in Science and Technology* (Oxford: Oxford University Press, 2014); Nancy Anderson, "Eye and Image: Looking at a Visual Studies of Science," *Historical Studies in the Natural Sciences* 39, no. 1 (2009): 115–25; Scott Curtis and Robert Lue, "Bridging Science, Art, and the History of Visualization," *Discourse* 37, no. 3 (2015): 193–206.

13. Samuel Taylor Coleridge, *Biographia Literaria; or Biographical Sketches of My Literary Life and Opinions*, vol. 1 (London: Rest Fenner, 1817). Coleridge condemns the wordy flourishes of a translation by Pope that loses sight of "the whole *visual* likeness" of Homer's imagination. He favors another translation that deploys an "allegory of visualized *Puns*" (48).

14. *Oxford English Dictionary*, 2nd ed. (1989), "visualization," https://www.oed.com/oedv2/00278329. Relatedly, *to envisage* was imported from

French into English in 1820 by Coleridge's friend John Keats, and John Herschel used it in an astronomical sense by 1836 (*Oxford English Dictionary,* "envisage," last updated September 2024, https://doi.org/10.1093/OED/1053207940). *To envision* was coined in 1921 as the word *television* came of use (*Oxford English Dictionary,* "envision," last updated July 2023, https://doi.org/10.1093/OED/1025927510).

15. Saint Augustine's dichotomy remained central in premodern optics: "There are two visions, one of perception (sentiensis), the other of thought (cogitantis)." A. Mark Smith, *From Sight to Light: The Passage from Ancient to Modern Optics* (Chicago: University of Chicago Press, 2015), 153.

16. For Enlightenment thinkers' instrumental belief that Blackness is abnormal and in need of a pathological explanation, see Andrew Curran, *The Anatomy of Blackness: Science and Slavery in an Age of Enlightenment* (Baltimore, MD: Johns Hopkins University Press, 2011).

17. See M. Norton Wise, "Making Visible," *Isis* 97, no. 1 (2006): 75–82.

18. Antje Pfannkuchen argues the same point in "When Nature Begins to Write Herself: German Romanticism Reads the Electroscope" (PhD diss., New York University, 2010).

19. Carl Hanser, *Georg Christoph Lichtenberg Schriften und Briefe* (Munich, Germany: Hanser Verlag, 1971), A2:220, 25; D:687, 107. Unless otherwise noted, all translations are my own.

20. [Wilhelm] Homberg, "Réflexions sur différentes végétations métalliques," *Mémoires de mathématique et de physique tirés des registres de l'Académie royale des sciences* (November 30, 1692): 145–52. Homberg also researched interactions of light with matter, including silver nitrate. Lawrence Principle, *The Transmutations of Chymistry: Wilhelm Homberg and the Académie royale des sciences* (Chicago: University of Chicago Press, 2020), 128.

21. Manuel Bonnet and Jean-Louis Marignier, *Niépce: Correspondance et papiers* (Saint-Loup de Varenne, France: Maison Nicéphore Niépce, 2003), 708, 712.

22. Albertus Magnus noted silver salts' darkening effect in the thirteenth century. Medical treatises well into the nineteenth century routinely mention such treatments. Ferenc Szabadváry, *History of Analytical Chemistry* (Oxford: Pergamon Press, 1966), 17.

23. Robert Boyle, *Experiments and Considerations Touching Colors* (London: Herringman, 1664), 151–53.

24. Everard Home, "On the Rete Mucosum," in *Supplement to the Foregoing Lectures on Comparative Anatomy,* vol. 5 (London: Longman et al., 1828), 284.

25. Everard Home, "On the Black Rete Mucosum of the Negro, Being a Defence Against the Scorching Effects of the Sun's Rays," *Philosophical Transactions of the Royal Society* 111 (1821): 1–6. Since the eclipse was

over England, the two Black men were likely free, since enslaved peoples on British soil could sue for emancipation after *Somerset v. Stewart* (1772) and *Knight v. Wedderburn* (1778).

26. André Bazin, "The Ontology of the Photographic Image," trans. Hugh Gray, *Film Quarterly* 13, no. 4 (1960): 7.

27. Charles Sanders Peirce, *Collected Papers of Charles Sanders Peirce,* vol. 2, ed. Charles Hartshorne and Paul Weiss (Cambridge, MA: Harvard University Press, 1952), 159. Peirce conducted stellar photometric research at the Harvard Observatory.

28. Commercial photographic film stocks were calibrated for white skin via Shirley cards, photos of white women's faces. Lorna Roth, "Looking at Shirley, the Ultimate Norm: Colour Balance, Image Technologies, and Cognitive Equity," *Canadian Journal of Communications* 34, no. 1 (2009): 111–36; Syreeta McFadden, "Teaching the Camera to See My Skin: Navigating Photography's Inherited Bias Against Dark Skin," *BuzzFeed News,* April 2, 2014, https://www.buzzfeednews.com/article/syreetamcfadden/teaching-the-camera-to-see-my-skin.

29. For artificial colorization of deep space images producing a false cosmic look, see Elizabeth A. Kessler, *Picturing the Cosmos: Hubble Space Telescope Images and the Astronomical Sublime* (Minneapolis: University of Minnesota Press, 2012).

30. Jessica Riskin, *The Restless Clock: A History of the Centuries-Long Argument over What Makes Living Things Tick* (Chicago: University of Chicago Press, 2016).

31. Descartes's "vortices" as rotating envelopes of ether currents were not kinemorphic.

32. Klaas van Berkel, *Isaac Beckman on Matter and Motion: Mechanical Philosophy in the Making* (Baltimore, MD: Johns Hopkins University Press, 2013), 105. For Ofer Gal, "motion" is "the great intellectual challenge of the early modern era" (Ofer Gal, "Two Bohemian Journeys: Real, Imaginary and Idealized Voyages at the Turn of the Seventeenth Century," in *Motion and Knowledge in the Changing Early Modern World,* ed. Ofer Gal and Yi Zheng [Dordrecht, Netherlands: Springer, 2014]).

33. George Berkeley, *An Essay Towards a New Theory of Vision* (Dublin: Aaron Rhames, 1709), 163. See Nicholas J. Wade, *A Natural History of Vision* (Cambridge, MA: MIT Press, 1998), 201–34. For Nicholas J. Wade, "a sequence of discrete images could not be observed in the natural environment" (202).

34. The mistaken idea that "retinal persistence" explains our perception of moving images as an illusion derived from quickly superimposed static images recurs in film historiography into the twentieth century. Max Wertheimer demonstrated in the 1910s that visual perception of motion involves not static or synthetic representations but a neural kinesthetic unity instead.

Cinema studies keep having to wrestle with this illusionistic persistence. See Rafe McGregor, "Cinematic Realism: A Defence from Plato to Gaut," *British Journal of Aesthetics* 58, no. 3 (2018): 225–39.

35. Long thought to be an original made by Janssen from Nagasaki, Japan, during the actual transit, this plate was recently shown to be only a test plate. Actual plates would look much the same. Françoise Launay and Peter D. Hingley, "Jules Janssen's 'Revolver Photographique' and Its British Derivative, 'the Janssen Plate,'" *Journal for the History of Astronomy* 31 (2005): 70–71.

36. Animated visualizations unfold in continuous visual streams, such as sequential images or temporal scenarios like visualizing the apsidal precession of the Moon's orbit around Earth in the 1740s (see Siegfried Bodenmann, "The 18th-Century Battle over Lunar Motion," *Physics Today* 63, no. 1 [2010]: 27–32). Nick Hopwood pinpoints the origin of sequential pictorial strategies "around 1800," stating it equally involves images and texts—thus polyvalent visualization (*Haeckel's Embryos: Images, Evolution, and Fraud* [Chicago: University of Chicago Press, 2015], 12).

37. For clouds as philosophical prototypes and metaphors of media environments, see John Durham Peters, *The Marvelous Clouds* (Chicago: University of Chicago Press, 2015).

38. Luke Howard, "On the Modifications of Clouds, and the Principles of Their Production, Suspension, and Destruction," *Philosophical Magazine* 16 (1802–1803): 97.

39. Jean-Baptiste Lamarck, *Annuaire météorologique pour l'An X* (Paris: Maillard, 1802), 115.

40. Johann Wolfgang von Goethe's coinage of the noun Morphologie in 1796 was inspired by dynamic physiologist Carl Friedrich Kielmeyer, who attempted to combine a body's "ability to turn the impression made on the nerves into images" with its growth and reproduction to explain the "simultaneous and successive metamorphosis" of plants and insects all the way to higher intelligence (Gabrielle Bersier, "Visualizing Carl Friedrich Kielmeyer's Organic Forces," *Monatshefte* 97, no. 1 [2005]: 20). Goethe found similar insights in *Zoonomia* (1794–1796) by Erasmus Darwin—the grandfather of Charles Darwin and the uncle and tutor of Thomas Wedgwood (32).

41. Lamarck hypothesized that Earth was hundreds of millions of years old, while his Catholic nemesis, Georges Cuvier, insisted on a divine origin of six millennia. See Richard Burckhardt Jr., "Lamarck, Evolution, and the Inheritance of Acquired Characters," *Genetics* 194 (August 2013): 793–805; Snait Gissis, "Interactions Between Social and Biological Thinking: The Case of Lamarck," *Perspectives on Science* 17, no. 3 (2009): 237–306; Koen B. Tanghe, "Leave Lamarck Alone! Why the Use of the Term 'Lamarckism' and Its Cognates Must Be Shunned," *Perspectives in Biology and Medicine* 62, no. 1 (2019): 72–94.

42. Howard debunked an apocryphal lunar theory of weather attributed to William Herschel (John R. Starr, "Herschel's Weather Table," *Weather* 57 [2002]: 99–100). Herschel and Howard published articles on the Sun in the same issue of the *Philosophical Magazine* (June 1800) and researched weather cycles. Similarities between morphic cosmologies of Herschel and Lamarck are mentioned in "Cosmogony," *Chamber's Encyclopedia,* vol. 3 (Edinburgh: R. Chambers, 1871), 262.

43. See Michael Hoskin, "Nebulae, Star Clusters and the Milky Way from Galileo to William Herschel," *Journal for the History of Astronomy* 34 (2008): 369.

44. See Teun Koetsier, *A History of Kinematics from Zeno to Einstein: On the Role of Motion in the Development of Mathematics* (Cham, Switzerland: Springer, 2023).

45. G. F. Rodwell, "On the Perception of the Unseen," in *Report of the Marlborough College Natural History Society,* vol. 17 (Marlborough, England: Perkins, 1873), 30.

46. Laurent Mannoni, *The Great Art of Light and Shadow: Archaeology of the Cinema,* trans. Richard Crangle (Exeter, England: Exeter University Press, 2000); Laurent Mannoni, Donato Pesenti Campagnoni, and David Robinson, *Light and Movement: Incunabula of the Motion Picture, 1420–1896* (Ann Arbor: University of Michigan Press, 1995).

47. For the telescope as a tool of visualization, see Antoni Malet, "Early Conceptualizations of the Telescope as an Optical Instrument," *Early Science and Medicine* 10, no. 2 (2005): 237–62. For temporal chemical images as part of the prehistory of photography, see Matthew C. Hunter, *Painting with Fire: Sir Joshua Reynolds, Photography, and the Temporally Evolving Chemical Object* (Chicago: University of Chicago Press, 2019).

48. Victor Fouque, *La Vérité sur l'invention de la photographie* (Paris: Librairie des auteurs, 1867).

49. Eliza Meteyard, *A Group of Englishmen (1795–1815)* (London: Longmans, Green, 1871); R. B. Litchfield, *Tom Wedgwood: The First Photographer* (London: Duckworth, 1903).

50. Josef Maria Eder, *History of Photography,* trans. Edward Epstean (1932; New York: Columbia University Press, 1945).

51. Beaumont Newhall, *The History of Photography from 1839 to the Present Day* (New York: Museum of Modern Art, 1949); Helmut Gernsheim and Alison Gernsheim, *The History of Photography* (Oxford: Oxford University Press, 1955); André Bazin, *What Is Cinema?,* vol. 1, trans. Hugh Gray (1958; Berkeley: University of California Press, 2004); George Sadoul, *L'Invention du cinéma* (Paris: Denoël, 1946).

52. Deac Rossell, "Quartet: Four Stories of Early Cinema Research," *Early Popular Visual Culture* 14, no. 4 (2016): 404. See also Deac Rossell,

Chronology of the Birth of Cinema 1833–1896 (Bloomington: Indiana University Press, 2022).

53. See Paul Virilio, *War and Cinema: The Logistics of Perception,* trans. Patrick Camiler (London: Verso, 1989); Friedrich Kittler, *Gramophone, Film, Typewriter,* trans. Geoffrey Winthrop-Young and Michael Wutz (Stanford, CA: Stanford University Press, 1999); Jonathan Crary, *Techniques of the Observer: On Vision and Modernity in the Nineteenth Century* (Cambridge, MA: MIT Press, 1990); François Albera and Maria Tortajada, *Cinema Beyond Film: Media Epistemology in the Modern Era* (Amsterdam: Amsterdam University Press, 2006).

54. See Thomas Elsaesser and Adam Barker, eds., *Early Cinema: Space, Frame, Narrative* (London: BFI, 1990); Larry J. Schaaf, *Out of the Shadows: Herschel, Talbot, and the Invention of Photography* (New Haven, CT: Yale University Press, 1992); Marta Braun, *Picturing Time: The Work of Étienne-Jules Marey (1830–1904)* (Chicago: University of Chicago Press, 1992); Bonnet and Marignier, *Niépce*; Tom Gunning, "Phantasmagoria and the Manufacturing of Illusions and Wonder: Towards a Cultural Optics of the Cinematic Apparatus," in *The Cinema: A New Technology for the 20th Century,* ed. André Gaudreault, Catherine Russell, and Pierre Veronneau (Lausanne, Switzerland: Editions Payot, 2004); Mannoni, *Great Art of Light and Shadow*; André Gaudreault, *Cinéma et attraction: Pour une nouvelle histoire du cinématographe* (Paris: CNRS, 2008); Zielinski, *Deep Time of the Media*; Stephen C. Pinson, *Speculating Daguerre: Art and Enterprise in the Work of L. J. M. Daguerre* (Chicago: University of Chicago Press, 2012).

55. Gabriel Rockhill, "Le Cinéma n'est jamais né," *Appareil* 1 (2008): 26, https://doi.org/10.4000/appareil.130.

56. Siegfried Zielinski, *Variations on Media Thinking* (Minneapolis: University of Minnesota Press, 2019); Zielinski, *Deep Time of the Media.*

57. Mary Ann Doane, *The Emergence of Cinematic Time: Modernity, Contingency, the Archive* (Cambridge, MA: Harvard University Press, 2002); Jussi Parikka, *Insect Media: An Archaeology of Animals and Technology* (Minneapolis: University of Minnesota Press, 2010); Erkki Huhtamo, *Illusion in Motion: Media Archaeology of the Moving Panorama and Related Spectacles* (Cambridge, MA: MIT Press, 2013); Jussi Parikka, *A Geology of Media* (Minneapolis: University of Minnesota Press, 2015).

58. Vivian Sobchack, "Afterword: Media Archaeology and Re-Presencing the Past," in *Media Archaeology: Approaches, Applications, and Implications,* ed. Erkki Huhtamo and Jussi Parikka (Berkeley: University of California Press, 2011).

59. Tom Gunning, introduction to Mannoni, *Great Art of Light and Shadow.*

60. Benjamin Schmidt, *Inventing Exoticism: Geography, Globalism, and*

Europe's Early Modern World (Philadelphia: University of Pennsylvania Press, 2015).

61. See Mary Baine Campbell, *Wonder & Science: Imagining Worlds in Early Modern Europe* (Ithaca, NY: Cornell University Press, 1999).

62. This explains how the rumor that Jesuits were planning on colonizing the Moon in the 1620s became credible (see chapter 1).

63. According to William B. Ashworth Jr., from the 1550s to the 1650s the "emblematic world view" dominated natural history through "the belief that every kind of thing in the cosmos has myriad hidden meanings" through secret connections, so that "the notion that a peacock should be studied in isolation from the rest of the universe" made little sense. "Natural History and the Emblematic World View," in *Reappraisals of the Scientific Revolution,* ed. David C. Lindberg and Robert S. Westman (Cambridge: Cambridge University Press, 1990), 312.

64. Cristina Malcolmson, *Studies of Skin Color in the Early Royal Society: Boyle, Cavendish, Swift* (New York: Routledge, 2016).

65. Faith E. Beasley, "Versailles Meets the Taj Mahal," in *French Global: A New Approach to Literary History,* ed. Christie McDonald and Susan Rubin Suleiman (New York: Columbia University Press, 2010).

66. François Bernier, "Nouvelle division de la terre par les différentes espèces ou races d'hommes qui l'habitent," *Journal des Sçavans* 12 (1684): 132.

67. Robert Bernasconi, "Crossed Lines in the Racialization Process: Race as Border Concept," *Research in Phenomenology* 42 (2012): 206–28. For Justin E. H. Smith, Bernier's classification was "the biogeographical starting point for the determination of geopolitical order" (*Nature, Human Nature & Human Difference: Race in Early Modern Philosophy* [Princeton, NJ: Princeton University Press, 2015], 143). See also Curran, *Anatomy of Blackness,* 20–21.

68. Siep Stuurman, "François Bernier and the Invention of Racial Classification," *History Workshop Journal* 50 (2000): 1–21.

69. François Bernier, *Abrégé de la philosophie de Gassendi,* 2nd ed., vol. 4 (Lyon, France: Anisson, Posuel & Rigaud, 1684), 361, 363.

70. François Bernier, "Des climats & de la diversité des habitants de la Terre," in *Abrégé de la philosophie de Gassendi.*

71. For the reconstruction of human pigmentation history, see William J. Pavan and Richard A. Sturm, "The Genetics of Human Skin and Hair Pigmentation," *Annual Review of Genomics and Human Genetics* 20 (2019): 41–72.

72. Denise Ferreira da Silva, *Toward a Global Idea of Race* (Minneapolis: University of Minnesota Press, 2007), xxviii.

73. Sylvia Wynter, *On Being Human as Praxis,* ed. Katherine McKittrick (Durham, NC: Duke University Press, 2015), 10–16.

74. Saidiya Hartman documents the public staging of Black life via

"coerced spectacles" in which "blacks were envisioned fundamentally as vehicles for white enjoyment" (*Scenes of Subjection: Terror, Slavery, and Self-Making in Nineteenth-Century America* [New York: Oxford University Press, 1997], 23). Calvin L. Warren presents this simulacral operation as an ontological law of modernity: the double imperative "to see the invisible" in order "not to see black being" (*Ontological Terror: Blackness, Nihilism, and Emancipation* [Durham, NC: Duke University Press, 2018], 70). Warren's double bind is partly based on Hortense J. Spillers's insight that "undecipherable markings on the captive body render a kind of hieroglyphics of the flesh whose severe disjunctures come to be hidden to the *cultural seeing* of skin color" (Hortense J. Spillers, *White, Black, and in Color: Essays on American Literature and Culture* [Chicago: University of Chicago Press, 2003], 207, quoted in Warren, *Ontological Terror,* 71). See chapter 3 for hieroglyphs and race in photoimaging.

75. [Benjamin Banneker], *Copy of a Letter from Benjamin Banneker to the Secretary of State, with His Answer* (Philadelphia: Daniel Lawrence, 1792).

76. For Douglass, see chapter 6. Frantz Fanon, *Black Skin, White Masks,* trans. Charles Lam Markmann (New York: Grove Press, 1967), 109; Édouard Glissant, *Poetics of Relation,* trans. Betsy Wing (Ann Arbor: University of Michigan Press, 1997), 189–94.

77. Fred Moten, *Black and Blur (consent not to be a single being)* (Durham, NC: Duke University Press, 2017), 76.

78. See Karen Beckman and Jean Ma, eds., *Still Moving: Between Cinema and Photography* (Durham, NC: Duke University Press, 2008).

79. Fred Moten, *In the Break: The Aesthetic of the Black Radical Tradition* (Minneapolis: University of Minnesota Press, 2003), 18.

80. Fred Moten, *Stolen Life (consent not to be a single being)* (Minneapolis: University of Minnesota Press, 2018), 194; Zielinski, *Deep Time of the Media,* 25–27.

81. Charles W. Mills, *Blackness Visible: Essays on Philosophy and Race* (Ithaca, NY: Cornell University Press, 1998), 3.

82. Katherine McKittrick, *Dear Science and Other Stories* (Durham, NC: Duke University Press, 2021), 170.

83. Michel Foucault, "Nietzsche, Genealogy, History," in *Language, Counter-Memory, Practice: Selected Essays and Interviews,* ed. D. F. Bouchard, trans. D. F. Bouchard and Sherry Simon (Ithaca, NY: Cornell University Press, 1977), 162.

84. *Oxford English Dictionary,* "matrix," last updated December 2024, https://doi.org/10.1093/OED/9397880093.

85. La Marr Jurelle Bruce, *How to Go Mad Without Losing Your Mind: Madness and Black Radical Creativity* (Durham, NC: Duke University Press, 2021), 6.

86. Nicholas Whittaker, "Case Sensitive: Why We Shouldn't Capital-

ize 'Black,'" *Drift,* September 17, 2021, https://www.thedriftmag.com/case-sensitive/.

87. Fred Moten, "Chromatic Saturation: The Case of Blackness," in *The Universal Machine* (Durham, NC: Duke University Press, 2018).

88. Thomas Clarkson, *An Essay on the Slavery and Commerce of the Human Species, Particularly the African,* 3rd ed. (Philadelphia: Joseph Crookshank, 1787), 131.

1. Photosophia

1. Antoni Malet, "Early Conceptualizations of the Telescope as an Optical Instrument," *Early Science and Medicine* 10, no. 2 (2005): 237–62.

2. *Ambassades du Roy de Siam envoyé à L'Excellence du Prince Maurice, arrivé à la Haye le 10 Septembre 1608* (N.p., 1608), 9. Unless otherwise noted, all translations are my own.

3. State representatives of France, Spain, Holland, and the Vatican understood the telescope as a powerful new military technology. In December 1608, Pierre Jeannin said a French soldier had mastered the art of telescope-making. Quoted in Engel Sluiter, "The Telescope Before Galileo," *Journal for the History of Astronomy* 27 (1997): 228.

4. For global Dutch ambitions, see Robert Parthesius, *Dutch Ships in Tropical Waters: The Development of the Dutch East India Company (VOC) Shipping Network in Asia 1595–1660* (Amsterdam: Amsterdam University Press, 2010).

5. See, for instance, Dhruv Raina, "French Jesuit Scientists in India: Historical Astronomy in the Discourse on India, 1670–1770," *Economic and Political Weekly* 34, no. 5 (1999): 30–38.

6. Jean-Jacques Gautier, *Jean le Noir ou le misanthrope* (Paris: Hôtel de Bouthillier, 1789), 82.

7. See Louis Sala-Molins, *Dark Side of the Light: Slavery and the French Enlightenment,* trans. John Conteh-Morgan (Minnesota: University of Minnesota Press, 2005).

8. See Anne T. Woolett and Ariane van Suchtelen, *Rubens and Brueghel: A Working Friendship* (Los Angeles: J. Paul Getty Museum, 2006), 94.

9. Laurent Mannoni, *The Great Art of Light and Shadow: Archaeology of the Cinema,* trans. Richard Crangle (Exeter, England: Exeter University Press, 2000), 5–6.

10. For Daniele Barbaro's *La pratica della perspettiva* (1567), see Vincent Llardi, *Renaissance Vision from Spectacles to Telescopes* (Philadelphia: American Philosophical Society, 2007), 220–21.

11. Tiemen Cocuyt, "The Camera Obscura and the Availability of Seventeenth Century Optics," in *Inside the Camera Obscura: Optics and Art Under the Spell of the Projected Image,* ed. Wolfgang Lefèvre (Berlin: Max Planck Institute for the History of Science, 2007).

12. John Gorman, "Projecting Nature in Early Modern Europe," in Lefèvre, *Inside the Camera Obscura,* 35.

13. From a 1621 text by astronomer Jean Leurechon, cited in Mannoni, *Great Art of Light and Shadow,* 12.

14. Johann Zahn, *Oculus artificialis teledioptricus sive telescopium* (Herbi Poli, Germany: Quirinus Heyl, 1685).

15. Ofer Gal and Raz Chen-Morris, "Nature's Drawing: Problems and Resolutions in the Mathematization of Motion," in *Baroque Science* (Chicago: University of Chicago Press, 2013).

16. Kathleen M. Crowther and Peter Barker, "Training the Intelligent Eye: Understanding Illustrations in Early Modern Astronomy Texts," *Isis* 104, no. 3 (2013): 447–48.

17. For motion visualization in late seventeenth-century mechanics, see Michael S. Mahoney, "Infinitesimals and Transcendent Relations: The Mathematics of Motion in the Late Seventeenth Century," in *Reappraisals of the Scientific Revolution,* ed. David C. Lindberg and Robert S. Westman (Cambridge: Cambridge University Press, 1990).

18. Omar W. Nasim, *Observing by Hand: Sketching the Nebulae in the Nineteenth Century* (Chicago: University of Chicago Press, 2013), 6, 10, 18.

19. See Norma Wenczel, "The Optical Camera Obscura II: Images and Texts," in Lefèvre, *Inside the Camera Obscura,* 27–29.

20. See Catherine Chevalley, "L'*Ars Magna Lucis et Umbrae* d'Athanase Kircher: Néoplatonisme, hermétisme et 'nouvelle philosophie,'" *Baroque* 12 (1987): http://baroque.revues.org/584; Roberto Buonanno, *The Stars of Galileo Galilei and the Universal Knowledge of Athanasius Kircher* (New York: Springer, 2014).

21. Siegfried Zielinski, *Deep Time of the Media: Toward an Archaeology of Hearing and Seeing by Technical Means,* trans. Gloria Custance (Cambridge, MA: MIT Press, 2006); Mannoni, *Great Art of Light and Shadow.*

22. John E. Fletcher, "Astronomy in the Life and Correspondence of Athanasius Kircher," *Isis* 61, no. 1 (1970): 64.

23. John Glassie, *A Man of Misconceptions: The Life of an Eccentric in an Age of Change* (New York: Riverhead Books, 2012), 98, 149.

24. Athanasii Kircheri, *Ars Magna Lucis et Umbrae in decem Libros digesta* (Roma: Sumptibus Hermanni Scheus, 1646), 840–70.

25. Athanasius Kircher, *Mundus subterraneus,* vol. 1 (Amsterdam: Joannes Jansson & Elizeus Weyerstraet, 1665), 327, cited in Hiro Hirai, "Kircher's Chymical Interpretation of the Creation and Spontaneous Generation," in *Chymists and Chymistry: Studies in the History of Alchemy and Early Modern Chemistry,* ed. Lawrence M. Principle (Sagamore Beach, MA: Watson Publishing, 2007), 79, 82.

26. See Dominique Demange and Yael Kedar, "Physical Action, Species,

and Matter: The Debate Between Roger Bacon and Peter John Olivi," *Journal of the History of Philosophy* 58, no. 1 (2020): 49–69.

27. A. Mark Smith, *From Sight to Light: The Passage from Ancient to Modern Optics* (Chicago: University of Chicago Press, 2015), 248–55.

28. Christoph Scheiner, *Oculus hoc est: Fundamentum Opticum, in quo ex accurata Oculi Anatome, abstrusarum experientiarum sedula pervestigatione, ex invisis specierum visibilium tam everso quam erecto situ spectaculis, necnon solidis rationum momentis Radius Visualis eruitur; sua Visioni in Oculo sedes decernitur; Anguli Visorii ingenium aperitur* [The eye, that is, the foundation of optics, in which the visual ray is extracted from the accurate anatomy of the eye, the diligent investigation of difficult experiments, the unseen spectacles of visible species both inverted and upright, as well as true instances of reason; its visual seat in the eye is determined; and the natural angle of vision revealed] (Innsbruck, Austria: Daniel Agricola, 1619).

29. Jean Tarde, *Les Astres de Borbon, et apologie pour le soleil* (Paris: Jean Gesselin, 1627), 8 (my translation).

30. [Antonie van] Leeuwenhoek, "Microscopical Observations," *Philosophical Transactions of the Royal Society* 112 (1675): 379.

31. Isaac Newton, *Opticks* (London: Smith & Walford, 1704), 136.

32. For crossovers of *species* between vision and race, see Mary Quinlan-McGrath, *Influences: Art, Optics, and Astrology in the Italian Renaissance* (Chicago: University of Chicago Press, 2013), 218fn25; Juliana Chow, *Nineteenth-Century American Literature and the Discourse of Natural History* (Cambridge: Cambridge University Press, 2021), 36.

33. Johannes Hevelius, *Selenographia: Sive lunae descriptio* (Gdańsk, Poland: Hünefeld, 1647).

34. See Kathrin Müller, "How to Craft Telescopic Observations in a Book: Hevelius's *Selenographia* (1647) and Its Images," *Journal for the History of Astronomy* 41 (2010): 355–79.

35. Because of its orbital libration (a slight figure-eight motion), the Moon exposes 59 percent of its surface to earthly observers, from 8 to 50 percent at a time.

36. Johannes Hevelius, *Cometographia* (Gdańsk, Poland: S. Reiniger, 1668); Patrick Feaster, "Early Motion Pictures of Eclipses (1639–1880)," *Griffonage-Dot-Com* (blog), March 30, 2017, https://griffonagedotcom.wordpress.com/2017/03/30/early-motion-pictures-of-eclipses-1639-1880/. *Selenographia*'s very long Latin subtitle affirms that "the native faces [nativa facies] of all other planets . . . most accurately cut from the air are placed under view [sub aspectum ponuntur]."

37. Alan E. Shapiro, "Images: Real and Virtual, Projected and Perceived, from Kepler to Dechales," *Early Science and Medicine* 13, no. 3 (2008): 270–312.

38. Jill H. Casid reminds us that the magic lantern likely existed already

(*Scenes of Projection: Recasting the Enlightenment Subject* [Minneapolis: University of Minnesota Press, 2015], 55). Huygens lists the magic lantern among instruments usable for solar eclipse and sunspot observation (61).

39. Michael Barth, "Huygens at Work: Annotations in His Rediscovered Copy of Hooke's *Micrographia,*" *Annals of Science* 52 (1995): 603.

40. See Allan Chapman, "'Micrographia' on the Moon," *Astronomy and Geophysics* 56, no. 5 (2015): 23–29.

41. Robert Hooke, *Micrographia, or Some Physiological Descriptions of Minute Bodies Made by Magnifying Glasses with Observations and Inquiries Thereupon* (London: John Martyn and James Allestry, 1665), iv.

42. Lorraine Daston and Peter L. Galison, "Truth-to-Nature," in *Objectivity* (Princeton, NJ: Princeton University Press, 2007).

43. For Wren, see Matthew C. Hunter, *Wicked Intelligence: Visual Art and the Science of Experiment in Restoration London* (Chicago: University of Chicago Press, 2013), 43–47; J. A. Bennett, *The Mathematical Science of Christopher Wren* (Cambridge: Cambridge University Press, 1982), 74–75.

44. Gregorio Astengo, "Parallelogrammum Prosopographicum," *Nexus Network Journal* 22 (2020): 735–53, https://doi.org/10.1007/s00004-020-00497-x.

45. George Sinclair, "Parallelogrammum Prosopographicum . . . ," *Philosophical Transactions of the Royal Society* 8, no. 96 (July 1673): 6080–85.

46. The *Encyclopédie* under "Objectif" indicates: "One can also simply say the objective [l'objectif]." Denis Diderot and Jean le Rond d'Alembert, eds., *L'Encyclopédie, ou dictionnaire raisonné des sciences, des arts et des métiers, etc.,* vol. 11 (1765), 301.

47. Hooke, *Micrographia,* 4; *Oxford English Dictionary,* "objective," last updated March 2025, https://doi.org/10.1093/OED/9609347108.

48. The original theological context for *objective* was progressively supplanted by its optical meaning. When an exegete of Gassendi writes in 1654 of "the Objective presence of all things at once, to the Divine Intellect," the transition from theology to optics is palpable (Walter Charleton, *Physiologica Epicuro-Gassendo-Charltoniana; or, The Fabrick of Science Natural upon the Thesis of Atoms* [London: Newcomb, 1654], 82). For how symbolism and ideology warped the perceptual understanding and simulation of perspective, see James Elkins, *The Poetics of Perspective* (Ithaca, NY: Cornell University Press, 1994).

49. For depth relations in Hooke's work, see Christa Knellwolf, "Robert Hooke's *Micrographia* and the Aesthetics of Empiricism," *Seventeenth Century* 16, no. 1 (2001): 177–200; Meghan C. Doherty, "Discovering the 'True Form': Hooke's *Micrographia* and the Visual Vocabulary of Engraved Portraits," *Notes and Records of the Royal Society of London* 66, no. 3 (2012): 211–34. See also Hunter, *Wicked Intelligence,* chaps. 1 and 2.

50. Meghan C. Doherty points to Hooke's familiarity with the "visual

vocabulary developed by engravers for translating a three-dimensional world into a two-dimensional representation." "Discovering the 'True Form,'" 211.

51. Margaret Cavendish, *The Description of a New World, Called the Blazing World* (London: A. Maxwell, 1668), 34. For race in Cavendish's celestial journey, see Cristina Malcolmson, *Studies of Skin Color in the Early Royal Society: Boyle, Cavendish, Swift* (New York: Routledge, 2016), 123–34.

52. Margaret Cavendish, *Observations on Experimental Philosophy* (1666), cited in Sujata Iyengar, "Royalist, Romanticist, Racialist: Rank, Gender, and Race in the Science and Fiction of Margaret Cavendish," *ELH: English Literary History* 69, no. 3 (2002): 655.

53. Malcolmson, *Studies of Skin Color,* 13, 44, 65–66; Jeremy Robin Schneider, "The First Mite: Insect Genealogies in Hooke's *Micrographia,*" *Annals of Science* 75, no. 3 (2018): 192n111.

54. See Mechthild Fend, "Skin Colour," in *Fleshing Out Surfaces: Skin in French Art and Medicine, 1650–1850* (Manchester, England: Manchester University Press, 2016).

55. Mari-Tere Álvarez, "Moon Shot: From Renaissance Imagination to Modern Reality," in *Renaissance Futurities: Science, Art, Invention,* ed. Charlene Villaseñor Black and Mari-Tere Álvarez (Berkeley: University of California Press, 2020). For Moon fictions (with race entirely omitted), see Frédérique Aït-Touati, *Fictions of the Cosmos: Science and Literature in the Seventeenth Century,* trans. Susan Emanuel (Chicago: University of Chicago Press, 2014).

56. See below and Eileen Reeves, "Jesuits on the Moon," in *Evening News: Optics, Astronomy, and Journalism in Early Modern Europe* (Philadelphia: University of Pennsylvania Press, 2014).

57. Johannes Kepler, *Kepler's Somnium: The Dream, or Posthumous Work on Lunar Astronomy,* trans. with commentary by Edward Rosen (New York: Dover, 2003), 12.

58. See Frédérique Aït-Touati, "Penser le ciel à l'âge Classique: Fiction, hypothèse et astronomie de Kepler à Huygens," *Annales: Histoire, sciences sociales* 65, no. 2 (2010): 325–44. Frédérique Aït-Touati terms lunar observers of Earth "geoscopes" (338).

59. Kepler, *Somnium,* 133. Kepler consulted chronicles from the West Indies (*Kepler's Somnium,* 133fn357). For Kepler, blackness is an excess rather than a lack because "light destroys matter" and "has more to remove in black things" (72fn146). This corresponds to the model of Black skin as an extra layer of tegument, ascribing "thick skin" to enslaved Black people and rationalizing inhumane mistreatment.

60. Raz Chen-Morris, "Shadows of Instruction: Optics and Classical Authorities in Kepler's *Somnium,*" *Journal of the History of Ideas* 66, no. 2 (2005): 225, 242.

61. For the implications of the Copernican revolution for racialization, see Sylvia Wynter. Race figures rarely in critical analyses of seventeenth-century astronomical rationality. An exception is Mary Baine Campbell, "Impossible Voyages: Seventeenth-Century Space Travel and the Impulse of Ethnology," *Literature and History* 6, no. 2 (1997): 1–17.

62. Francis Godwin, *The Man in the Moone*, ed. William Poole (1638; Toronto: Broadview, 2009), 76.

63. See Alexander Hugo Schulenburg, "Transient Observations: The Textualizing of St Helena Through Five Hundred Years of Colonial Discourse" (PhD diss., University of St Andrews, 1999), 184–85.

64. In 1638, John Wilkins, a future cofounder of the Royal Society, published a pro-heliocentric treatise: *The Discovery of a World in the Moone, or A Discourse Tending to Prove That 'Tis Probable There May Be Another Habitable World in That Planet* (London: Michael Sparl & Edward Forrest, 1638). In the second edition, he asserted that "Colonies" on the Moon would bring "inconceivably" more "Pleasure and Profit" than the "Discoveries in America," underlining the overall colonial mindset of lunar speculations. John Wilkins, *A Discourse Concerning a New World & Another Planet*, 2nd ed. (London: John Maynard, 1640), 206, 242. See David Cressy, "Early Modern Space Travel and the English Man in the Moon," *American Historical Review* 111, no. 4 (2006): 961–82.

65. In the second edition, Godwin added an essay on telegraphy, "The Inanimate Messenger," an expression synonymous with our "media." Francis Godwin, *The Man in the Moone; or, A Discourse of a Voyage Thither*, 2nd ed. (London: Joshua Kirton, 1657).

66. Cyrano de Bergerac, *Histoire comique, contenant les Estats & Empires de la Lune* (Paris: Charles de Sercy, 1657), 2 (unless otherwise noted, all translations are my own). In the preface, Cyrano claims ruefully that his book provides "as large an increase of goods for the Republic of Letters as the discovery of New lands was useful for old ones" (n.p.).

67. The 1687 English translation renders "les yeux sont inutiles, on n'a besoin que des oreilles [eyes are useless, only ears are required]" by the ominous formula "made wholly for the Ears and not the Eyes" (Cyrano Bergerac, *The Comical History*, trans. A. Lovell [London: Henry Rhodes, 1687], 121). I return to this formula made famous by Thomas Edison in chapter 7.

68. See, for instance, H. van Hetten [Jean Leurechon?], *Récréation mathématique* (Pont-à-Mousson, France: Jean Appier Hanzelet, 1626).

69. The oppositions of civilized versus uncivilized language, phonic versus graphic meaning, verbal language versus music, and, finally, writing versus speech point to "silent black *mater*iality" and the "aural aesthesis" or "phonic substance" that, for Fred Moten, haunt optical media. Fred Moten, "Black Mo'nin' in the Sound of the Photograph," in *In the Break: The*

Aesthetic of the Black Radical Tradition (Minneapolis: University of Minnesota Press, 2003), 197, 203.

70. [Bernard Le Bovier, sieur de Fontenelle], *Entretiens sur la pluralité des mondes* (Paris: Veuve C. Blageart), 1686 (unless noted, all translations are my own). Alain Niderst lists Fontenelle's verbatim borrowings from François Bernier, *Abrégé de la philosophie de Gassendi,* 2nd ed., vol. 4 (Lyon, France: Anisson, Posuel & Rigaud, 1684) (*Fontenelle à la recherche de lui-même [1657–1702]* [Paris: Nizet, 1972], 107). See Jean Dagen, "Fontenelle et l'épicurisme," *Revue d'Histoire Littéraire de la France* 103, no. 2 (2003): 397–414.

71. For dialogues as a new educational genre addressed to women, see Juliette Cherbuliez, "On Letting Sleeping Blonds Lie: Gender, Leisure Literature, and the Imagination in Fontenelle," *Romanic Review* 102, no. 1–2 (2011): 145–68.

72. Sylvia Wynter, "Unsettling the Coloniality of Being/Power/Truth/Freedom: Towards the Human, After Man, Its Overrepresentation—An Argument," *New Centennial Review* 3, no. 3 (2003): 257–337.

73. Madame Deloge de la Mézange was a close friend of Fontenelle's, and he sojourned at her castle. Deloge was interested in skin color change and protogenetics. The physiologist Claude-Nicolas Le Cat mentions a "eugenic" experiment in which she was involved: The gray spots on a white male dog were painted orange-brown, and the puppies it had with a black-and-white female were reported to have been black, white, and orange-brown. Le Cat adds that she kept one of the puppies and had its portrait painted. Claude-Nicolas Le Cat, *Traité de la couleur de la peau humaine en général, et de celle des nègres en particulier, et de la métamorphose d'une de ces couleurs en l'autre, soit de naissance, soit naturellement* (Amsterdam: n.p., 1765), 19.

74. The Code Noir commissioned by Jean-Baptiste Colbert in 1682 was drafted by two colonial officials who uniformized disparate local practices (see Vernon Valentine Palmer, "The Origins and Authors of the Code Noir," *Louisiana Law Review* 56 [1995]: 363–406). Prior to Newton, the Heavens and Earth were not thought to share uniform mechanical laws according to Ofer Gal and Raz Chen-Morris (*Baroque Science,* chaps. 4 and 5). They describe Newton's work as "the human enforcement of mathematical order on a messy nature" (184). (See also, Nicholas Campion, "Astronomy and Culture in the Eighteenth Century: Isaac Newton's Influence on the Enlightenment and Politics," *Mediterranean Archaeology and Archaeometry* 16, no. 4 [2016]: 497–502). Newton's reorganization of silver coinage in England after the East India Company's silver devalued home currency attests to his global purview (see Allison Margaret Bigelow, *Mining Language: Racial Thinking, Indigenous Knowledge, and Colonial Metallurgy in the Early Modern Iberian World* [Chapel Hill: University of North Carolina Press, 2020], 2–3). Denise Ferreira da Silva theorizes Newton's contribution as a global field of forces: "The plenum is now inhabited by moving things, bodies, which obey the

invisible forces or powers that determine how they affect and how they are affected by other bodies" (*Toward a Global Idea of Race* [Minneapolis: University of Minnesota Press, 2007], 48).

75. Tryon quoted in Philippe Rosenberg, "Thomas Tryon and the Seventeenth-Century Dimensions of Antislavery," *William and Mary Quarterly* 61, no. 4 (2004): 609–42.

76. "A Discourse in a Way of a Dialogue, Between an Ethiopian or Negro-Slave and a Christian, That Was His Master in America," in *Friendly Advice to the Gentlemen-Planters of the East and West Indies* (London: Andrew Sowle, 1684), 148–49.

77. Gabriel Daniel, *Voyage du monde de Descartes* (Paris: Veuve Simon Bénard, 1690), 46 (unless otherwise noted, all translations are my own).

78. Justin E. H. Smith, "Gabriel Daniel: Descartes Through the Mirror of Fiction," in *The Oxford Handbook on Descartes and Cartesianism,* ed. Steven Nadler, Tad M. Schmaltz, and Delphine Antoine-Mahut (Oxford: Oxford University Press, 2019). The Jesuit order nominally rejected slavery (see Timothy J. Reiss, "Descartes's Silences on Slavery and Race," in *Race and Racism in Modern Philosophy,* ed. Andrew Valls [Ithaca, NY: Cornell University Press, 2005]).

79. M. de Fontenelle, *A Discovery of New Worlds,* trans. A. Behn (London: William Canning, 1688).

80. Aphra Behn, *Emperor of the Moon: A Farce* (London: R. Holt, 1687), 59.

81. See Catherine Ingrassia, "Aphra Behn, Captivity, and *Emperor of the Moon,*" *Restoration: Studies in English Literary Culture, 1660–1700* 41, no. 2 (2017): 53–67.

82. François de Salignac de La Mothe-Fénelon, *Oeuvres,* vol. 4 (Paris: Didot, 1787), 571–72 (unless otherwise noted, all translations are my own).

83. Fénelon outlines elsewhere his approach to "correct" imaging: "[Water] receives without alteration all the images of various objects, and it keeps none of them. The pure and tranquil soul is the same. God imprints his image on it and that of all other objects that he wishes to imprint. Everything is imprinted; everything is erased. . . . Everything disappears as in water as soon as God wishes to make new impressions." *Fénelon: Selected Writings,* ed. and trans. Chad Helms (Mahwah, NJ: Paulist Press, 2006), 278 (my translation).

2. Kinemorphosis

1. For both real and fictional racial shifting, see Katy L. Chiles, *Transformable Race: Surprising Metamorphosis in the Literature of Early America* (Oxford: Oxford University Press, 2014).

2. Alan W. Hirshfeld, *Parallax: The Race to Measure the Cosmos* (New York: Dover, 2013), 157.

3. Quoted in Laurence Bobis and James Lequeux, "Cassini, Rømer and

the Velocity of Light," *Journal of Astronomical History and Heritage* 11, no. 2 (2008): 100.

4. Jean Deschamps, *Court abrégé de philosophie wolffienne* (Amsterdam and Leipzig: Arkstée et Merkus, 1743), 23 (my translation).

5. Maupertuis, *Oeuvres de Mr. de Maupertuis,* 4 vols. (Lyon, France: Jean-Marie Bruyset, 1756), 1:26, 226 (unless otherwise noted, all translations are my own).

6. J. B. Shank, "The Invention of French Newtonianism: Maupertuis and Voltaire," in *The Newton Wars and the Beginning of the French Enlightenment* (Chicago: University of Chicago Press, 2009).

7. It was known since a 1670s expedition to Peru that clocks were slower near the equator, a crucial argument for the equatorial bulge.

8. Jessica Riskin, *The Restless Clock: A History of the Centuries-Long Argument Over What Makes Living Things Tick* (Chicago: University of Chicago Press, 2016), 87–188.

9. Mary Terrall, "Mathematics and Mechanics in the Paris Academy of Sciences," in *The Man Who Flattened the Earth: Maupertuis and the Sciences in the Enlightenment* (Chicago: University of Chicago Press, 2002).

10. Maupertuis, *Discours sur les différentes figures des Astres* (Paris: Imprimerie royale, 1732), 46.

11. Maupertuis, "Essai de cosmologie," in *Oeuvres,* 1:xiv.

12. See Ansgar Lissy, "L'Économie de la nature: Maupertuis et Euler sur le principe de moindre action," *Philosophiques* 42, no. 1 (2015): 37–38.

13. In an essay on the origins of language, Maupertuis explores psychological "duration [durée]" in pre-Bergsonian terms: "But could not immense times have elapsed between two perceptions that I would consider as following closely on each other?" *Oeuvres,* 1:285.

14. This debate focuses on visual reproduction as well. Preformist Leibniz had a predilection for the pantograph inflecting models of human reproduction. Matthew Jones, *The Good Life in the Scientific Revolution: Descartes, Pascal, Leibniz, and the Cultivation of Virtue* (Chicago: University of Chicago Press, 2006), 208. For epigenesis, see Terrall, *Man Who Flattened the Earth*; Stéphane Schmitt, "Mécanisme et épigenèse: Les conceptions de Bourguet et Maupertuis sur la génération," *Dix-Huitième Siècle* 46, no. 1 (2014): 477–99.

15. See Terrall, *Man Who Flattened the Earth,* 211–20. Maupertuis connects biological and chemical growth in *System of Nature: An Essay on the Formation of Organized Bodies* ([1751] in *Oeuvres,* 2:139–68), arguing that "elements themselves, endowed with intelligence, arrange and gather themselves [s'arrangent & s'unissent] in order to fulfill the aims of the Creator" (168). The French "remplir les vues" means "fulfill the aims" but also "fill up the views," combining teleology and visualization. Denis Diderot took such vitalism to be a frightening "universal copulation" (172, all translations

my own). Maupertuis, "Réponse aux objections de M. Diderot," in *Oeuvres,* 2:169–84; Charles T. Wolfe, "Endowed Molecules and Emergent Organization: The Maupertuis-Diderot Debate," *Early Science and Medicine* 15, nos. 1–2 (2010): 38–65.

16. See Andrew Curran, "Rethinking Race History: The Role of the Albino in the French Enlightenment Life Sciences," *History and Theory* 48 (2009): 151–79.

17. On Johann Nicolas Pechlin and Albinus, see [Maupertuis], *Vénus physique contenant deux dissertations, l'une sur l'origine des Hommes et des Animaux; et l'autre sur l'origine des Noirs* (La Haye, Netherlands: Jean Martin Husson, 1746), 117fnA. See also Andrew S. Curran, *The Anatomy of Blackness: Science & Slavery in the Age of the Enlightenment* (Baltimore: Johns Hopkins University Press, 2011); Craig Koslofsky, "Superficial Blackness? Johann Nicolas Pechlin's *De Habitu et Colore Aethiopum Qui Vulgo Nigritae* (1677)," *Journal of Early Cultural Studies* 18, no. 1 (2018): 140–58.

18. Maupertuis's monogenism contrasts with the polygenism of his nemesis Voltaire. In 1734, Voltaire penned a metaphysical treatise in which an extraterrestrial rejects monogenism after a flyover of Earth. Nicholas Cronk et al., *Oeuvres complètes de Voltaire,* 20C (Oxford: Voltaire Foundation, 2017).

19. See Bronwen Douglas, "Notes on 'Race' and the Biologisation of Human Difference," *Journal of Pacific History* 40, no. 3 (2005): 331–38. For the influence of Maupertuis's theory of generation on Buffon, David Hume, and Erasmus Darwin, see Peter Knox-Shaw, "Hume's 'Farther Scenes': Maupertuis and Buffon in the *Dialogues,*" *Hume Studies* 34, no. 2 (2008): 209–30.

20. *Le Code noir ou Édit du Roy* (Paris: Claude Girard, 1735), 5. See Martha Hodes, *White Women, Black Men: Illicit Sex in the Nineteenth-Century South* (New Haven, CT: Yale University Press, 1998).

21. In her otherwise impeccable intellectual biography of Maupertuis, Mary Terrall surprisingly omits this fact. See Philippe Haudrère, "L'origine du personnel de direction générale de la Compagnie française des Indes, 1719–1794," *Revue française d'histoire d'outre-mer* 248 (1980): 356; René Kerviler, *La Bretagne à l'Académie française au XVIIIe siècle* (Paris: Victor Palmé, 1889), 287.

22. Maupertuis, "Lettre sur l'âme des bêtes," in *Oeuvres,* 2:218.

23. We know only of Wright that he invented a quadrant for Moon observation in 1733 (the pannauticon) and published *Universal Architecture* (1755) on building and grotto design (Michael Hoskin and George D. Rochester, "Thomas Wright and the Royal Society," *Journal for the History of Astronomy* 23 [1992]: 167–72). He was a pansophist and a freemason and had a speech impediment (Judy Preston, "A Polymath in Arcadia: Thomas Wright (1711–86)," *Garden History* 38, no. 2 [2010]: 159–76).

24. Thomas Wright of Durham, *An Original Theory or New Hypothesis of the Universe Founded upon the Laws of Nature and Solving by Mathematical*

Principles the General Phaenomena of the Visible Creation and Particularly the Via Lactea (London: H. Chapelle, 1750), 1fn.

25. William Hastie, ed. and trans., *Kant's Cosmogony* (Glasgow: John Maclehose and Sons, 1900), 204–5.

26. Simon Schaffer, "The Phoenix of Nature: Fire and Evolutionary Cosmology in Wright and Kant," *Journal for the History of Astronomy* 9 (1978): 180–200.

27. Wright claims he observed the Great Comet of 1744 in a telescope (*Original Theory,* 40). But the magnification of his drawing far exceeds what reflectors of the time could discern, so he likely extrapolated from descriptions of the comet's head and "parabolic" hoods found in Jean-Philippe Loÿs de Chéseaux, *Traité de la comète* (Genève, Switzerland: Marc-Michel Bousquet, 1744), 145–47.

28. J. H. Lambert, *La Perspective affranchie du plan géométral* (Zürich, Switzerland: Heideggeur, 1759).

29. Johann Heinrich Lambert, *Photometria, sive de Mensura et Gradibus Luminis, Colorum et Umbrae* (Augsburg, Germany: Klett, 1760).

30. [Johann Heinrich] Lambert, *The System of the World,* trans. James Jacque (London: Vernor and Hood, 1800), 16. For visualization, see Maarten Bullynck, "Johann Lambert's Scientific Tool Kit," *Science in Context* 23, no. 1 (2010): 65–89; [Johann Heinrich] Lambert, "Construction d'une échelle ballistique," *Nouveaux mémoires de l'académie royale des sciences et belles-lettres* (1773): 34–41.

31. Immanuel Kant, "Thoughts of the True Estimation of Living Forces . . . ," in *Natural Science,* ed. Eric Watkins (Cambridge: Cambridge University Press, 2012), 103.

32. Immanuel Kant, *Universal Natural History and Theory of the Heavens or Essay on the Constitution and Mechanical Origin of the Whole Universe According to Newtonian Principles,* trans. William Hastie (1900; Ann Arbor: University of Michigan Press, 1969); Immanuel Kant, "Universal Natural History and Theory of the Heavens," in *Natural Science,* by Immanuel Kant, ed. Eric Watkins, trans. Lewis White Beck et al. (Cambridge: Cambridge University Press, 2012) (I cite from this edition).

33. For Kant's knowledge of and thought about magic lanterns, see Stefan Andriopoulos, *Ghostly Apparitions: German Idealism, the Gothic Novel, and Optical Media* (New York: Zone Books, 2013).

34. Michela Massimi states that Maupertuis is the source of Kant's nebular theory ("Kant's Dynamical Theory of Matter in 1755, and Its Debt to Speculative Newtonian Experimentalism," *Studies in the History and Philosophy of Science* 42 [2011]: 525–43). According to Michael Friedman, *Kant's Construction of Nature: A Reading of the Metaphysical Foundations of Natural Science* ([Cambridge: Cambridge University Press, 2013], 485n125), Stanley Jaki, who translated *The Universal Natural History of the Heavens,* considers

that Kant copied a passage from Maupertuis's *Elements of Geography* (1742) about the flattening of Earth (Immanuel Kant, *Universal Natural History of the Heavens*, trans. and ed. Stanley L. Jaki [Edinburgh: Scottish Academic Press, 1981], 273n26.)

35. See Martin Schonfeld, *The Philosophy of the Young Kant: The Precritical Project* (Oxford: Oxford University Press, 2000), 82–83.

36. That expression figures on his letterhead. Maurice Bessy and Lo Duca, *Georges Méliès* (Paris: Prisma, 1945), 132.

37. Alexander Pope's *An Essay on Man* (1734): "Superior Beings, when of late they saw / A mortal Man unfold all Nature's Law, / Admir'd such Wisdom in an earthly shape, / And show'd a NEWTON, as we show an *Ape*." Schonfeld, *Philosophy of the Young Kant*, 123.

38. Cited in Jon M. Mikkelsen, "Recent Works on Kant's Race Theory," in *Kant and the Concept of Race: Late Eighteenth-Century Writings*, trans. and ed. Jon M. Mikkelsen (Albany: State University of New York Press, 2013), 8.

39. See Bernard Boxill, "Kantian Racism and Kantian Teleology," in *The Oxford Handbook of Philosophy and Race*, ed. Naomi Zack (Oxford: Oxford University Press, 2017), 45.

40. Immanuel Kant, "Physical Geography," in *Natural Science*, 573–74.

41. On this point, see Sally Hatch Gray, "Kant's Race Theory, Forster's Counter, and the Metaphysics of Color," *Eighteenth Century* 53, no. 4 (2012): 393–412.

42. See Robert J. Richards, "Kant and Blumenbach on the Bildungstrieb: A Historical Misunderstanding," *Studies in History and Philosophy of Biological and Biomedical Sciences* 31, no. 1 (2000): 11–32.

43. Michela Massimi, "The Legacy of Newton for the Pre-Critical Kant," in *The Oxford Handbook of Newton*, ed. C. Smeenk and E. Schliesser, online ed. (Oxford Academic, 2017), https://doi.org/10.1093/oxfordhb/9780199930418.001.0001. Friedman points out that Kant was also interested in Euler's optical theory for his model of ether. Friedman, *Kant's Construction of Nature*, 195fn151.

44. James Delbourgo, "The Newtonian Slave Body: Racial Enlightenment in the Atlantic World," *Atlantic Studies: Literary, Cultural and Historical Perspectives* 9, no. 2 (2012): 185–207. Mitchell's essay in answer to the infamous 1743 contest by the Académie de Bordeaux (the second city in France for the slave trade)—"What is the physical cause of the color of negroes, the nature of their hair, and the degeneration of both?"—set aside prior explanations as fantastic and prejudicial, explaining skin color through anatomy and Newtonian optics. He deemed that white skin was actually "white" and "transparent" while "the Skins of Negroes transmit no color" and hence is pure black—another instance of optical physiology. The cause of Blackness is simply that "the Skin [of Negroes] is deprived of its white Colour," for lack of clothing, housing, and refinements (John Mitchell, "An Essay upon

the Causes of the Different Colours of People in Different Climates," *Philosophical Transactions of the Royal Society* 43 [1744]: 133). Mitchell considered Black and white people equally degenerated from an original middle-color complexion in Middle Eastern ancestors (147–48).

45. See Alan E. Shapiro, "The Evolving Structure of Newton's Theory of White Light and Color," *Isis* 71, no. 2 (1980): 211–35.

46. Isaac Newton, *Opticks*, vol. 1 (London: Smith & Walford, 1704), 106.

47. Immanuel Kant, "Of the Different Human Races: An Announcement (1775)," in Mikkelsen, *Kant and the Concept of Race*, 54.

48. Johann Gottlieb von Herder, *Outlines of a Philosophy of the History of Man*, trans. T. Churchill (1784; New York: Bergman Publishers, 1966), 166.

49. David Bindman, *Ape to Apollo: Aesthetics and the Idea of Race in the 18th Century* (Chicago: University of Chicago Press, 2002), 168–71.

50. For Kant's racialization as invested in technics of visuality, see Denise Ferreira da Silva, *Toward a Global Idea of Race* (Minneapolis: University of Minnesota Press, 2007), 60–61; David Lloyd, *Under Representation: The Racial Regime of Aesthetics* (Bronx, NY: Fordham University Press, 2019), 51; Achille Mbembe, *The Critique of Black Reason*, trans. Laurent Dubois (Durham, NC: Duke University Press, 2017).

51. Michael Hoskin, *Discoverers of the Universe: William and Caroline Herschel* (Princeton, NJ: Princeton University Press, 2011).

52. See Simon Schaffer, "Herschel in Bedlam: Natural History and Stellar Astronomy," *British Journal for the History of Science* 13, no. 3 (1980): 211–39. For religious implications, see Michael Hoskin, "William Herschel and God," *Journal for the History of Astronomy* 45, no. 2 (2014): 247–52.

53. William Herschel compares his telescopic observation of nebulae with playing George Frideric Handel's fugues. Schaffer, "Herschel in Bedlam," 216.

54. 5/12 to 5/14, "Telescopes," Papers of William Herschel, 1936, GBR/0180/RGO 35/170/22, Cambridge University Library, Cambridge University, Cambridge, UK.

55. Joseph Priestley's 1772 *The History and Present State of Discoveries Relating to Vision, Light, and Colours* was influential for William Herschel's ideas about light. Simon Schaffer, "'The Great Laboratories of the Universe': William Herschel on Matter Theory and Planetary Life," *Journal for the History of Astronomy* 9 (1980): 81.

56. William Herschel, "Catalogue of a Second Thousand of New Nebulae and Clusters of Stars; with a Few Introductory Remarks on the Construction of the Heavens," *Philosophical Transactions of the Royal Society* 79 (January 1, 1789): 213. See Omar Nasim, *Observing by Hand: Sketching the Nebulae in the Nineteenth Century* (Chicago: University of Chicago Press, 2013), 26–27.

57. "Appendix to the Paper on the Power of Penetrating into Space by

Telescope," Papers of William Herschel, RGO 35/170/23, 75, Cambridge University Library.

58. See Serena Keshavjee, "'La Vie renaissant de la mort': Albert Besnard's 'Non-Miraculous' History of Creation," in *Picturing Evolution and Extinction: Regeneration and Degeneration in Modern Visual Culture,* ed. Fae Brauer and Serena Keshavjee (Cambridge: Cambridge Scholars Publishing, 2015).

59. From the 1770s on, Bode worked with Lambert on the *Astronomisches Jahrbuch* and was a close acquaintance of Kant's. In a 1781 letter, Kant mentions that his and Lambert's cosmologies were reviewed in Bode's new edition of *Anleitung zur Kenntnis des gestirnten Himmels* (Introduction to the knowledge of the starry heavens) (Immanuel Kant, *Correspondence,* trans. Arnulf Zweig [Cambridge: Cambridge University Press, 1999], 184–85). Starting in 1783, Bode corresponded with William Herschel (Index to the Correspondence of William Herschel A-C, RAS MSS Herschel W.1/BODE, Johann Elert [1747–1826], July 9, 1783, 13.B.104, Royal Astronomical Society Library, London). In 1788, Bode compared Lambert's and Kant's systems with the Herschels' (M. Bode, "Observations sur la distribution des nébuleuses et des groupes d'étoiles dans le firmament," in *Mémoires de l'académie royale des sciences et belles-lettres de Berlin, 1794–5* [1788; Berlin: George Decker, 1799]). A French commentator of Kant well informed of his philosophy and cosmology states that William Herschel even translated Kant's *Universal Natural History* into English (Nicolas-Louis François de Neuchâteau, *Le Conservateur, ou recueil de morceaux inédits,* vol. 2 [Paris: Crapelet, 1799], 32–35).

60. William Herschel, "On the Construction of the Heavens," *Transactions of the Royal Society* 75 (1785): 253.

61. William Herschel, "On the Proper Motion of the Sun and Solar System," *Philosophical Transactions of the Royal Society* 73 (January 1, 1783): 243.

62. Edwin Hubble's 1930s discovery of the red shift in spectrographs reinstated proper motion and hastened the theory of the Big Bang. But for roughly 150 years, the universe had no overarching movement.

63. See the Illustris project, a digital simulation—indeed, a film—of seven billion years of cosmic evolution with an Oculus-like mobile point of view (https://www.illustris-project.org/).

64. See royal astronomer Alexis-Marie Rochon, who traveled to Morocco, India, Madagascar, and the southern Atlantic and Pacific Islands. He built a new prismatic micrometer and was placed in charge of the King's collection of instruments. Danielle Fauque, "Alexis-Marie Rochon (1741–1817), savant, astronome, et opticien," *Revue d'Histoire des Sciences* 38, no. 1 (1985): 3–36.

65. Christopher J. Berry, "Adam Smith and Science," in *The Cambridge Companion to Adam Smith,* ed. Knud Haakonssen (Cambridge: Cambridge University Press, 2006), 117.

66. Adam Smith, "The Principles Which Lead and Direct Philosophical Enquiries; Illustrated by the History of Astronomy," in *Essays on Philosophical Subjects,* ed. Joseph Black and James Hutton (London: Cadell & Davies, 1795), 15.

67. See Jessica Riskin, *Science in the Age of Sensibility: The Sentimental Empiricism of the French Enlightenment* (Chicago: University of Chicago Press, 2002), 114–15. Riskin documents the correspondence between Franklin, Barbeu-Dubourg, and Joseph Priestley mixing slavery, politics, and physics.

68. Jacques Barbeu-Dubourg, *Chronographie, ou description des tems; contenant toute la suite des Souverains de l'Univers, & des principaux événements de chaque siècle, depuis la Création du monde jusqu'à présent* (Paris: chez l'auteur, 1753).

69. Denis Diderot, "Chronologique (machine)," in *L'Encyclopédie, ou dictionnaire raisonné des sciences, des arts et des métiers, etc.,* ed. Denis Diderot and Jean le Rond d'Alembert, vol. 3 (1765), 400–01; Stephen Ferguson, "The 1753 Carte chronographique of Jacques Barbeu-Dubourg," *Princeton University Library Chronicle* 52 (1990–1991): 190–230. The Torah scroll was clearly the model, as Barbeu-Dubourg was the French authority for Old Testament translations (Paul Delaunay, "Vieux médecins mayennais: Barbeu Du Bourg," *Bulletin de la Commission historique et archéologique de la Mayenne* 19 [1903]: 16).

70. Cited in Alfred Owen Aldridge, "Jacques Barbeu-Dubourg: A French Disciple of Benjamin Franklin," *Proceedings of the American Philosophical Society* 95, no. 4 (1951): 346–47.

71. Eran Shalev, "'A Republic Amidst the Stars': Political Astronomy and the Intellectual Origins of the Stars and Stripes," *Journal of the Early Republic* 31, no. 1 (2011): 39–73. The red-and-white broad stripes of the flag come from the navy flag of the British East India Company.

72. [Thomas Paine], *Common Sense Addressed to the Inhabitants of America* (Philadelphia: W. and T. Bradford, 1776), 45.

73. David Rittenhouse, *An Oration Delivered February 24, 1775 Before the American Philosophical Society Held at Philadelphia, for Promoting Useful Knowledge* (Philadelphia: John Dunlap, 1775), 8–20.

74. Brooke Hindle, *David Rittenhouse* (Princeton, NJ: Princeton University Press, 1964), 112.

75. When shown Banneker's corrections of two well-known astronomy manuals, Rittenhouse was very impressed, adding, "considering the colour of the Author." Banneker retorted: "I am annoyed that the subject of my race is so much stressed: the work is either correct or it is not." Charles A. Cerami, *Benjamin Banneker: Surveyor, Astronomer, Publisher, Patriot* (New York: John Willey, 2002), 136, 150. For Banneker, see Britt Rusert, "The Banneker Age: Black Afterlives of Early National Science," in *Fugitive Science:*

Empiricism and Freedom in Early African American Culture (New York: New York University Press, 2017).

76. Jean-Nicolas Rieucau, "Condorcet's Science Obscured: Shadows Cast by the Enlightenment," *Proceedings of the Western Society for French History* 32 (2004): 82–106.

77. M. Schwartz [Marie-Jean-Antoine-Nicolas de Caritat, marquis de Condorcet], *Réflexions sur l'esclavage des nègres* (Neuchâtel, Switzerland: Société typographique, 1781).

78. For a critique of Condorcet, see Louis Sala-Molins, *Dark Side of the Light: Slavery and the French Enlightenment,* trans. John Conteh-Morgan (Minneapolis: University of Minnesota Press, 2006); David Williams, *Condorcet and Modernity* (Cambridge: Cambridge University Press, 2004), 139–58.

79. Condorcet, "Sur l'Admission des femmes au droit de cité," *Journal de la société de 1789* 5 (July 3, 1789): 2.

80. Condorcet worked on a global history of knowledge since the 1770s. See Keith Michael Baker, *Condorcet: From Natural Philosophy to Social Mathematics* (Chicago: University of Chicago Press, 1975).

81. Condorcet, *Esquisse d'un tableau historique des progrès de l'esprit humain,* new ed. (Paris: Bibliothèque choisie, 1829), 7; Marquis de Condorcet, *Outlines of an Historical View of the Progress of the Human Mind* (London: J. Johnson, 1795), 3–4.

82. L. M. Henriquez, *Voyage et adventures de Frondeabus, fils d'Herschell, dans la cinquième partie du monde, ouvrage traduit de la langue Herschellique* (Paris: Cailleau, 1799).

83. *Mercure de France: Journal littéraire et politique* 7 (Paris: Cailleau, 1799): 108–11; *Magasin encyclopédique ou journal des sciences, des lettres et des arts* 5 (Paris: Fuchs, 1801): 430.

3. Photoimaging Hieroglyphs

1. See François Brunet, *The Birth of the Idea of Photography,* trans. Shane B. Lillis (Cambridge, MA: MIT Press, 2019).

2. Reputed experimentalist and theoretician Hermann von Helmholtz still attributed the origin of all forces to the Sun in the 1860s. Jessica Riskin, *The Restless Clock: A History of the Centuries-Long Argument Over What Makes Living Things Tick* (Chicago: University of Chicago Press, 2016), 211.

3. For pictures or images analyzable as chemical objects rather than as visual representations, see Matthew C. Hunter, *Painting with Fire: Sir Joshua Reynolds, Photography, and the Temporally Evolving Chemical Object* (Chicago: University of Chicago Press, 2020), 18–19, 39–40.

4. For the importance of the Caribbean buccaneer and maroon communities, see Julius C. Scott, *The Common Wind: Afro-American Currents in the Age of the Haitian Revolution* (London: Verso, 2018).

5. Trevor Burnard and John Garrigus convincingly propose that poisoning resulted from ergotism in stale wheat due to the wartime disruption of wheat deliveries. *The Plantation Machine: Atlantic Capitalism in French Saint-Domingue and British Jamaica* (Philadelphia: University of Pennsylvania Press, 2016), 97–136.

6. Maria Alessandra Bollettino, "Slavery, War, and Britain's Atlantic Empire: Black Soldiers and Rebels in the Seven Years' War" (PhD diss., University of Texas at Austin, 2009).

7. Vincent Brown, *Tacky's Revolt: The Story of an Atlantic Slave War* (Cambridge, MA: Belknap Press, 2020), 11.

8. Marjoleine Kars, *Blood on the River: A Chronicle of Mutiny and Freedom on the Wild Coast* (New York: New Press, 2022).

9. Torture involved scientific tools like magic lanterns and electric shocks. Kieran Murphy, "Haiti and the Black Box of Romanticism," *Studies in Romanticism* 56, no. 1 (2017): 41.

10. Boubacar Barry, *Senegambia and the Atlantic Slave Trade* (Cambridge: Cambridge University Press, 1997), 79, 116–18, 121–24. For the rise of the Euro-African diaspora or "habitants," see James F. Searing, "The Seven Years' War in West Africa: The End of Company Rule and the Emergence of the *Habitants*," in *The Seven Years' War: Global Views,* ed. Mark H. Danley and Patrick J. Speelman (Leiden, Netherlands: Brill, 2012).

11. Gene E. Ogle, "'The Eternal Power of Reason' and 'The Superiority of Whites': Hilliard d'Auberteuil's Colonial Enlightenment," *French Colonial History* 3 (2003): 43.

12. For instance, see Abbé [Lazzaro] Spallanzani, *Essay on Animal Reproductions,* trans. M. Matty (London: T. Becket, 1769).

13. For instance, Abbé Poncelet, *La Nature dans la formation du tonnerre et la reproduction des êtres vivants,* vol. 1 (Paris: Le Mercier, 1766). The expression *sexual reproduction* is associated with Erasmus Darwin in *Zoonomia* (1794) and "The Temple of Nature" (1803). We find reproduction des espèces in *Journal de politique et de littérature* (Brussels: n.p., 1776), 1:468. In a 1780 book on plants of Paris, we find reproduction de l'espèce (M. Bulliard, *Flora Parisiensis* [Paris: Didot, 1780], 5:631). We find the expression procédés techniques de reproduction (mechanical reproduction process) in legal proceedings of 1826 (*Commission de la propriété littéraire* [Paris: Pillet, 1826], 287). T. K. Hervey mentions "the reproduction, in every form, of these specimens [of sculpture]" ("Illustrations of Modern Sculpture," *Literary Gazette* 795 [April 14, 1832]: 240). "The State of the Art of Lithography" mentions "the reproduction of original sketches and drawings by the hundreds and thousands" (*Art-Union* 6 [July 15, 1839]: 97).

14. See Marie-Hélène Huet, *Monstrous Imagination* (Cambridge, MA: Harvard University Press, 1993); Raymond Stephanson and Darren N.

Wagner, eds., *The Secrets of Generation: Reproduction in the Long Eighteenth Century* (Toronto: Toronto University Press, 2015).

15. Louis de la Caze, *Idée de l'homme physique et moral pour servir d'Introduction à un traité de médecine* (Paris: Guérin et Delatour, 1760), 87.

16. Denis Diderot, "Génération (physiologie)," in *L'Encyclopédie, ou dictionnaire raisonné des sciences, des arts et des métiers, etc.*, ed. Denis Diderot and Jean le Rond d'Alembert, vol. 7 (1757), 572–73.

17. Buffon, *Histoire naturelle* (Paris: Imprimerie royale, 1749), 2:35–53.

18. [Charles François Tiphaigne de la Roche], *Giphantie* (Paris: Durand, 1760) (I cite from this edition; all translations are my own); *Giphantia, or A View of What Has Passed, What Is Now Passing, and, During the Present Century, What Will Pass in the World* (London: Robert Horsfield, 1761) (Horsfield also published Granville Sharp's 1769 *A Representation of the Injustice and Dangerous Tendency of Tolerating Slavery*); T. L. R., *Giphantie oder die Erdbeschauung* (Ulm, Germany: Auf Rosten der Bartholomdichten Handlung, 1761); [Tiphaigne de la Roche], *Amilec, ou la graine d'homme* (n.p., 1753) (I cite from this edition; all translations are my own); *Amilec, or the Seeds of Mankind* (London: Needham, 1754). Reviews include L'Abbé Raynal, *Correspondence littéraire, philosophique et critique* (1753; Paris: Furne, 1829), 1, 78–79; *Aus der anmuthigen Gelehrsamkeit* (Leipzig, Germany: Breitkopf, 1754), 1, 132–40. *Amilec* is in the vein of Voltaire's 1752 *Micromégas.*

19. Christopher L. Miller, *Blank Darkness: Africanist Discourses in French* (Chicago: University of Chicago Press, 1985).

20. The spirit-guide whom the protagonist meets materializes like a mirage image, "a sort of stain [tache], a sort of shadow fixed in the air" (1:16). Because humans interpreted them as divinities, the elemental spirits "took measures to no longer be visible: they imagined a kind of filter, a sort of sieve [filière]" that rid them of materiality (1:35–36). For the narrative itself, materialization/dematerialization and visibility/invisibility characterize the primitive nation of Africa.

21. Élie Fréron, "Giphantie," in *L'Année littéraire,* vol. 8 (Amsterdam: n.p., 1760), 3–21 ("To obtain durable paintings representing people realistically, one would need only to fix these fugitive images" [9]); "Giphantie," in *L'Avant-coureur, feuille hebdomadaire* (Paris: Lambert, 1760), 512–16; *Mémoires pour l'histoire des Sciences et des Beaux-Arts* (Paris: Chaubert, 1760), 2869–71; *Journal des sçavans* 55, no. 13 (Amsterdam: Michel Rey, 1760), 501–2; *"Giphantia," Monthly Review, or Literary Journal* 24 (London: Griffith, 1761), 222–26; [Tobias Smollett], *"Giphantia," Critical Review, or Annals of Literature* 11 (London: Hamilton, 1761), 109–15. For Tobias Smollett's authorship, see Valerie Wainwright, "Additions to Smollett's Journalism: Further Attributions for *The Critical Review,* 1757–1763," *Notes and Queries* 59, no. 2 (2012): 226–47.

22. The Lunar Society counted the likes of Joseph Priestley, James Watt, Erasmus Darwin, and Thomas Wedgwood as members, many of whom were published in *The Monthly Review.* Wedgwood reported on experiments on phlogiston for coloring ceramics and bankrolled fellow members (Robert Schofield, *The Lunar Society of Birmingham: A Social History of Provincial Science and Industry in Eighteenth-Century England* [Oxford: Clarendon Press, 1963], 290–91). The Masonic Lodge of the Nine Sisters gathered hundreds of key liberal French thinkers and leading scientists in the two decades before the Revolution (Louis Amiable, *Une loge maçonnique d'avant 1789: Les Neuf Soeurs* [Paris: Germer Baillère, 1897]).

23. Pernille Røge, *Economistes and the Reinvention of Empire: France in the Americas and Africa, c. 1750–1802* (Cambridge: Cambridge University Press, 2019), 179.

24. Joseph-Roger de Benoist, *Histoire de l'église Catholique au Sénégal: Du milieu du XVè siècle à l'aube du troisième millénaire* (Paris/Dakar: Karthala/Claireafrique, 2007), 71–75.

25. Abbé Demanet, *Nouvelle histoire de l'Afrique françoise,* 2 vols. (Paris: Veuve Duchesne, 1767), 1:239–66.

26. Andrew S. Curran, "Rethinking Race History: The Role of the Albino in the French Enlightenment Life Sciences," *History and Theory* 48 (2009): 117, 242, 249.

27. Fred Moten, *Black and Blur (consent not to be a single being)* (Durham, NC: Duke University Press, 2017), 74–76.

28. Achille Mbembe, *Critique of Black Reason,* trans. Laurent Dubois (Durham, NC: Duke University Press, 2017), 69.

29. Ann Thomson, "Colonialism, Race and Slavery in Raynal's *Histoire des deux Indes,*" *Global Intellectual History* 2, no. 3 (2017): 251–67, https://doi.org/10.1080/23801883.2017.1370233. Ann Thomson shows that Raynal first explained racial difference with inherited genetics ("germs") before adopting Demanet's environmental chemistry through the intermediary of physiocrat Abbé Pierre-Joseph-André Roubaud. It is not excluded that Immanuel Kant's telic idea of whiteness owes much to Demanet via Raynal.

30. Jean Senebier, *Mémoires physico-chymiques, sur l'influence de la lumière solaire pour modifier les êtres des trois règnes de la* NATURE, *& sur-tout ceux du règne végétal* (Genève, Switzerland: Barthelemy Chirol, 1782), 1:viii.

31. Carole Huta, "Un dialogue entre l'ombre et la lumière. L'art d'observer à la fin du XVIIIe siècle: Jean Sénebier (1742–1809)," *Revue d'Histoire des Sciences* 51, no. 1 (1998): 94. See also the special issue on Senebier, Marc J. Ratcliff et al., eds., *Archive des sciences* 63 (2010); Jean Pierre Maunoir, *Éloge historique de Monsieur Sénebier* (Paris: Paschoud, 1810), 14–15; Geerdt Magiels, *From Sunlight to Insight: Jan IngenHousz, the Discovery of Photosynthesis & Science in the Light of Ecology* (Brussels: Brussels University Press, 2010).

32. See Curran, *Anatomy of Blackness,* 22–23, 90–95.

33. Senebier repeats: "White colors blacken. Black colors are invariable/ unalterable." The French original fits colors as well as peoples: "Les *blancs* noircissent. Les *noirs* sont invariables"; "Les *blancs* noircissent. Les *noirs* sont inaltérables"; "Les *blancs* ont noircis. Les *noirs* ont été inaltérables" (3:220, 222, 224).

34. Miriam Claude Meijer, "Petrus Camper on the Origin of Color of Blacks," *History of Anthropology Newsletter* 24, no. 2 (1997): 8.

35. Roxann Wheeler glosses *complexion* as a range of bodily differences related to anatomy, humor theory, climate, culture, etc., arguing it was reduced to skin color only in the 1770s, making race "a science of surfaces" (*The Complexion of Race: Categories of Difference in Eighteenth-Century British Culture* [Philadelphia: University of Pennsylvania Press, 2000], 26, 29). See Kary L. Chiles, *Transformable Race: Surprising Metamorphoses in the Literature of Early America* (Oxford: Oxford University Press, 2013).

36. Denise Ferreira da Silva, *Toward a Global Idea of Race* (Minneapolis: University of Minnesota Press, 2007), xv, 44–48.

37. Senebier's experiments with silver chloride were made in 1778 or 1779. Jean Sénebier, "Réponse à la lettre de Madame de V***," *Observations sur la physique* 14, no. 3 (September 1779): 200–215; James Priestley, *The History and Present State of Discoveries Relating to Vision, Light, and Colours* (London: J. Johnson, 1772), 378–80.

38. Jean Senebier, *Essai sur l'art d'observer et de faire des expériences* (Paris: Fuchs, 1802), 1:6, 110. See Patrick Singy, "The Art of Scientific Observation Before the Emergence of Positivism," *Representations* 95, no. 1 (2006): 54–75.

39. Senebier knows Johann Heinrich Lambert's research on photometry, cosmology, and computing instruments' margin of deviation (Senebier, *Essai,* 1:10, 72, 405–9; 2:192, 215–18); he knows William Herschel's working protocols in mirror-making (3:220–22) and telescope coverage: "Herschel, who knows all the movements he can give to his telescope, uses them to range over [parcourir] the sky scrupulously, by following carefully all of its parts, and by sweeping [balayant] it, as he says, to express the rigor with which he observes it" (1:207).

40. See Antje Pfannkuchen, "Image, Language, Science: Hieroglyphs and the Romantic Quest for Primordial Truth," in *Before Photography,* ed. Kirsten Belgum, Vance Byrd, and John D. Benjamin (New York: De Gruyter, 2021), https://doi.org/10.1515/9783110696448-013.

41. Both Senebier and Lichtenberg corresponded with Joseph Priestley, a key member of the Lunar Society led by the father of Thomas Wedgwood. Linde Katritzky, "Georg Christoph Lichtenberg," *Notes and Records of the Royal Society of London* 39, no. 1 (1984): 41–49.

42. Georg Christoph Lichtenberg, *Novi Commentarii Societatis Regiae*

Scientiarum Gottingensis. Commentationes physicae et mathematicae classis (Göttingen, Germany: Johann Christian Dieterich, 1778), 8:168–80, translation by Steven Tester.

43. Georg Christoph Lichtenberg, *Nova Methodo Naturam Ac Motum Fluidi Electrici Investigandi* (Göttingen, Germany: Johann Christian Dietrich, 1778), pl. 1. See Antje Pfannkuchen, "A Science of Hieroglyphs, or the Test of Bildung," in *The Technological Introject: Friedrich Kittler Between Implementation and the Incalculable,* ed. Jeffrey Champlin and Antje Pfannkuchen (Bronx, NY: Fordham University Press, 2018). A correspondent of William Herschel compared electrophorus images with nebulae in 1785 (Simon Schaffer, "'The Great Laboratories of the Universe': William Herschel on Matter Theory and Planetary Life," *Journal for the History of Astronomy* 9 [1980]: 86–87).

44. Antje Pfannkuchen, "A Matter of Visibility—G. Chr. Lichtenberg's Art and Science of Observation," *Configurations* 24, no. 3 (2016): 387.

45. Liselotte Dieckmann, "The Metaphor of Hieroglyphics in German Romanticism," *Comparative Literature* 7, no. 4 (1955): 306–12; Frances S. Connelly, "Poetic Monsters and Nature Hieroglyphics: The Precocious Primitivism of Philipp Otto Runge," *Art Journal* 52, no. 2 (1993): 31–39; Byron Ellsworth Hamann, "How Maya Hieroglyphs Got Their Name: Egypt, Mexico, and China in Western Grammatology Since the Fifteenth Century," *Proceedings of the American Philosophical Society* 152, no. 1 (2008): 1–68; J. Michele Molina, "Athanasius Kircher's *China Illustrata* and the Life Story of a Mexican Mystic," in *Athanasius Kircher: The Last Man Who Knew Everything,* ed. Paula Findlen (New York: Routledge, 2004).

46. Siegfried Zielinski examines these in *Deep Time of the Media: Toward an Archaeology of Hearing and Seeing by Technical Means,* trans. Gloria Custance (Cambridge, MA: MIT Press, 2006), 179.

47. E. F. F. Chladni, *Traité d'acoustique* (Paris: Courcier, 1809), vii (my translation).

48. Lichtenberg wrote two long essays on William Herschel. Georg Christoph Lichtenberg, *Vermischte Schriften,* vols. 6–7 (Göttingen, Germany: Johann Christian Dietrich, 1800–1806).

49. Mark Littman, *The Heavens on Fire: The Great Leonid Meteor Storms* (Cambridge: Cambridge University Press, 1998), 45–52.

50. E. F. F. Chladni, *Die Akustik* (Leipzig, Germany: Breitkopf und Hartel, 1802).

51. Johann Wilhelm Ritter, *Key Texts of Johann Wilhelm Ritter (1776–1810) on the Science and Art of Nature,* trans. Jocelyn Holland (Leiden, Netherlands: Brill, 2010), 305.

52. Lorenz Oken, *Isis: Encylopädische Zeitschrift, vorzügl. Für Naturgeschichte, vergleichende Anatomie u. Physiologie* (Jena, Germany: Expedition der Isis, 1826), 957. For Müller, see G. E. Berrios, "On the Fantastic

Apparitions of Vision by Johannes Müller," *History of Psychiatry* 16, no. 2 (2005): 229–46.

53. Georges Vigarello, *The Silhouette from the 18th Century to the Present Day,* trans. Augusta Dörr (London: Bloomsbury, 2012), 16.

54. This "black manner" was inherently racial: William Hogarth connects it to the "network" of "threads" producing color in Black skin. *Analysis of Beauty* (London: J. Reeves, 1753), 114–15.

55. See Marie-Madeleine Martinet, "Ombres et transparences, de Vinci aux calques numériques: Imitation par analogie ou par contiguïté?," *Sillages Critiques* 14 (2012): https://doi.org/10.4000/sillagescritiques.2788.

56. See Andrea Wulf, *Chasing Venus: The Race to Measure the Heavens* (New York: Vintage Books, 2013); Simone Dumont and Monique Gros, "The Important Role of the Two French Astronomers J.-N. Delisle and J.-J. Lalande in the Choice of Observing Places During the Transits of Venus in 1761 and 1769," *Journal of Astronomical Data* 19, no. 1 (2013): 131–44.

57. See René Sigrist, "Scientific Networks and Frontiers in the Golden Age of Academies (1700–1830)," in *Networking Across Borders and Frontiers,* ed. Jürgen Barkhoff and Helmut Eberhart (Frankfurt, Germany: Peter Lang, 2009); Jean-Pierre Martin and Anita McConnell, "Joining the Observatories of Paris and Greenwich," *Notes and Records of the Royal Society* 62 (2008): 355–72.

58. See Lisa Lowe, *The Intimacies of Four Continents* (Durham, NC: Duke University Press, 2015); Tony Ballantyne, ed., *Science, Empire and the European Exploration of the Pacific* (London: Routledge, 2018).

59. Camille Blachère, "Discours scientifique et récit de voyage: Les observations des passages de Vénus en 1761 et 1769 et les modalités de la communication des données astronomiques acquises lors d'expéditions extra-européennes," paper presented at Narrative Matters 2014: Narrative Knowing/Récit et Savoir Conference, June 2014, Paris, France, available at HAL Open Science, https://hal.archives-ouvertes.fr/hal-01099094, accessed June 10, 2025.

60. M. Le Gentil, *Voyage dans les mers de l'Inde fait par ordre du roi, à l'occasion du passage de Vénus sur le disque solaire, le 6 juin 1761, & le 3 du même mois 1769* (Paris: Imprimerie royale, 1779), 1:39–40.

61. Jimena Canales, *A Tenth of a Second: A History* (Chicago: University of Chicago Press, 2009); Wulf, *Chasing Venus,* 93. See B. E. Schaefer, "The Transit of Venus and the Notorious Black Drop Effect," *Journal for the History of Astronomy* 32, no. 4 (109) (2001): 325–36. It was called "a black ligament" and "black fibers" by Samuel Dunn ("A Determination of the Exact Moments of Time When the Planet Venus Was at External and Internal Contact with the Sun's Limb," *Philosophical Transactions of the Royal Society* 60 [1770]: 65–73). M. de la Lande calls it "obscure extension [prolongement obscur]" and "black ligament [ligament noir]" ("Explication du prolongement obscur

du disque de Vénus," *Mémoires de l'Académie Royale des sciences* [January 31, 1770]: 406–12). The earliest mention of *black drop* was by Anders Johan Lexell in 1769 as gutta nigra in Latin (Johan Sten, *A Comet of the Enlightenment: Anders Johan Lexell's Life and Discoveries* [Espoo, Finland: Birkhäuser, 2014], 71fn12). The "gutta nigra" originally named an opium concoction and thus has Orientalist connotations (Thomas Castle, *Lexicon Pharmaceuticum* [London: Cox and Sons, 1828], 337). For the connection between Venus, the black-drop effect, a hypothetical Venus atmosphere, and possible features showing life, see David Dunér, "Venusians: The Planet Venus in the 18th-Century Extraterrestrial Life Debate," *Journal of Astronomical Data* 19, no. 1 (2013): 145–67.

62. The eclipsed Moon was known as "luna niger," while a basic operation in alchemy (with Egypt as its purported source) was attaining blackness (calcinatio) to regain a purer whiteness (see Stanton J. Linden, ed., *The Alchemy Reader: From Hermes Trismegistus to Isaac Newton* [Cambridge: Cambridge University Press, 2003]). On Carl Jung's racialized construct of the "nigredo" stage, see Graham Richards, *"Race," Racism and Psychology: Towards a Reflexive History* (Hove, England: Psychology Press, 2012).

63. Don Sanchez Cetquero was the first to use the English expression in "Observation of the Transit of Mercury of May 4, 1832," *Monthly Notices of the Royal Astronomical Society* 2 (1833): 140. The one-drop rule came into effect in the U.S. South in the 1830s before being codified in Thurman v. State, 18. Ala. 276 (1850) (Frank Sweet, *Legal History of the Color Line: The Rise and Triumph of the One-Drop Rule* [Palm Coast, FL: Backintyme, 2005], 175–76).

64. Others followed under names such as Eidograph, Prosopographus, Delineator, etc. Vigarello, *Sihouette,* 23.

65. Henry Vivarez, "Un Précurseur de la photographie dans l'art du portrait à bon marché," *Le Vieux Papier: Bulletin de la Société Archéologique, Historique & Artistique* 4 (Lille, France: Lefebvre-Ducrocq, 1906), 181–88, 289–96, 358–69, 453–57.

66. See Gwendolyn DuBois Shaw, "'Interesting Characters by the Lines of Their Faces': Moses Williams's Profile Portrait Silhouettes of Native Americans," in *Black Out: Silhouettes Then and Now,* ed. Asma Naeem (Washington, DC: National Portrait Gallery, 2018).

67. John B. Lyon, "'The Science of Sciences': Replication and Reproduction in Lavater's Physiognomics," *Eighteenth-Century Studies* 40, no. 2 (2007): 258.

68. Johann Kaspar Lavater, *Physiognomische Fragmente zur Beförderung des Menschenliebe,* 4 vols. (Leipzig, Germany: Weidmanns Erben und Reich, 1775–1778), 2:90, quoted in Lyon, "Science of Sciences," 262.

69. Laurence Chatel de Brancion, *Carmontelle's Landscape Transparencies: Cinema of the Enlightenment* (Los Angeles: J. Paul Getty Museum, 2008).

70. Barbara Maria Stafford, "'Peculiar Marks': Lavater and the Countenance of Blemished Thought," *Art Journal* 46, no. 3 (1987): 185–92.

71. Quoted in David Bindman, *Ape to Apollo: Aesthetics and the Idea of Race in the 18th Century* (Chicago: University of Chicago Press, 2002), 102. David Bindman provides an excellent treatment of Lavater's overall views on race at 92–123.

72. Victor I. Stoichita, "Johann Caspar Lavater's *Essays on Physiognomy* and the Hermeneutics of Shadow," *Res* 31 (1997): 134.

73. Asma Naeem, "Black Out," in *Black Out,* 21.

74. The earliest depiction of an individual enslaved African American is a 1796 cutout silhouette of the head of a woman named Flora. Naeem, "Black Out," 92–93, 97, 103.

75. François Arago, *Rapport de M. Arago sur le daguerréotype* (Paris: Bachelier, 1839), 13.

76. Arago and Charles sat together on numerous review commissions at the Académie des Sciences from the 1810s to the 1820s, and there is no reason to believe that Arago was misinformed.

77. Gaston Tissandier, *Les Merveilles de la photographie* (Paris: Hachette, 1874), 13fn1.

78. R. B. Litchfield, "The Story of Professor Charles's Silhouettes," in *Tom Wedgwood, the First Photographer* (London: Duckworth, 1903).

79. "Cours de physique de Jacques-Alexandre-César Charles," Ms 2104, D90300, 1781, 2, Bibliothèque de l'Institut, Paris.

80. "Décret à l'offre faite par M. Charles," in *Collection Générale des décrets rendus par l'Assemblée nationale* (Paris: Baudouin, 1792), 77. In 1806, he chose 243 instruments to be preserved at the Institut de France, some of which found their way to the Conservatoire National des Arts et Métiers (J.-A.-C. Charles, "Cours de physique de Jacques-Alexandre-César Charles," Ms 2104 XX, Bibliothèque de l'Institut de France, Paris).

81. Frédéric Jean Laurent Meyer [Friedrich Johann Lorenz Meyer], "Le Cabinet de Charles," in *Fragments sur Paris,* trans. Général Dumouriez, vol. 2 (Hamburg, Germany: n.p., 1798), 2:139–43. A longer description of Charles's camera obscura is found in *Mémoires de Madame la duchesse d'Abrantès,* 2nd ed. (Paris: Mame, 1835), 4:319–21. Charles writes pithily: "At the bottom of my camera obscura I made a hole to look at people walking in the Louvre, then I look at their specter [sur leur spectre] and they are six times larger" ("Cours de physique de Jacques-Alexandre-César Charles," Ms 2104, MSS-NS 2104 tCIV pièce 3, 1784, 196, Bibliothèque de l'Institut, Paris).

82. L. Babonneix, "Julie Bouchaud des Hérettes à la 'Maison Coigny' (juin 1796-octobre 1800)," *Revue d'histoire littéraire de la France* 30, no. 4 (1923): 466–89. Her grandfather brought an enslaved man named François Jan to Nantes (Dominique Le Page, review of "Dictionnaire des gens de couleur dans la France moderne," *Annales de Bretagne* 121, no. 2 [2014]: 166).

83. Joseph Fourier, “Eloge historique de M. Charles,” *Mémoire de l’académie royale des sciences* 8 (1829): lxxiii–lxxxviii; Claude Joseph Blondel, *Un Enfant illustre de Beaugency: Le physicien et aéronaute Jacques Charles (1746–1823)* (Orléans, France: Académie d’Orléans, 2003), with uneven scholarship.

84. Laurent Mannoni, *The Great Art of Light and Shadow: Archaeology of the Cinema,* trans. Richard Crangle (Exeter, England: Exeter University Press, 2000).

85. Charles, “Cours de physique de Jacques-Alexandre-César Charles,” Ms 2104, MSS-NS 2104 tCIV pièce 17, 1784, 185–88, Bibliothèque de l’Institut, Paris.

86. Charles, “Cours de physique de Jacques-Alexandre-César Charles,” Ms 2104, MSS-NS 2104 tCIV pièce 17, 1784, 120–21; Hachette, “De l’héliostate,” *Journal de l’école polytechnique* 9 (1813): 263–79. See Allan Mills, “Portable Heliostats (Solar Illuminators),” *Annals of Science* 43, no. 4 (1986): 386. Charles’s heliostat was constructed and sold by the optician Dumotiez according to Monge, Cassini, and Bertholon, eds., *Dictionnaire de physique* (Paris: Hôtel de Thou, 1816), under “heliostat,” 3:454.

87. Charles, “Cours de physique de Jacques-Alexandre-César Charles,” Ms 2104, MSS-NS 2104 tCIV pièce 17, 1784, 130–31. Mannoni misinterpreted this “artificial candle” as a paraffin lamp.

88. Henri de Parville, “Gaston Tissandier,” *La Nature* 1372 (September 9, 1899): 226.

89. Étienne Malus, “De l’héliostate de Sgravesande perfectionné par M. Charles,” in *Mémoires de mathématiques et de physique* (Paris: Baudouin, 1811), 279.

90. “Charles’ mégascope” was placed in the “shutter of a dark room,” confirming it was integrally attached to a solar microscope. Charles Chossat, “Sur la Courbure des milieux réfringents de l’oeil chez le boeuf,” *Annales de physique et de chimie* 10 (1819): 339.

91. After doing my own archival research on Charles, I discovered the concurring work of Stephen C. Pinson, *Speculating Daguerre: Art and Enterprise in the Work of L. J. M. Daguerre* (Chicago: University of Chicago Press, 2012).

92. “Cours de physique de Jacques-Alexandre-César Charles,” Ms 2104, MSS-NS 2104 tCIV pièce 3, 1784, folio 20, Bibliothèque de l’Institut, Paris.

93. “In general a camera obscura is not very good for drawing, but it is excellent for taking down a topographical position.” “Cours de physique de Jacques-Alexandre-César Charles,” Ms 2104, MSS-NS 2104 tCIV pièce 3, 1784, 227, Bibliothèque de l’Institut, Paris.

94. “Cours de physique de Jacques-Alexandre-César Charles,” Ms 2104, MSS-NS 2104 tCIV pièce 17, 1784, 231, Bibliothèque de l’Institut, Paris.

95. "Cours de physique de Jacques-Alexandre-César Charles," Ms 2104, MSS-NS 2104 tCIV pièce 17, 1784, 231, 234, Bibliothèque de l'Institut, Paris.

96. A manual of home entertainment explains "the Art of making silhouette portraits in the English manner using a camera obscura [chambre obscure]" (Decremps, *Codicile de Jérôme Sharp* [Paris: Desoer, 1791], 56–57). According to Henry Vivarez, the *Encyclopédie méthodique* of Panckoucke indicates under "physionotrace": "We may consider as physionotrace the shadow of a figure's profile. The optical instrument known as the *megascope,* with which may be obtained in a camera obscura the exact tracings of all reliefs, is a true *physionotrace*" (I am unable to locate this entry, but it is cited in Vivarez, "Un Précurseur de la photographie," 290–91).

4. Photology

1. Scheele investigated the effects of light on silver chloride, publishing his results in 1777. He demonstrated that silver was the blackening agent in silver chloride (luna cornua) exposed to the Sun, that ammonia dissolves silver chloride, and that the blue end of the spectrum blackens silver chloride the fastest. Carl William Scheele, *Chemical Observations and Experiments on Air and Fire,* trans. Johann Reinhold Forster (London: J. Johnson, 1780), 81–82, 90–91.

2. Trevor H. Levere, "Dr Thomas Beddoes: Chemistry, Medicine, and the Perils of Democracy," *Notes and Records of the Royal Society of London* 63, no. 3 (2009): 221.

3. Dorothy Stansfield, *Thomas Beddoes M.D. (1760–1808): Chemist, Physician, Democrat* (Dordrecht, Netherlands: D. Reidel Publishing, 1984), 74, 128, 220.

4. See Trevor H. Levere, "Between Enlightenment and Romanticism: The Case of Dr. Thomas Beddoes," in *Hans Christian Ørsted and the Romantic Legacy in Science,* ed. R. M. Brain, R. S. Cohen, and O. Knudsen (New York: Springer, 2007).

5. *The Chemical Essays of Charles-William Scheele,* trans. Thomas Beddoes (London: John Murray, 1786).

6. Mrs. [Elizabeth] Fulhame, *An Essay on Combustion with a View to a New Art of Dying and Painting* (London: Cooper, 1794).

7. Thomas Beddoes and James Watt, *Considerations on the Medicinal Use of Factitious Airs* (Bristol, England: Bulgin and Rosser, 1796), 6:32.

8. For a keen reading of this case, see Rana Hogarth, "Of Black Skin and Biopower: Lessons from the Eighteenth Century," *American Quarterly* 71, no. 3 (2019): 837–47.

9. Thomas Thomson, *System of Chemistry,* 5th ed. (London: Baldwin, 1814), 4:480.

10. John Edmond Stock, "Appendix: Docteur Beddoes Commonplace

Books," in *Memoirs of the Life of Thomas Beddoes, M.D.* (London: John Murray, 1811), lxvi.

11. Doctor Biett et al., *Abrégé pratique des maladies de la peau* (Paris: Béchet jeune, 1838). Tattoo removal with a silver nitrate pencil is mentioned in Charles Perrier, *Les Criminels* (Lyon, France: Storck, 1905), 2:393.

12. Pierre François Olive Rayer, *Traité théorique des maladies de la peau* (Paris: Baillère, 1827), 2:215, 218.

13. Rana Hogarth documents cases of vitiligo in the 1790s in "The Strange Case of Hannah West: Skin Colour and the Search for Racial Difference," *Social History of Medicine* 29, no. 3 (2016): 557–72. For argyria, see I. A. Albers, "Observation of a Change in Colour in the Skin, Produced by the Internal Use of Nitrate of Silver," *Eclectic Repertory and Analytical Review* 7 (Philadelphia: Thomas Dobson, 1817), 209.

14. William Charles Wells, "An Account of a Female of the White Race of Mankind, Part of Whose Skin Resembles that of a Negro," in *Two Essays* (London: Constable, 1818). It was presented to the Royal Society in 1813.

15. Nicholas J. Wade and Benjamin W. Tatler nonetheless champion Wells's work without a word on his racism in *The Moving Tablet of the Eye: The Origins of Modern Eye Movement Research* (Oxford: Oxford University Press, 2005), 71. Editors Nicholas J. Wade et al. celebrate Wells's "admirable personal qualities" in "The Singular Vision of William Charles Wells (1757–1817)," *Journal of the History of Neuroscience* 20 (2011): 13.

16. Edward Bancroft, *Experimental Researches Concerning the Philosophy of Permanent Colours* (London: Cadell, Jun. and W. Davies, 1794), 1:34, 45.

17. See Sybille Fisher, *Modernity Disavowed: Haiti and the Cultures of Slavery in the Age of Revolution* (Durham, NC: Duke University Press, 2004).

18. Clarkson wrote in 1785: "Suppose we were to take a common globe; then begin at the equator to paint every country along the meridian line in succession from thence to the poles; and to paint them with the same colour which prevails in the respective inhabitants of each, we should see black, with which we had been obliged to begin, insensibly turn to an olive, and the olive, through as many intermediate colours, to a white. . . . The difference would consist wholly in shades of the same colour" (Thomas Clarkson, *An Essay on the Slavery and Commerce of the Human Species, Particularly the African*, 3rd ed. [Philadelphia: Joseph Crukshank, 1787], 131). Delany proposed a pigment called "rouge" to explain the skin color spectrum, arguing that all humans share the same pigmentation in differing degrees. He chose the term after the Hebrew word *Adam* meaning "red earth" but also because human blood is red and because "the color of the blackest African is produced by *identically the same* essential coloring matter that gives the 'rosy cheeks and ruby lips' to the fairest and most delicately beautiful white lady" (Martin Delany, *Principia of Ethnology: The Origin of Races and Color*, 2nd ed. [Philadelphia: Harper & Brother, 1880], 27). See Mandy A. Reid, "Utopia Is

in the Blood: The Bodily Utopias of Martin R. Delany and Pauline Hopkins," *Utopian Studies* 22, no. 1 (2011): 91–103.

19. Thomas Wedgwood, "Experiments and Observations on the Production of Light from Different Bodies, by Heat and by Attrition," *Philosophical Transactions of the Royal Society* 82 (1792): 28–47, 270–82.

20. Ritter's article "Chemical Polarity in Light" makes confusing claims about optics, phlogiston, and metaphysics, hampering its discovery in England and France in 1802–1803. See Jan Freks, Heiko Weber, and Gerhard Wiesenfeldt, "Reception and Discovery: The Nature of Johann Wilhem Ritter's Invisible Rays," *Studies in History and Philosophy of Science* 40 (2009): 143–56; Antje Pfannkuchen, "The Dynamic Polarity of Romantic Light," *Germanic Review* 92 (2017): 355–67.

21. "Modifications of Light," Papers of William Herschel, RGO/35/170/24, folio 10, microfilm, Cambridge University Library, Cambridge, UK. I am unable to identify "G. W. I."

22. Herschel notes of Marat's work, "This contradicts known facts," or "M. Marat proceeds now in his mistaken reasoning upon appearances he does not understand," but he also drafted a "Memorandum of M. Marat's Good Experiments." "Miscellaneous Notes," Papers of William Herschel, RGO/35/170/24, folios 55, microfilm, 142–46, Cambridge University Library, Cambridge, UK.

23. See Jacques de Cock, *Marat avant 1789* (Geneva: Fantasques éditions, 2003), 331–32.

24. In 1783, Marat congratulated his friend Philippe Rose Roume de Saint-Laurent for being "the creator of a great and new colony" in Trinidad (de Cock, *Marat,* 341).

25. See Charles Coulston Gillispie, *Science and Polity in France at the End of the Old Regime* (Princeton, NJ: Princeton University Press, 2004), 291–328; de Cock, *Marat,* 1437–62.

26. Jean-Paul Marat, *Recherches physiques sur le feu* (Paris: Jombert, 1780).

27. One experiment used a large portable camera obscura moved by a clock mechanism to follow the Sun. Jean-Paul Marat, *Découvertes de M. Marat sur le feu, l'électricité et la lumière* (Paris: Clousier, 1779), 13n1.

28. Alfred Bonnardot, *Histoire artistique et archéologique de la gravure en France* (Paris: Deflorenne, 1845), 134–35.

29. Jean-Paul Marat, *Découvertes de M. Marat, docteur en médecine & médecin des gardes-du-corps de Monseigneur le Comte d'Artois, sur la lumière* (Londres et Paris: Jombert, 1780), iv.

30. See Hasok Chang, "The Hidden History of Phlogiston," *Hyle* 16, no. 2 (2010): 47–79; Simon Schaffer, "'The Great Laboratories of the Universe': William Herschel on Matter Theory and Planetary Life," *Journal for the History of Astronomy* 9 (1980): 93.

31. William Hyde Wollaston, "A Method of Examining Refractive and Dispersive Powers, by Prismatic Reflection," *Philosophical Transactions of the Royal Society* 92 (1802): 378, 379.

32. Andrew Robinson, *The Last Man Who Knew Everything: Thomas Young, the Anonymous Genius Who Proved Newton Wrong and Deciphered the Rosetta Stone, Among Other Surprising Feats* (New York: Plume Books, 2007), 27.

33. George Peacock, *Life of Thomas Young* (London: John Murray, 1855), 44.

34. Thomas Young, "Outlines of Experiments and Inquiries Respecting Sound and Light," *Philosophical Transactions of the Royal Society* 90 (1800): 106–54. See the excellent article by Peter Pesic, "Thomas Young's Musical Optics: Translating Sound into Light," *Osiris* 28, no. 1 (2013): 15–39.

35. Young stated in 1807 that interferences were analogous to tides "in the harbor of Batsha" (Robinson, *Last Man,* 251n108). The Bai Chay estuary of Hanoi Bay has unique tide patterns due to multiple inlets. In 1684, Edmond Halley puzzled over these patterns, which Newton interpreted as interferences (the first use of this concept) in the *Principia* (Isaac Newton, *The Principia,* trans. I. Bernard Cohen and Anne Whitman [Berkeley: University of California Press, 1999], 238–42). A British captain was "informed by the inhabitants hereabouts" that the annual cycle of tides was tied to the Moon, adding, "I have found the predictions of the natives confirmed by my own observations." This translation of Native navigational and astronomical knowledge into the WTL is a striking example of transcultural transfer to and appropriation by Western science ("An Account of the Course of the Tides at Tonqueen in a Letter from M. Francis Davenport July 15, 1678, with the Theory of Them, at the Barr of Tonqueen, by the Learned Edmund Halley F. R. S.," *Philosophical Transactions of the Royal Society* 14, no. 162 [1684]: 677–84).

36. Thomas Young, "Experiments and Calculations Relative to Physical Optics," *Philosophical Transactions of the Royal Society* 94 (1804): 16.

37. Thomas Young, "On the Theory of Light and Colour," *Philosophical Transactions of the Royal Society* 92 (1802): 42.

38. "An Account of a Method of Copying Paintings upon Glass, and of Making Profiles, by the Agency of Light upon Nitrate of Silver. Invented by T. Wedgwood, Esq. With Observations by Humphry Davy," *Journal of the Royal Institution* I (1802): 167–70. See Richard Buckley Litchfield, *Tom Wedgwood, the First Photographer* (London: Duckworth, 1903), 187.

39. "Experiments on the Separation of Light and Heat by Refraction. In a Letter from Sir H. C. Englefield, Bart. F. R. S. to Thomas Young, M. D. F. R. S. From the Journal of the Royal Institution, p. 202," *Journal of Natural Philosophy, Chemistry, and the Arts* 3 (1802): 125–30. Sir H. C. Englefield writes:

"I have only to add that in the course of the month of June 1802, I repeated most of these experiments with the same apparatus [solar microscope, camera obscura, prism, three thermometers], in presence of Mr. Davy, with the most complete success. . . . At the suggestion of Mr. Davy, we tried several experiments with respect to the power of the several coloured rays in rendering Canton's phosphorus luminous" (129). He concludes: "There was great reason to suspect that this power, like that of blackening the nitrate of silver, extended beyond the visible blue ray" (130).

40. Beaumont Newhall opts for Lewis (*Latent Image: The Discovery of Photography,* [Albuquerque: University of New Mexico Press, 1983], 23). For Wedgwood workshop workers, see Larry Stewart, "Assistants to Enlightenment: William Lewis, Alexandre Chisholm and Invisible Technicians in the Industrial Revolution," *Notes and Records of the Royal Society* 62 (2008): 17–29. Photochemical reactions are described in Joseph Priestley's classic *The History and Present State of Discoveries Relating to Vision, Light, and Colors* (London: Johnson, 1772).

41. Watt to Josiah Wedgwood: "Your instructions as to the Silver Pictures about which, when at home, I will make experiments" (Litchfield, *Tom Wedgwood,* 186). The letter was lost after Eliza Meteyard published it (*Life of Josiah Wedgwood* [London: Hurst and Backett, 1866], 2:585–86). Meteyard writes: "Dr. Turner of Liverpool, as it was well known, had either invented or brought to tolerable perfection the art of copying prints upon glass by striking off impressions with a coloured solution of silver, and fixing them on glass by baking on an iron plate in a heat sufficient to incorporate the solution with the glass" (586). This is copied verbatim (without attribution!) from a footnote of an 1831 biography of Joseph Priestley that begins, "I believe it was Dr. Turner of Liverpool who first invented or brought . . . ," the passage then being the same, with one crucial added sentence: "Some of them are very neatly performed, producing transparent copies in a bright yellow upon clear glass" (John Towill Rutt, *Life and Correspondence of Joseph Priestley,* vol. 1 [London: R. Hunter, 1831], 76). Meteyard conveniently leaves out mention of the "bright yellow" pictures. Matthew Turner was a chemist who taught at the Warrington Academy from 1762 to 1765 and taught Priestley chemistry (Jan Golinski, *Science as Public Culture: Chemistry and Enlightenment in Britain, 1760–1820* [Cambridge: Cambridge University Press, 1992], 54, 95).

42. In 1788, Josiah Wedgwood (son) reported to his father Matthew Boulton's use of fulminating silver for plating (Katherine Eufemia Farrer, *Correspondence of Josiah Wedgwood, 1781–1794* [London: Women's Printing Society, 1906], 73–74). Barnes mentions the experiments of Josiah Wedgwood Sr. with George Stubbs on projecting silhouettes onto ceramic to make cameos (Alan Barnes, "Negative and Positive Images: Erasmus Darwin, Tom

Wedgwood, and the Origins of Photography," in *The Genius of Erasmus Darwin,* ed. C. U. M. Smith and Robert Arnott [Aldershot, England: Ashgate, 2005], 241n13).

43. Wedgwood Museum, Barlaston (#17737–96), cited in Robert E. Schofield, "Josiah Wedgwood, Industrial Chemist," *Chymia* 5 (1959): 191.

44. R. W. Darwin, "New Experiments on the Ocular Spectra of Light and Colours," *Philosophical Transactions of the Royal Society* 76 (1786): 313–48.

45. E. Darwin, *The Botanic Garden: A Poem* (London: J. Johnson, 1796), vii.

46. Francis Doherty, "Tom Wedgwood, Coleridge and 'Metaphysics,'" *Neophilogus* 71, no. 2 (1987): 305–15.

47. [Thomas Wedgwood], "An Enquiry into the Origin of Our Notion of Distance. Drawn Up from Notes Left by the Late Thomas Wedgwood, Esq.," *Quarterly Journal of Science and the Arts* 3 (1817): 1–12. This essay belongs to many unpublished writings of Thomas Wedgwood on education, philosophy, and perception.

48. Matthew C. Hunter, *Painting with Fire: Sir Joshua Reynolds, Photography, and the Temporally Evolving Chemical Object* (Chicago: University of Chicago Press, 2020), 122–28.

49. November 12, 1800, Coleridge to Josiah Wedgwood Jr., quoted in Litchfield, *Tom Wedgwood,* 111.

50. September 16, 1803, Coleridge to Thomas Wedgwood, quoted in Litchfield, 146.

51. Samuel Taylor Coleridge, *Biographia Literaria* (New York: Leavitt, Lord, and Co., 1834), 36fn256.

52. Philippe R. Girard, "Napoléon Bonaparte and the Emancipation Issue in Saint-Domingue, 1799–1803," *French Historical Society* 32, no. 4 (2009): 587–618.

53. Loi relative à la traite des Noirs et au régime des Colonies [Law pertaining to the slave trade and to the slaving regime of the colonies], 30 Floréal, an X [May 20, 1802]. See Jean-François Niort and Jérémy Richard, "A propos de la découverte de l'arrêté consulaire du 16 juillet 1802 et du rétablissement de l'ancien ordre colonial (spécialement de l'esclavage) à la Guadeloupe," *Bulletin de la Société d'Histoire de la Guadeloupe* 152 (2009): 31–59.

54. Jennifer Heuer, "The One-Drop Rule in Reverse? Interracial Marriages in Napoleonic and Restoration France," *Law and History Review* 27, no. 3 (2009): 515–48.

55. See Serge Sochon, *Pierre-Simon de Laplace, un savant issu des Lumières* (Paris: Christian, 2004), 77–79, 96–97.

56. That point is underlined by Casper Hakfoort, *Optics in the Age of Euler: Conceptions of the Nature of Light, 1700–1795* (Cambridge: Cambridge University Press, 1995), 184.

57. Maurice Crosland, *The Society of Arcueil: A View of French Science at the Time of Napoleon I* (London: Heinemann, 1967), 121, 254–59.

58. See James Lequeux, *François Arago, un savant généreux: Physique et astronomie au XIXè siècle* (Paris: EDP Sciences, 2008), 30–40.

59. See Paul Murdin, *Full Meridian of Glory: Perilous Adventures in the Competition to Measure the Earth* (New York: Springer, 2009).

60. See Jeff Z. Buchwald, *The Rise of the Wave Theory of Light: Optical Theory and Experiment in the Early Nineteenth Century* (Chicago: University of Chicago Press, 1989); Theresa Leavitt, *A Short Bright Flash: Augustin Fresnel and the Birth of the Modern Lighthouse* (New York: Norton, 2013).

61. Manuel Bonnet and Jean-Louis Marignier, *Niépce: Correspondance et papiers* (Saint-Loup de Varenne, France: Maison Nicéphore Niépce, 2003), 1:336–56.

62. For reprography technology and copying machines at that time, see Hunter, *Painting with Fire.*

63. Augustin Fresnel, "Mémoire sur la diffraction de la lumière," *Annales de physique et de chimie* 1 (1816): 245. Arago and Fresnel conducted a stealthy campaign for the WTL, publishing an essay on polarized light in 1819 accompanied by a translation of Francesco Grimaldi's 1665 proposition on interferences stating that "a lit body can become darker when a new light is added to that which it receives" (François Arago and Augustin Fresnel, "Sur l'action que les rayons de lumière polarisée exercent les uns sur les autres," and "Extrait d'un ouvrage du P. Grimaldi," *Annales de physique et de chimie* 10 [1819]: 288–306, 306–312).

64. Augustin Fresnel, "De La Lumière," in Jean Riffaut, *Supplément à la traduction française de la cinquième edition du Système de chimie par Th. Thomson* (Paris: Méquignon-Marvis, 1822), 64.

65. Augustin Fresnel, "Post-Scriptum," in Riffaut, *Supplément,* 536.

66. Arago made only the following note in the procès-verbaux of the Bureau des Longitudes on August 22, 1821: "A sunray falling on silver muriate decomposes that salt. But two rays falling together on that point under conditions of interference prevents decomposition." Arago, *Oeuvres complètes* (Paris: Gide, 1858), 10:484–85.

67. Cited in Larry Schaaf, "Sir John Herschel's 1839 Royal Society Paper on Photography," *History of Photography* 3, no. 1 (January 1979): 57–58. John Herschel submitted "Note of the Art of Photography, or the Application of the Chemical Rays of Light to the Purpose of Pictorial Representation" to the Royal Society in March 1839 but quickly withdrew it out of deference for Talbot (*Proceedings of the Royal Society of London* 4 [1837–43]: 131–33). It was thought lost until Larry Schaaf located it in 1979 in St John's College Library, where I consulted it.

68. J. F. H. Herschel, "John Herschel à François Arago 1839," Correspondance classée, X2(H5), Bibliothèque de l'Observatoire de Paris. See François

Arago, "William Herschel," in *Oeuvres completes,* vol. 3 (Paris: Gide et Baudry, 1855).

69. Berthollet, "Extraits de la Bibliothèque Britannique," *Annales de chimie* 45 (1802): 256. "An Account of a method, etc. Description of a process for copying paintings on glass, and make silhouettes through the action of light on silver nitrate, by T. Wedgwood." Berthollet comments: "White skin on which the silver solution is spread is more apt than paper to receive the impression of light which produces variegated hues all the way to black depending on the intensity of its transmission: blue rays exert the strongest action." C. L. Berthollet, *Essai de statique chimique* (Paris: Didot, 1803), 1:204–5.

70. The table of contents of *Annales de chimie* (Paris: Bernard, 1807), 333, reads: "Wedgwood. Description of a process for making silhouettes through the action of light on silver nitrate." Bulletin des sciences, *Société philomatique* 3 (Paris: J. Klostermann, 1811), 167: "Action of light on silver nitrate, by T. Wedgwood" (excerpt from Nicholson's Journal, November 1802) signed "I. B" (Jean-Baptiste Biot), originally published in *Bulletin des sciences* 69 (1802). William Henry, *Élémens de chimie expérimentale,* trans. H. F. Gaultier-Claubry (Paris: Magimel, 1812), 2, 46: "This process was described by M. T. Wedgwood in Nicholson's Journal, in-8, III, 167."

71. "Système de chimie, de M. Th. Thomson, Translated by M. Riffault, Preceded by an Introduction by M. C. L. Berthollet," *Annales de chimie* 69 (1809): 100–12.

72. Étienne Bérard, "Mémoire sur le muriate d'argent," *Annales de chimie* 68 (1808): 78–87.

73. [Étienne-Louis Malus], "*Le Traité des couleurs* de Goethe," *Annales de chimie* 79 (1811): 199–219; William Alschuler, "Color Theory and Practice 1800–1860," in *Encyclopedia of Nineteenth-Century Photography,* ed. John Hannavy (New York: Routledge, 2007), 316; Keld Nielsen, "Another Kind of Light: The Work of T. J. Seebeck and His Collaboration with Goethe," part 1, *Historical Studies in the Physical and Biological Sciences* 20, no. 1 (1989): 146–47.

74. Berthollet, Chaptal, and Biot, "Rapport sur un mémoire de M. Bérard, relatif aux propriétés physiques et chimiques des divers rayons qui composent la lumière solaire," *Annales de chimie* 85 (1813): 309–25.

75. J. E. Bérard, "Mémoire sur les propriétés des différentes espèces de rayons qu'on peut séparer au moyen du prisme de la lumière solaire," *Mémoires de physique et de chimie de la Société d'Arcueil* 3 (1817): 43.

76. Larry John Schaaf, *Tracings of Light: Sir John Herschel and the Camera Lucida* (London: Friends of Photography, 1989), 31.

77. Thomas Thomson, *Éléments de chimie* (Paris: Bernard, 1809), 8:262–70.

78. Larry J. Schaaf, *Out of the Shadows: Herschel, Talbot, and the Invention of Photography* (New Haven, CT: Yale University Press, 1992), 9–11. Correspondence shows his efforts at professionalization. See, for example, Franz Xaver von Zach to William Henry Fox Talbot, June 29, 1822, WCT 988, available at Correspondence of William Henry Fox Talbot Project, accessed June 12, 2025, https://foxtalbot.dmu.ac.uk/letters. A recent collection on Talbot's nonphotographic pursuits omits astronomy altogether (Mirjam Brusius, Katrina Dean, and Chitra Ramalingam, eds., *William Henry Fox Talbot: Beyond Photography* [New Haven, CT: Yale University Press, 2013]).

79. William Henry Fox Talbot, Notebook 'A', 1817–1844, Add MS 88942/1/183, Western Manuscripts, British Library, London, UK.

80. William Henry Fox Talbot, Notebook 'B', 1822–1824, Add MS 88942/1/184, 94, 103, 112–13, Western Manuscripts, British Library, London, UK.

81. William Henry Fox Talbot, Notebook 'C', 1825, Add MS 88942/1/185, 15–35, Western Manuscripts, British Library, London, UK.

82. William Henry Fox Talbot, Notebook 'C', 1825, Add MS 88942/1/185, 19 (dated between March 22 and 29, 1825), Western Manuscripts, British Library, London, UK.

83. John Herschel to William Henry Fox Talbot, November 1, 1827, Letter ID 8807, available at Adler Planetarium Calendar of the Correspondence of Sir John Herschel Database, accessed June 12, 2025, http://historydb.adlerplanetarium.org/herschel.

84. John Herschel, "Light," *Encyclopaedia Metropolitana,* ed. Edward Smedley (London: Baldwin and Cradock, 1830), 2:582; J.-F.-W. Herschel, *Traité de la lumière,* trans. P.-F. Verhulst and Adolphe Quételet (Paris: De Malher, 1829), 328.

85. Dozens of letters between John Herschel and Talbot in 1826–1827 include topics such as light absorption, spectra, light bands, refraction, Fraunhofer, telescopes, microscopes, and astronomy.

86. William Henry Fox Talbot, pocket notebook (1829–1830), Add MS 88942/5/1/12, Western Manuscripts, British Library, London, UK.

87. Christine Blondel, "Electrical Instruments in 19th Century France, Between Makers and Users," *History and Technology* 13 (1997): 157–82.

88. John Herschel considered the Lerebours dioptric telescope at the Observatoire de Paris to be on par with Fraunhofer's Dorpat telescope. *Bibliothèque universelle des sciences, belles-lettres et arts* 30 (Genève: Bibliothèque universelle, 1825), 447.

89. [Jean Nicolas Pierre Hachette], "Rapport fait par M. Hachette sur un microscope composé à objectif achromatique présenté par M. Vincent Chevalier," *Bulletin de la société d'encouragement pour l'industrie nationale* 254 (August 1825): 239–42.

90. Paolo Brenni, "19th-Century French Instrument Makers: XIII: Soleil, Dubosq, and Their Successors," *Bulletin of the Scientific Instrument Society* 51 (1996): 7–16.

91. For instance, the catalog of the Utzschneider and Fraunhofer firms in *Astronomische Nachtrichten* in 1829. Paolo Brenni, "19th-Century Scientific Instrument Advertising," *Nuncius* 17, no. 2 (2002): 499.

92. An 1839 account of Froment's photographs mentions "various drawings obtained by the action of light. These drawings are fixed on paper treated with silver nitrate and represent samples of gauze, muslin and other fabrics, tree leaves, etc. . . . Last year, in Manchester, the Academy of Sciences of this city invited him to one of its sessions, where his experiments were compared advantageously to those of M. Talbot. . . . M. Bourcier declares that M. Froment does not know the Daguerre process, only shared with M. Arago and not the public. . . . He can make numberless prints without fearing any alterations. He continues his research begun three years ago at Polytechnique. . . . Right now, he is seeking to render leaves with their green tint and hopes to succeed. He has obtained indoor views, views of landscapes with shadows and natural perspective, of statues, busts, and buildings reproduced in the camera obscura" (Bottex and Lecoq, "Séance du 14 juin," in *Annales des sciences physiques et naturelles, d'agriculture et d'industrie, publiées par la Société royale d'agriculture, etc. de Lyon* [Lyon, France: Barret, 1839], 2:276–77). This raises important questions. Did Froment present his work with Talbot's in 1836 in Manchester? Was photographic research conducted at École Polytechnique under the aegis of Arago? Another source confirms that Froment presented his photographs "without a camera obscura" at the Société philosophique de Manchester in January 1839 ("Froment [Gustave]," *Biographie nationale des contemporains,* ed. Ernest Glaeser [Paris: Glaeser, 1878], 270).

93. Aimé Laussédat, *Notice biographique sur Gustave Froment* (Paris: J. Hetzel, 1865), 10.

94. Arthur Chevalier, *Étude sur la vie et les travaux scientifiques de Charles Chevalier* (Paris: Bonaventure et Ducessois, 1862), 15.

5. Selenography

1. Charles Chevalier, *Guide du photographe* (Paris: Charles Chevalier, 1854), 3:19. The statement is dated to "the first days of the year 1826" by his son Arthur Chevalier, *Étude sur la vie et les travaux scientifiques de Charles Chevalier* (Paris: Bonaventure et Ducessois, 1862), 19; Helmut Gernsheim and Alison Gernsheim, *The History of Photography* (Oxford: Oxford University Press, 1955), 49. An erroneous (back-translated) French quote with the wrong date (1839) and source ("letter") figures as an epigraph in Roger Watson and Helen Rappaport, *Capturing the Light: The Birth of Photography, a*

True Story of Genius and Rivalry (New York: St. Martin's Press, 2013). The misquote originates with Éric Michaud, "Daguerre, un Prométhée chrétien," *Études photographiques* 2 (1997): 1.

2. Fred Moten, *Black and Blur (consent not to be a single being)* (Durham, NC: Duke University Press, 2017), 76. See introduction.

3. Lawrence Jennings, *French Anti-Slavery: The Movement for the Abolition of Slavery in France, 1802–1848* (Cambridge: Cambridge University Press, 2000).

4. The French nègre was occasionally used since the eighteenth century for *ghostwriter,* but the usage was enthroned in 1845 by Eugène de Mirecourt, who made numerous racist statements about best-selling mixed-race novelist Alexandre Dumas. Dumas sued him and won. See Edmund Birch, "Alexandre Dumas's Odyssey: Race, Slavery, Narrative," *PMLA* 137, no. 5 (2022): 809–23.

5. Franco-Brazilian experimenter Hercules Florence coined the term for his photocopy process in 1832–1834 (photographia/la photographie). Two commentators from Edinburgh (Andrew Fyfe and John Robison) did so independently in 1839 about Talbot's and Daguerre's processes (*Oxford English Dictionary,* under "photography," updated July 2023, https://doi.org/10.1093/OED/3795670947). John Herschel used *photography* first in his unpublished 1839 draft titled "Note on the Art of Photography, or the Application of the Chemical Rays of Light to the Purpose of Pictorial Representation" (*Proceedings of the Royal Society of London* 4, no. 37 [1839]: 132–33), then in "On the Chemical Action of the Rays of the Solar Spectrum on Preparations of Silver and Other Substances, Both Metallic and Non-Metallic, and on Some Photographic Processes" (*Philosophical Transactions of the Royal Society of London* 130 [1840]: 1–59).

6. For Lorenz Oken, see chapter 3. "Photography [photographie]: part of natural history dealing with light" (François Raymond, *Supplément au dictionnaire de l'Académie française* [Paris: Gustave Barba, 1836], 619), with similar entries in other 1830s dictionaries.

7. Josef Maria Eder, *History of Photography,* trans. Edward Epstean (1932; New York: Columbia University Press, 1945), 259.

8. Wilhelm Beer and Johannes Heinrich Mädler, *Mappa Selenographica* (Berlin: S. Schropp, 1834).

9. R. B. Litchfield, *Tom Wedgwood: The First Photographer* (London: Duckworth, 1903), 21.

10. Eugène Hubert, "M. Daguerre, the Camera Obscura, and the Drawings That Make Themselves," in *First Exposures: Writings from the Beginning of Photography,* ed. Steffen Siegel (Los Angeles: J. Paul Getty Museum, 2017), 26–27 (translation amended).

11. Stephen Pinson, "Daguerre, expérimentateur du visuel," *Etudes photo-*

graphiques 13 (July 2003): 110–35; Léopold Chandezon and Jean-Guillaume-Antoine Cuvelier, *Les Machabées, ou la prise de Jérusalem* [Maccabees, or the taking of Jerusalem] (Paris: Delaguette, 1817).

12. D. Sulik, A. Kaplan, and H. Khanjian, "The First Scientific Investigation of Niépce's Images from UK and US Collections: Image Layer and Image Formation," *Imaging Science Journal* 61 (2012): 626n1.

13. François Arago, "Fixation des images qui se forment au foyer d'une chambre obscure," *Compte rendus hebdomadaires des séances de l'Académie des sciences* 8 (January–June 1839): 6; François Arago, *Oeuvres complètes,* ed. M. J.-A. Barral, 13 vols. (Paris: Gide, 1854–1862), 7:456.

14. L. M. Dougherty and A. Dollfus, "F. D. Arago's Polarimeter and His Original Observation of Extraterrestrial Polarisation in 1811," *Journal of the British Astronomy Association* 99, no. 4 (1989): 185.

15. Arago, *Oeuvres complètes,* 8:73–74.

16. Tanya Sheehan, *Study in Black and White: Photography, Race, Humor* (College Park: Pennsylvania State University Press, 2018), 1 (see also 2, 15, 25–26).

17. Alessandra Raengo, *On the Sleeve of the Visual: Race as Face Value* (Hanover, NH: Dartmouth College Press, 2013), 27.

18. Niépce cited in [Louis-Mandé] Daguerre, *Historique et description des procédés du Daguerréotype et du Diorama* (Paris: Susse Frères/Lerebours, 1839), 39.

19. Steffen Siegel, ed., *First Exposures: Writings from the Beginning of Photography* (Los Angeles: J. Paul Getty Museum, 2017), 167.

20. Arago, *Oeuvres complètes,* 7:457, 467.

21. J. F. W. Herschel, diary entry for February 14, 1839, Manuscript Library, Harry Ransom Humanities Research Center, University of Texas at Austin, quoted in Mike Ware, "Luminescence and the Invention of Photography," *History of Photography* 16, no. 1 (2002): 15n53.

22. Le Baron de Vastey, *Réflexions sur une lettre de Mazères, ex-colon français, adressée à M. J. C. L. Sismonde de Sismondi, sur les Noirs et les Blancs, la Civilisation de l'Afrique, le Royaume d'Hayti, etc.* (Au Cap-Henry, Haiti: P. Roux, 1816), 31–32; *Reflexions on the Blacks and Whites,* trans. W. H. M. B. (London: Hatchard, 1817).

23. See Marlene L. Daut, *Baron de Vastey and the Origins of Black Atlantic Humanism* (New York: Palgrave Macmillan, 2017).

24. Le Baron de Vastey, *Le Système colonial dévoilé* (Au Cap-Henry, Haiti: P. Roux, 1814), 32.

25. Joseph von Fraunhofer, *VIII. Bestimmung des Brechungs- und Farbenzerstreuungs-Vermögens verschiedener Glasarten, in Bezug auf die Vervollkommnung achromatischer Fernröhre* (München, Germany: n.p., 1817). In the 1860s, these absorption bands were understood to index the chemical composition of light sources.

26. See Jean-Michel Racault, "La Cosmologie poétique des Harmonies de la Nature," *Revue d'histoire littéraire de France* 89, no. 5 (1989): 825–42.

27. Jacques-Bernardin-Henri de Saint-Pierre, *Harmonies de la nature,* 3 vols. (Paris: Méquignon-Marvis, 1815), 3:407–612.

28. Bernardin de Saint-Pierre, *Empsael et Zoraïde, ou les Blancs esclaves des Noirs au Maroc* (Caen, France: Louis Jouan, 1905), 3. This edition is preferable to the flawed first publication mentioned above.

29. Trevor Burnard and John Garrigus, *The Plantation Machine: Atlantic Capitalism in French Saint-Domingue and British Jamaica* (Philadelphia: University of Pennsylvania Press, 2016).

30. See Matthew Goodman, *The Sun and the Moon* (New York: Basic Books, 2008), 10, 40–41, 84–85.

31. William N. Griggs, *The Celebrated "Moon Story"* (New York: Bunnell and Price, 1852), 42.

32. Cited in Lynda Walsh, *Sins Against Science: The Scientific Media Hoaxes of Poe, Twain, and Others* (Albany: State University of New York Press, 2006), 66.

33. Matthew Goodman mentions a parallel P. T. Barnum exhibition of an African American woman named Joice Heth who was born into slavery and claimed to be 160 years old (*Sun and the Moon,* 9–10, 251–64).

34. Quoted in Louis P. Masur, *1831 Year of the Eclipse* (New York: Hill and Wang, 2001), 32.

35. Thomas R. Gray, *The Confessions of Nat Turner* (Baltimore, MD: Lucas & Deaver, 1831), 11.

36. Scot French, *The Rebellious Slave: Nat Turner in American Memory* (Princeton, NJ: Princeton University Press, 2004).

37. Linda K. Kerber, "Abolitionists and Amalgamators: The New York City Race Riots of 1834," *New York History* 48, no. 1 (1967): 28–39. Anti-Black riots also took place in Philadelphia in August 1834.

38. William N. Griggs, *The Celebrated "Moon Story"* (New York: Bunnell and Price, 1852).

39. Novelist Honoré de Balzac, a friend of Arago, debunked the story, pointing out that Locke's "megascope" was nonsensical since the lamp drowns the image, leaving on the screen but "a uniform and very intense lighting." Honoré de Balzac, "Des Découvertes faites dans la lune et attribuées à Herschell fils," and "Réponse aux auteurs des découvertes dans la lune faussement attribuéees à Sir John Herschell fils," in *Oeuvres completes,* vol. 22 (Paris: Calmann-Lévy, 1886), 255–59.

40. Illustrations from Leopoldo Galluzzo, *Altre scoverte fatte nella luna dal Sigr. Herschel* (Napoli, Italy: L. Gatti e Dura, 1836).

41. Both John and William Herschel believed in extraterrestrial life. Steven Ruskin, *John Herschel's Cape Voyage* (Aldershot, UK: Ashgate, 2004), 94–95.

42. Elizabeth Green Musselman, "Swords into Ploughshares: John Herschel's Progressive View of Astronomical and Imperial Governance," *British Society for the History of Science* 31, no. 4 (1998): 424–25.

43. For the pro-Native sentiments of John and his wife Margaret, see Ruskin, *John Herschel's Cape Voyage,* 52–57.

44. Henry Brougham, *The Life and Times of Henry, Lord Brougham,* vol. 1 (New York: Harper Bros., 1871), 59.

45. Helmut Gernsheim and Alison Gernsheim, *The History of Photography* (Oxford: Oxford University Press, 1955), 23–24.

46. John Stewart, "Chemistry and Slavery in the Scottish Enlightenment," *Annals of Science* 77, no. 2 (2020): 155–68.

47. Henry Brougham, "Experiments and Observations on the Inflection, Reflection, and Colours of Light," *Philosophical Transactions of the Royal Society* 86 (1796): 227–77; Henry Brougham "Further Experiments and Observations on the Affections and Properties of Light," *Philosophical Transactions of the Royal Society* 87 (1797): 352–85.

48. Henry Brougham, "Further Experiments and Observations on the Properties of Light," *Abstracts of the Papers Communicated to the Royal Society of London* 6 (1850–1854): 312–19.

49. Papers of Charles Blagden, CB/1/2/193 and 195, Royal Society Library, London, UK.

50. See Thomas Young, "Reply to the Edinburgh Reviewers," in *Miscellaneous Works,* vol. 1 (London: John Murray, 1855).

51. Henry Brougham, *An Inquiry into the Colonial Policy of the European Powers,* 2 vols. (Edinburgh: E. Balfour et al., 1803), 2:412.

52. Monroe H. Freedman, "Henry Lord Brougham: Advocating at the Edge for Human Rights," *Hofstra Law Review* 36 (2007): 311–21.

53. W. Lewis Hyde, "John William Draper 1811–1882, Photographic Scientist," *Applied Optics* 15, no. 7 (1976): 1727.

54. John William Draper, "Early Contributions to Spectrum Photography and Photo-Chemistry," *Nature* 10, nos. 243–44 (July 30, 1874): 243–44.

55. William John Draper, "Experiments on Solar Light," *Journal of the Franklin Institute* 24, no. 1 (July 1837): 46.

56. Draper used a beam going through a small hole in a plate turned at an acute angle, so it produced diffraction at both sides of the hole.

57. See John William Draper, *A Treatise on the Forces Which Produce the Organization of Plants,* 2nd ed. (New York: Harper Bros., 1845), 137–60; K. Hentschel, "Why Not One More Imponderable? John William Draper's Tithonic Rays," *Foundations of Chemistry* 4 (2002): 5–59.

58. Lawrence C. Jennings, *French Anti-Slavery: The Movement for the Abolition of Slavery in France, 1802–1848* (Cambridge: Cambridge University Press, 2000), 276.

59. See Ariella Aïsha Azoulay, *Potential History: Unlearning Imperialism* (London: Verso, 2019), 3–5.

60. Though not much is known of the Arago sisters, James Lequeux insists that Marguerite, who married astronomer Claude-Louis Mathieu, and their daughter Lucie exerted a strong political influence on the brothers. James Lequeux, *François Arago, un savant généreux: Physique et astronomie au XIXè siècle* (Paris: EDP Sciences, 2008), 32.

61. See François Sarda, *Les Arago: François et les autres* (Paris: Tallandier, 2002), 241–55.

62. É. Arago et al., *Paris dans la comète* (Paris: Donday-Dupré, 1836), 12.

63. Jacques Arago, *Promenade autour du monde* (Paris: Leblanc, 1822); Jacques Arago, *Narrative of a Voyage Around the World* (London: Treuttel and Wurtz, 1823).

64. For a recent assessment of Jacques Arago's Romantic exoticism, see Peter Brown, "Jacques Arago: The Artist as Social Scientist in a World in Transition," *Great Circle* 39, no. 2 (2017): 120–48.

65. Cited in Benjamin Fagan, "*The North Star* and the Atlantic 1848," *African American Review* 47, no. 1 (2014): 56.

66. Frederick Douglass, "Colored Newspapers," *North Star,* January 1848, 1, Frederick Douglass Papers: Speech, Article, and Book File, 1846–1894, mss11879, box 21, reel 13, Library of Congress, http://hdl.loc.gov/loc.mss/mfd.21015.

67. See Maurice O. Wallace et al., *Pictures and Progress: Early Photography and the Making of African American Identity* (Durham, NC: Duke University Press, 2012).

68. Frederick Douglass, "Pictures and Progress," in *Frederick Douglass Papers: Series One,* ed. John W. Blassingame, vol. 3 (New Haven, CT: Yale University Press, 1985), 452–53.

69. Henry Louis Gates Jr., "Frederick Douglass's Camera Obscura: Representing the Antislave 'Clothed and in Their Own Form,'" *Critical Inquiry* 42 (2015): 31–60.

70. Ginger Hill, "'Rightly Viewed': Theorizations of Self in Frederick Douglass's Lectures on Pictures," in Wallace et al., *Pictures and Progress,* 42–45.

6. The Graphic Method

1. Henri Langlois relied on exhibitions centered on Marey in 1948, 1963, and 1966 to secure state financing for the Cinémathèque Française as a key national cultural institution. This entailed aesthetically elevating Marey's black-and-white shorts: "Nothing is more secret, more lyrical, more explosive, more contemporary than the silence of his blacks and the lightness of his whites," Langlois declared, opening the 1963 event. Langlois quoted in

Laurent Mannoni, *Histoire de la cinémathèque française* (Paris: Gallimard, 2006), 327fn232 (my translation). See also Henri Langlois, *E. J. Marey, sa vie, son oeuvre* (Beaune, France: Les Amis de Marey, 1974), with a section titled "Marey: Precursor of 20th-century Art," 19–20.

2. See, for instance, Anson Rabinbach, *The Human Motor: Energy, Fatigue, and the Origins of Modernity* (Berkeley: University of California Press, 1992); François Dagognet, *Étienne-Jules Marey: A Passion for the Trace,* trans. Robert Galeta and Jeanine Herman (New York: Zone Books, 1992); Francesco Casetti, *The Eye of the Century: Film, Experience, Modernity,* trans. Erin Larkin (New York: Columbia University Press, 2005); Mary Ann Doane, *The Emergence of Cinematic Time: Modernity, Contingency, the Archive* (Cambridge, MA: Harvard University Press, 2002).

3. See Marta Braun, *Picturing Time: The Work of Étienne-Jules Marey (1830–1904)* (Chicago: University of Chicago Press, 1992), xviii.

4. Jacques Besson's richly illustrated *Theatrum Instrumentorum et Machinarum* (1569) was the model. See Mark Andrews, *The Science and Engineering of Materials: Theater of Machine Books, 1472–1800* (Toronto: AE Publications, 2023).

5. Hebbel E. Hoff and L. A. Geddes conjecture that both friction and insufficient practical application sidelined these specimens. "The Beginnings of Graphic Recording," *Isis* 53, no. 3 (1962): 287–324.

6. Jean-Dominique Augarde, "The Scientific Cabinet of Comte d'Ons-en-Bray and a Clock by Domenico Cucci," *Cleveland Studies in the History of Art* 8 (2003): 80–95.

7. H. E. Hoff, L. A. Geddes, and Roger Guillemin, "The Anemograph of Ons-en-Bray: An Early Self-Registering Predecessor of the Kymograph," *Journal of the History of Medicine and Allied Sciences* 12, no. 10 (1957): 424–48.

8. James Dewey and Perry Byerly, "The Early History of Seismometry," *Bulletin of the Seismological Society of America* 59, no. 1 (1969): 183–227.

9. Alexander Keith, "Descriptions of a Thermometer Which Marks the Greatest Degrees of Heat and Cold, from One Time of Observation to Another, and May Also Register Its Own Height at Every Instant," *Transactions of the Royal Society of Edinburgh* 4 (1798 [1795]): 211.

10. The revival of self-tracing devices is often attributed to John Southern, an employee of the firm Boulton & Watt, who, in 1796, modified a pantograph with a weight-driven synchronized horizontal mechanism, affixing an inked stylus to a steam piston to register on a sheet of paper a closed loop, representing one continuous cycle of steam pressure variation. Southern was likely influenced by Keith. See Klaus Hentschel, *Visual Cultures in Science and Technology* (Oxford: Oxford University Press, 2014), 180–84.

11. Thomas Young, *A Course of Lectures on Natural Philosophy and the Mechanical Arts,* 2 vols. (London: Joseph Johnson, 1807), 190–91.

12. Emmanuel Breguet, "Who Was Abraham-Louis Breguet?," in *Breguet: Art and Innovation in Watchmaking*, ed. Emmanuel Breguet and Martin Chapman (New York: Prestel, 2015).

13. *Registre des séances du Bureau des longitudes pour les années 1810–1830*, Ms. 1060, s.v. 29 Sept. 1813 and 3 Feb. 1819, Archives de l'Observatoire de Paris, Bibliothèque de l'Observatoire de Paris, Paris Observatory, Paris, France.

14. Louis Moinet, *Nouveau traité général, élémentaire, pratique et théorique d'horlogerie pour les usages civils et astronomiques*, vol. 2, 2nd ed. (Paris: Dutertre, 1853).

15. [Étienne-Jules] Marey, "V. Des Appareils Enregistreurs (Histoire naturelle des corps organisés)," *Revue des cours scientifiques de la France et de l'étranger* 4 (1867): 567fn1.

16. Eytelwein's device used "the tip of a stylus pushing against a paper strip rolled around two vertical-axis cylinders" (Hippolyte Sonnet, *Dictionnaire des mathématiques appliquées* [Paris: Lahure, 1867], 469). H. E. Hoff and L. A. Geddes point out that the decisive steps took place in Paris at École Polytechnique and Conservatoire National des Arts et Métiers in the 1830s and 1840s ("Graphic Registration Before Ludwig: The Antecedents of the Kymograph," *Isis* 50, no. 1 [1959]: 5–21).

17. Arthur Morin, *Nouvelles Expériences sur le frottement* (Paris: Bachelier, 1834), 2:73. A report on Morin's experiments in the *Comptes rendus de l'Académie des Sciences* is signed by Arago.

18. [Étienne-Jules] Marey, "Production du movement chez les animaux," *Revue des cours scientifiques de la France et de l'étranger* 14 (March 2, 1867): 213; [Étienne-Jules] Marey, "Du Mouvement dans les fonctions de la vie," *Revue des cours scientifiques de la France et de l'étranger* 10 (February 3, 1866): 174.

19. Charles Wheatstone, "Notes sur le chronoscope électromagnétique," in *The Scientific Papers of Sir Charles Wheatstone* (London: Taylor and Francis, 1879).

20. For setup versus machine, see Henning Schmidgen, "Physics, Ballistics, and Psychology: A History of the Chronoscope in/as Context, 1845–1890," *History of Psychology* 8, no. 1 (2005): 46–78.

21. C. C. Adley, "The Electric Telegraph," *Minutes of Proceedings of the Institution of Civil Engineers* 9 (1852): 326.

22. Adolphe Quételet, "Expériences de M. Wheatstone," *Compte-rendus de l'Académie de Bruxelles* 7 (October 17, 1840): 131–32.

23. L'Abbé Moigno, *Traité de télégraphie électrique* (Paris: Franck, 1849), 88.

24. John F. Herschel, "On the Chemical Action of the Rays of the Solar Spectrum on Preparations of Silver and Other Substances, Both Metallic and Non-Metallic, and on Some Photographic Processes," *Philosophical*

Transactions of the Royal Society of London 130 (1840): 46, 50. John Herschel devised an actinometer in 1824, which he used until 1839 (Adelheid Voskuhl, "Recreating Herschel's Actinometry: An Essay in the Historiography of Experimental Practice," *British Journal for the History of Science* 30, no. 3 [1997]: 350). He was a central actor in spectroscopy in the 1830s with John William Draper and David Brewster (M. A. Sutton, "Sir John Herschel and the Development of Spectroscopy in Britain," *British Journal for the History of Science* 7, no. 1 [1974]: 42–60).

25. See Thomas L. Hankins, "A 'Large and Graceful Sinuosity,'" *Isis* 97, no. 4 (2006): 605–33.

26. Britt Salvesen, "Charles Wheatstone," in *Encyclopedia of 19th-Century Photography,* ed. John Hannavy (New York: Routledge, 2008), 1492–93.

27. O. J. R. Howarth, *The British Association for the Advancement of Science: A Retrospect 1831–1921* (London: BAAS, 1922), 158.

28. For an extensive list of chronoscope-chronograph applications, see P.-A. Daguin, *Traité élementaire de physique,* vol. 3 (Toulouse, France: Privat, 1855), 251–64. For the history of the drum kymograph for physiology research by Carl F. W. Ludwig, see Merriley Borell, "Instrumentation and the Rise of Modern Physiology," *Science & Technology Studies* 5, no. 2 (1987): 53–62.

29. Edward S. Holden, *Memorial of William Cranch Bond and George Phillips Bond* (San Francisco: Murdoch and Co., 1897), 250.

30. See Peter Galison, *Einstein's Clocks and Poincaré's Maps: Empires of Time* (New York: Norton, 2003), 101–7. The expression came from royal astronomer George Biddell Airy in England (J. A. Bennett, "George Biddell Airy and Horology," *Annals of Science* 37, no. 3 [1980]: 269–85). Jimena Canales explains why, in the words of an 1857 commentator, "astronomers" pioneered "the ways of measuring thoughts." She shows that astronomer Adolphe Hirsch was instrumental in developing chronographic and telegraphic methods for the transnational astronomical synchronization of timekeeping ("Exit the Frog, Enter the Human: Physiology and Experimental Psychology in Nineteenth-Century Astronomy," *British Journal for the History of Science* 34, no. 2 [2001]: 186).

31. John Herschel, "Instantaneous Photography," *Photographic News* 4, no. 88 (May 11, 1860): 13. *The Bulletin de la Société Française de photographie* and *The Photographic News* translated each other's noteworthy news items throughout the 1860s. Pierre-Hubert Desvignes patented in France a direct application of Herschel's idea: "The views being placed in the said cylinder, and the cylinder being caused to rotate, will show to the eye the steam engine as if in motion" ("Scientific Gossip," *Photographic News* 4, no. 109 [October 5, 1860]: 269).

32. Étienne-Jules Marey, "Recherches sur le pouls," *Comptes rendus des séances de la société de biologie* 1, no. 3 (1860): 281–309.

33. See Nicholas Wade and Josef Brozek, *Purkinje's Vision: The Dawning of Neuroscience* (Mahwah, NJ: Lawrence Elbaum Associates, 2001).

34. Quetelet knew Herschelian cosmology very well and was a personal friend of John Herschel. Adolphe Quételet, *Astronomie élémentaire* (Paris: De Malher, 1826), 66–67; H. Elkhadem, "La Correspondance d'Adolphe Quételet avec sir John Herschel: Un exemple de la richesse du fond Quételet," in *Adolphe Quételet 1796–1874, Hommages et contributions* (Brussels: Académie Royale de Belgique, 1975).

35. Joseph Plateau, *Dissertation sur quelques propriétés des impressions produites par la lumière sur l'organe de la vue* (Liège, Belgium: Dessain, 1831), 5 (unless otherwise stated, all translations are my own).

36. J[oseph] Plateau, *Essai d'une théorie générale comprenant des apparences visuelles qui succèdent à la contemplation des objets colorés et de celles qui accompagnent cette contemplation: C'est-à-dire la persistance des impressions de la rétine, les couleurs accidentelles, l'irradiation, les effets de la juxtaposition des couleurs, les ombres colorées, etc.* [Essay of a general theory including visual appearances that follow the contemplation of colored objects and of those that accompany this contemplation, that is, the persistence of impressions of the retina, accidental colors, irradiation, effects from juxtaposed colors, colored shadows, etc.] (Brussels: Hayez, 1834), 3–4. The dissertation is included as the second part of the essay. (Unless otherwise stated, all translations are my own.)

37. Jonathan Crary, *Techniques of the Observer: On Vision and Modernity in the Nineteenth Century* (Cambridge, MA: MIT Press, 1990), 70. For a critique of Crary on that point, see Brooke Belisle, "The Dimensional Image: Overlaps in Stereoscopic, Cinematic, and Digital Depth," *Film Criticism* 37, no. 3/1 (2013): 117–37; Jens Schröter, *3D: History, Theory and Aesthetics of the Transplanar Image,* trans. Brigitte Pichon and Dorian Rudnystky (New York: Bloomsbury, 2014), 4–27.

38. Nicholas J. Wade and Benjamin W. Tatler, eds., *The Moving Tablet of the Eye: The Origins of Modern Eye Movement Research* (Oxford: Oxford University Press, 2005), 177–78.

39. Laurent Mannoni, *The Great Art of Light and Shadow: Archaeology of the Cinema,* trans. Richard Crangle (Exeter, England: Exeter University Press, 2000), 206–7.

40. Nicholas Wade, *A Natural History of Vision* (Cambridge, MA: MIT Press, 1998), 195–97.

41. Michael Faraday, "On a Peculiar Class of Optical Deceptions," *Journal of the Royal Institution* 1 (1831): 210.

42. C[harles]. W[heatstone]., "Contributions to the Physiology of Vision, 1," *Journal of the Royal Institution* 1 (1831): 101.

43. Adolphe Quételet, *Notes extraites d'un voyage en Angleterre* (n.p., 1833), 8–9.

44. Chitra Ramalingam, "Fixing Transience: Photography and Other Images of Time in 1830s London," in *Time and Photography,* ed. Jan Baetens, Alexander Streitberger, and Hilde Van Gelder (Leuven, Belgium: Leuven University Press, 2018), 4.

45. Beverley F. Ronalds, *Sir Francis Ronalds: Father of the Electric Telegraph* (London: Imperial College Press, 2016), 57.

46. Beverley F. Ronalds, "The Beginnings of Continuous Scientific Recording Using Photography: Sir Francis Ronalds' Contribution," *European Society for the History of Photography* (2016): 2, http://www.eshph.org/wp-content/uploads/2016/05/ronalds_camera.pdf.

47. See Larry Schaaf, "Henry Collen and the Treaty of Nanking," *History of Photography* 6, no. 4 (1982): 353–66.

48. Francis Ronalds, "On Photographic Self-Registering Meteorological and Magnetic Instruments," *Philosophical Transactions of the Royal Society* 137 (1847): 111–17.

49. Charles Brooke, "On the Automatic Registration of Magnetometers, and Other Meterological Instruments, by Photography," *Philosophical Transactions of the Royal Society* 137 (1847): 59–68. See also Isabel Marília Peres et al., "The Photographic Self-Recording of Natural Phenomena in the Nineteenth Century," in *The Circulation of Science and Technology: Proceedings of the 4th International Conference of the ESHS,* ed. A. Roca-Rosell (Barcelona: Societat Catalana d'Història de la Ciència i de la Tècnica, 2012).

50. For the duplicity of astronomer Airy trying to dissuade Ronalds from using photographic self-registration while supporting Brooke at Greenwich, while John Herschel and Edward Sabine, who ran the British Association for the Advancement of Science and financed Kew, sided with Ronalds, see Ronalds, *Sir Francis Ronalds,* 483–93.

51. Étienne-Jules Marey, "Inscription photographique des indications de l'électromètre de Lippmann," *Comptes Rendus Hebdomadaires des Séances de l'Académie des Sciences* 83, no. 4 (1876): 278–80.

52. Étienne-Jules Marey, *Développement de la méthode graphique par l'emploi de la photographie* (Paris: Masson, 1884).

53. Henri Zuber, "Une Expédition en Corée," *Le Tour du monde* 25 (1873): 407.

54. Alex Soojung-Kim Pang, *Empire and the Sun: Victorian Solar Eclipse Expeditions* (Stanford, CA: Stanford University Press, 2002).

55. John McAleer, "'Stargazers at the World's End': Telescopes, Observatories and 'Views' of Empire in the Nineteenth-Century British Empire," *British Journal for the History of Science* 46, no. 3 (2013): 389–413.

56. Enfantin, *Oeuvres de Saint-Simon et d'Enfantin,* vols. 13–16 (Paris: Dentu, 1867–1868), 16:49–50.

57. Henri de Saint-Simon, *Introduction aux travaux scientifiques du dix-neuvième siècle* (n.p., 1808), 1:94–95.

58. Henri de Saint-Simon, *Oeuvres choisies de C.-H. de Saint-Simon* (Brussels: Van Meenen and Co., 1859), 1:xxi, 290–96.

59. Robert Chambers, *Vestige of the Natural History of Creation* (London: John Churchill, 1844), 296, 309.

60. In his best-selling 1830 *Consolations in Travel, or The Last Days of a Philosopher,* Humphry Davy sketches an Oculus-like perspective on world history from astronomy, asserting the "superiority" of the "Caucasian stock" over "the negro or flat-nosed race" that would require "a hundred generations, successively improved" to reach the level of the Greeks. Humphry Davy, *Consolations in Travel, or The Last Days of a Philosopher* (London: John Murray, 1830), 38–39.

61. John William Draper, *Human Physiology, Statical and Dynamical: or, The Conditions and Course of the Life of Man* (New York: Harper's and Brothers, 1856), v.

62. John William Draper, *History of the Intellectual Development of Europe* (New York: Harper & Brothers, 1863).

63. See Adam Dewbury, "The American School and Scientific Racism in Early American Anthropology," *Histories of Anthropology Annual* 3 (2007): 121–47.

64. William John Draper, *Thoughts on the Future Civil Policy of America* (New York: Harper's and Brothers, 1865), 143–44, emphasis added.

65. Stephen Jay Gould, *The Mismeasure of Man,* rev. and exp. ed. (1981; New York: W. W. Norton, 1996).

66. In *Human Physiology, Statical and Dynamical,* Draper foregrounds optics at every turn: "In that phantasmagorical exhibition which we call history, events give birth to events as in dissolving views" (623), adding later, "He who has visited the dark Chamber of Baptista Porta, and seen with his own eyes the fairy but inverted landscapes . . . the magical spectres of things which the fingers could not grasp" can only hope that on these screens he will "find reflected all the future events of his life" appearing to him "now so little that the eye could scarcely discern their form, and now expanding to a gigantic stature and rushing forth" (633–34). A proponent of the "multiple worlds hypothesis," Draper relativizes white supremacy from the eyes of "a stranger from another planet" who would undoubtedly conclude that "wherever we look man is the same" (569–70). That macroscopic scale dilutes his biases, leading him to recognize that "the old white inhabitants of Europe were not able to commence their civilization from their own interior resources, but were thrown in that career by the example and aid of a more southern and darker people" (634). Draper's astronomical purviews on natural history whimsically dictate his opinions on the racial vectors of human history.

67. Charles Darwin, *On the Origin of Species by Means of Natural Selection,*

or The Preservation of Favoured Races in the Struggle for Life (London: John Murray, 1859), 1.

68. Niles Eldridge, *Eternal Ephemera: Adaptation and the Origin of Species from the Nineteenth-Century Through Punctuated Equlibria and Beyond* (New York: Columbia University Press, 2015), 8.

69. John Herschel, *Preliminary Discourse on the Study of Natural Philosophy* (London: Longman and Rees, 1833), 151.

70. Marey makes the same paradigmatic division between "static" and "dynamic" physiological research. "Du Mouvement dans les fonctions de la vie," 170.

71. [Étienne-Jules] Marey, "Évolution historique des sciences (Histoire naturelle des corps organisés) (1)," *Revue des cours scientifiques de la France et de l'étranger* 4 (1867): 257–61.

72. In 1855, Arthur de Gobineau published *Essay on the Inequality of Human Races,* propounding the Aryan origins of white Europeans. In 1863, Gustave Flourens, the son of Marie-Jean-Pierre Flourens, gave on behalf of his father a lecture series titled "The Natural History of Organized Bodies" where he echoed Gobineau's unscientific racist theories. This may be why Marey steered clear of race. Gustave Flourens, "Histoire de l'homme," *Revue des cours scientifiques de la France et de l'étranger* 1 (1863): 46–48, and following installments in vol. 2.

73. Airy quoted in Holly Rothermel, "Images of the Sun: Warren De la Rue, George Biddell Airy and Celestial Photography," *British Journal for the History of Science* 26, no. 2 (1993): 137.

74. Christopher Ray Carter, *Magnetic Fever: Global Imperialism and Empiricism in the Nineteenth Century* (Philadelphia: American Philosophical Society, 2009), xv, 97.

75. Alan Hirschfeld, *Parallax: The Race to Measure the Cosmos* (New York: Henry Holt, 2001), 61.

76. Aimé Laussedat, "Les Applications de la perspective au lever des plans—vues dessinées à la chambre claire—photographies," *Annales du conservatoire des arts et métiers,* series 2 (Paris: Gauthiers-Villars, 1890), 2:2.

77. *Expériences faites avec l'instrument à mesurer les bases appartenant à la commission de la carte d'Espagne,* trans. from Spanish by A. Laussédat (Paris: Librairie militaire Dumaine, 1860), 3.

78. *Notice sur les travaux scientifiques de M. Aimé Laussédat* (Paris: Gauthiers-Villars, 1883), 11fn2.

79. Aimé Laussedat, *Mémoire fondamental sur l'application de la chambre claire au lever des plans, Mémorial de l'officier du génie 16* (Paris: Mallet-Bachelier, 1854), 18–20.

80. E. Monet, *Application de la photographie à la topographie* (Paris: n.p, 1894), 25.

81. Warren De la Rue, *The Bakerian Lecture on the Total Solar Eclipse of July 18th, 1860* (London: Taylor and Francis, 1862), 82.

82. A. Laussedat, *La Lunette astronomique horizontale* (Paris: E. Martinet, 1874), 4.

83. A. Laussedat et al., "Rapport sur l'observation de l'éclipse solaire du 18 juillet 1860," *Compte-rendus des séances de l'Académie des sciences* 51 (1860): 993.

84. Astronomer Arthur Eddington became famous for his total solar eclipse photographs in 1919, which experimentally proved Albert Einstein's relativity theory through the "lensing" of starlight around the Sun. Eddington went to Príncipe Island in the Gulf of Guinea, an old way station for slaving ships to the Americas. He and his team were hosted by the owner of the island's largest plantation, Jerónimo José Carneiro. In 1905–1906, the inhumane exploitation of Angolan workers on Príncipe and São Tomé islands was called "Modern Slavery" by activist Henry Woodd Nevinson and caused an international uproar and a boycott (Henry W. Nevinson, *A Modern Slavery* [New York: Harper & Brothers, 1906). Although the worst practices stopped after WWI, by the time of Eddington's visit, Angolan workers were still working in near-enslavement conditions with high mortality rates. Accounts of the expedition make no mention of this context. Lowell J. Satre, *Chocolate on Trial: Slavery, Politics, and the Ethics of Business* (Athens: Ohio University Press, 2005).

85. *Bulletin de la Société française de photographie* 22 (1876): 99.

7. Flammarion's Telechronoscope

1. *St. Louis Post Dispatch,* August 9, 1896, 4.

2. Camille Flammarion, "Lumen, récit d'outre-terre," *L'Artiste* 11 (February 1, 1867): 163–84; "Lumen, les paradoxes de la science," *L'Artiste* 13 (May 1, 1867): 163–78; "Lumen, les paradoxes de la science," *L'Artiste* 14 (June 1, 1867): 338–50. Several passages and a fourth part were added to the collated novella in Camille Flammarion, *Récits de l'infini* (Paris: Didier, 1873), the text used in this chapter (unless otherwise stated, all translations are my own). *Récits de l'infini* includes two appended short stories: "History of a Comet" and "To Infinity." That collection was how *Lumen* first appeared in English (Camille Flammarion, *Stories of Infinity,* trans. S. R. Crocker [Boston: Robert Brothers, 1873]).

3. Danielle Chaperon was the first to revive *Lumen*'s "cosmic cinema," albeit outside the purview of media studies. *Camille Flammarion, entre astronomie et littérature* (Paris: Imago, 1998).

4. Camille Flammarion, *Mémoires biographiques et philosophiques d'un astronome* (Paris: Flammarion, 1911), 22–55.

5. See Philippe de la Cotardière, *Camille Flammarion* (Paris: Flammarion, 2001), 46.

6. Lynn L. Sharp, *Secular Spirituality: Reincarnation and Spiritism in Nineteenth-Century France* (Lanham, MD: Lexington Books, 2006).

7. For an excellent treatment of astronomy and Flammarion in late nineteenth-century visual culture, see Lynda Nead, *The Haunted Gallery: Painting, Photography, Film c. 1900* (New Haven, CT: Yale University Press, 2007), 199–244.

8. Victor Hugo, *Proses philosophiques* (Paris: Albin Michel, 1937), 610.

9. See Helge S. Kragh, *Entropic Creation: Religious Contexts of Thermodynamics and Cosmology* (Hampshire, UK: Ashgate, 2008).

10. In *Les Merveilles célestes, lectures du soir* (Paris: Hachette, 1867), 241, Flammarion collates and edits (without attribution) three passages on comets from the fourth part of *Les Posthumes,* citing the same collated passage in *Récits de l'infini* (282fn1) (Restif de la Bretonne, *Les Posthumes* [Paris: Duchêne, 1802], 4:74–76). In *Les Mondes imaginaires et les mondes réels* (Paris: Didier, 1865), Flammarion mentions three other works by Restif: *Les Hommes volants, Monsieur Nicolas,* and *La Découverte australe* (173, 524–32).

11. Colin Montgomery et al., "Michell, Laplace and the Origin of the Black Hole Concept," *Journal of Astronomical History and Heritage* 12, no. 2 (2009): 90–96.

12. See Karl Clausberg, "A Microscope for Time: What Benjamin, Klages, Einstein and the Movies Owe to Distant Stars," in *Given World and Time: Temporalities in Context,* ed. Tyrus Miller (Budapest: Central European University Press, 2008). Karl Clausberg argues that Flammarion read Eberty's *The Stars and the Earth* and advocates for Eberty's prescience and influence. Clausberg suggests that Flammarion included a vignette of the Battle of Waterloo seen in backward motion in his 1873 version of *Lumen* after reading a similar episode in Richard A. Proctor's 1870 book *Other Worlds than Ours* (itself also influenced by Eberty, according to Clausberg). However, the Waterloo episode figures already in the 1867 version of *Lumen* ("Lumen, les paradoxes de la science" [May 1, 1867], 175–76), so Flammarion is the source of Proctor, not the reverse. Johann Wolfgang von Goethe's *Faust* (finished in 1832) and Charles Babbage's *Ninth Bridgewater Treatise* (1838) also proposed waves of sound and light reaching infinity (see Chaperon, *Camille Flammarion,* 68–77). Eberty's description of his "microscope of time" is nontechnical: "As the magnifying glass apparently enlarges a thousand times the space which a minute object occupies, and thus renders it possible to separate the small contiguous portions of which it consists . . . so [the observer] is able to follow the reflected images of the stages of a rapid development" (*The Stars and the Earth: Thoughts upon Space, Time, and Infinity* [London: H. Baillere, 1846], 2:12).

13. Benoît Turquety, *Inventing Cinema: Machines, Gestures and Media History,* trans. Timothy Barnard (Amsterdam: Amsterdam University Press, 2019), 107–18.

14. They were based on illustrations for the second edition (1867) of his book *Les Merveilles célestes* (1865). Flammarion indicates that the second edition replaced a number of long verse citations by illustrations as "the poetry of direct spectacle." Camille Flammarion, *Les Merveilles célestes, lectures du soir,* 2nd ed. (Paris: Hachette, 1867), i.

15. Camille Flammarion, "La Composition chimique des astres, révélée par l'analyse de leur lumière," *Le Siècle,* January 12, 1866, 3.

16. Fulgence Marion [Camille Flammarion], *L'Optique* (Paris: Hachette, 1867). The *Fantasmagorie* of Robertson takes roughly a sixth of the entire book (209–63).

17. Several optical scientists and photographers, from Plateau in the late 1840s to Antoine-François-Jean Claudet in the 1850s, proposed stereoscopic disk photography combined with the phenakistoscope to produce short motion effects, notably John Herschel, "Instantaneous Photography," *Photographic News* 4, no. 88 (May 11, 1860): 13. Ernest de Saint-Elme reported on Aimé Laussedat's idea of a panoramic two-reel paper camera: "A strip of negative paper rolled around a dispensing cylinder placed on the side at the back of the apparatus is tensed from this cylinder to another which is the receptor on the other side. . . . We thus obtain a series of juxtaposed panoramic views on the same paper strip" ("Chronique photographique," *Cosmos* 4, no. 2 [1866]: 40–41). See Caroline Chik, "La Photographie stéréoscopique animée, avant la chronophotographie," *Cinémas* 25, no. 1 (2014): 133–56.

18. Camille Flammarion, *L'Atmosphère: Description des grands phénomènes de la nature* (Paris: Hachette, 1872), 283.

19. Camille Flammarion, "Eclipse de soleil du 22 décembre 1870," *Comptes rendus de l'Académie des Sciences* 71 (1870): 941–44.

20. The archivist of Flammarion's Juvisy Observatory and I visited the holding room where Flammarion's machines are stored, but we couldn't locate the photometer.

21. Self-registering photographic setups for meteorology were reported already in the 1860s, notably simultaneous photographic measurements of magnetism between England and Portugal in 1867. See Isabel Marília Peres et al., "The Photographic Self-Recording of Natural Phenomena in the Nineteenth Century," in *The Circulation of Science and Technology,* ed. A. Roca-Rosell (Barcelona: SCHCT-IES, 2010).

22. Félix Nadar, *When I Was a Photographer,* trans. Eduardo Cadava and Liana Theodoratou (Cambridge, MA: MIT Press, 2015), 231.

23. "Jan Evangelista Purkyně," Monoskop, last edited May 25, 2022, monoskop.org/Jan_Evangelista_Purkyně.

24. For enlarger-heliostat setups, see Désiré von Monckhosen, *Photographic Optics* (London: Robert Hardwicke, 1867).

25. Françoise Launay, *The Astronomer Jules Janssen: A Globetrotter of Celestial Physics,* trans. Storm Dunlop *(New York: Springer, 2012), 182.*

26. Helium was subsequently found in caves. Norman Lockyer's wife and collaborator, Winifred Lockyer, translated one of Flammarion's books into English. Camille Flammarion, *The Wonders of the Heavens,* trans. by Mrs. Norman Lockyer (New York: Scribner, 1871).

27. Françoise Launay and Peter D. Hingley, "Jules Janssen's 'Revolver Photographique' and Its British Derivative, 'the Janssen Slide,'" *Journal for the History of Astronomy* 31 (2005): 58.

28. For the intersection of the Venus transit, psychophysiology, and astronomers' personal equations, see Jimena Canales, *A Tenth of a Second: A History* (Chicago: University of Chicago Press, 2009).

29. Hervé Faye, "Sur l'observation photographique du passage de Vénus et sur un appareil de M. Laussédat," *Comptes rendus de l'Académie des Sciences* 70 (1870): 541–48. See Jimena Canales, "Photogenic Venus: The 'Cinematographic Turn' and Its Alternatives in Nineteenth-Century France," *Isis* 93, no. 4 (2002): 597fn24. Camille Flammarion singles out the Laussedat setup with a heliostat in *Études et lectures sur l'astronomie* (Paris: Gauthier-Villars, 1873), 4:48–51.

30. Richard Proctor, "On the Application of Photography as a Means of Determining the Solar Parallax from the Transit of Venus in 1874," *Monthly Notices of the Royal Astronomical Society* 30, no. 3 (January 1870): 62–67; Richard A. Proctor, *Other Worlds than Ours: The Plurality of Worlds Studied Under the Light of Recent Scientific Researches* (1870; London: Longmans, Green, and Co. 1872), xii.

31. Théodose du Moncel, "Rapport [. . .] sur les appareils électriques présentés par M. Deschiens," *Bulletin de la Société d'Encouragement* (July 1875): 333–49 [meeting of July 10, 1874].

32. *Bulletin de la Société française de Photographie* 7 (August 2, 1867): 201–2. See also Ray Zone, *Stereoscopic Cinema and the Origins of 3-D Film, 1838–1952* (Lexington: University of Kentucky Press, 2007), 28.

33. Rédier accompanied Janssen in the 1868 mission to Japan. His father Antoine [Antonin] Rédier was a clockmaker brought to Paris by Arago (see "Antoine Rédier," *La Nature* 1024 [January 14, 1893]: 107). Janssen's motivation may have been proprietary: In 1862 he suggested a new spectroscope design that his instrument-maker Jean George Hofmann patented (Françoise Launay, *The Astronomer Jules Janssen: A Globetrotter of Celestial Physics,* trans. Storm Dunlop [New York: Springer, 2012], 22–23, 77), and the next year his stellar spectral analysis method was similarly snatched and patented by Pietro Angelo Secchi (Biman B. Nath, *The Story of Helium and the Birth of Astrophysics* [New York: Springer, 2012], 84–88).

34. See C. Wall-Romana, "Translation of Charles Cros, 'Process for Recording and Reproducing Colors, Forms and Movement' (1867) with an Introduction," *Early Popular Visual Culture* 19, no. 1 (2021): 53–66.

35. Charles Cros and Tristan Corbière, *Oeuvres complètes* (Paris: Gallimard, 1970), 535.

36. Charles Cros, "Un Drame interastral," *La Renaissance littéraire et artistique* 1, no. 18 (1872): 139–41. Unless otherwise noted, all translations are my own.

37. Another contributor of *L'Artiste* and very close friend of Cros was Auguste, comte de Villiers de L'Isle-Adam. Shortly after Edison's coinvention of the phonograph, Villiers extrapolated Cros's tale into his *Eve of the Future,* which combines the phonograph, a cinema apparatus, and "plastic substances" into a full-fledged cyborg. Ana Oancea cites two short stories of Villiers on Edison from 1877 and 1878 as precursors to the installment version in 1880–1881 and the 1886 novel ("Edison's Modern Legend in Villiers' *L'Ève future,*" *Nordlit* 28 [2011]: 173–87).

38. Camille Flammarion, "Le Passage de Vénus, résultats des expéditions françaises," *La Nature* 101 (1875): 356–58. When Janssen explained how he changed from Deschiens to Rédier, he indicated that rather than "alternative and sudden motions" he opted for a disk with a "continuous rotating motion" (*Comptes rendus de l'Académie des Sciences* 59 [July 6, 1874]). While the Deschiens design had an electrical intermittent mechanism, the Rédier design used a softer clockwork with a Maltese cross—but it was of course not continuous at all.

39. In a 1893 patent, Léon Bouly, the inventor of the "cinématographe" (whose trade name the Lumière brothers bought from him), describes: "a reversible photographic and optical device enabling the automatic and continuous capture on any kind of sensitive surface of a series of analytical shots of a motion . . . and providing subsequently, directly or by projection, the synthesis of these motions." Cited in Laurent Mannoni, Donata Presenti Campagnoni, and David Robinson, eds., *Light and Movement: Incunabula of the Motion Picture* (Gemona, Italy: La Giornate del Cinema Muto, 1995), 352.

40. "Patent Caveat," QM001348; TAEM 116:191, 349–51, illustration is on 350, Thomas Edison Papers, available at www://edison.rutgers.edu.

41. In 1875, Edison mistook electromagnetic interference for a new force he called "etheric." See Ian Wills, "Edison and Science: A Curious Result," *Studies in History and Philosophy of Science* 40 (2009): 157–66.

42. I will address these connections in a forthcoming essay.

43. See Wall-Romana, "Translation of Charles Cros."

44. Anon., "The Phonograph, etc.: Mr. Edison at Home in Menlo Park," *Daily Evening Traveller,* May 23, 1878, available at Thomas A. Edison Papers Digital Edition, accessed June 20, 2025, https://edisondigital.rutgers.edu/document/MBSB10620. An unsigned article from *The Boston Evening Transcript,* "Edison's Laboratory," dated Thursday, May 23, 1878, mentions that "THE TELEPHONOSCOPE/To do for the ear what the telescope does for the

eye, and upon somewhat similar principles (substituting waves of sound for waves of heat), was explained" (available at Thomas A. Edison Papers Digital Edition, accessed June 20, 2025, https://edisondigital.rutgers.edu/document/SM029089a). Edison was feeding these lines to journalists. See *Half-Hour Recreations in Popular Science*: "The Telephonoscope / Is to the ear what the telescope is to the eye" (ed. Dana Estes [Boston: Estes and Lauriat, 1879], 31).

45. Camille Flammarion, *Uranie* (Paris: C. Marpon and E. Flammarion, 1889).

46. Camille Flammarion, *La Fin du monde* (Paris: E. Flammarion, 1894).

47. Camille Flammarion, "Le Mouvement de rotation de la terre reproduit par le cinématographe," *Bulletin de la Société astronomique de France* (January 1898): 34.

48. L. Reverchon, "Le Kosmokinétographe," *Cosmos* 693 (May 7, 1898): 587–88.

49. Danielle Chaperon, "Le Cinématographe astronomique, Camille Flammarion: un parcours de 1864 à 1898," *1895, Revue d'histoire du cinéma* 18 (1995): 52–65.

50. "A Night Condensed into Two Minutes: Latest Details of How Camille Flammarion's Cinematograph Photographs the Heavenly Bodies," *Los Angeles Herald*, February 20, 1898, 17.

51. Camille Flammarion, *Lumen*, trans. A. A. M. and R. M., with portion of the last chapter written specially for the English edition (New York: Dodd, Mead & Co., 1897), 220–21.

52. See Jean Epstein, *The Intelligence of a Machine*, trans. Christophe Wall-Romana (1947; Minneapolis: Univocal, 2014).

53. See John Warne Monroe, *Laboratories of Faith: Mesmerism, Spiritism, and Occultism in Modern France* (Ithaca, NY: Cornell University Press, 2008).

54. Janvier trained as a medical doctor in France and became a Haitian diplomat in England. His book *A Black People Confronting White Peoples* was published by Flammarion's brother in 1883. Louis-Joseph Janvier, *Un Peuple noir devant les peuples blancs* (Paris: Marpon et Flammarion, 1883).

55. Anténor Firmin, *De l'égalité des races humaines* (Paris: Pichon, 1885), 12, 18. See Robert Bernasconi, "A Haitian in Paris: Anténor Firmin as a Philosopher Against Racism," *Patterns of Prejudice* 42, nos. 4–5 (2008): 367–83.

56. Susan Gillman, "Pauline Hopkins and the Occult: African-American Revisions of Nineteenth-Century Sciences," *American Literary History* 8, no. 1 (1996): 57–82.

57. Flammarion, *Mondes imaginaires*, 36, 555.

58. Flammarion's text traffics in Orientalism, describing a young Ottoman woman accompanied by "a small kneeling black slave playing a string instrument" (*Récits de l'infini*, 197). Lumen states that "indeed, there is not

so much distance as you presume between the mind of a negro and the mind of a brain of the Latin race" (159).

59. Camille Flammarion, *Dieu dans la matière* (Paris: Didier, 1869), 267.

60. In *Starry Dreams* (1888), recounting an interstellar journey where the narrator discovers new life-forms on celestial bodies, Flammarion critiques religion and politics as equally divisive and militaristic, berating German people for "being the slaves of military leaders, neither less nor more than those of a king of central Africa" (*Rêves étoilés* [Paris: Marpon et Flammarion, 1888], 128). In *Mémoires,* he denounces the antisemitism of his mother (24), but in the novel *The End of the World,* a money-grubbing press magnate is described as "an American Israelite" (Flammarion, *La Fin du monde,* 216). He also mentions "the German race" and "Greco-Latin races" in several works, refracting the political animosity of France and Prussia, but without any biological justification. Flammarion's brother, two years after championing Janvier's affirmation of the Black diaspora, published the antisemitic manifesto of the Third Republic: Édouard Drumont, *La France juive,* 2 vols. (Paris: Marpon et Flammarion, 1885–1886).

Conclusion

1. Michel Foucault, "Discursive Formations," in *The Archaeology of Knowledge and the Discourse on Language,* trans. A. M. Sheridan Smith (New York: Pantheon Books, 1972).

2. Roland Barthes, *Camera Lucida: Reflections on Photography,* trans. Richard Howard (New York: Farrar, Strauss & Giroux, 1981); Shawn Michelle Smith, "Race and Reproduction in *Camera Lucida,*" in *At the Edge of Sight: Photography and the Unseen* (Durham, NC: Duke University Press, 2013).

3. Susan Buck-Morss, *Hegel, Haiti, and Universal History* (Pittsburgh: University of Pittsburgh Press, 2009), 22, 145. See also Sybille Fisher, *Modernity Disavowed: Haiti and the Cultures of Slavery in the Age of Revolution* (Durham, NC: Duke University Press, 2004), 25–32.

4. Siegfried Zielinski, *Deep Time of the Media: Toward an Archaeology of Hearing and Seeing by Technical Means,* trans. Gloria Custance (Cambridge, MA: MIT Press, 2006); Jussi Parikka, *A Geology of Media* (Minneapolis: University of Minnesota Press, 2015).

5. Arjun Appadurai, *Modernity at Large: Cultural Dimensions of Globalization* (Minneapolis: University of Minnesota Press, 1996); Denise Ferreira da Silva, *Toward a Global Idea of Race* (Minneapolis: University of Minnesota Press, 2007); Édouard Glissant, *Poetics of Relation,* trans. Betsy Wing (Ann Arbor: University of Michigan Press, 1997); Lisa Lowe, *The Intimacies of Four Continents* (Durham, NC: Duke University Press, 2015); Achille Mbembe, *The Critique of Black Reason,* trans. Laurent Dubois (Durham, NC: Duke University Press, 2017); Fred Moten, *Black and Blur (consent not to be*

a single being) (Durham, NC: Duke University Press, 2017); Fred Moten, *Stolen Life (consent not to be a single being)* (Minneapolis: University of Minnesota Press, 2018); Dipesh Chakrabarty, *Provincializing Europe: Postcolonial Thought and Historical Difference* (Princeton, NJ: Princeton University Press, 2000); Sylvia Wynter, *On Being Human as Praxis,* ed. Katherine McKittrick (Durham, NC: Duke University Press, 2015).

6. Olúfẹ́mi O. Táíwò, *Reconsidering Reparations* (Oxford: Oxford University Press, 2022), 20.

7. I called for Europe's reparations as a prolegomenon to Europe's unification. Christophe Wall-Romana, "Metaschuld, 1999, das Jahr der Unverjährbarkeit," *Lettre International* 47, no. 4 (1999): 35–43.

8. Albert Vanloo, Eugène Leterrier, and Arnold Mortier, *Le Voyage dans la Lune* (Paris: Tresse, 1877), 53–54.

9. H. G. Wells, *The First Men in the Moon* (London: George Newnes, 1901).

10. See Matthew Solomon, ed., *Fantastic Voyages of the Cinematic Imagination: Georges Méliès's Trip to the Moon* (Buffalo: State University of New York Press, 2011).

11. White explorers on the Moon carry umbrellas in Offenbach's operetta and in the novel of A. Ville d'Avray, *Voyage dans la lune avant 1900* (Paris: Furne, Jouvet & Cie, 1892). In Wells's novel, Selenites carry "terrestrial-looking umbrellas" (Wells, *First Men in the Moon,* 296). Umbrellas clearly stand for weaponry, disguising as a "civilizing mission" the military nature of conquest.

12. M. J. Charles-Roux, *Exposition universelle 1900: Les colonies françaises* (Paris: Imprimerie nationale, 1902), 171, 174. Malagasy music was first recorded by the Société d'Anthropologie at the occasion of the fair, and several musicians stayed in Paris after the fair, including Raony Lalao, who studied at the Conservatoire National and brought Malagasy music to the attention of musicologists (J. Tiersot, "La Musique chez les nègres d'Afrique," *Encyclopédie de la musique* [Paris: Delagrave, 1922], 3216).

13. In the revival of Moon travel narratives after the 1835 Great Moon Hoax, racial discourses are prominent, for instance in Louis Desnoyers, *Robert-Robert* (1843; Paris: L. Passard, 1853). White shipwreck survivors describe an accidental trip to the Moon in a balloon by a man afraid of people who "do not look like him . . . mainly negroes" (1:262). Lunarians are described as having "blue hair, red eyes, green skin, purple lips and black teeth" (2:25–26), the same color spectrum for Lunarians as Francis Godwin, *The Man in the Moone,* ed. William Poole (1638; Toronto: Broadview, 2009), 100 (see chap. 1). The survivors land in Africa—tacitly equivalent to the Moon—where they are captured by cannibal "savages" before bringing peace among African tribes, justifying French colonization as peacekeeping (2:92–101, 145–47). They escape Africa in a ship smuggling enslaved peoples

whose bondage condition is described graphically, including their murder by being thrown overboard when a British cutter takes pursuit (2:200–09). The narrative ends in Paris, with a pithy conclusion that "history looks like these magic lanterns whose lens have the property of enlarging objects immeasurably however small they may be to the naked eye" (2:295). In another Moon travel narrative, "lunar humanity displayed only a single race always subject to the same influences of temperature and environment," by contrast with developmental gaps "on Earth between the refined scions of our European civilizations and the barbarous ruffians erring in the bush of central Africa or Australian deserts." Lunar technics include telegraphic television (Pierre de Sélènes [A. Bétolaud de la Drable], *Un Monde inconnu, deux ans sur la Lune* [Paris: Ernest Flammarion, 1896], 106, 119–20, 162–63).

14. *Charleston* [*Sur un air de Charleston*], dir. Jean Renoir, France, 1927.

15. Hudgins was a friend of Josephine Baker, who introduced the Charleston to France, based on African music and African American communal dancing. On Hudgins, see Anthea Kraut, "The Black Body as Object and Subject of Property," in *Choreographing Copyright: Race, Gender, and Intellectual Property Rights in American Dance* (Oxford: Oxford University Press, 2016).

16. See Henry Louis Gates Jr., *The Signifying Monkey: A Theory of African-American Literary Criticism* (Oxford: Oxford University Press, 1988), 108–10.

17. [Charles François Tiphaigne de la Roche], *Giphantie* (Paris: Durand, 1760).

18. W. E. B. Du Bois, "The Comet," in *Darkwater: Voices from Within the Veil* (New York: Harcourt, Brace & Howe, 1920).

19. See Laurent Mannoni and Ben Brewster, "The Phantasmagoria," *Film History* 8, no. 4 (1996): 390–415. Robertson took lessons from Jacques-Alexandre-César Charles and adapted his megascope (see Françoise Levie, *Étienne-Gaspard Robertson, la vie d'un fantasmagore* [Brussels: Le Préambule, 1990], 27–52). Sited in a former convent and ossuary confiscated during the Revolution, *Fantasmagorie* shows inserted the traumas of the revolution within larger historical developments. Programs ranged from gory mythology to biblical and Koranic miracles, the witches of *Macbeth,* semierotic idylls, Egyptian scenes and walking skeletons, Gothic episodes ("The Bloody Nun") and bloody dreams, vignettes from the Reign of Terror ("the head of Danton"), and evocations of Enlightenment heroes such as Voltaire, Jean-Jacques Rousseau, Marie-Jean-Antoine-Nicolas de Caritat, marquis de Condorcet, and Benjamin Franklin. News events were included, like the death of Pierre-Augustin Caron de Beaumarchais and the fire of the Odeon Theater. The first lady of the day, Joséphine de Beauharnais, Napoleon Bonaparte's wife, attended the first run (Levie, *Étienne-Gaspard Robertson,* 105–7, 291–99). My point is that the *Fantasmagorie* was a kinesthetic vision-machine and a history-machine all in one.

20. Shawn Michelle Smith, *Photographic Returns: Racial Justice and the Time of Photography* (Durham, NC: Duke University Press, 2020), 173.

21. W. E. B. Du Bois, "The Princess Steel," *PMLA* 130, no. 3 (2015): 819–29.

22. Du Bois took astronomy at Fisk University in 1887–1888, practicing on a "3-in. telescope," studying "Trouvelot's astronomical drawings." W. E. B. Du Bois, *Against Racism: Unpublished Essays, Papers, Addresses, 1887–1961,* ed. Herbert Aptheker (Amherst: University of Massachusetts Press, 1985), 11–12.

23. W. E. Burghardt Du Bois, "The American Negro at Paris," *American Monthly Review of Reviews* 22, no. 5 (1900): 575–77. See Alexander G. Weheliye, "Diagrammatics as Physiognomy: W. E. B. Du Bois's Graphic Modernities," *CR: The New Centennial Review* 15, no. 2 (2015): 23–58.

24. Émile Picard, *Exposition universelle international de 1900 à Paris, Rapports du Jury International* (Paris: Imprimerie Nationale, 1903), 2:145.

25. See David C. Wall, "Close-Up: Jordan Peele, the 'Looking Trilogy,'" *Black Camera* 15, no. 1 (2023): 182–88.

Index

Page numbers in italics indicate photographs and other illustrations.

Christophe Wall-Romana is professor of French in the Department of French and Italian at the University of Minnesota. His previous books include *Cinepoetry: Imaginary Cinemas in French Poetry* and *Jean Epstein: Corporeal Cinema and Film Philosophy*. He has translated or cotranslated books by Judy Blume, Philip K. Dick, William Merwin, Norbert Wiener, Jean Epstein, and, most recently, with Joe Hughes, Gilbert Simondon's *Imagination and Invention* (Univocal/Minnesota, 2023).